The Historical Bible

THE MAKERS AND TEACHERS
OF JUDAISM

FROM THE FALL OF JERUSALEM TO THE DEATH OF HEROD THE GREAT

BY

CHARLES FOSTER KENT, Ph. D.

WOOLSEY PROFESSOR OF BIBLICAL LITERATURE IN YALE UNIVERSITY

WITH MAPS AND CHARTS

CHARLES SCRIBNER'S SONS

NEW YORK   CHICAGO   BOSTON

PREFACE

THE period represented by this volume is in many ways the most complex and confusing in Israel's history. The record is not that of the life of a nation but of the scattered remnants of a race. It was inevitable that under the influence of their varied environment, the survivors of the Jewish race should develop very different beliefs and characteristics. The result is that many different currents of thought and shades of belief are reflected in the literature of this period; some of it is dross, but much of it is purest gold. While the period following the destruction of Jerusalem was a reflective and a retrospective age in which the teaching of the earlier priests and prophets gained wide acceptance, it was also a creative era. Fully half of the literature of the Old Testament and all of the important writings of the Apocrypha come from these tragic five centuries. Although the historical records are by no means complete, the great crises in Israel's life are illuminated by such remarkable historical writings as the memoirs of Nehemiah, the first book of Maccabees, and the detailed histories of Josephus.

The majority of the writings, however, reveal above all the soul of the race. Out of its anguish and suffering came the immortal poems found in Isaiah 40–66, the book of Job, and the Psalter. Instead of the distinctly nationalistic point of view, which characterizes practically all of the writings of the pre-exilic period, the interest becomes individual and the outlook universal. During these centuries Israel's prophets, priests, and sages became not merely teachers of the nation but of humanity. Conspicuous among the great teachers of his day stands the noble sage, Jesus the son of Sirach, who gleaned out and presented in effective form that which was most vital in the earlier teaching of his race. In his broad, simple faith in God and man, in his emphasis on deeds and character, as well as ceremonial, and in his practical philosophy of life he was a worthy forerunner of the Great Teacher whose name he bore.

This period represents the culmination and fruition of the divine influences at work in Israel's early history. It was during this period

PREFACE

that Judaism was born and attained its full development, Israel accepted the absolute rule of the written law, and the scribes succeeded the earlier prophets and sages. Out of the heat and conflict of the Maccabean struggle the parties of the Pharisees and Sadducees sprang into existence and won their commanding place in the life of Judaism. Hence this period is the natural historical introduction to the study of the birth and early development of Christianity. It is also the link that binds the revelation found in the Old Testament to that of the New.

The volume of literature coming from this period is so vast that it has been necessary to abridge it at many points in order to utilize that which is most valuable. This has been done by leaving out those passages which are of secondary origin or value, and by preserving at the same time the language and logical thought of the original writers. In the verbose and voluminous writings of Josephus the resulting text is in most cases far clearer and more useful; for the repetitious clauses found in the original often obscure the real thought of the writer. No apology or explanation is required for the use of such apocryphal writings as I Maccabees, Ben Sira, the Wisdom of Solomon, or Josephus's histories, for these are required to bridge the two centuries which intervene between the latest writings of the Old Testament and the earliest writings of the New. They make it possible to study biblical history as an unbroken unit from the days of Moses to the close of the first Christian century, and thus concretely to emphasize the significant but often the forgotten fact that God was revealing himself unceasingly through the life of his people, and that the Bible which records that revelation consists not of two disconnected parts but is one book.

To two of my former students, the Reverend Harold B. Hunting and Ralph H. Pierce, I am under obligation for valuable aid and suggestions in preparing this volume for press.

C. F. K.

YALE UNIVERSITY,
October, 1911.

CONTENTS

THE EXILE AND REVIVAL OF THE JUDEAN COMMUNITY

PAGE

§ XCI. THE JEWS IN PALESTINE AND EGYPT............ 1

Lam. 2¹⁻¹⁰, 5¹⁻¹⁸, Jer. 43⁸⁻¹², 44¹⁻¹⁴, ²⁸.
I. The Significance of the Destruction of the Hebrew
State.—II. The Book of Lamentations.—III. Author-
ship and Date of the Book.—IV. Its Real Character.—
V. Numbers and Fortunes of the Jews Who Remained
in Palestine.—VI. Fortunes of the Jews in Egypt.—
VII. The Jewish Colony at Elephantine.—VIII. The
Temple of Jahu at Elephantine.

§ XCII. EZEKIEL'S MESSAGE TO HIS SCATTERED COUNTRY-
MEN...................................... 12

Ezek. 37, 40¹, ¹³, ¹⁵, ¹⁷, ¹⁹, ²⁰, ²¹ᵇ, ²⁴ᵇ, ⁴⁴⁻⁴⁷, 41¹⁻³ᵃ, 43¹⁻⁹,
44⁹⁻¹⁶, ²³, ²⁴, 45¹⁻⁸.
I. The Home of the Exiles in Babylon.—II. Their New
Conditions and Occupations.—III. Their Religious Life.
IV. The Prophecies of Ezekiel.—V. The Resurrection
of the Dead Nation.—VI. The Divine Shepherd.—VII.
Ezekiel's Plan of the Restored Temple.

§ XCIII. THE CLOSING YEARS OF THE BABYLONIAN RULE.. 23

II Kings 25²⁷⁻³⁰, Isa. 9¹⁻⁷, 11¹⁻¹⁰, 13²⁻⁴, ¹¹, ¹⁷, ¹⁸ᵇ, ¹⁹⁻²², Ezra
6³⁻⁵, 5¹⁴, ¹⁵, ¹⁵, ⁶, I Esdr. 5⁴⁻⁶, Ezra 3²⁻⁴, ⁶ᵇ.
I. The Transformation of the Jews into a Literary
People.—II. The Literary Activity of the Babylonian
Period.—III. The Holiness Code.—IV. The Liberation
of Jehoiachin and the Hopes of the Jews.—V. The Rule
of Nabonidus.—VII. Rise and Conquests of Cyrus.—
VII. His Capture of Babylon.—VIII. His Treatment
of Conquered Peoples.

§ XCIV. THE REBUILDING OF THE TEMPLE.............. 35

Hag. 1, 2, Ezra 5²⁻6¹⁴.
I. The Books of Ezra and Nehemiah.—II. The Chronicler's Conception of the Restoration.—III. Convulsions in the Persian Empire.—IV. Haggai's Effective
Addresses.—V. The Attempt to Stop the Rebuilding
of the Temple.—VI. The Significance of the Restoration of the Temple.

CONTENTS

PAGE

§ XCV. ZECHARIAH'S VISIONS AND ENCOURAGING ADDRESSES — 43

Zech. 1⁷⁻⁴⁶ᵃ, ¹¹⁻¹⁴, ⁶ᵇ⁻¹⁰, 6⁹⁻¹⁵, 7, 8¹⁻⁸.
I. Zechariah's Ancestry and Point of View.—II. The Book of Zechariah.—III. Problems and Hopes of the Judean Community.—IV. Zechariah's Assurances of Jehovah's Care.—V. Preparations for the Crowning of Zerubbabel.—VI. Disappointment of these Patriotic Hopes.—VII. Zechariah's Later Exhortations and Predictions.

§ XCVI. ISRAEL'S TRAINING AND DESTINY — 53

Is. 40¹⁻⁴, ⁶, ²¹, 41¹⁻⁴, ⁸⁻¹⁰, 42¹⁻⁷, ¹³⁻²⁵, 43¹⁻⁷, ¹⁰⁻¹⁵, ²²⁻²⁸, 44¹⁻⁵.
I. The Seventy Years Following the Rebuilding of the Temple.—II. Spiritual Forces in Judaism.—III. Evidences that Isaiah 40–66 Were Written in Palestine.—IV. Their Probable Date.—V. Their Literary Characteristics.—VI. Their Theme and Purpose.—VII. Reasons Why Jehovah Will Restore His People.

§ XCVII. CONDITIONS AND PROBLEMS WITHIN THE JUDEAN COMMUNITY — 64

Mal. 1⁶⁻¹⁴, 2, 3, 4¹⁻³, Ps. 22¹⁻¹⁸.
I. Date of the Book of Malachi.—II. Neglect of the Temple Service.—III. The Need of a Great Moral Awakening.—IV. The Lot of the Faithful.—V. The Problem of Suffering in the Literature of the Period.

§ XCVIII. THE PROBLEM AND TEACHINGS OF THE BOOK OF JOB — 73

Job 1, 2, 3², ¹¹, ¹³, ¹⁵, ¹⁷, ¹⁹, ²⁰⁻²², ²⁵, ²⁶, 4¹⁻⁷, ¹⁷⁻¹⁹, 5¹⁷⁻²², ²⁶, ²⁷, 6¹⁻⁴ᵇ, ¹⁴, ¹⁵, ²⁰⁻³⁰, 7¹⁻⁶, ⁹⁻¹⁸, ²⁰, ²¹, 8¹⁻⁶, 9¹⁻⁷, ¹⁵⁻²⁰, ²⁴, ³¹⁻³⁵, 10⁹⁻¹⁵, ²⁰⁻²², 11¹, ⁷⁻⁹, ¹³⁻¹⁵, 12¹⁻³, 13⁷⁻¹⁸, ²¹⁻²⁵, 14⁷⁻¹⁰, ¹³⁻¹⁵, ¹⁸, ¹⁹, 15⁴⁻⁶, 16¹⁻⁴, ¹¹⁻¹³ᵃ, ¹⁸⁻²¹, 18¹, ⁵⁻⁷, 19¹, ¹³⁻¹⁶, ²²⁻²⁷, 20¹⁻⁵, 21¹, ⁷⁻⁹, 22¹⁻⁵, ²³, ²⁷, ²⁸, 23¹⁻⁶, 25¹⁻⁴, 26¹, 27², ⁴, ⁵, ⁷⁻⁹, 29¹⁻⁵, 30¹⁶⁻²¹, 31¹⁻⁸, ³⁵⁻³⁷, 40², ⁸, ⁹, 38²⁻⁷, ⁸⁻¹¹, ³⁹⁻⁴¹, 42², ³, ⁵, ⁶.
I. The Structure of the Book of Job.—II. Dates of the Different Parts.—III. The Prose Story.—IV. The Poem of Job.—V. Progress in Job's Thought.—VI. Significance of the Speeches of Job.

§ XCIX. THE TRAINING AND MISSION OF THE TRUE SERVANT OF JEHOVAH — 94

Is. 49¹⁻¹³, 50⁴⁻¹⁰, 52¹³⁻¹⁵, 53.
I. The Different Portraits of Jehovah's Servant.—II. The Prophet's Purpose.—III. The Character and Condition of Those to Whom the Prophet Appealed.—IV. The Task and Training of Jehovah's Servant.—V. Methods of Jehovah's Servant.—VI. Realization of the Ideal of Service.

CONTENTS

PAGE

§ C. NEHEMIAH'S WORK IN REBUILDING THE WALLS OF
JERUSALEM.............................. 104

Neh. 1-4, 6, 7¹⁻⁵ᵃ, 12³¹, ³², ³⁷⁻⁴⁰.
I. Nehemiah's Memoirs.—II. Nehemiah's Response to
the Call to Service.—III. Obstacles that Confronted
Him.—IV. His Plan of Work.—V. The Restored Walls.
—VI. Completion and Dedication of the Walls.

§ CI. NEHEMIAH'S SOCIAL AND RELIGIOUS REFORMS.... 117

Is. 56, 58²⁻¹², Neh. 5, 13⁴⁻³¹.
I. Cruelty and Hypocrisy of the Jewish Leaders.—II.
Nehemiah's Method of Correcting the Social Evils in
the Community.—III. The Historical Value of Nehemiah 13.—IV. Regulations Regarding the Temple Service.—V. Provisions Regarding Sabbath Observance
and Foreign Marriages.—VI. Significance of Nehemiah's
Work.

§ CII. TRADITIONAL ACCOUNT OF THE ADOPTION OF THE
PRIESTLY LAW............................. 126

Ezra 7¹, ⁶⁻¹⁰, Neh. 7⁷³ᵇ⁻⁸⁴ᵃ, ⁵, ⁶, ⁹⁻¹⁸, 9¹⁻³, ⁶⁻⁸, ³²⁻³⁸, 10²⁸⁻³⁹ᵇ.
I. The Ezra Tradition.—II. The Historical Value of the
Ezra Tradition.—III. The Facts Underlying It.—IV.
Origin and Aims of the Priestly Laws.—V. Their Im-
portant Regulations.—VI. Their Practical Effects.

§ CIII. THE JEWISH STATE DURING THE LAST CENTURY
OF PERSIAN RULE.......................... 134

Ps. 36⁵⁻¹⁰, Joel 2¹⁻²⁹, Jos. Ant. XI, 7–8².
I. Prosperity of the Judean Community.—II. The
Growth of the Psalter.—III. The Prophecy of Joel.—
IV. Hopes of the Jews.—V. Rule of the High Priests.
—VI. The Date of the Samaritan Schism.—VII. Its
Nature and Consequences.

THE GREEK AND MACCABEAN AGE

§ CIV. THE JEWS UNDER THEIR GREEK RULERS........ 146

I Mac. 1¹⁻⁴, Jos. Ant. XI, 8⁷ᵃ, ᵉ, XII, 1¹ᵇ⁻ᵈ, ᵍ⁻ʲ, 2¹ᵃ, ⁵ᵈ, ᵉ,
4¹ᵈ⁻ᶠ, 3ᵃ⁻ᶠ, 3ᵇ, 4ᵃ⁻ᶜ, 5ᵃ⁻ᶜ, ᵉ, 6ᵃ, 3³ᵃ, ᵇ, ᵉ⁻ᵉ.
I. Josephus's Histories.—II. Alexander's Conquests.—
III. The Jews in Egypt and Alexandria.—IV. The
Rule of the Ptolemies.—V. Fortunes of the Jews of
Palestine.—VI. Conquest of Palestine by the Seleucids
in 311 B.C.

CONTENTS

PAGE

§ CV. THE WISE AND THEIR TEACHINGS............. 155

Prov. 1²⁻⁶, 8¹⁻⁶, ¹³⁻²⁷, ²⁹⁻³⁵, 13¹⁴, ²⁰, 24⁵, 12¹⁰, 20¹³, 23¹⁶, ²⁹⁻³⁵, 29²⁰, 15²³, 19¹¹, 16³², 23²⁶⁻²⁸, 4²⁵⁻²⁷, 14¹⁵, 26¹², 27², 4³³, 11⁶, 21³, 15¹, 3²⁷, 14²¹, 19¹⁷, 25²¹, ²², 3¹¹, ¹², 1⁵, ⁶.
I. Structure and Authorship of the Book of Proverbs.—
II. Date of the Different Collections.—III. The Wise in Israel's Early History.—IV. Their Prominence in the Greek Period.—V. Their Aims.—VI. Their Methods.—
VII. Their Important Teachings.

§ CVI. THE DIFFERENT CURRENTS OF THOUGHT IN JUDA-
ISM DURING THE GREEK PERIOD............. 167

Ps. 19⁷⁻¹⁴, 46, 22²⁷⁻³⁰, Jonah 1, 2¹, ¹⁰, 3, 4, Eccles. 1¹²⁻¹⁸, 2¹⁻¹⁷, ²⁴⁻²⁶.
I. The Ritualists.—II. The Legalists.—III. The Dis-
ciples of the Prophets.—IV. The Date and Character of the Book of Jonah.—V. Its Teachings.—VI. The Book of Ecclesiastes.—VII. Koheleth's Philosophy of Life.

§ CVII. THE TEACHINGS OF JESUS THE SON OF SIRACH.... 177

B. Sir. 1¹⁻¹⁰, 2¹⁻⁹, 3¹⁷⁻³⁰, 4², ⁹, ¹⁰, ²⁰⁻²⁵, ²⁸⁻³¹, 5¹⁻², 6², ⁴⁻⁸, ¹⁴⁻¹⁶, 7¹², ¹³, ²⁰⁻²², ²³⁻³⁰.
I. Date and Character of Jesus the Son of Sirach.—II.
His Writings.—III. The History of the Book.—IV. Its Picture of Jewish Life.—V. Rise of the Scribes.—VI.
The Teachings of Ben Sira.

§ CVIII. THE CAUSES OF THE MACCABEAN STRUGGLE..... 186

I Mac. 1¹⁰⁻²², ²⁴⁻⁶³.
I. The Character and Contents of I Maccabees.—II.
Character and Contents of II Maccabees.—III. Aggressive Character of Hellenic Culture.—IV. Contrast be-
tween Hellenism and Judaism.—V. Apostasy of the Jews and Perfidy of the High Priests.—VI. Character of Antiochus Epiphanes.—VII. His Policy toward the Jews.

§ CIX. THE EFFECT OF PERSECUTION UPON THE JEWS... 194

I Mac. 2, Dan. 7¹⁻²⁷, 12¹⁻³.
I. The Uprising Led by Mattathias.—II. Party of the Hasideans or Pious.—III. Date of the Visions in Daniel 7-12.—IV. Their Real Character and Aim.—V. The Four Heathen Kingdoms and the Kingdom of God.

§ CX. THE VICTORIES THAT GAVE THE JEWS RELIGIOUS
LIBERTY.................................... 203

I Mac. 3¹⁻⁴³, ⁴⁶⁻⁶⁰, 4.
I. The Character of Judas.—II. Obstacles against which Judas Contended.—III. Defeat of Apollonius and Se-
ron.—IV. The Battle of Emmaus.—V. The Battle at Bethsura.—VI. Restoration of the Temple Service.—
VII. The New Spirit in Judaism.

x

CONTENTS

PAGE

§ CXI. THE LONG CONTEST FOR POLITICAL INDEPEN-
DENCE 215

I Mac. 5¹⁻²³, ⁴⁵, ⁵⁴, ⁶⁵⁻⁶⁸, ⁶³, 6¹⁸⁻⁶³, 7, 9¹⁻³¹, 10¹⁻²¹, ⁶⁷⁻⁷¹, ⁷⁴⁻⁷⁶,
11²⁰⁻²⁹.
I. The Political Situation.—II. The Jewish Attitude
toward the Heathen Reflected in the Book of Esther.—
III. Campaigns against the Neighboring Peoples.—IV.
The Battle of Beth-zacharias.—V. Victories Over Nicanor.—VI. The Death of Judas.—VII. Dissensions in
the Syrian Court.—VIII. Concessions to Jonathan.

§ CXII. PEACE AND PROSPERITY UNDER SIMON 231

I Mac. 11³⁸⁻⁴⁰, ⁵⁴⁻⁵⁶, 12³⁹⁻⁵³, 13¹⁻¹¹, ²⁰⁻³⁰, ³³, ⁴³⁻⁵³, 14¹⁶⁻¹⁸,
³⁸⁻⁴⁹, ⁴⁻¹⁵.
I. Capture and Death of Jonathan.—II. Character and
Policy of Simon.—III. His Conquests.—IV. His Authority.—V. Completion of the Psalter.—VI. The Religious Life Reflected in the Later Psalms.

§ CXIII. THE RULE OF JOHN HYRCANUS AND ARISTOBULUS 240

I Mac. 16¹¹⁻²², Jos. Jew. War, I, 2³ᶜ⁻⁴ᵇ, ⁴ᵈ, ⁵, ⁶, Ant. XIII,
9¹ᵈ, ᵉ, Jew. War, I, 2⁷ᵃ, ᵇ, Ant. XIII, 10⁵, 6ᵃ⁻ᶜ, ⁷, 11¹ᵃ⁻ᶜ,
³ᵃ, ³ᵉ.
I. Murder of Simon.—II. The Syrian Invasion.—III.
John's Military Policy and Conquests.—IV. The Break
with the Pharisees.—V. The Reign of Aristobulus.

§ CXIV THE PHARISEES, SADDUCEES, AND ESSENES 247

Jos. Ant. XVIII, 1², ³ᵃ⁻ᶜ, ³ᵈ, ⁴ᵃ, ᵇ, ⁵ᵃ, ᵇ, Jew. War, II, 8²⁻⁸,
⁹ᵃ⁻ᶜ, ¹⁰ᵇ, ᶜ, ¹¹ᵇ, ¹².
I. Influences that Gave Rise to the Jewish Parties.—
II. Character and Beliefs of the Pharisees.—III. Of the
Sadducees.—IV. Of the Essenes.

§ CXV. THE LIFE AND FAITH OF THE JEWS OF THE DIS-
PERSION 255

Jos. Ant. XII, 3¹ᵃ, VII, 3³ᵃ, ᵇ, 10²ᵈ⁻³ᵉ, XIII, 10⁴, Wisd. of
Sol. 6¹²⁻¹⁶, 7²⁵⁻8¹, ⁷, 1¹⁻⁸, 12⁻¹⁵, 2²³⁻3¹, 5¹⁵, ¹⁶, 11²⁴⁻12², 15¹⁻³.
I. Conditions of the Jews in Antioch and Asia Minor.—
II. In Egypt.—III. The Jewish Temple at Leontopolis.
—IV. Translation of the Hebrew Scriptures into Greek.
—V. Apologetic Jewish Writings.—VI. The Wisdom of
Solomon.—VII. Its Important Teachings.

§ CXVI. THE DECLINE OF THE MACCABEAN KINGDOM..... 264

Jos. Jew. War, I, 4¹⁻⁴ᶜ, ⁵ᶜ, ⁶ᵃ, ᵉ, ⁸ᶜ, ᵈ, 5¹⁻7⁷.
I. The Character and Policy of Alexander Janneus.—
II. The Effects of His Rule.—III. Alexandra's Reign.

xi

CONTENTS

PAGE

—IV. Quarrels between Hyrcanus and Aristobulus.—
V. Rome's Intervention.—VI. Cause of the Fall of the
Jewish Kingdom.—VII. Political, Intellectual, and Re-
ligious Effects of the Maccabean Struggle.

THE RULE OF ROME

§ CXVII. THE RISE OF THE HERODIAN HOUSE............ 275

Jos. Jew. War, I, 8[2, 4a, 5-7, 9b], 9[1, 3a-6b], 10[1, 2a, 3a, 4, 5a, b],
11[1, 4, 6], 12[3-5], 13[1a], Ant. XIV, 13[1], Jew. War, I, 13[7, 8c],
14[1b, 2, 4], 15[3, 4], 16[1], 17[1, 8, 9a], 18[1, 2c, 4a].
I. The Fruitless Struggle against Rome.—II. Antipater's Policy.—III. Herod's Early Record.—IV. The
Parthian Conquest.—V. Herod Made King of the Jews.

§ CXVIII. HEROD'S POLICY AND REIGN.................... 285

Jos. Jew. War, I, 19[1, 2a], 20[1, 2, 3b-4a], 21[1[2, 1-4, 6a-8a, 9a-10a, 11],
22[1-4], 23[1a, d, 2ae, d-3a], 24[1a], 27[1, 2a, 6b], 28[1a], 29[3c], 30[5a], 31[1a],
33[1, 7, 8a].
I. Herod's Character.—II. His Attitude toward Rome.
III. His Building Activity.—IV. His Attitude toward
His Subjects.—V. The Tragedy of His Domestic Life.
—VI. Effects of His Reign.

§ CXIX. HEROD'S TEMPLE................................ 297

Jos. Ant. XV, 11[1a, 2c, 3a-1, 4a, g, 5a-g, h-k, 6].
I. Herod's Motives.—II. Preparations for the Rebuilding of the Temple.—III. The Approaches to the Temple.—IV. The Organization of the Temple.

§ CXX. THE MESSIANIC HOPES AND THE RELIGIOUS BE-
LIEFS OF JUDAISM.......................... 303

Sibyl. Oracles, III, 767-84, 1723-46, Enoch 46[1-3], 48[3-6], 49[27-29],
51[1, 2].
I. The Growth of Israel's Messianic Hopes.—II. The
Kingly, Nationalistic Type of Messianic Hope.—III.
The Apocalyptic, Catastrophic Type.—IV. The Ethical
and Universalistic Type.—V. The Messianic Hopes of
Judaism at the Beginning of the Christian Era.

APPENDIX I. A PRACTICAL BIBLICAL REFERENCE LIBRARY 311

APPENDIX II. GENERAL QUESTIONS AND SUBJECTS FOR
SPECIAL RESEARCH..................... 312

CONTENTS

LIST OF MAPS AND CHARTS

JEWISH AND CONTEMPORARY CHRONOLOGY FROM 597 TO 165 B.C.
Frontispiece

THE EMPIRES OF BABYLONIA, PERSIA, AND ALEXANDER
to face page 1

THE JEWISH COMMUNITY IN PALESTINE DURING THE PERSIAN
AND GREEK PERIODS.........................to face page 40

THE JERUSALEM OF NEHEMIAH..................to face page 106

CHRONOLOGY OF THE MACCABEAN AND ROMAN PERIODS
to face page 186

PALESTINE DURING THE MACCABEAN PERIOD......to face page 194

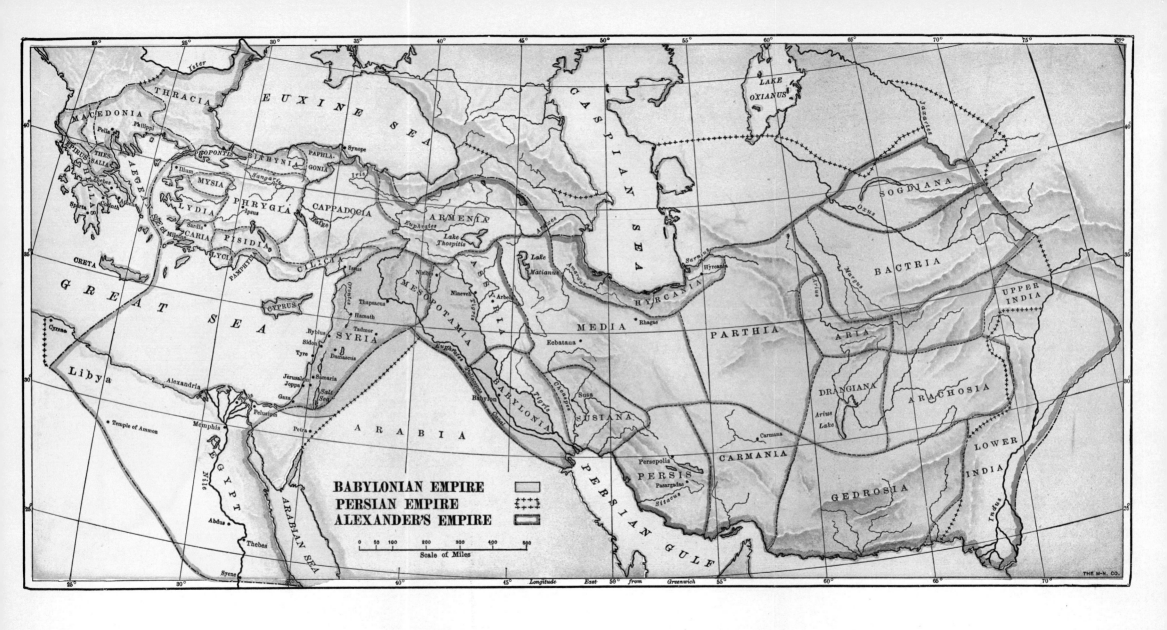

THRACIA

EUXINE SEA

CASPIAN SEA

LAKE OXIANUS

MACEDONIA
Pella• •Philippi
EPIRUS THES.
THESSALIA
HELLAS
Thebes• •Corinth
Sparta• Athens•
AEGEAN SEA

PROPONTIS BITHYNIA
PAPHLA.
GONIA •Synope

MYSIA
Illum•
Sangarius
Iris

SOGDIANA

LYDIA PHRYGIA
Sardis•
Ipsus•
Halys

CAPPADOCIA

ARMENIA
Euphrates
Lake Thospitis
Araxes

Oxus

BACTRIA

Marpus

UPPER INDIA

CARIA PISIDIA
Miletus•
LYCIA
PAMPHYLIA

CILICIA
Issus•

Nisibis•
MESOPOTAMIA
ASSYRIA
Nineveh•
•Arbela
Tigris

Lake Matianus

Amardus

Sarnius
HYRCANIA

Jaxartes

ARIA

CRETA

CYPRUS

GREAT SEA

Orontes
Thapsacus•
•Hamath
SYRIA
Tadmor•
•Byblus
Sidon•
Tyre• •Damascus

HYRCANIA

MEDIA
•Rhagae

PARTHIA

Arius Lake

DRANGIANA

ARACHOSIA

LOWER INDIA

Libya

Cyrene•
•Alexandria

Jerusalem• •Samaria
Joppa•
Salt Sea
Gaza•
Petra•

Euphrates
Pelusiyna

BABYLONIA
Babylon•
Cunal

Ecbatana•

Tigris
Choaspes
Susa•
SUSIANA

Carmana•

CARMANIA

GEDROSIA

Indus

Memphis•
•Temple of Ammon

ARABIA

Persepolis•
PERSIS
Pasargadae•
Sittacus•

EGYPT
Nile
Abdus•
•Thebes

ARABIAN SEA

PERSIAN GULF

Syene•

BABYLONIAN EMPIRE
PERSIAN EMPIRE
ALEXANDER'S EMPIRE

0 50 100   200   300   400   500
Scale of Miles

THE M-N. CO.

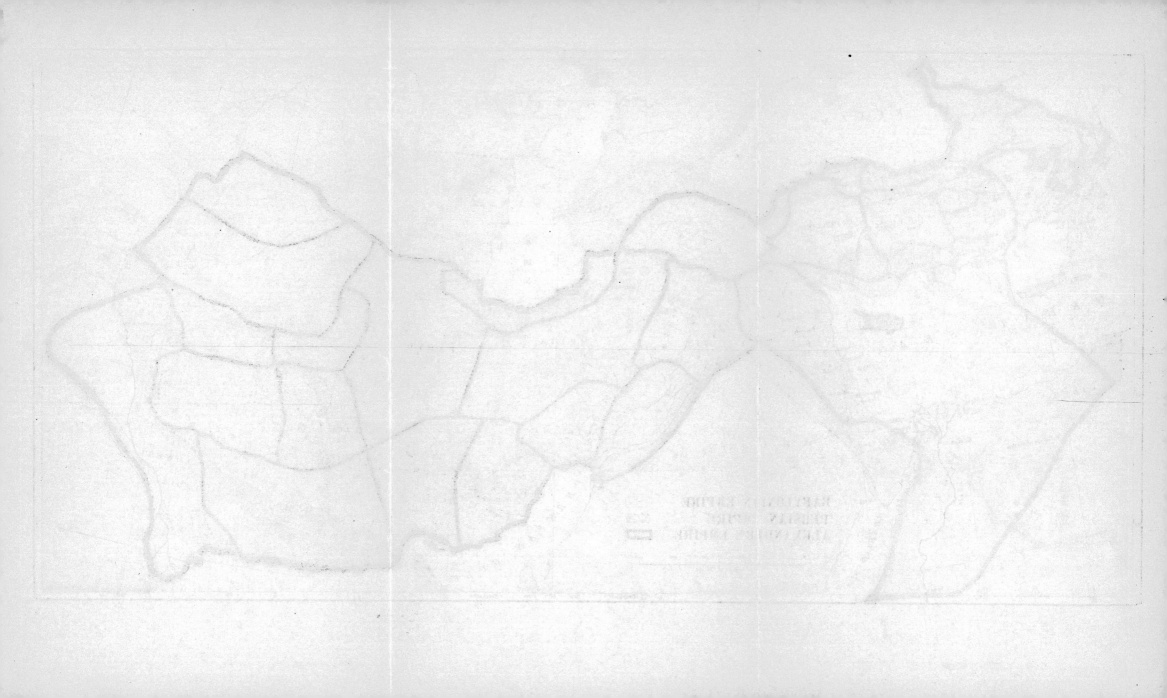

THE EXILE AND THE REVIVAL OF THE JUDEAN COMMUNITY

§ XCI. THE JEWS IN PALESTINE AND EGYPT

How the Lord hath beclouded in his anger the daughter of Zion!

He hath cast down from heaven to earth the beauty of Israel,

And he hath not kept in remembrance his footstool in the day of his anger.

The Lord hath swallowed up without mercy every habitation of Jacob,

He hath thrown down in his wrath the strongholds of the daughter of Judah,

He hath struck to the ground, he hath polluted her king and her princes.

He hath cut off in the fierceness of his anger all of Israel's strength,

He hath drawn back his right hand from before the enemy,

He hath burnt in Jacob like a flame, which devours on all sides.

He hath bent his bow as an enemy, he hath stood as an adversary,

He hath slain all the desirable men in the tent of Zion,

He hath poured out his fury as fire [on the daughter of Judah].

The Lord hath become like an enemy, he hath swallowed up Israel,

He hath swallowed up all of his palaces, he hath destroyed his fortresses,

And he hath multiplied in the daughter of Judah sighing and lamentation.

1. Jehovah's dire judgment upon Judah (Lam. 2¹⁻⁵)

1

2. Also upon the temple and its service (6, 7)

He hath torn down as a vine his dwelling, he hath destroyed his assembling place,

He hath caused to be forgotten in Zion, fast day and sabbath,

And hath spurned in his indignant anger, king and priest.

The Lord hath rejected his altar, he hath abhorred his sanctuary,

He hath given up into the hands of the enemy the ark of the covenant,

They have made a din in Jehovah's house, as in the solemn feast day.

3. Upon Jerusalem and its defences (8-10)

Jehovah hath determined to destroy the wall of Zion,

He hath stretched out the line, he hath not held back his hand from destroying,

He hath made rampart and wall lament, they mourn together,

Her gates have sunk into the ground, he hath destroyed her defences,

Her king and her princes are among the heathen, there is no law.

Her prophets also receive from Jehovah no vision.

Silent, upon the earth sit the elders of Zion;

They cast dust upon their heads; they are girded with sackcloth;

With heads bowed to earth are the daughters of Jerusalem.

4. The great calamity a punishment for the nation's sins (5¹⁻⁷)

Remember, O Jehovah, what has befallen us,

Look and see our disgrace.

Our inheritance is turned over to aliens,

Our homes belong to foreigners.

We are orphans and fatherless,

Our mothers are like widows.

We drink our water for money,

Our wood comes to us by purchase.

The yoke upon our necks harasses us,

We are weary, but find no rest.

We have given the hand to the Egyptians,

And to the Assyrians, that we might be sated with food.

Our fathers sinned and are no more,

While we bear their guilt.

2

Slaves have dominion over us,
With none to deliver from their hand.
We get our bread at the peril of our lives,
Because of the sword of the wilderness.
Our skin becomes hot like an oven,
Because of the glowing heat of famine.
They ravish the women in Zion,
The virgins in the cities of Judah.
Princes are hanged up by the hand.
The person of the elders is not honored.
The young men bear up the mill,
And the children stumble under the wood.

5. Pitiable fate of the survivors (8-12)

The elders have ceased from the gate,
The young men from their music.
The joy of our heart has ceased,
Our dance is turned into mourning.
The crown has fallen from our head;
Woe to us! for we have sinned.
For this reason our heart is faint,
For these causes our eyes are dim;
For the mountain of Zion is desolate;
The jackals walk over it.

6. The tragic contrast with Judah's former prosperity (14-18)

The word of Jehovah also came to Jeremiah in Tahpanhes, saying, Take great stones in thy hand, and bury them in the loose foundation in the brick-covered place before Pharaoh's palace door in Tahpanhes in the sight of the men of Judah; and say to them, 'Thus saith Jehovah of hosts, the God of Israel, "Behold, I will send and bring Nebuchadrezzar the king of Babylon, my servant, and will set his throne upon these stones that you have buried, and he shall spread his royal pavilion over them. And he shall come and shall smite the land of Egypt; such as are for death shall be given to death, and such as are for captivity shall be given to captivity, and such as are for the sword shall be given to the sword. And he will kindle a fire in the houses of the gods of Egypt, and will burn them and carry them away. And he shall wrap himself in the land of Egypt, as a shepherd puts on his mantle, and shall go

7. Prediction of Egypt's conquest by Nebuchadrezzar (Jer. 43 8-13)

3

forth from there in peace. He shall also break the obelisks of Heliopolis and the temples of the gods of Egypt shall he burn with fire." '

8. Failure of the Jews to learn the lessons from the past (44¹⁻¹⁰)

The word that came to Jeremiah concerning all the Jews who dwelt in the land of Egypt, who dwelt at Migdol, Tahpanhes, Memphis, and in upper Egypt, saying, Thus saith Jehovah of hosts, the God of Israel, 'Ye have seen all the evil that I have brought upon Jerusalem and upon all the cities of Judah; and behold, they are this day a desolation, and no man dwelleth in them, because of their wickedness which they have committed to provoke me to anger in that they went to offer sacrifices to other gods, that they knew not, neither they nor ye, nor your fathers. However, I constantly sent to them all my servants the prophets, saying, "Oh, do not this abominable thing that I hate." But they neither hearkened nor inclined their ear to turn from their wickedness, to offer no sacrifice to other gods. And so my wrath and mine anger was poured forth and was kindled against the cities of Judah and the streets of Jerusalem, and they were wasted and desolate, as is now the case.' Therefore now thus saith Jehovah, the God of hosts, the God of Israel, 'Why do you commit a great crime against yourselves to cut off from you man and woman, infant and sucking child, out of the midst of Judah so that ye leave none remaining, in that ye provoke me to anger with the work of your hands, offering sacrifice to other gods in the land of Egypt, whither ye have gone to sojourn, that ye may be cut off, and that ye may be an object of cursing and a reproach among all the nations of the earth? Have ye forgotten the crimes of your fathers, and the crimes of the kings of Judah, and the crimes of their princes, which they committed in the land of Judah and in the streets of Jerusalem? They are not humbled even to this day, neither have they feared nor walked in my law nor in my statutes that I set before you and before your fathers.

9. Fate awaiting the refugees in Egypt (¹¹⁻¹⁴, ²⁸)

'Therefore thus saith Jehovah of hosts, the God of Israel: "Behold, I set my face against you for evil to cut off the remnant of Judah in the land of Egypt, and they shall fall by the sword and by famine; they shall die, small and great, and they shall be an object of execration, of astonishment,

4

of cursing, and of reproach. For I will punish those who
dwell in the land of Egypt, as I have punished Jerusalem,
by the sword, by famine, and by pestilence, so that none of
the remnant of Judah, who have gone into the land of
Egypt to reside there, shall escape or be left to return to
the land of Judah, to which they have a desire to return;
for none shall return except as fugitives. And they who
escape the sword shall return from the land of Egypt to the
land of Judah, few in number; and all the remnant of Judah,
who have gone into the land of Egypt to sojourn there shall
know whose word shall be confirmed, mine or theirs."

I. The Significance of the Destruction of the Hebrew State.
The destruction of Jerusalem in 586 B.C. resulted in a mighty transformation of the life and thought of Israel. It marked the final overthrow of the old Hebrew kingdoms, and the gradual rise of that new
and important factor in human history known as Judaism. For over
three centuries the Jews who survived the great catastrophe were
helpless under the rule of the great world powers which in succession
conquered southwestern Asia. For the great majority of the Jewish
race it represented the beginning of that long exile which has continued
until the present. Scattered from the desert of Sahara to the distant
land of China, and from the Black Sea to the Indian Ocean, the different groups of exiles quickly began to adapt themselves to their changed
surroundings and to absorb the new knowledge and the powerful influences which gradually transformed their beliefs and ideals. While
their vision was vastly broadened by this contact, the danger and horror
of being completely engulfed in the great heathen world bound the
faithful more closely together, and in time made Judaism the solid,
unbreakable rock that has withstood the assaults and the disintegrat-
ing forces of the ages. At first the survivors of the great catastrophe
were stunned by the blow that had shattered their nation. They lived
only in their memories of the past and in their hopes for the future.
At last, in the long period of misery and enforced meditation, they began not only to accept but also to apply the eternal principles proclaimed by their earlier prophets. Thus amidst these entirely new
conditions they gained a broader and deeper faith and were still further
trained for the divine task of teaching mankind.

II. The Book of Lamentations. After describing the destruction
of the little kingdom established at Mizpah under Gedaliah, the Hebrew

historical records suddenly become silent. This silence is due to the fact that there was little of external interest to record. The real history of this tragic half-century is the record of the anguish and doubts and hopes in the hearts of the scattered remnants of the race. The little book of Lamentations expresses dramatically and pathetically the thoughts of the people as they meditated upon the series of calamities which gathered about the great catastrophe of 586 B.C. Like the ancient Torah, or five books of the Law, it contains a quintet of poems. These are very similar in theme and form to many of the psalms of the Psalter. In the first four the characteristic five-beat measure, by which the deep emotions, especially that of sorrow, were expressed, is consistently employed. Each of these four is also an acrostic, that is, each succeeding line or group of lines begins with a succeeding letter of the Hebrew alphabet. This acrostic form was probably adopted in order to aid the memory, and suggests that from the first these poems were written to be used in public. Even so the Jews of Jerusalem to-day chant them on each of their sabbaths beside the foundation walls of the great platform on which once stood their ruined temple. Although the artificial character of these poems tends to check the free expression of thought and feeling, it is possible to trace in them a logical progress and to feel the influence of the strong emotions that inspired them.

III. **Authorship and Date of the Book.** In theme and literary form these poems are so strikingly similar to Jeremiah's later sermons that it was almost inevitable that tradition should attribute them to the great prophet of Judah's decline. This tradition, to which is due the position of the book of Lamentations in the Greek and English Bibles, cannot be traced earlier than the Greek period. The evidence within the poems themselves strongly indicates that they were not written by Jeremiah. It is almost inconceivable that he would subject his poetic genius to the rigid limitations of the acrostic structure. Moreover, he would never have spoken of the weak Zedekiah, whose vacillating policy he condemned, in the terms of high esteem which appear in Lamentations 4²⁰. These poems also reflect the popular interpretation of the great national calamity, rather than Jeremiah's searching analysis of fundamental causes. A careful study of Lamentations shows that chapters 2 and 4 were probably written by one who was powerfully influenced by Ezekiel's thought. They both follow in their acrostic structure an unusual order of the Hebrew alphabet, differing in this respect from chapters 1 and 3. They have so many close points of contact with each other that it is safe to say that they are both from the same author. They reveal an intimate familiarity with events immediately following the destruction of Jerusalem and were probably written between 580 and 561 B.C., when Jehoiachin was liberated. Chapters 1 and 3 follow the regular order of the Hebrew alphabet and apparently represent the work of a later author or authors. Chapter 1 is full of pathos and religious feeling and is closely parallel in thought to such psalms as 42 and 137. Chapter 3 is a poetic monologue describing the fate and voicing the contrition of the righteous within the Judean community. Chapter 5, on the contrary, is in the three-beat measure and lacks the acrostic structure of the preceding chapters. Its style and point of view are so different from those of the preceding chapters that it must be the work of another author, who probably lived in the Persian period.

IV. **Its Real Character.** The purpose of the book of Lamentations was evidently, (1) to give appropriate expression to the feelings of the Jews who survived the destruction of Jerusalem, 586 B.C.; (2) to drive home the great lessons taught by their past history, and thus to arouse true repentance; and (3) to kindle in turn hopes regarding their future. Through them Jeremiah and Ezekiel live and speak again, but from the point of view of the people. These tragic poems also throw contemporary light upon the horrors of the final siege and capture of Jerusalem and upon the fate of those who survived.

V. **Numbers and Fortunes of the Jews Who Remained in Palestine.** The Jews actually carried into captivity constituted only a small part of the total population of Judah (*cf.* § XC[ii]). The peasants and the inhabitants of the towns outside Jerusalem remained undisturbed, except as some of them were doubtless drafted into the army which under Zedekiah undertook to defend Jerusalem against the Chaldeans. From the later record of Nehemiah's work the names of many of these towns can be determined. In the north were Jericho, Geba, Mizpah, Anathoth, and Kirjath-jearim; in the centre, Netophah and Bethlehem; and in the south Tekoa, Keilah, and Bethzur. The lot of these, who are later known as the people of the land, was pitiable indeed. There are many references in Lamentations and Ezekiel to the persecutions to which they were subjected by their malignant foes, the Moabites and Ammonites on the east and the Philistines on the west. Even more cruel and aggressive were the Edomites, who had suffered many wrongs at the hands of the Hebrews. It was probably about this time that this half-nomadic people began to be driven northward by the advance of the Nabateans, an Arab people who came from the south. Dislodged from their homes, the Edomites took advantage of the weakness of the Jews and seized southern Judah, including the ancient capital Hebron. The doom which Ezekiel pronounces upon the Edomites in 25[12] is because of the revenge that they wreaked upon the Jews at this time. It is significant that Ezekiel's sermons in the period immediately following the fall of Jerusalem contain dire predictions of divine vengeance upon all these foes. After the overthrow of Gedaliah's kingdom, the Jews who remained in Palestine appear to have been left wholly without defences or defenders. Ezekiel, in 33[23-29], speaks of those who inhabit the waste places in the land of Israel, who live in the strongholds and the caves. Some of them appear to have turned robbers. Foreign settlers came in from every side and in time intermarried with the natives and led them into idolatry. Ezekiel sternly condemns their immorality and apostasy.

From the references in Jeremiah 41[5] and Ezra 3[3] it is clear that even during this reign of terror many of the people continued to offer sacrifices to Jehovah at the great altar cut in native rock which stood before the ruins of their temple in Jerusalem. Priests were also doubtless found in the land to conduct these services. The ancient feasts, however, with their joyous merrymaking and the resulting sense of divine favor, were no longer observed. Instead, the people celebrated in sackcloth and ashes the fasts commemorating the successive stages in the destruction of their city (Zech. 7[3-7]). While their lot was pitiable and their character seemingly unpromising, these people of the land were important factors in the re-establishment of the Judean community.

VI. **Fortunes of the Jews in Egypt.** The narrative in Jeremiah states definitely that the large proportion of those who had rallied about Gedaliah after his death found a temporary asylum on the eastern borders of Egypt. Here they were beyond the reach of Chaldean armies and within the territory of the one nation which offered a friendly asylum to the Jewish refugees. Most of this later group of exiles settled at the towns of Tahpanhes and Migdol. The latter means tower and is probably to be identified with an eastern outpost, the chief station on the great highway which ran along the southeastern shore of the Mediterranean directly to Palestine and Syria.

The excavations of the Egypt Exploration Fund at Tahpanhes, which was the Daphnæ of Herodolus, has thrown much light upon the home of this Jewish community. The town was situated in a sandy desert to the south of a marshy lake. It lay midway between the cultivated delta on the west and what is now the Suez Canal on the east. Past it ran the main highway to Palestine. Its founder, Psamtik I, the great-grandfather of Hophra, had built here a fort to guard the highway. Herodotus states that he also stationed guards here, and that until late in the Persian period it was defended by garrisons whose duty was to repel Asiatic invasions (II, 30). Here the Ionian and Carian mercenaries, who were at this time the chief defence of the Egyptian king, were given permanent homes. By virtue of its mixed population and its geographical position, Tahpanhes was a great meeting place of Eastern and Western civilization. Here native Egyptians, Greek mercenaries, Phœnician and Babylonian traders, and Jewish refugees met on common ground and lived side by side. It corresponded in these respects to the modern Port Said.

Probably in remembrance of the Jewish colony that once lived here, the ruins of the fort still bear an Arab name which means The Palace of the Jew's Daughter. The term palace is not altogether inappropriate, for apparently the fort was occasionally used as a royal residence. Many wine-jars, bearing the seals of Psamtik, Hophra, and Amasis, have been found in the ruins. In the northwestern part of these ruins has been uncovered a great open-air platform of brickwork, referred to in Jeremiah 43[8-10]. It was the place of common meeting found in connection with every Egyptian palace or private home. When Amasis, in 564 B.C., came to the throne of Egypt he withdrew the privileges granted by his predecessors to foreigners. The Greek colonists were transferred to Naukratis, and Tahpanhes lost most of its former glory. About this time, if not before, the great majority of the Jewish refugees, who had settled in these frontier towns, probably returned to Palestine to find homes in its partially depopulated towns.

Ezekiel from distant Babylon appears to have regarded the Jews in Egypt with considerable hope (Ezek. 29[21]). But Jeremiah, who knew them better, was keenly alive to their faults. In their despair and rage many of them evidently rejected the teachings of the prophets and became devotees of the Aramean goddess, the Queen of Heaven, mentioned in the recently discovered Aramean inscription of Zakar, king of Hazrak (cf. § LXV[vii]). Jeremiah's closing words to them, therefore, are denunciations and predictions that they should suffer even in the land of Egypt, at the hand of Nebuchadrezzar, the same fate that had overtaken their fellow-countrymen at Jerusalem. Both Jeremiah and Ezekiel (Ezek. 30) predicted that Nebuchadrezzar would invade and conquer Egypt. In 568 B.C. his army actually did appear

on the borders of Egypt; but how far he succeeded in conquering the
land is unknown. The complete conquest of Egypt certainly did
not come until the Persian period under the leadership of the cruel
Cambyses.

VII. **The Jewish Colony at Elephantine.** Jeremiah and Ezekiel
also refer to the Jewish colonists at Memphis and at Pathros, which is
the biblical designation of upper Egypt. Many of the colonists who
had settled there had doubtless fled before the conquests of Jerusalem.
The presence of a great number of Jews in Egypt at a later period indicates that even at this early date more exiles were probably to be found
in Egypt than in Babylon. Recent discoveries on the island of Elephantine in the upper Nile, opposite the modern Assuan, have thrown
new light upon the life of these Jewish colonists. These records con-
sist (1) of a series of beautifully preserved legal documents written in
Aramaic on papyrus and definitely dated between the years 471 and
411 B.C. They include contracts between the Jews residing on the
island of Elephantine regarding the transfer of property and other
legal transactions. They contain many familiar Jewish names, such
as Zadok, Isaiah, Hosea, Nathan, Ethan, Zechariah, Shallum, Uriah,
and Shemaiah. They indicate that by the earlier part of the Persian
period a large and wealthy colony of Jewish traders and bankers was
established on this island. They appear to have lived in a community
by themselves, but in the heart of the city, side by side with Egyptians,
Persians, Babylonians, Phœnicians, and Greeks, whose property in
some cases joined their own. The Jews had their own court which
ranked equally with the Persian and Egyptian law courts. Even
native Egyptians, who had cases against the Jews, appeared before
it. The names of Arameans and Arabs also appear in its lists of witnesses. From these contemporary documents it is clear that the Jews
of upper Egypt enjoyed great privileges and entered freely into the life
of the land. Ordinarily they married members of their own race;
but the marriage of a Jewess with a foreigner is also reported. He
appears, however, to have been a proselyte to Judaism. Another Jewess married an Egyptian and took oath by the Egyptian goddess Sati,
suggesting that she had nominally at least adopted the religion of her
husband. One Hebrew also bears the suggestive name of Hosea,
the son of Petikhnum (an Egyptian name meaning *Gift of the god
Khnum*).

VIII. **The Temple of Yahu at Elephantine.** These Aramaic legal
documents also contain many references to Yahu (the older form of

Yahweh or Jehovah), the god worshipped by the Jews, and to Yahu's temple situated on King's Street, one of the main thoroughfares of the city. These references have been signally confirmed by a most remarkable letter recently discovered by the Germans at this site. It was written in November of the year 408 B.C., by the members of the Jewish colony at Elephantine to Bagohi (the Bagoas of Josephus), the Persian governor of Judah. It states, among other things, that "Already in the days of the kings of Egypt our fathers had built this temple in the fortress of Elephantine. And when Cambyses (529–522 B.C.) entered Egypt he found this temple built, and, though the temple of the gods of Egypt were all at that time overthrown, no one injured anything in this temple." It further states that recently (in the year 411 B.C.), in the absence of the Persian governor in Egypt, the foreigners in Elephantine had stirred up a certain minor official to instruct his son, who was commander of a neighboring fortress, to destroy the Jewish temple.

The Aramaic letter was intended to be sent, together with rich gifts, to influence the powerful Persian governor of Judah, Bagohi, to issue an order permitting the Jews to rebuild their temple. From this letter we learn that the temple of the God Yahu was built of hewn stone with pillars of stone in front, probably similar to those in the Egyptian temples, and had seven great gates built of hewn stone and provided with doors and bronze hinges. Its roof was wholly of cedar wood, probably brought from the distant Lebanon, and its walls appear to have been ceiled or adorned with stucco, as were those of Solomon's temple. It was also equipped with bowls of gold and silver and the other paraphernalia of sacrifice. Here were regularly offered cereal-offerings, burnt-offerings, and frankincense. The petitioners also promised that, if the Persian officials would grant their request, "we will also offer cereal-offerings and frankincense and burnt-offerings on the altar in your name, and we will pray to God in your name, we and our wives and all the Jews who are here, if you do thus until the temple is built. And you shall have a portion before the God Yahu, the God of Heaven, from every one who offers to him burnt-offerings and sacrifices."

Historical students have long been familiar with the fact that late in the Greek period the Jews of Egypt built a temple to Jehovah at Leontopolis, in the Delta (*cf.* § CXV[viii]); but these recent discoveries open an entirely new chapter in Jewish history. They indicate that probably within a generation after the destruction of the Jerusalem temple,

11

in 586 B.C., the Jewish colonists in Egypt built for themselves far up the Nile, and possibly at other points in this land of their exile, a temple or temples to Jehovah; that they remained loyal to God and the institutions of their race; and that in the midst of cosmopolitan Egypt they preserved intact their racial unity. In the light of these discoveries it is also clear that because of their character and numbers and nearness to Palestine the Jews of Egypt, even at this early period, were a far more important factor in the life and development of Judaism than they have hitherto been considered. These discoveries also afford definite grounds for the hope that from this unexpected quarter much more valuable material will come to illumine this otherwise dark period of post-exilic Jewish history.

§ XCII. EZEKIEL'S MESSAGE TO HIS SCATTERED COUNTRYMEN

1. Vision of the dead bones representing the scattered people (Ezek. 37[1-6])

The hand of Jehovah was upon me, and he brought me by the spirit and set me down in the midst of the valley; and it was full of bones. And he caused me to pass by them round about; and, behold, there were very many on the surface of the valley; and, lo, they were very dry. And he said to me, Son of man, can these bones live? And I answered, O Lord Jehovah, thou knowest. Again he said to me, Prophesy over these bones, and say to them, O ye dry bones, hear the word of Jehovah. 'Thus saith Jehovah to these bones: "Behold I am about to put breath into you, that ye may live. And I will put sinews on you, and will clothe you with flesh, and cover you with skin, and put breath in you, that ye may live; and know that I am Jehovah." '

2. Revival of the scattered bones (7-10)

So I prophesied as he commanded me: and as I prophesied, there was an earthquake; and the bones came together, bone to its bone. And I beheld, and, lo, there were sinews upon them, and flesh had clothed them, and skin covered them; but there was no breath in them. Then he said to me, Prophesy to the breath, prophesy, son of man, and say to the breath, 'Thus saith Jehovah: "Come from the four winds, O breath, and breathe upon these slain, that they may live." ' So I prophesied as he commanded me, and

12

the breath came into them, and they lived, and stood upon their feet, an exceedingly great host.

Then he said to me, O man, these bones are the whole house of Israel; behold, they say, 'Our bones are dried up, and our hope is lost; we are completely ruined.' Therefore prophesy, and say to them, 'Thus saith Jehovah: "Behold, I will open your graves, and raise you from your graves, O my people; and I will bring you into the land of Israel. And ye shall know that I am Jehovah, when I have opened your graves, and raised you from your graves, O my people. And I will put my spirit in you, that ye may live, and I will restore you to your own land: that ye may know that I, Jehovah, have spoken it and performed it," is the oracle of Jehovah.'

3. Symbolic of the revival of the nation (11-14)

This word also came to me from Jehovah: Do thou, O man, take a stick, and write upon it, JUDAH AND THE ISRAELITES ASSOCIATED WITH HIM: then take another stick, and write upon it, JOSEPH, AND ALL THE HOUSE OF ISRAEL ASSOCIATED WITH HIM. Then join them together, so that they may become one stick in thy hand. And when the children of thy people shall say to thee, 'Wilt thou not show us what this means?' say to them, 'Thus saith Jehovah: "Behold, I am about to take the stick of Joseph, which is in the hand of Ephraim, and the tribes of Israel associated with him; and I will unite them with the stick of Judah, and make them one stick, and they shall be united in my hand."' And let the sticks on which thou writest be in thy hand before their eyes. And say to them, 'Thus saith the Lord Jehovah: "Behold, I am about to take the Israelites from among the nations, whither they are gone, and gather them from all sides, and bring them into their own land: and I will make them one nation in the land, upon the mountains of Israel; and there shall be one king over them all; and they shall be no longer two nations, neither shall they be divided into two kingdoms any longer; nor shall they defile themselves any more with their idols, nor with their detestable things, nor with any of their transgressions; but I will save them from all their apostasies wherein they have sinned, and will cleanse them; so shall they be my people, and I will be their God.

4. Union of the southern and northern Israelites (15-23)

13

5. Renewal of the covenant under a Davidic ruler (24-28)

And my servant David shall be king over them; and they all shall have one shepherd: they shall also walk in mine ordinances, and observe my statutes, and do them. And they shall dwell in the land that I have given to my servant Jacob, wherein their fathers dwelt; and they shall dwell therein, they and their sons, forever. And David my servant shall be their prince forever. Moreover I will make a covenant of peace with them; it shall be an everlasting covenant with them; and I will establish them, and multiply them, and set my sanctuary in the midst of them forevermore. My dwelling place also shall be with them; and I will be their God, and they shall be my people. And the nations shall know that I am Jehovah who sanctifieth Israel, when my sanctuary shall be in the midst of them forevermore." '

6. Ezekiel's vision (40¹⁻⁴)

In the twenty-fifth year of our captivity, in the beginning of the year, in the tenth day of the month, in the fourteenth year after the city was taken, on that very day, the hand of Jehovah was laid upon me, and he brought me in an inspired vision to the land of Israel, and set me down upon a very high mountain, on which was a city-like building toward the south. Thither he brought me, and there was a man whose appearance was like the appearance of bronze, with a flaxen line and a measuring reed in his hand; and he was standing in the gateway. And the man said to me, Son of man, behold with thine eyes, and hear with thine ears, and give heed to all that I shall show thee; for, in order that thou shouldst be shown it wert thou brought hither; declare all that thou seest to the house of Israel.

7. Encircling wall (5)

There was a wall encircling a temple, and in the man's hand a measuring reed six cubits long, each cubit being equal to about twenty-one inches. And he measured the thickness of the building one reed (about ten and one-half feet); and the height one reed.

8. Outer gateway on the east (6-12)

Then he came to the east gateway and went up its steps and measured the threshold of the gate one reed wide. And each guard-room was one reed long, and one reed broad; and between the guard-rooms were spaces of five cubits; and the threshold of the gate at the vestibule of the gate on the inner side was one reed. Then he measured the

14

vestibule of the gate, eight cubits, and its jambs, two cubits; and the vestibule of the gate was on the inner side. And the guard-rooms of the east gate were three on each side; and all three were of the same dimensions; and the posts were on both sides. And he measured the breadth of the entrance to the gateway, ten cubits; and the width of the gate, thirteen cubits; and there was a sill one cubit wide, before the guard-rooms on each side; and the guard-rooms, six cubits on both sides.

And he measured the gate from the outer wall of the one guard-room to the outer wall of the other, twenty-five cubits wide [about forty-four feet]; door opposite door. And from the front of the gateway at the entrance to the front of the inner vestibule of the gate were fifty cubits. 9. Dimensions of the gateway (13, 15)

Then he brought me to the outer court, and there were chambers and a pavement made round about the court; thirty chambers were upon the pavement. And he measured its breadth from the front of the lower gate to the front of the inner court without, one hundred cubits on the east and on the north. 10. Outer court of the temple (17, 19)

And the north gateway of the outer court, he measured its length and breadth. And its measurements were the same as those of the east gateway. The dimensions of the gateway on the south were also the same as the others. 1. Outer gateways (20, 21b, 24b)

He brought me outside the gate and into the inner court, and there were two chambers on the inner court, one by the north gate, facing the south, and the other by the south gate, facing the north. And he said to me, This chamber which faces the south is for the priests who have charge of the temple; and the chamber which faces the north is for the priests who have charge of the altar; they are the sons of Zadok, those of the sons of Levi who may be near to Jehovah to serve him. And he measured the court, a hundred cubits wide, and a hundred cubits broad—a perfect square. The altar was in front of the temple. 12. Chambers for the ministering priests (44-47)

Then he brought me into the hall of the temple and measured the jambs, six cubits on each side. And the breadth of the entrance was ten cubits; and the sides of the entrance were five cubits on each side; and he measured its length, forty cubits; and its width, twenty cubits. 13. Main hall (41¹, ²)

14.
Most
holy
place
(3, 4)

Then he went into the inner room and measured the jambs of its entrance, two cubits; and the entrance, six cubits; and the side-walls of the entrance, seven cubits on each side. And he measured its length, twenty cubits, and its breadth, twenty cubits, before the hall of the temple. And he said to me, This is the most holy place.

15. The
side-
cham-
bers;
plan
and
dimen-
sions
(5-8a)

Then he measured the thickness of the wall of the temple, six cubits; and the width of the side-chambers, four cubits, round about the temple on every side. And the side-chambers were in three stories, one above another, and thirty in each story; and there were abatements all around the walls of the temple that the side-chambers might be fastened to them and not to the walls of the temple. And the side-chambers became wider as they went up higher and higher, for the temple grew narrower higher up; and there was an ascent from the lowest story to the highest through the middle story. And I saw also that the temple had a raised platform round about.

16.
Vision
of Je-
hovah
(43¹⁻⁵)

Then he brought me to the east gate. And behold the glory of the God of Israel came from the east; and his voice was like the sound of many waters; and the earth shone with his glory. And the vision which I saw was like that which I saw when he came to destroy the city; and the visions were like that which I saw by the River Chebar; and I fell on my face. Then the glory of Jehovah came into the temple through the east gate. And the spirit took me up, and brought me into the inner court; and, behold, the glory of Jehovah filled the temple.

17.
Temple
sancti-
fied by
Jeho-
vah's
pres-
ence
(6-9)

Then I heard One speaking to me from the temple, as he stood by me. And he said to me, O man, this is the place of my throne, and the place for the soles of my feet, where I will dwell in the midst of the Israelites forever. And the house of Israel, they and their kings, shall no more defile my holy name with their idolatry and with the corpses of their kings by placing their thresholds by my threshold, and their door-posts by my door-post, with only a wall between me and them, thus defiling my holy name by the abominations which they have committed; therefore I have destroyed them in mine anger. Now let them put away their idolatry, and the corpses of their kings far from me, that I may dwell in the midst of them forever.

Therefore thus saith the Lord Jehovah, 'No foreigner, consecrated neither in heart nor flesh, of all the foreigners who are among the Israelites, shall enter my sanctuary. But those Levites who went far from me, when Israel went astray, who went astray from me after their idols, shall bear their guilt. Yet they shall be ministers in my sanctuary, having oversight at the gates of the temple, and ministering in the temple; they shall slay the burnt-offering and the sacrifice for the people, and they shall stand before them and minister to them. Since they were wont to minister to them before their idols and were a stumbling block of iniquity to the house of Israel; therefore I have taken a solemn oath against them,' is the oracle of the Lord Jehovah, 'and they shall bear their guilt. And they shall not approach me to act as priests to me, so as to come near any of my sacred things, or to those which are most sacred; but they shall bear their shame and the punishment for the abominations which they have committed; I will make them responsible for the care of the temple, for all its service, and for all that shall be done therein. 18. Duties of the priests from the ancient sanctuaries (44⁹⁻¹⁴)

But the priests, the Levites, the sons of Zadok, who took charge of my sanctuary when the Israelites went astray from me, shall come near to me to minister to me, and they shall stand before me to offer to me fat and blood,' is the oracle of the Lord Jehovah. 'They shall enter my sanctuary, and they shall approach near to my table to minister to me, and they shall keep my charge. 19. Duties of the sons of the Jerusalem priests (¹ᵇ, ¹⁶)

And they shall teach my people the difference between the sacred and the common, and instruct them how to discern between the clean and the unclean. And in a controversy they shall act as judges, judging it according to my ordinances. And they shall keep my laws and my statutes in all my appointed feasts; and they shall maintain the sanctity of my sabbaths.' 20. As guardians of the laws and ritual (²³, ²⁴)

When ye allot the land as inheritance, ye shall offer as a special gift to Jehovah, a sacred portion of the land, five thousand cubits long, and twenty thousand cubits wide; it shall be sacred throughout its entire extent. And out of this area shalt thou measure off a space twenty-five thousand cubits long and ten thousand cubits wide, and on it 21. Apportionment of the land to the temple and its ministers (45¹⁻⁵)

17

shall the most holy sanctuary stand. It is a holy portion of the land; it shall belong to the priests who are the ministers in the sanctuary, who draw near to minister to Jehovah; and it shall be a place for their houses, and an open space for the sanctuary. Out of this a square of five hundred cubits shall be for the sanctuary, with an open space fifty cubits wide around it. And a space twenty-five thousand cubits long and ten thousand wide shall belong to the Levites, the ministers of the temple; it shall be their possession for cities in which to dwell.

22. To the city and prince (6-8) And as the possession of the city, ye shall assign a space five thousand cubits wide, and twenty-five thousand long, beside the sacred reservation; it shall belong to the whole house of Israel. And the prince shall have the space on both sides of the sacred reservation and the possession of the city, on the west and on the east, and of the same length as one of the portions of the tribes, from the west border to the east border of the land. It shall be his possession in Israel; and the princes of Israel shall no more oppress my people, but shall give the land to the house of Israel according to their tribes.

I. **The Home of the Exiles in Babylon.** From the references in the contemporary writers it is possible to gain a reasonably definite idea regarding the environment of the Jewish exiles in Babylon. Ezekiel describes the site as "a land of traffic, a city of merchants, a fruitful soil, and beside many waters," where the colony like a willow was transplanted (17^5). The Kabaru Canal (the River Chebar of Ezekiel) ran southeast from Babylon to Nippur through a rich alluvial plain, intersected by numerous canals. Beside it lived a dense agricultural population. On the tells or artificial mounds made by the ruins of earlier Babylonian cities were built the peasant villages. Ezekiel speaks of preaching to the Jewish colony of Tel-Abib (Storm-hill), and the lists of those who later returned to Judah contain references to those who came from Tel-Melah (Salt-hill) and Tel-Harsha (Forest-hill).

II. **Their Condition and Occupations.** It is probable that these mounds were not far from each other and that the adjacent fields were cultivated by the Jewish colonists. Thus they were enabled, under even more favorable conditions than in Judah, to continue in their old occupations and to build houses and rear families as Jeremiah had

18

advised (Jer. 29; § LXXXVII[35]). In Babylonia, as at Elephantine, so long as they paid the imperial tax and refrained from open violence they were probably allowed to rule themselves in accordance with their own laws. The elders of the different families directed the affairs of the community and acted as judges, except in the case of capital offences which were punished in the name of Nebuchadrezzar (Jer. 29[22]). Thus for a long time the exiles constituted a little Judah within the heart of the Babylonian empire, maintaining their racial integrity even more completely than the Jews resident in Egypt.

Babylonia was the scene of an intense commercial activity. The opportunities and allurements of the far-reaching traffic which passed up and down the great rivers and across the neighboring deserts were eventually too strong for the Jews to resist. Hence in Babylonia, as in Egypt, they gradually abandoned their inherited agricultural habits and were transformed into a nation of traders. In the recently discovered records of the transactions of the famous Babylonian banking house which flourished during the earlier part of the Persian period, under the direction of succeeding generations of the Murashu family, are found many familiar Jewish names. These indicate that within a century after the fall of Jerusalem many sons of the exiles had already won a prominent place in the commercial life of that great metropolis.

III. **Their Religious Life.** With this transformation in their occupation came a great temptation to forget their race and to lose sight of its ideals. The temptation was all the greater because their capital city and temple were in ruins and the belief was widely held that Jehovah had forsaken his land and people and retired to his "mount in the uttermost parts of the north" (Is. 14[13] Ezek. 1[4]). Their actual experiences had proved so fundamentally different from their hopes that there was undoubtedly in the minds of many a dread doubt as to whether Jehovah was able to fulfil his promises. False prophets were also present to mislead the people (Jer. 39[21-23] Ezek. 13[1-7] 14[8-10]). There is also no indication that the Jews of Babylon ever attempted to build a temple to Jehovah in the land of their captivity. Hence there were no ancient festivals and public and private sacrifices and impressive ceremonials to kindle their religious feelings and to keep alive their national faith. Instead, the imposing religion of the Babylonians, with its rich temples, its many festivals, its prosperous and powerful priesthood, and its elaborate ritual must have profoundly impressed them and led them to draw unfavorable comparisons between it and the simple services of their pre-exilic temple. Nevertheless, in spite of these temptations, there were many who proved themselves loyal to Jehovah. Prayer and fasting and sabbath observance took the place of sacrificial rites. A strong emphasis is laid by Ezekiel on the sabbath (20^{12-21} 22^{26} 23^{38}). From this time on it became one of the most important and characteristic institutions of Judaism. Under the influence of the new situation it lost much of its original, philanthropic, and social character and became instead a ceremonial institution. In faithfully observing it the exiles felt that even in captivity they were paying homage to their divine King. The more it took the place of the ancient feasts and sacrifices, the more they forgot that the sabbath was God's gift to toiling man rather than man's gift to God. From the Babylonian exile, also, probably dates that custom of assembling on the sabbath to read the ancient scriptures which represents the genesis of the later synagogue and its service.

IV. **The Prophecies of Ezekiel.** The priest-prophet Ezekiel was the interpreter, pastor, and guide of the Babylonian exiles. He met their problems and proposed the solutions which became the foundation principles of later Judaism. His prophecies fall naturally into four distinct groups: (1) Chapters 1 to 24, which recount his call and deal with the issues at stake in the different Judean communities in the critical years between the first and second captivities. They represent the prophet's work between the years 592 and 586 B.C. (2) Chapters 25 to 32, include seven oracles regarding Ammon, Moab, Edom, Philistia, Tyre, and Egypt, the nations which had taken part in the destruction of Jerusalem or else, like Egypt, had lured Judah to its ruin. The complete destruction of these foes is predicted, and chapter 32 concludes with a weird picture of their fate, condemned by Jehovah to dwell in Sheol, the abode of the shades. (3) Chapters 33 to 39 contain messages of comfort and promise to Ezekiel's fellow-exiles in Babylonia and in the distant lands of the dispersion. They are dated between the years 586 and 570 B.C. (4) Chapters 40 to 48 present Ezekiel's plan for the restored temple and service and for the redistribution of the territory of Canaan, and his belief that Judah's fertility would be miraculously increased. This plan is definitely dated in the year 572 B.C., two years before the prophet's death.

V. **The Resurrection of the Dead Nation.** Ezekiel dealt with the problems of his fellow-exiles concretely and from a point of view which they could readily understand. He fully realized that if the faith of the people was to be saved in this crisis a definite hope, expressed in objective imagery, must be set before them. With the same inspired insight that had prompted Jeremiah to purchase his family estate in the hour of Jerusalem's downfall, Ezekiel saw that Jehovah would yet restore his people, if they would but respond to the demands of this crisis. His message was, therefore, one of hope and promise. In the memorable chapter in which he pictures a valley filled with dry bones, he aimed to inspire their faith by declaring that Jehovah was not only able but would surely gather together the dismembered parts of the nation and impart to it new life and activity. The prophet was clearly speaking of national rather than of individual resurrection. Like Jeremiah, he anticipated that the tribes of the north and south would again be united, as in the days of David, and that over them a scion of the Davidic house would rule as Jehovah's representative. He also assured them that Jehovah would come again to dwell in the midst of his purified and restored people.

VI. **The Divine Shepherd.** In the thirty-fourth chapter Ezekiel deals with the same theme under a different figure. First he traces the cause of the exile to the inefficiency and greed and oppression of the earlier shepherds, the rulers like Jehoiakim, who had scattered rather than gathered and led the people intrusted to them. Now Jehovah himself, the great Shepherd of the People, will arise and gather his flock, and lead them back to their home and give them a rich pasture. Over them he will appoint a descendant of David, but this prince shall be shorn of his ancient kingly power.

Ezekiel also presents in his characteristic, symbolic form the promise that Jehovah will now fulfil the popular hopes and destroy the wicked foes who have preyed upon his people, and thus vindicate his divine rulership of the world. In one passage Judah's worst foes, the Edomites, represent aggressive heathendom. Again, in a still more impressive picture, suggested by an experience in his own childhood when the dread Scythians swept down from the north, he portrays the advance of the mysterious foes from the distant north under the leadership of Gog (38, 39). When they are already in the land of Palestine, the prophet declares, Jehovah will terrify them with an earthquake, so that in panic they shall slay each other, as did the Midianites in the days of Gideon, until they shall all fall victims of Jehovah's judgment. Ezekiel thus revived in the changed conditions of the exile that popular conception of the day of Jehovah which the earlier prophets had refused to countenance. It was the prophet's graphic way of declaring that Jehovah would prepare the way for the return of his people, if they would but respond when the opportune moment should arrive.

21

Later Judaism, however, and especially the apocalpytic writers, interpreted literally and developed still further this picture of Jehovah's great judgment day until it became a prominent teaching of later Jewish and Christian thought.

Similarly Ezekiel declared that the barren lands of Judah would be miraculously transformed and rendered capable of supporting the great numbers of the exiles who should return. In this respect Ezekiel became the father of the later priestly school to which belongs the author of the book of Chronicles, in whose thought the events of Israel's history came to pass, not through man's earnest effort and in accordance with the established laws of the universe, but through special divine interposition. It is difficult to determine whether Ezekiel himself was simply endeavoring to state dramatically that Jehovah would fully anticipate the needs of his people, or whether he did actually anticipate a series of prodigious miracles.

VII. Ezekiel's Plan of the Restored Temple. Ezekiel, being a true prophet, fully realized that the fundamental question regarding the future of his race was not whether they would be restored to their home but whether or not they would guard against the mistakes and sins of the past and live in accord with Jehovah's just demands. The solution of this question which he proposes reveals his priestly training. With infinite pains and detail he develops the plan of a restored temple and ritual. The details were doubtless in part suggested by his remembrance of the temple at Jerusalem and in part taken from the great temples of Babylon. By means of this elaborate picture he declared his firm conviction that his race would surely be restored. His chief purpose, however, was to impress upon the minds of his people the transcendent holiness of Jehovah and the necessity that he be worshipped by a holy people. The entire plan of the temple, of the ritual, and even of the allotment of the territory of Canaan was intended to enforce this idea. His plan, if adopted, was calculated to deliver the people from the temptations and mistakes of the past. With this end in view Jehovah's sacred abode was guarded with massive double walls and huge gateways. Only the priests were allowed to enter the inner court, and a sharp distinction was made between the priests who were the descendants of Zadok and the Levites whose fathers had ministered at the many sanctuaries scattered throughout the land of Israel. The territory immediately adjacent to the temple was assigned to the priests and Levites, and its sanctity was further guarded on the east and west by the domains of the prince. His chief function was, not to rule, as had the selfish and

inefficient tyrants who had preceded him, but to provide the animals
and the material requisite for the temple service. The territory on the
north and the south of the temple was assigned to the different tribes
of Israel.

No political or social problems clouded the prophet's vision. The
entire energies of priest, Levite, prince, and people were to be devoted
to the worship of the Holy One, whose restored and glorified sanctuary
stood in their midst. Thus it was that Ezekiel reversed the ideals of
the pre-exilic Hebrew state and presented that programme which with
many modifications was adopted in principle at least by the post-exilic
Judean community. In place of the monarchy appeared the hierarchy;
instead of the king the high priest became both the religious and the
civil head of the nation. Soon the Davidic royal line disappeared
entirely, and the interests of the people centred more and more about
the temple and its ritual. Although Ezekiel's vision was not and could
not be fully realized, except by a series of miracles, this devoted priest-
prophet of the exile was in a large sense the father of Judaism.

§ XCIII. THE CLOSING YEARS OF THE BABYLONIAN RULE

Now it came to pass in the thirty-seventh year of the
captivity of Jehoiachin king of Judah, in the twenty-seventh
day of the twelfth month, Evil-merodach king of Babylon,
in the year in which he became king, (561 B.C.) lifted up
Jehoiachin king of Judah from prison to a position of
honor. And he spoke kindly to him and placed his seat above
the seats of the kings who were with him in Babylon, and
changed his prison garments. And Jehoiachin ate with
him continually as long as he lived. And for his support a
continual allowance was given him by the king, each day
a portion, as long as he lived.

1. Libera-
tion of
King
Jehoi-
achin
(II
Kings.
2$5^{27-30}$)

The people who have been walking in darkness see a great
  light,
Those who dwell in the land of deepest gloom, upon them a
  light shines.
Thou multipliest the exultation, thou makest great the
  rejoicing,
They rejoice before thee as men rejoice at harvest time,
As men are wont to exult when they divide spoil.

2. Hope
for the
people
in
gloom
Is. 9$^{1-3}$

3. Deliverance from foreign conquerors (4, 5)

For the burdensome yoke and the crossbar on his shoulder,
The rod of his taskmaster, thou breakest as in the day of Midian.
For every boot of the warrior with noisy tread,
And every war-cloak drenched in the blood of the slain
Will be completely burned up as fuel for the flame.

4. Rise of a divinely gifted prince to establish a just rule (6, 7)

For a child is born, to us a son is given,
And dominion shall rest upon his shoulder;
And his name will be Wonderful Counsellor,
Godlike Hero, Ever-watchful Father, Prince of Peace.
To the increase of his dominion and to the peace there shall be no end,
On the throne of David and throughout his kingdom,
To establish and uphold it by justice and righteousness
Henceforth and forever. The jealousy of Jehovah will accomplish this.

5. The divinely gifted scion of the Davidic house (11¹, ²)

A sprout shall spring from the stock of Jesse,
And a shoot from his roots shall bear fruit.
The spirit of Jehovah shall rest upon him.
A spirit of wisdom and insight,
A spirit of counsel and might,
A spirit of knowledge and the fear of Jehovah.

6. His just rule (³⁻⁵)

He will not judge according to what his eyes see,
Nor decide according to what his ears hear;
But with righteousness will he judge the helpless,
And with equity will he decide for the needy in the land.
He will smite an oppressor with the rod of his mouth,
And with the breath of his lips will he slay the guilty.
Righteousness will be the girdle about his loins,
And faithfulness the band about his waist.

7. Effects of that rule upon the world (⁶⁻⁸)

Then the wolf will be the guest of the lamb,
And the leopard will lie down with the kid;
The calf and the young lion will graze together,
And a little child shall be their leader.
The cow and the bear shall become friends,
Their young ones shall lie down together,

And the lion shall eat straw like the ox;
The suckling will play about the hole of the asp,
And the weaned child will stretch out his hand toward
the viper's nest.

Men shall not harm nor destroy
In all my holy mountain;
For the earth shall have been filled with knowledge of
Jehovah
As the waters cover the sea.
And it shall come to pass in that day,
That the root of Jesse who is to stand as a signal to
the peoples—
To him shall the nations resort,
And his resting-place shall be glorious.

8. Upon all mankind (9, 10)

Upon a treeless mountain lift up a signal, raise a cry to them,
Wave the hand that they may enter the princely gates.
I myself have given command to my consecrated ones, to
execute my wrath,
I have also summoned my heroes, my proudly exultant ones.
Hark, a tumult on the mountains, as of a mighty multitude!
Hark, an uproar of kingdoms, of gathered nations!
It is Jehovah of hosts mustering the martial hosts.

9. Jehovah rallying the hosts against Babylon (13²⁻⁴)

I will punish the earth for its wickedness, and the wicked
for their iniquity,
I will still the arrogance of the proud, and lay low the pre-
sumption of tyrants.
Behold, I stir up against them the Medes,
Who consider not silver, and take no pleasure in gold,
On children they will look with no pity, they have no com-
passion on the fruit of the womb,
And Babylon, the most beautiful of kingdoms, the proud
glory of the Chaldeans, shall be,
As when God overthrew Sodom and Gomorrah.

10. Its coming overthrow by the Medo-Persian army (11b, 17-19)

It shall be uninhabited forever, and tenantless age after age;
No nomad shall pitch there his tent, nor shepherds let their
flocks lie down there,

11. Its utter destruction (20-22)

But wild cats shall lie there, and their houses shall be full of jackals;

Ostriches shall dwell there, and satyrs shall dance there,

Howling beasts shall cry to each other in its castles, and wolves in its revelling halls;

Its time is near at hand, its day shall not be extended.

12. Cyrus's command to rebuild the temple (Ezra 6³⁻⁵)

In the first year of Cyrus the king, Cyrus the king made a decree: Concerning the house of God in Jerusalem—this house shall be rebuilt, where they offer sacrifices and bring him offerings made by fire. Its height shall be sixty cubits and its breadth sixty cubits, It shall be constructed with three layers of huge stones and one layer of timber. And let the expenses be paid out of the king's treasury. Also let the gold and silver vessels of the house of God, which Nebuchadrezzar took from the temple at Jerusalem and brought to Babylon, be restored and brought again to the temple which is at Jerusalem, each to its place, and you shall put them in the house of God.

13. Restoration of the vessels of the temple (5¹⁴, ¹⁵)

Now the gold and silver vessels of the house of God which Nebuchadrezzar took from the temple at Jerusalem and brought to the temple in Babylon, those Cyrus the king took out of the temple in Babylon, and they were delivered to one by the name of Sheshbazzar, whom he had made governor. And he said to him, Take these vessels; go, put them in the temple at Jerusalem, and let the house of God be rebuilt in its place.

14. The exiles who returned to Jerusalem (1⁵, ⁶ I Esdr. 5⁴⁻⁸)

Then the heads of the fathers' houses of Judah and Benjamin, and the priests and the Levites, even all whose spirit God had stirred to go up to build the temple of Jehovah which is at Jerusalem, arose. And all those who were about them supplied them with silver vessels, with gold, with goods, and with beasts, and with precious things, besides all that was voluntarily offered.

These are the names of the men who went up, according to their tribes, by their genealogy. Of the priests the sons of Phinehas, the son of Aaron: Jeshua the son of Jozadak, the son of Seriah. And there rose up with him Zerubbabel the son of Shealtiel of the house of David, of the family of Peres, of the tribe of Judah; in the second year of Cyrus king of Persia in the first day of the month Nisan.

Then Jeshua the son of Jozadak, and his kinsmen the priests, and Zerubbabel the son of Shealtiel and his kinsmen arose and built the altar of the God of Israel, to offer burnt-offerings on it, as prescribed in the law of Moses the man of God. And they set up the altar in its place; for fear, because of the peoples dwelling in the land, had come upon them, but they plucked up courage and offered burnt-offerings to Jehovah, even burnt-offerings morning and evening. And they kept the feast of booths as it is prescribed, and offered the fixed number of daily burnt-offerings according to the direction for each day; but the foundation of the temple of Jehovah was not yet laid.

15. Renewal of the altar service (Ezra 3$^{1-4, 6b}$)

I. **The Transformation of the Jews into a Literary People.** The destruction of Jerusalem transformed the Jewish peasants of Palestine into a literary race. Before the final destruction of Jerusalem they had lived together in a small territory where communication was easy and the need of written records but slight. The exile separated friends and members of the same families, and scattered them broadcast throughout the then known world. The only means of communicating with each other in most cases was by writing, and this necessity inevitably developed the literary art. The exiles in Babylonia and Egypt were also in close contact with the two most active literary peoples of the ancient world. In countries where almost every public or private act was recorded in written form, and where the literature of the past was carefully preserved and widely transcribed, it was inevitable that the Jews should be powerfully influenced by these examples. Furthermore, the teachers of the race, prophets and priests alike, prevented by the destruction of the temple from employing their former oral and symbolic methods of instruction, resorted, as did the priest Ezekiel, to the pen. Thus the religious thought and devotion of the race began to find expression in its literature.

The incentives to collect the earlier writings of the priests and prophets were also exceedingly strong, for the experiences and institutions of their past, together with their hopes for the future, were the two main forces that now held together the Jewish race. Fortunately, the more intelligent leaders realized, even before 586 B.C., that the final catastrophe was practically certain, and therefore prepared for it in advance.

27

The decade between the first and second captivities also gave them an opportunity to collect the more important writings of their earlier prophetic and priestly teachers, while the Judean state was still intact and while these earlier writings could be readily consulted.

II. **The Literary Activity of the Babylonian Period.** The literary work of this period took three distinct forms: (1) The collection, compilation, and editing of earlier historical writings. It was probably during this period that the narratives of Judges, of Samuel, and Kings, which carried the history down into the exile itself, received their final revision. (2) Earlier writings were revised or supplemented so as to adapt them to the new and different conditions. Thus the sermons of the pre-exilic prophets, as for example those of Amos and Isaiah, were then revised and supplemented at many points. These earlier prophets had predicted doom and destruction for their nation; but now that their predictions had been realized what was needed was a message of comfort and promise. The fulfilment of their earlier predictions had established their authority in the minds of the people. The purpose of the later editors was evidently to put in the mouth of these earlier prophets what they probably would have said had they been present to speak at the later day to their discouraged and disconsolate countrymen. Studied in the light of these two fundamentally different points of view, the glaring inconsistencies which appear in the prophetic books are fully explained and the consistency of the earlier prophets vindicated.

The third form of literary activity is represented by the writings of Ezekiel. With the authority of a prophet, he dealt directly with the problem of his day, and the greater part of his book consists of the records of his prophetic addresses or of epistles which he sent to his scattered fellow-countrymen, even as Jeremiah wrote from Judah a letter to the distant exiles in Babylon. His new constitution for the restored Jewish state was also based on earlier customs and laws, but was adapted to the new needs of the changed situation. He was not the only one to undertake this task. Other priests gathered earlier groups of oral laws and put in written form the customs and traditions of the pre-exilic temple. At the same time they modified these earlier customs so as to correct the evils which past experience had revealed.

III. **The Holiness Code.** The chief product of the literary activity of the earlier part of the exile is the collection of laws found in the seventeenth to the twenty-sixth chapters of Leviticus. Because of its strong emphasis on the holiness of Jehovah and on the necessity that he be worshipped by a people both ceremonially and morally holy, it is now commonly designated as the Holiness Code. In theme, in point of view, in purpose, and in literary form it has many close points of contact with the writings of Ezekiel. In its original unity it evidently came from the period and circle of thought in which the great priest-prophet lived. His sermons, however, suggest that he was acquainted with its main teachings. In distinguishing sharply between the Jerusalem priests and the ministering Levites, and in prohibiting the marriage of a priest with a widow, Ezekiel shows that his work represented a slightly later stage in the development of Israel's religious standards. The most probable date, therefore, for the Holiness Code is the decade between the first and second capitvity (597–586 B.C.).

Like every ancient lawbook the Holiness Code contains many laws and regulations which evidently come from a much earlier period in Israel's history. Some of its enactments are very similar to those of the primitive codes of Exodus 21–23. In spirit it is closely related to the book of Deuteronomy. It also reproduces many of the laws found in this earlier code. Both codes represent the fruitage of the teaching of the pre-exilic prophets and priests. Each contains ceremonial, civil, and moral laws; but the emphasis on the ritual is more pronounced in the Holiness Code. It consists of ten or eleven distinct groups of laws. In Leviticus 18 and 19 are found certain short decalogues. They probably represent the united efforts of the Judean prophets and priests during the Assyrian period to inculcate the true principles of justice, service, and worship in the minds of the people. Some of the laws in these earlier decalogues are the noblest examples of Old Testament legislation:

DUTIES TO OTHERS

I. Thou shalt not wholly reap the corners of thy fields.
II. Thou shalt not gather the gleanings of thy harvest.
III. Thou shalt not glean thy vineyard.
IV. Thou shalt not gather the fallen fruit of thy vineyard.
V. Thou shalt leave them for the poor and the resident alien.

Kindness to the needy

VI. Ye shall not steal.
VII. Ye shall do no injustice, in measures of length, weight or of quantity.
VIII. Ye shall not deal falsely with one another.

Honesty in business relations

IX. Ye shall not lie to one another.
X. Ye shall not swear falsely by my name.

JUSTICE TO ALL MEN

Toward dependents

I. Thou shalt not oppress thy neighbor.
II. Thou shalt not rob thy neighbor.
III. The wages of a hired servant shall not remain with thee all night until the morning.
IV. Thou shalt not curse the deaf.
V. Thou shalt not put a stumbling-block before the blind.

Toward equals

VI. Thou shalt not do injustice in rendering a judicial decision.
VII. Thou shalt not show partiality to the poor.
VIII. Thou shalt not have undue consideration for the powerful.
IX. Thou shalt not go about as a tale-bearer among thy people.
X. Thou shalt not seek the blood of thy neighbor [by bearing false testimony in court].

ATTITUDE TOWARD OTHERS

In the heart

I. Thou shalt not hate thy fellow-countryman in thy heart.
II. Thou shalt warn thy neighbor and not incur sin on his account.
III. Thou shalt not take vengeance.
IV. Thou shalt not bear a grudge against the members of thy race.
V. Thou shalt love thy neighbor as thyself.

IV. **The Liberation of Jehoiachin and the Hopes of the Jews.** The liberation of Jehoiachin, the grandson of Josiah, from the Babylonian prison where he had been confined since the first capture of Jerusalem was the one event in the Babylonian period deemed worthy of record by the biblical historians. The occasion was the accession of Nebuchadrezzar's son Evil-merodach (Babylonian, Amil-Marduk). The act possessed little political importance, for the Jews were helpless in the hands of their Babylonian masters; but it evidently aroused the hopes of the exiles, and especially that type of hope which centred in the house of David.

Ezekiel, in his ideal programme, assigned to the Davidic prince only minor duties in connection with the temple, and transferred the chief authority to the high priest and his attendants. But it is evident that Ezekiel did not fully voice the hopes of the majority of the exiles. The late passage in II Samuel 7¹⁰, which contains the promise to David:

> Thy house and kingdom shall always stand firm before me,
> Thy throne shall be established forever,

expresses the prevailing belief in the days immediately preceding the exile. The national hopes which looked to the descendants of the house of David for fulfilment were inevitably modified, however, by the experiences of the exile and strengthened by the liberation of Jehoiachin. The rule of such kings as Manasseh and Jehoiakim had revealed the overwhelming evils that unworthy rulers, even though of the house of David, could bring upon their subjects. Josiah's reign, on the other hand, established new and higher standards. The noble ethical and social ideals of Amos, Hosea, and Isaiah had not wholly failed to awaken a response.

All of these varied influences are traceable in the two prophecies found in Isaiah 9¹⁻⁷ and 11¹⁻¹⁰. Embodying as they do many of the social principles for which Isaiah contended, it was natural that these anonymous writings should afterward be attributed to that great statesman-prophet. Jehovah, however, was the one supreme king whom Isaiah acknowledged; and it was difficult to find in his strenuous life a logical or historical setting for these kingly oracles. They also imply that the royal house of Judah had been struck down, and that the new king is to rise out of a background of gloom and is to inaugurate an entirely new era. The character and rule of this king of popular hopes reflect many of the traits of David and Josiah; but his aims and methods are in accord with the moral and social standards of the great pre-exilic prophets. They portray a temporal ruler; but the spirit which actuates him and the principles which guide him are noble and unselfish. As subsequent history clearly shows, the prophet or prophets who painted these portraits apparently hoped that a son or grandson of Jehoiachin would realize them. It is exceedingly probable in the light of the later predictions of Haggai and Zechariah (§§ XCIV,

XCV) that these prophecies were written not long after the birth of Zerubbabel. The kingdom over which he was to rule and to which he was to bring perfect justice and peace was the prophetic counterpart of Ezekiel's priestly plan of the restored and redeemed community. The ethical ideals thus concretely set forth were never fully realized in Israel's troubled history; but they remain as valid and commanding to-day as they were far back in the Babylonian period. The abolition of all the insignia of war, the high sense of official responsibility, the protection of the weak by the strong, and the reign of perfect peace and harmony throughout all the earth are the goals for which all earnest, consecrated souls in every age and race are striving. It is natural and proper that the Christian Church should see in Jesus the fullest and truest realization of these ancient kingly ideals.

V. The Rule of Nabonidus. The successors of Nebuchadrezzar proved weak and inefficient. His dissolute son, Amil-Marduk, was soon murdered by his brother-in-law Nergalsharuzur (Gk. Neriglissar). This ruler is probably the Nergal-sharezer of Jeremiah 39³ who directed the final capture and destruction of Jerusalem in 586 B.C. After reigning four years he died, leaving the Babylonian empire to his young son, who soon fell a victim to a conspiracy of his nobles. They placed on the throne a certain Nabuna'id, who is known to the Greek historians as Nabonidus. He appeared to be more interested in excavating ancient ruins and in rebuilding old temples than in ruling his subjects. By his arbitrary religious policy and his neglect of the popular gods of the Babylonians, he completely alienated the loyalty of his people. During the latter part of his reign, which extended from 555 to 538 B.C., he left the government largely in charge of his son Belsharuzur, the Belshazzar of the story in Daniel.

VI. Rise and Conquests of Cyrus. While the Babylonian empire was sinking into decay, the Median kingdom on the north and east experienced a sweeping revolution. Its cause was the discontent of the older Median population under the rule of the more barbarous Umman-Manda. These later Scythian conquerors had, under their king Cyaxares, broken the power of Assyria and fallen heir to its eastern territory. The older elements found a leader in Cyrus, the king of Anshan, a little state among the mountains of Elam, northeast of Babylonia. From contemporary inscriptions it appears that the followers of Astyages, who succeeded Cyaxares to the Median throne, rebelled against their king and delivered him over into the hands of Cyrus. As soon as Cyrus became master of the Median Empire, he proved an able commander, a skilful politician, and a wise statesman. Recognizing that he could hold in control the diverse and turbulent elements in his heterogeneous kingdom only as he kept them actively occupied, he at once entered upon a series of campaigns which in the end left him undisputed master of southwestern Asia. In 547 B.C., two years after he became king of Media, he crossed the Tigris and conquered Mesopotamia, which had been held for a time by the Babylonians. Apparently he did not assume the title King of Persia until 546. Appreciating the great strength of Babylon, he did not at first attempt its capture, but began at once by intrigue to pave the way for its ultimate overthrow. In 545 he set out on a western campaign against Crœsus, the king of Lydia, the ancient rival of Media. After a quick and energetic campaign, Sardis, the rich Lydian capital, was captured, and Cyrus was free to advance against the opulent Greek colonies that lay along the eastern shores of the Ægean. These in rapid succession fell into his hands, so that by 538 B.C. he was in a position to advance with a large victorious army against the mistress of the lower Euphrates.

VII. **His Capture of Babylon.** The campaigns of Cyrus were naturally watched with keen interest by the Jewish exiles in Babylonia. The songs in Isaiah 14, 15, and 21[1-10], and Jeremiah 51[29-31], voice their joyous expectation of Babylon's impending humiliation. In a contemporary inscription Cyrus has given a vivid account of the fall of the capital. Early in October of the year 538 B.C. he assembled a large army on the northern borders of Babylonia. Here a battle was fought in which the Babylonians were completely defeated. The town of Sippar quickly surrendered to Cyrus's general, and two days later the Persian army entered Babylon. The record states that the gates of the mighty city were opened by its inhabitants, and Cyrus and his followers were welcomed as deliverers. King Nabonidus was captured and banished to the distant province of Carmania, northeast of the Persian Gulf. In the words of Cyrus: "Peace he gave the town; peace he proclaimed to all the Babylonians." In the eyes of the conquered, he figured as the champion of their gods, whose images he restored to the capital city. The temples as well as the walls of Babylon were rebuilt, and the king publicly proclaimed himself a devoted worshipper of Marduk and Nebo, the chief gods of the Babylonians. Thus from the first the policy of Cyrus in treating conquered peoples was fundamentally different from that of the Babylonians and Assyrians. They had sought to establish their power by crushing the conquered rather than by furthering their well-being; but

33

Cyrus, by his many acts of clemency, aimed to secure and hold their loyalty.

VIII. His Treatment of Conquered Peoples. Cyrus showed the same wisdom in his treatment of the many petty peoples who had been ground down under the harsh rule of Babylon. In one of his inscriptions he declares: "The gods whose sanctuaries from of old had lain in ruins I brought back again to their dwelling-places and caused them to reside there forever. All of the citizens of these lands I assembled and I restored them to their homes" (Cyrus Cyl., 31, 32). In the light of this statement it is clear that the Jews, in common with other captive peoples, were given full permission to return to their homes and to rebuild their ruined temple. The decree of Cyrus recorded in the Aramaic document preserved in Ezra 6³⁻⁵ is apparently the Jewish version of the general decree which he issued. It is also possible that he aided the vassal peoples in rebuilding their sanctuaries; for such action was in perfect accord with his wise policy. He also intrusted the rulership of different kingdoms as far as possible to native princes. In the Greek book of I Esdras has been preserved a list (which has fallen out of the biblical book of Ezra) of those who availed themselves of Cyrus's permission to return to Palestine. It includes simply the priest Jeshua, or Joshua, the lineal heir of the early Jerusalem priestly line of Zadok, and Zerubbabel, a descendant of the Judean royal family. They doubtless took with them their immediate followers and were probably accompanied by a few exiles whose loyalty impelled them to leave the attractive opportunities in Babylon to face the dangers of the long journey and the greater perils in Palestine.

From Jeremiah 41⁵ and Haggai 2¹⁴ it appears that a rude altar had been built on the sacred rock at Jerusalem and that religious services were held on the site of the ruined temple soon after its destruction in 586 B.C. With the gifts brought back by Zerubbabel and his followers, daily sacrifices were probably instituted on the restored altar under the direction of the priest Joshua (cf. Hag. 2¹⁰⁻¹⁴). In the light, however, of the oldest records it is clear that the revival of the Judean community in Palestine was gradual and at first far from glorious. The Jews were a broken-hearted, poverty-stricken, persecuted people, still crushed by the great calamity that had overtaken their nation. The general return of the exiles was only a dream of the future, and, despite the general permission of Cyrus, the temple at Jerusalem still lay in ruins.

34

§ XCIV. THE REBUILDING OF THE TEMPLE

In the second year of Darius the king, in the first day of the sixth month, this word of Jehovah came by Haggai the prophet: Speak to Zerubbabel the son of Shealtiel, governor of Judah, and to Joshua the son of Jehozadak the high priest, saying, 'Thus saith Jehovah of hosts, "This people say: The time has not yet come to rebuild the temple of Jehovah."' Then this word of Jehovah came by Haggai the prophet: Is it a time for you yourselves to dwell in your own ceiled houses, while this temple lies in ruins? Now therefore, thus saith Jehovah of hosts, 'Consider your past experiences. Ye sow much, but bring in little; ye eat, but ye do not have enough; ye drink, but ye are not filled; ye clothe yourselves, but not so as to be warm; and he who earneth wages, earneth wages in a bag with holes.' <sub/> 1. Jehovah's disapproval of the delay in rebuilding the temple (Hag. 1¹⁻⁶)

Thus saith Jehovah of hosts, 'Consider your experiences. Go up to the mountains, and bring wood and rebuild the temple; then I will be pleased with it, and I will reveal my glory,' saith Jehovah. 'Ye looked for much, and it came to little; and when ye brought it home, I blew upon it. Why?' saith Jehovah of hosts. 'Because of my temple that lieth in ruins, while ye are running each to his own house. Therefore the heavens withhold the dew, and the earth withholdeth its fruit. And I have called forth a drought upon the land and upon the mountains, and upon the grain and the new wine and the oil and upon that which the ground bringeth forth, and upon m⸱⸱ and animals, and upon all the labor of the hands.' 2. The cause of the prevailing calamities (7-11)

Then Zerubbabel the son of Shealtiel and Joshua the son of Jehozadak the high priest, with all the rest of the people, obeyed the command of Jehovah their God and the words of Haggai the prophet, as Jehovah their God had sent him to them. The people also feared before Jehovah. And Jehovah stirred up the spirit of Zerubbabel the son of Shealtiel, governor of Judah, and the spirit of Joshua the son of Jehozadak the high priest, and the spirit of all the rest of the people, so that they came and worked on the temple of Jehovah of hosts, their God, in the twenty-fourth day of the sixth month. 3. Initiation of the work (12-15a)

4. Assurance of Jehovah's approval (1¹⁵ᵇ⁻2⁹)

In the second year of Darius the king, on the twenty-first day of the seventh month, this word from Jehovah came by Haggai the prophet: Speak to Zerubbabel son of Shealtiel, governor of Judah, and to Joshua, the son of Jehozadak, the high priest, and to all the remnant of the people, saying, 'Who is left among you that saw this temple in its former glory? and how do you see it now? Is it not in your eyes as nothing? Yet now be strong, O Zerubbabel,' is the oracle of Jehovah; 'and be strong, O Joshua, son of Jehozadak, the high priest, and be strong, all ye people of the land,' is the oracle of Jehovah, 'and work, for I am with you,' is the oracle of Jehovah of hosts, 'and my spirit abideth in your midst; fear not.'

5. Promises of rich blessings (2⁶⁻⁹)

For thus saith Jehovah of hosts: 'Yet a little while, and I will shake the heavens, and the earth, and the sea, and the dry land. And I will shake all nations, and the precious things of all nations shall come; and I will fill this temple with glory,' saith Jehovah of hosts. 'The silver is mine, and the gold is mine,' is the oracle of Jehovah of hosts. 'The later glory of this temple shall be greater than the former,' saith Jehovah of hosts; 'and in this place will I grant prosperity,' is the oracle of Jehovah of hosts.

6. Past pollution of the nation (10)

In the twenty-fourth day of the ninth month, in the second year of Darius, this word of Jehovah came by Haggai the prophet: Thus saith Jehovah of hosts: 'Ask of the priests a decision, saying, " If one bear holy flesh in the skirt of his garment, and with his skirt touch bread, or pottage, or wine, or oil, or any food, shall it become holy?"' And the priests answered and said, No. Then said Haggai, If one that is unclean by reason of a dead body touch any of these, shall it be unclean? And the priests answered and said, It shall be unclean. Then answered Haggai and said, So is this people and so is this nation before me, is the oracle of Jehovah; and so is every work of their hands; and that which they offer there is unclean.

7. Its cause the failure to rebuild the temple (15-19)

And now, I pray you, think back from this day, before a stone was laid upon a stone in the temple of Jehovah; how were ye? When ye came to a heap of twenty measures, there were but ten; when ye came to the wine vat to draw out fifty vessels, there were but twenty. I smote with

36

blasting and with mildew and with hail all the work of your hands; yet ye turned not to me, is the oracle of Jehovah. Think back from this day, think! Is the seed yet in the granary, yea, the vine and the fig tree and the pomegranate and the olive tree have not brought forth; from this day will I bless you.

This word of Jehovah came the second time to Haggai in the twenty-fourth day of the month: Speak to Zerubbabel, governor of Judah, and say: 'I will shake the heavens and the earth; and I will overthrow the throne of kingdoms; and I will destroy the strength of the kingdoms of the nations; and I will overthrow the chariots, and those who ride in them; and the horses and their riders shall come down, each by the sword of his brother. *8. World-wide upheaval (20-22)*

'In that day,' is the oracle of Jehovah of hosts, 'I will take thee, O Zerubbabel, my servant, the son of Shealtiel,' is Jehovah's oracle, 'and will make thee as a seal-ring, for I have chosen thee,' is the oracle of Jehovah of hosts. *9. Rôle of Zerubbabel (23)*

At that time Tattenai, the governor of the province beyond the River, and Shethar-bozenai and their associates came to them, and spoke thus to them, Who gave you permission to build this temple and to finish this wall? And who are the builders who are carrying this through? But the eye of their God was upon the elders of the Jews, so that they did not make them cease, until a report should come to Darius and a written decision concerning it be returned. *10. Inquiries of the Persian officials (Ezra 5³⁻⁵)*

Then Darius the king made a decree, and search was made in the archives where the official documents from Babylon had been deposited. And at Ecbatana, the royal palace in the province of Media, a roll was found, and in it was thus written: A record: In the first year of Cyrus the king, Cyrus the king made a decree: 'Concerning the house of God at Jerusalem, let the house be rebuilt, where they offer sacrifices and bring him offerings made by fire; its height shall be sixty cubits, and its breadth sixty cubits. It shall be constructed with three layers of huge stones and one layer of timber; and let the expenses be paid out of the king's treasury. Also let the gold and silver vessels of the house of God, which Nebuchadnezzar took from the temple at Jerusalem and brought to Babylon, be restored and *11. Result of the investigation by Darius (6¹⁻⁵)*

brought to the temple which is at Jerusalem, each to its place; and you shall put them in the house of God.'

12. His command to aid in the rebuilding of the temple (6-12)

Now therefore, Tattenai, governor of the province beyond the River, Shethar-bozenai, and the rulers of the province beyond the River, go away from there; let the work of this house of God alone; let the elders of the Jews rebuild this house of God in its place. Moreover I make a decree in regard to what you shall do for these elders of the Jews for the building of this house of God: that out of the king's wealth from the tribute of the province beyond the River the expenses be exactly paid to these men, and that without delay. And whatever is needed, both young bullocks and rams and lambs for burnt-offerings to the God of heaven, also wheat, salt, wine, and oil, according to the direction of the priests at Jerusalem, let it be given to them day by day without fail, that they may regularly offer sacrifices of sweet savor to the God of heaven, and pray for the life of the king and of his sons. Also I have made a decree, that whoever shall make this command invalid, a beam shall be pulled out from his house, and he shall be impaled upon it, and his house shall for this be made a refuse heap. And the God who hath caused his name to dwell there shall overthrow all kings and peoples who shall put forth their hand to make invalid the command or to destroy the house of God at Jerusalem. Exactly will it be executed.

13. Completion of the temple (13, 14)

Then Tattenai, the governor of the province beyond the River, and Shethar-bozenai, and their associates did exactly as Darius the king had given command. And the elders of the Jews built and prospered. And they finished the building according to the command of the God of Israel and according to the decree of Cyrus and Darius.

I. **The Books of Ezra and Nehemiah.** The books of Ezra and Nehemiah are the chief sources of information regarding Jewish history during the Persian period. They fall into nine general divisions: (1) the return of the Babylonian exiles and the revival of the Judean community, Ezra 1–4; (2) the rebuilding of the temple, 5–6; (3) Ezra's expedition and the priestly reformation, 8–10, and Nehemiah 8–10; (4) Nehemiah's work in rebuilding the walls, Nehemiah 1^1–7^5; (5) census of the Judean community, 7^{6-69}; (6) measures to secure the repopuration of Jerusalem, 11; (7) genealogy of the priests and Levites, 12^{1-26}; (8) dedication of the walls, 12^{27-43}; and (9) Nehemiah's later reform measures, $12^{44}-13^{31}$. It is evident that Ezra and Nehemiah were originally one book, and that they come from the same author as I and II Chronicles. This important fact is demonstrated by the presence of the same marked characteristics of thought and literary style in both of these books. The closing verses of II Chronicles are also repeated verbatim at the beginning of Ezra.

Throughout these books the interest is religious and ceremonial rather than civil and national. They constitute in reality a history of the Jerusalem temple and its institutions. The whole may properly be designated as the "Ecclesiastical History of Jerusalem." It traces the history of Jerusalem and the southern kingdom from the earliest times to the close of the Persian period. Its author, who is commonly known as the Chronicler, evidently lived during the earlier part or middle of the Greek period. Certain characteristics of his literary style and point of view indicate that he wrote about 250 B.C. His peculiarities and methods of writing are clearly revealed by a comparison of the older parallel history of Samuel-Kings with the books of Chronicles. In general he lacks the historical spirit and perspective of the earlier prophetic historians. He also freely recasts his record of earlier events in order to bring it into accord with the traditions current in his own day. Above all he aimed to establish the authority and prestige of the Jerusalem temple, and to prove that Jehovah "was not with Israel" (II Chron. 25^7), which was represented in his day by the hated Samaritans. The hatred engendered by the Samaritan feud explains many of the peculiarities of the Chronicler. He was, in fact, an apologist rather than a historian. Thus post-exilic institutions, as, for example, the temple song service with its guilds of singers, are projected backward even to the days of David, and the events of early Hebrew history are constantly glorified. The numbers found in the earlier, prophetic sources are magnified, and at every point it is easy to recognize the influence of the Chronicler's familiarity with the splendor and magnificence of the great Persian and Greek empires, and of his desire to inspire his fellow-Jews with national pride and with loyalty to their religious institutions.

II. **The Chronicler's Conception of the Restoration.** Fortunately the Chronicler did not depend entirely upon traditions current in his day, or upon his own conceptions of the early history, but quoted freely from earlier sources. As a result a large portion of the prophetic history of Samuel and Kings is reproduced verbatim in I and II Chronicles. For the Persian period, regarding which he is our chief authority, he apparently quoted from three or four documents. In Ezra 4^{7-23} is found a brief description in Aramaic of the opposition of Judah's neighbors to the rebuilding of the walls, probably in the days of Nehemiah. In Ezra 5 and 6 there is another long quotation from an Aramaic document that describes a similar attempt to put a stop to the rebuilding of the temple in the days of Haggai and Zechariah. The Chronicler evidently believed that the second temple was rebuilt, not by the people of the land to whom Haggai and Zechariah spoke, but by Jewish exiles who on the accession of Cyrus had returned in great numbers from Babylon. He assumed that Judah had been depopulated during the Babylonian exile, and that the only people left in Palestine were the heathen and the hated Samaritans. He also pictures the return of the exiles, not as that of a handful of courageous patriots, but of a vast company laden with rich gifts and guarded by Persian soldiers.

A careful examination of Ezra 2, which purports to contain the list of the 42,360 exiles who returned immediately after 538 B.C., quickly demonstrates that, like its duplicate in Nehemiah 7^{6-69}, its historical basis, if it has any outside the fertile imagination of the Chronicler, is a census of the Judean community. This census was taken, not at the beginning, but rather at the end of the Persian period. Thus in the list of the leaders appear the names not only of Joshua and Zerubbabel, but also of Nehemiah and Ezra (Azariah). Certain leaders, such as Mordecai and Bigvai, bear Persian names which clearly imply that they lived far down in the Persian period. The family of the high priest Joshua already numbers nine hundred and ninety-three. In this census are also included the inhabitants of many towns outside Jerusalem, as, for example, Jericho, Gibeon, and Bethlehem. Moreover, certain towns are mentioned, such as Lud and Ono, which were not added to the Judean community until the latter part of the Persian period. In view of these facts and the unmistakable implications in the sermons of Haggai and Zechariah that in their day there had been no general return of their kinsmen from Babylon, the prevailing popular interpretation of this period of Israel's history is clearly untenable and misleading. If there was a general return of exiles from Babylon, it certainly did not come until after the walls had been rebuilt under the inspiring leadership of Nehemiah. The Jews to whom Haggai and Zechariah preached, and who rebuilt the second temple, were the people of the land who had sur-

THE BOOKS OF EZRA AND NEHEMIAH

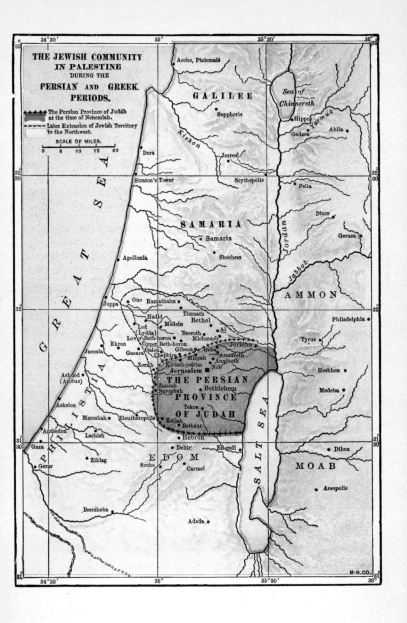

THE JEWISH COMMUNITY
IN PALESTINE
DURING THE
PERSIAN AND GREEK
PERIODS.

The Persian Province of Judah
at the time of Nehemiah.
Later Extension of Jewish Territory
to the Northwest.

SCALE OF MILES.
0   5   10   15   20

GALILEE

Sea of
Chinnereth

Accho, Ptolemais

Sephoris

Hippos

Gadara

Ahila

Jezreel

Kishon

Dora

Straton's Tower

Scythopolis

Pella

SAMARIA

Dium

Samaria

Gerasa

Shechem

Apollonia

AMMON

Joppa

Ono   Ramathaim

Hadid

Timnath

Bethel

Philadelphia

Lod
(Lydda)

Modein

Beeroth

Ai

Michmash

Tyrus

Ekron

Upper Beth-horon

Lower Beth-horon

Gibeon

Geba

Jericho

Jamnia

Gazara

Ajalon

Chephira

Mizpah

Asmaveth

Anathoth

Heshbon

Zorah

Kiriath-jearim

Nob

Jerusalem

THE PERSIAN

Medeba

Zanoah

Netophah

Bethlehem

PROVINCE

Ashdod
(Azotus)

Tekoa

OF JUDAH

Askelon

Mareshah

Eleutheropolis

Keilah

Bethsur

Anthedon

Lachish

Hebron

SALT SEA

Gaza

Debir

En-gedi

Dibon

Ziklag

E D O M

Gerar

Socho

Carmel

MOAB

Areopolis

Beersheba

Adada

GREAT SEA

PHILISTIA

Jordan

Jabbok

Yarmuk

M·N·CO.

vived the destruction of Jerusalem, or else had returned from their temporary refuge on the borders of the land of Egypt.

III. **Convulsions in the Persian Empire.** After a brilliant and successful reign Cyrus died in 529 B.C., leaving his vast empire to his son Cambyses. The new king lacked the wisdom and statesmanship of his father, but inherited his love of conquest. Most of his short reign was devoted to the conquest of Egypt. From their hill-tops the Jews doubtless witnessed the march of the great armies of Persia, and were forced to contribute to their support. It was a period of change and transition, when old empires went down in ruin and new forces gained the ascendancy.

On his return from Egypt, Cambyses, finding a pretender contending for the throne, committed suicide, thus leaving the empire without any legitimate head. During this crisis, in the autumn of 521 B.C., a Persian noble, Darius, was raised to the kingship by conspirators, who had slain the pretender. Darius claimed relationship with the Persian royal family, and strengthened his position by marrying Atossa, the daughter of Cyrus. The beginning of his reign was signalized by a series of revolts throughout the whole extent of the empire. In Susiana a certain Athrina proclaimed himself king. In Babylonia a native prince rallied his countrymen and assumed the title of Nebuchadrezzar III. The Median revolt was led by a certain Pharaortes; while among the Persians themselves a pretender, who claimed to be a son of Cyrus, gained a wide following. Fortunately for Darius there was no concerted action among the leaders of these different rebellions, so that he was able to subdue them in succession; but to the ordinary on-looker the task seemed wellnigh impossible. Not until the spring of 519 did Darius become fully master of the situation.

IV. **Haggai's Effective Addresses.** It was in the autumn of 520 B.C., when the rebellions in the Persian Empire were at their height, that Haggai made his stirring appeal to the members of the Judean community. From the references in his addresses and in those of his contemporary, Zechariah, it is evident that he and his hearers were profoundly influenced by these great world movements. The situation seemed to give promise not only of deliverance from Persian rule, but an opportunity at last to realize the national hopes of the Jewish race. Haggai's message was simple, direct, and practical. According to the belief suniversally accepted in his day his logic was unanswerable. On the one hand Jehovah, through poor crops and hard times, had plainly showed his displeasure with his people in Judah. The reason

41

THE REBUILDING OF THE TEMPLE

was obvious; although they had built comfortable houses for themselves, Jehovah's temple still lay in ruins. If they would win his favor, it was plainly their duty to arise and rebuild his sanctuary. The upheavals in the Persian Empire also gave promise that, if they were true to their divine King, he would at last fulfil the predictions voiced by their earlier prophets.

The words of Haggai, uttered in September of 520, met with an immediate response. Work was begun on the temple in October of the same year. When the energy and enthusiasm of the builders began to wane, the prophet appeared before them again in November of 520 with the declaration that Jehovah was about to overthrow the great world powers and to destroy the chariots, horses, and riders of their Persian masters, "each by the sword of his brother." He also voiced the popular expectations that centred in Zerubbabel, who had already been appointed governor of Judah. The prophet declared boldly that this scion of the house of David would be Jehovah's seal-ring, the earthly representative of that divine power which was about to work great revolutions in the history of the world. During the same period Zechariah also uttered his messages of encouragement and spurred the people on to continued efforts (§ XCV).

V. **The Attempt to Stop the Rebuilding of the Temple.** The Aramaic document preserved in Ezra 5 and 6 describes in detail an attempt of the Persian governor, who ruled over the province west of the Euphrates, to put a stop to the temple building. The narrative, the letter, and decrees which it contains reveal at many points their Jewish origin. While the tradition may be comparatively late, its circumstantial character favors the conclusion that it preserves the memory of a definite historical event. The action of the Jews in rebuilding their temple was in perfect accord with the policy of Cyrus and also of Darius, as is shown by contemporary inscriptions. The attempt, therefore, to stop the building of the temple failed; and in 516 B.C., four years after the work was begun, it was completed.

VI. **The Significance of the Restoration of the Temple.** The rebuilding of the Jerusalem temple appears to have been of immediate significance chiefly to the Jews of Palestine. The Jews of Egypt, or at least those of Elephantine, had their own temple. From Zechariah 6[9-11] it is evident that the Jewish exiles in Babylon sent certain gifts to the Jerusalem temple; but the hundreds of miles of desert that intervened made communication exceedingly difficult, so that except at rare intervals there was apparently little interchange between Baby-

42

lonia and Palestine. For all Jews, however, the rebuilding of the temple meant that at last they had a common rallying-place, and that Jehovah was again being worshipped by his own people at his traditional place of abode. In a sense it bridged the seventy years that had intervened since the destruction of the pre-exilic Hebrew state, and made it possible to revive the ancient religious customs. In time it attracted from the lands of the dispersion patriotic Jews whose interest was fixed upon the ceremonial side of their religious life. It also furnished a centre about which gradually grew up a hierarchy with an increasingly elaborate ritual, and a body of laws which ultimately became the characteristic features of Judaism.

§ XCV. ZECHARIAH'S VISIONS AND ENCOURAGING ADDRESSES

In the twenty-fourth day of the eleven. ᵗʰ [February], in the second year of Darius [519 B.C.], this word Jehovah came to the prophet Zechariah, the son of Berechiah, the son of Iddo: I saw in the night and there was a man standing among the myrtle trees that were in the valley-bottom, and behind him there were horses, red, sorrel, and white. Then said I, O my Lord, what are these? And the angel who talked with me said to me, I will show you what these are. And the man who was standing among the myrtle trees answered and said, These are they whom Jehovah hath sent to go to and fro through the earth. And they answered the angel of Jehovah who was standing among the myrtle trees and said, We have gone up and down through the earth and behold, all the earth is still and at peace.

1. Report of uni-al peace (Zec. 1⁷⁻¹¹)

Then the angel of Jehovah answered and said, O Jehovah of hosts, how long hast thou no pity on Jerusalem and the cities of Judah with which thou hast been wroth these seventy years? And Jehovah answered the angel who was talking with me with good words, even comforting words. So the angel who was talking with me said to me, Proclaim now, 'Thus saith Jehovah of hosts: "I am jealous for Jerusalem and for Zion with a great jealousy. But with great wrath am I wroth with the arrogant nations; for I was only a little angry [with Israel], but they helped

2. Jehovah's promise yet to exalt and bless his holy city (12-17)

43

to make greater the calamity." Therefore, thus saith Jehovah: "I am turning to show mercy to Jerusalem; my temple shall be built in it," saith Jehovah of hosts, "and a measuring line shall be stretched over Jerusalem. Proclaim again, Thus saith Jehovah of hosts: My cities shall yet overflow with prosperity; and Jehovah shall yet comfort Zion and choose Jerusalem." '

3.
Israel's
hostile
foes
(18, 19)

Now I lifted mine eyes and looked, and there were four horns. And I said to the angel who was talking with me, 'What are these?' And he assured me, 'These are the horns with which he scattered Judah.'

4.
Their
promised destruction
(20, 21)

Then Jehovah showed me four smiths. And I said, What are these coming to do? And he said, These are the horns which scattered Judah, so that none lifted up his head; but these are come to terrify them, to strike down the horns of the nations, which lifted up their horn against the land of Judah to scatter it.

5.
Jerusalem
to be
populous
and
well
guarded
(2¹⁻⁵)

Then I lifted up mine eyes, and looked, and there was a man with a measuring line in his hand. Then I said, Where are you going? And he said to me, To measure Jerusalem, to see what is its breadth and length. Thereupon the angel who talked with me stood still, and another angel went out to meet him, and said to him, Run, speak to this young man, saying, 'Jerusalem shall be inhabited as villages without walls, because of the multitude of men and cattle in her midst. For I,' saith Jehovah, 'will be a wall of fire round about her, and I will be the glory in the midst of her.'

6.
Summons
to the
exiles
to return
(6-9)

Ho, ho, flee from the land of the north, is Jehovah's
 oracle.
For I have spread you abroad as the four winds of the heavens, is Jehovah's oracle.
Ho, escape to Zion, ye who dwell in Babylon.
For thus saith Jehovah of hosts to the nations which plundered you:
He that toucheth you toucheth the apple of mine eye.
'or, behold, I am about to shake my hand over them,
And they shall be a spoil to those who served them;
And ye shall know that Jehovah of hosts hath sent me.

44

Sing and rejoice, O daughter of Zion, for, lo, I come,
And I will dwell in the midst of thee, is Jehovah's oracle.
And many nations shall join themselves to Jehovah in that day,
And shall be his people, and he will dwell in the midst of thee,
And thou shalt know that Jehovah of hosts hath sent me to thee.
And Jehovah shall inherit Judah as his portion in the holy land,
And he shall yet comfort Zion and choose Jerusalem.
Be silent, all flesh, before Jehovah;
For he hath waked up out of his holy habitation.

7. Jehovah's return to dwell among his people (10-13)

Then he showed me Joshua, the high priest, standing before the angel of Jehovah and the adversary standing at his right hand to accuse him. And the angel of Jehovah said to the adversary, Jehovah rebuke thee, O adversary; yea, Jehovah, who hath chosen Jerusalem, rebuke thee. Is not this a brand plucked out of the fire? Now Joshua was clothed with filthy garments and was standing before the angel.

8. The polluted priesthood and nation (3¹⁻²)

And [the angel] answered and spoke to those who stood before him, saying, Take the filthy garments from off him, and clothe him with robes of state; set a clean turban upon his head. So they set a clean turban upon his head, and clothed him with garments; and the angel of Jehovah was standing by.

9. Their reconsecration (4, 5)

And the angel of Jehovah testified to Joshua, saying, Thus saith Jehovah of hosts: 'If thou wilt walk in my ways, and if thou wilt keep my charge, then thou also shalt rule my house and shalt also keep my courts and I will give thee a place of access among these who stand by. Hear now, O Joshua the high priest, thou and thy associates who sit before me; for they are men who are a sign; for behold, I am about to bring forth my servant the Branch. For, behold, the stone that I have set before Joshua; upon one stone are seven facets: behold, I will engrave it,' saith Jehovah of hosts, 'and I will remove the iniquity of that

10. Promise of an established king and kingdom (6-10)

land in one day. In that day,' saith Jehovah of hosts, 'ye shall each invite his neighbor under the vine and under the fig tree.'

11. Jehovah's presence in the midst of his people (4¹⁻⁶)

Then the angel who talked with me came again and waked me, as a man who is wakened out of his sleep. And he said to me, What seest thou? And I said, I see there a candlestick, all of gold, with a bowl upon the top of it, and its seven lamps upon it; there are seven pipes to each of the lamps, which are upon the top of it, and two olive trees by it, one on the right side of the bowl, and the other on its left side. And I spoke and said to the angel who talked with me, What are these, my lord? Then the angel who talked with me answered and said to me, Knowest thou not what these are? And I said, No, my lord. Then he answered and spoke to me, saying, The eyes of Jehovah, which rove to and fro through the whole earth.

12. The two leaders (11-14)

Then I answered, and said to him, What are these two olive trees upon the right side of the candlestick and upon its left side? And he answered me and said, Knowest thou not what these are? And I said, No, my lord. Then said he, These are the two anointed ones, who stand by the Lord of the whole earth.

13. Zerubbabel to complete the temple (6b-10)

This is the word of Jehovah regarding Zerubbabel, Not by might, nor by power, but by my spirit, saith Jehovah of hosts, will I make the great mountain before Zerubbabel a plain; and he shall bring forth the top stones with shoutings of, 'Grace, grace, to it.' Moreover this word of Jehovah came to me: The hands of Zerubbabel have laid the foundations of this temple; his hands shall also finish it; and ye shall know that Jehovah of hosts hath sent me to you. For who hath despised the day of small things? for they shall rejoice, and shall see the plummet in the hand of Zerubbabel.

14. Making the crown (6⁹⁻¹¹)

Now this word of Jehovah came to me: Take of them of the captivity, even of Heldai, of Tobijah, of Jedaiah and of Josiah the son of Zephaniah who have come from Babylon, yea, take of them silver and gold in order to make a crown and set it on the head of Zerubbabel the son of Shealtiel.

Thou shalt also say to them: 'Thus saith **Jehovah** of hosts: "Behold, the man whose name is the Branch; and he shall grow up out of his place; and he shall build the temple of Jehovah; and he shall bear the glory and shall sit and rule upon his throne; and Joshua the son of Jehozadak shall be a priest upon his right, and the counsel of peace shall be between them both. And the crown shall be to Heldai and Tobijah and Jedaiah, and Josiah the son of Zephaniah, as a memorial in the temple of Jehovah. And they who are far off shall come and build in the temple of Jehovah; and ye shall know that Jehovah of hosts hath sent me to you. And this shall come to pass, if ye will diligently obey the voice of Jehovah your God."' 15. Predictions concerning the glory of Zerubbabel's rule (12-15)

In the fourth year of King Darius, on the fourth day of the ninth month, the city of Bethel sent Sharezer and Regemmelech and their men, to entreat the favor of Jehovah, and to speak to the priests of the house of Jehovah of hosts, and to the prophets, saying, should I weep in the fifth month [in memory of the destruction of the temple] separating myself, as I have done these many years? Then this word of Jehovah of hosts came to me: Speak to all the people of the land, and to the priests, saying, 'When ye fasted and mourned in the fifth and in the seventh month [when Gedaliah was murdered], even these seventy years, did ye at all fast to me, even to me? And when ye eat and when ye drink, do ye not eat for yourselves, and drink for yourselves? 16. Jehovah asks not for formal worship (7¹⁻⁶)

Should ye not hear these words which Jehovah cried by the former prophets, when Jerusalem was inhabited and in prosperity, and her cities round about her, and the South Country, and the lowland were inhabited? Execute true judgment, and show kindness and pity each to his brother; and oppress not the widow nor the fatherless, the resident alien nor the poor; and let none of you devise evil against your brother in his heart. But they refused to heed, and turned a stubborn shoulder, and stopped their ears, that they might not hear. Yea, they made their hearts as an adamant lest they should hear the teaching, and the words which Jehovah of hosts had sent by his spirit through the former prophets. Therefore there came great wrath from 17. Only for deeds of justice and mercy (7⁻¹⁴)

Jehovah of hosts. And even when I cried they would not hear, so when they cried I did not hear, saith Jehovah of hosts. And I scattered them by a whirlwind among the nations which they did not know. Thus the land was left desolate behind them, so that no man passed to or fro; for they made the pleasant land a desolation.

18.
Glories
of re-
stored
Jeru-
salem
(8¹⁻⁵)

Now this word of Jehovah of hosts came to me:
Thus saith Jehovah of hosts,
'I cherish for Zion a great jealousy,
And I am jealous for her with great indigna*i*on.'
Thus saith Jehovah, 'I have returned to Z⁻⁻n,
And will dwell in the midst of Jerusalem
And Jerusalem shall be called, "The C⁻⁻ of Truth;"
And the mountain of Jehovah of h⁻⁻s, "The Holy Mountain." '
Thus saith Jehovah of hosts:
'Old men and old women sha⁻⁻ again sit in the broad places of Jerusalem,
Each man with his staff ⁻n his hand because of old age.
And the streets of the ⁻ty shall be full of boys,
And of girls playing ⁻ its broad places.'

19. Je-
hovah
himself
to
gather
his
scat-
tered
people
(⁶⁻⁸)

Thus saith Jeho⁻ n of hosts:
Because it see⁻eth impossible to the remnant of this people,
Is it also i⁻ ⁻ssible for me? saith Jehovah of hosts.
Thus sait⁻ Jehovah of hosts:
I am a⁻ ⁻t to rescue my people,
Fro⁻ ⁻he land of the east and the land of the west,
An⁻ ⁻ will bring them and they shall dwell in the midst of Jerusalem.
And they shall be my people in truth and righteousness,
And in turn I will be their God.

I. **Zechariah's Ancestry and Point of View.** Haggai's contemporary, the prophet Zechariah, was evidently a priest. In the genealogy of Nehemiah 12⁴, it is stated that he belonged to the priestly family of Iddo. This conclusion is confirmed by the character of his prophecies. Like the priest-prophet Ezekiel he is exceedingly fond of apocalyptic symbolism. He is also deeply interested in the priesthood and in its

48

ceremonial purity. Furthermore, it is exceedingly probable that he was a descendant of one of the many priests carried as exiles to Babylon. This is shown by his keen interest in and exact knowledge of the great political movements that were then shaking the Persian Empire. His conception of Jehovah is also strongly influenced by the analogies drawn from the Persian court. In his thought Israel's God is a transcendental ruler, who communicates with his subjects not directly, but through angelic messengers, and who, like the Persian kings, is dependent for information regarding his great kingdom upon the reports of the different members of his heavenly court. Thus Zechariah marks a wide departure from the simple theology of the pre-exilic prophets who thought of Jehovah as dwelling in the midst of his people and communicating directly with all who turned to him in faith.

II. **The Book of Zechariah.** The book which records the prophet's sermons contains four distinct divisions: (1) An exhortation addressed to the people in December, 520, three months after Haggai first appealed to them to rise and rebuild the temple, Zechariah 1^{1-6}; (2) symbolic visions dealing with the problems in the Judean community, $1^{7}-6^{8}$; (3) practical counsel, exhortations, and promises, $6^{9}-8^{23}$; (4) a later appendix coming from a prophet who probably lived during the earlier part of the Maccabean period, 9–14. All of Zechariah's recorded sermons probably date from the three or four years between 520 and 516 B.C., during which the temple was being rebuilt. They throw a remarkably clear light upon an exceedingly critical and significant period in the life of the Jews of Palestine. They are also in many ways the best Old Testament source for the study of the unfolding of Israel's messianic hopes.

III. **Problems and Hopes of the Judean Community.** Four or five practical problems confronted and disturbed the temple-builders. The first was: Would Jerusalem and the temple, still without walls, be protected from the attack of the hostile foes that encircled them. A second and larger question was: What was to be the outcome of the great tempest through which the Persian Empire was passing, and did it mean for the Jews deliverance from the powerful conquerors who for centuries had oppressed and crushed them? The third was: Would the necessarily modest service of the restored temple, already sadly polluted by heathen hands, be acceptable to Jehovah? Another problem was: What were the relations and the respective duties of Zerubbabel and Joshua, the civil and religious authorities in the community? It was also inevitable that at this time the hope of securing their independence under the leadership of Zerubbabel should come prominently to the front. To each of these problems Zechariah addressed himself, and his book records his convictions and public utterances.

IV. Zechariah's Assurances of Jehovah's Care. In his initial vision concerning the angelic horsemen he recognizes that the storms that have swept over the Persian Empire are beginning to subside, but he tells his fellow-laborers that, if they persist, Jehovah's temple shall be rebuilt and that the lands about Jerusalem shall again be sold to eager buyers, and the cities of Judah shall enjoy their former prosperity, for "Jehovah will surely comfort Zion." In the vision of the four horns and of the four smiths whose mission it is to smite the horns, he assures the people that Jehovah in his good time and way will overthrow the nations that now wrong and oppress them. Although there is no promise that Jerusalem will be surrounded by walls, he declares that it shall enjoy a prosperity and a growth which no walls can confine, and that Jehovah himself will be its protection, as well as its glory, that he will gather the scattered exiles, and that they, together with the nations which shall acknowledge Jehovah's rule, shall yet come streaming back to Judah.

In his next vision the prophet graphically presents a scene in Jehovah's court. Joshua the priest, representing the ceremonial service of the polluted temple, is charged by the adversary with uncleanness. Here for the first time in Hebrew literature we catch a glimpse of Satan, who is regarded not as hostile to God but as the prosecuting attorney of heaven. As in the prologue of the book of Job, he is an accredited member of the divine hierarchy. His task is to search out and report to Jehovah the misdeeds of men. In Zechariah's vision, however, the divine judge acquits Joshua of the charge, and causes him to be clad with clean garments, thus proclaiming the divine approval of the modest yet devoted service of the Judean community.

V. Preparations for the Crowning of Zerubbabel. Regarding Zerubbabel, Zechariah declares, in language highly figurative, that he shall yet be crowned and rule over a happy and prosperous people. He is spoken of as Jehovah's servant, the Branch. The term is probably original with Zechariah, although again used in the supplementary passages in Jeremiah 23^5 and 33^{15}. The word is akin to the term "shoot of the house of Jesse" used in Isaiah 11, to describe a certain scion of the house of David, who in all probability was the young Zerubbabel. Zechariah's figure describes the prince as an offshoot of the same royal tree. The obscure passage seems to mean that upon the stone, with its seven facets, which was to be set in the crown prepared 'or the head of Zerubbabel, Jehovah himself would engrave a fitting title.

In Zechariah's fifth vision he defined the relations between the civil and priestly authorities. The golden candlestick represented the temple and its service. The two olive trees beside it stood for Zerubbabel, the civil ruler, and for Joshua, the high priest. The duty of each was to contribute his part toward the support of the temple service. They were both Jehovah's Messiahs, that is, men anointed as a symbol of the task which each was to perform.

In this connection Zechariah declared that Jehovah would remove all obstacles from before Zerubbabel, and that he who had begun the work should live to see its completion. In an address recorded in the latter part of the sixth chapter of his prophecy (intentionally revised by a later scribe), Zechariah threw aside all symbolism and gave directions to make a crown for the head of Zerubbabel from the silver and gold that had been brought as a gift by a deputation from the Jews of Babylon. He also plainly predicted that this descendant of David should sit on the throne of Judah and that Joshua the priest should be his minister like the priests in the pre-exilic kingdom.

VI. **Disappointment of These Patriotic Hopes.** With Zechariah's prediction that Zerubbabel should reign on the throne of Judah the descendants of the house of David suddenly and forever disappear from Old Testament history. Whether the Jews made the attempt to shake off the yoke of Persia or whether Zerubbabel was quietly set aside cannot be determined. Contemporary history states that within at least six months after Zechariah voiced the patriotic hopes of his people the authority of Darius was fully established throughout the empire. He at once began thoroughly to organize the vast realm. Post roads bound together the distant provinces, and satraps, appointed largely from the ranks of the royal family, unified the whole empire and held it under firm control. As a rule Persian governors were substituted for the native princes. With the institution of this policy Zerubbabel may well have been quietly set aside. The event evidently made a profound impression upon the messianic expectations of the Jews. Henceforth, for three or four centuries, the temporal, kingly type of messianic hope, which had been inspired by the glories of the reign of David, entirely disappeared. It was not revived until the military victories of the Maccabean era had again brought prominently to the front this phase of national glory (cf. § cxvi). As a result of these disappointments

Israel's hopes were universalized and spiritualized. Jehovah, instead of a scion of the house of David, was henceforth regarded as the one supreme King of Israel.

VII. **Zechariah's Later Exhortations and Predictions.** In chapters 7 and 8, which conclude the original sermons of Zechariah, the apocalyptic language with which he clothed his earlier predictions regarding the future of the Judean community disappeared, and he spoke as did Amos and Haggai, plainly and directly regarding the questions which were then stirring the people. When a deputation came from the north to inquire whether or not, now that the temple was being rebuilt, they should continue to observe their fasts in memory of the destruction of Jerusalem and the death of Gedaliah, the prophet raised the searching question of whether their motive in these services was to please Jehovah or to please themselves. He then went on to declare that the only effective way to serve Jehovah was by deeds of justice and kindness, especially to the dependent classes in the community, and that the horrors of the exile had come because their fathers had failed to worship Jehovah by righteous deeds.

The prophet concludes with a brilliant picture of the coming restoration of Jerusalem and of the peace and prosperity which should be the lot of all, because Jehovah was about to gather his scattered people from the east and the west and to establish them in the midst of his sacred city. Other nations should eagerly come to Jerusalem to seek the favor of Jehovah and to ally themselves with his faithful followers, the Jews. In a prophecy, preserved in Micah 4$^{1-4}$ and Isaiah 2$^{1-4}$ (which probably comes from this period) the same thought is nobly expressed:

> It shall come to pass in the latter days,
> That the mountain of Jehovah shall be established,
> Even the house of our God on the top of the mountain,
> And it shall be lifted above the hills.
> All the nations shall flow to it,
> And many peoples shall go and say,
> Come, let us go up to Jehovah's mount,
> To the house of the God of Jacob,
> That he may instruct us in his ways,
> And that we may walk in his paths.
> For from Zion proceeds instruction,
> And Jehovah's word from Jerusalem.

§ XCVI. ISRAEL'S TRAINING AND DESTINY

Comfort ye, comfort ye my people, saith your God,
Speak tenderly to Jerusalem, and declare to her,
That her hard service is accomplished, her guilt is expiated,
That she hath received from Jehovah's hand double for all her sins.

1. Prologue: message of comfort (Isa. 40¹·²)

A voice is proclaiming: In the wilderness prepare the way of Jehovah,
Make straight in the desert a highway for our God!
Let every mountain and hill sink down, and every valley be lifted up,
And the crooked ᵗ ᵤₐde straight and the rough ridges a plain.

2. Preparations for the restoration (³·⁴)

A voice is saying, Proclaim! and I said, What shall I proclaim?
All flesh is grass and all its beauty like a flower of the field.
Grass withers, flower fades, when Jehovah's breath blows upon it,
Grass withers, flower fades, but the word of our God endureth forever.

3. Jehovah alone infinite and eternal (⁶⁻⁸)

To a high mountain, get thee up, Zion's herald of good news;
Lift up mightily thy voice, Jerusalem's herald of good news,
Lift up fearlessly, say to the cities of Judah: Behold your God!

4. Announcement of the good news (⁹)

Behold, Jehovah cometh in might, and his arm is maintaining his rule;
Behold, his reward is with him and his recompense is before him,
As a shepherd he will tend his flock, with his arm he will gather it,
The lambs in his bosom he will bear, the ewe-mothers he will lead.

5. Jehovah's deliverance of his people (¹⁰·¹¹)

6. His incomparable superiority to nature (12)

Who hath measured in the hollow of his hand the waters,
And ruled off the heavens with a span,
Or enclosed the dust of the earth in a measure,
And weighed the mountains in scales,
And the hills in a balance?

7. To man (13, 14)

Who hath determined the spirit of Jehovah,
And as his counsellor advised him?
With whom hath he consulted for enlightenment,
And to be instructed in the right,
And to be shown the way of discernment?

8. To the heathen nations (15-17)

Lo the nations! as a drop from a bucket,
And as dust on a balance are they reckoned.
Lo the isles! as a mote he uplifteth,
And Lebanon is not enough for fuel,
And its wild beasts for a burnt-offering.
All the nations are as nothing before him,
They are reckoned by him as void and nothingness.

9. To the heathen gods (18-20)

To whom then will ye liken God,
And what likeness place beside him?
An image! a craftsman cast it,
And a smelter o'erlays it with gold.
He who is too poor to do this
Chooses a tree that is not decayed,
Seeks for himself a skilled craftsman,
To set up an image that shall not totter.

10. To all the inhabitants of the universe (21, 22)

Do ye not know?   Do ye not hear?
Hath it not been told you from the beginning?
Have ye not been aware from the founding of the earth?
It is he who is enthroned above the vault of the earth,
And its inhabitants are as locusts;
Who stretcheth out the heavens as a thin veil,
And spreadeth them out like a habitable tent.

11. To the rulers of the earth (23, 24)

It is he who bringeth princes to naught,
The rulers of the earth he maketh as waste.
Scarcely have they been planted, scarcely have they
    been sown,

Scarcely hath the stock taken root in the earth,
But he bloweth upon them and they wither,
And a whirlwind carries them away like stubble.

To whom then will ye liken me
That I should equal him? saith the Holy One.
Lift up your eyes on high and see:
Who hath created these?
He who bringeth forth their host by number,
And calleth each by his name;
Of the many mighty and strong,
Not one is missing.

12.
To the stars
(25, 26)

Why sayest thou, O Jacob, and speakest, O Israel:
My way is hid from Jehovah
And my right is unnoticed by my God?
Hast thou not known?   Hast thou not heard?
An everlasting God is Jehovah.
The creator of the ends of the earth.
He fainteth not, neither is weary
His wisdom cannot be fathomed
He giveth vigor to the fainting.
And upon the powerless he layeth strength.
Young men may faint and grow weary,
And the strongest youths may stumble,
But they who trust in Jehovah renew their vigor,
They mount on pinions like eagles,
They run but are never weary,
They walk but never faint.

13. Jehovah's ability to save his people
(27-31)

Listen to me in silence, ye coastlands,
Let the peoples come near; then let them speak;
Together let us approach the tribunal.
Who raised up that one from the east
Whose steps victory ever attended,
Giving up peoples before him,
And letting him trample down kings?
His sword made them as dust,
And his bow like driven stubble;
He pursued them, passing on in safety,

14. Jehovah's leadership of his people in the past
(41 1-4)

Not treading the path with his feet.
Who hath wrought and accomplished this?
He who called the generations from the beginning,
I, Jehovah, who am the first,
And with those who come after I am the same.

15. Je-
hovah's
assur-
ance of
help
in the
present
and
future
(8-18)

And thou, Israel, my servant
Jacob, whom I have chosen,
Offspring of Abraham, my friend,
Thou, whom I brought from the ends of the earth,
And called from its most distant parts;
To whom I said, Thou art my servant,
I have chosen and have not rejected thee.
Fear not, for I, indeed, am with thee,
Be not terrified, for I am thy God.
I will strengthen thee; yea, I will help thee;
Yea, I will uphold thee with my righteous hand.

16.
Type of
servant
Jeho-
vah
desires
(42¹)

Behold, my servant whom I uphold,
My chosen, in whom I take delight;
I have put my spirit upon him,
That he may set forth law to the nations.

17. His
method
(2-3b)

He will not cry aloud nor roar,
Nor let his voice be heard in the street.
A crushed reed he will not break,
And a dimly burning wick he will not quench.

18. His
task
(3c, 4)

Faithfully will he set forth law;
He will not lose vigor nor be crushed,
Until he establish law in the earth,
And for his teaching the coastlands are waiting.

19. His
com-
mission
from
Jeho-
vah
(5-7)

Thus saith the one God, Jehovah,
He who spread out the heavens and stretched them forth,
Who created the earth and its products,
Who giveth breath to the people upon it,
And spirit to those who walk upon it:
I, Jehovah, have called thee in righteousness,
I have taken thee by the hand and kept thee,

56

I have made thee a pledge to the people, a light to the
  nations,
To open eyes that are blind,
To bring captives out from confinement,
From the prison house dwellers in darkness.

Ye who are deaf hear,
And ye blind look up that ye may see,
Who is blind but my servants,
And deaf as their rulers?
Much have ye seen, without observing it,
Though your ears were open, ye did not hear.

20.
Blind-
ness of
Jeho-
vah's
people
(18-20)

Jehovah was pleased for his righteousness' sake
To make his teaching great and glorious,
Yet it is a people spoiled and plundered,
They are all snared in holes,
And hidden in prison houses,
They have become a spoil, with none to rescue,
An object of plunder, with none to say, Restore.

21
Conse-
quences
of their
blind-
ness
(21, 22)

Who among you will give ear to this,
Will attend and hear for time to come?
Who gave up Jacob to plunderers,
And Israel to those who spoiled him,
And poured out upon him the heat of his anger,
And his violence like a flame,
So that it scorched him round about, but he knew it not,
And it burned him, but he laid it not to heart?

22.
Israel's
calam-
ities
due to
Jeho-
vah's
judg-
ments
(23-24)

And now thus saith Jehovah,
He who created thee, O Jacob, and formed thee,
Fear not, O Israel, for I redeem thee,
I call thee by name, thou art mine.
When thou passeth through the waters, I will be with
  thee,
Through the rivers, they shall not overflow thee;
When thou goest through the fire, thou shalt not be
  scorched,
Neither shall the flame burn thee.

23. By
Jeho-
vah
Israel
will be
pro-
tected
(43 1-2)

24.
Ransomed
(3, 4)

For I, Jehovah, am thy God.
I, Israel's Holy One, am thy deliverer;
I give Egypt as thy ransom,
Ethiopia and Seba for thee.
Because thou art precious in mine eyes,
Art honored and I love thee,
I will give lands in thy stead,
And peoples for the sake of thy life.

25.
And restored
(5-7)

Fear not for I am with thee,
From the east I will bring thine offspring,
And from the west I will gather thee;
I will say to the north, Give up!
And to the south, Withhold not!
Bring my sons from afar,
And my daughters from the ends of the earth,
Every one who is called by my name,
Whom for my glory I have created and formed.

26. Jehovah's witnesses
(10, 11)

Ye are my witnesses, is Jehovah's oracle,
And my servants, whom I have chosen,
That ye may acknowledge and believe me,
And that ye may perceive that I am ever the same,
Before me no God was formed,
Nor shall there be after me,
I, even I, am Jehovah,
And beside me there is no deliverer.

27. Jehovah's irrevocable purpose
(12, 13)

It was I who announced and brought deliverance,
And I declared, and there was no strange god among you,
Ye are my witnesses, is Jehovah's oracle,
I am God, yea, from henceforth the same;
And there is none who can snatch from my hand,
When I work, who can reverse it?

28. Revealed in the overthrow of Babylon
(14, 15)

Thus saith Jehovah,
Your redeemer, Israel's Holy One,
For your sake I have sent to Babylon,
And have brought them all down as fugitives.
Even the Chaldeans with their piercing cries of lamen-
    tation,

It is I, Jehovah, your Holy One,
The Creator of Israel, your King.

But thou, O Jacob, hast not called upon me,
Nor hast thou wearied thyself about me, O Israel;
Thou hast not brought me the sheep of thy burnt-
    offerings,
Nor honored me with thy sacrifices.
With offerings I have not burdened thee,
Nor with incense wearied thee.
Thou broughtest me no sweet cane with thy money,
Nor with the fat of thy sacrifices sated me.
Rather thou hast only burdened me with thy sins,
And wearied me with thine iniquities.

29.
Israel
alone
faith-
less
(22-24)

But it is I alone who blot out thy transgressions,
And I do not remember thy sins.
Remind me, let us plead together,
Do thou set forth the matter that thou mayest be
    justified:
Thy first father sinned,
And thy mediators rebelled against me.
Thy rulers profaned my sanctuary,
And I gave up Jacob to the ban,
And Israel to revilings!

30.
Israel's
disas-
ters the
result
of past
sins
(25-28)

But now hear, O Jacob, my servant,
And Israel whom I have chosen;
Thus saith Jehovah, thy maker,
Even he who formed thee from the womb, who helpeth
    thee:
' Fear not, my servant Jacob,
And thou, Jeshurun, whom I have chosen;
For I will pour water upon the thirsty land
And streams upon the dry ground.

31. Je-
hovah
now
ready
to re-
store
(44¹⁻³ᵇ)

I will pour out my spirit upon thy children,
And my blessing upon thy descendants,
So that they shall spring up as grass in the midst of waters,
As willows by water-courses.

32. Ea-
ger to
honor
his
people
before
all men
(3c-5)

59

One shall say, "I am Jehovah's,"
And another shall call himself, "Jacob,"
And another will inscribe on his hand, "Jehovah's,"
And receive the surname, "Israel."'

I. The Seventy Years Following the Rebuilding of the Temple.
Regarding the seventy years which intervened between the rebuilding
of the temple in 516 B.C. and the appearance of Nehemiah in 445 the
biblical historians are silent. This silence is probably because there
were no important political events in the life of the Judean community
to be recorded. During the latter part of his reign Darius bridged the
Hellespont and undertook the conquest of the western world. Later,
under the reign of his son Xerxes, the mighty hordes of eastern warriors
were turned back, and the growing weakness of the great Persian Empire
was revealed. In 486 Egypt rebelled, and Persian armies marched
along the eastern shore of the Mediterranean, probably levying heavy
taxes for their support upon the Jews as well as upon the other peoples
of Palestine. The suppression of the rebellion in Egypt illustrated how
impossible it was for any of the eastern peoples to withstand even the
decadent power of the Persian Empire.

In Palestine the Jews were still the prey of their hostile neighbors.
No walls protected the temple and city of Jerusalem. The Jews were
probably ground down under their greedy Persian governors. With
the disappearance of Zerubbabel the local control fell naturally into
the hands of the high priest and his followers, whose civil authority
from this time on constantly increased. The words of II Isaiah well
describe the lot of the Jews of Palestine during this period:

It is a people spoiled and plundered,
They are all snared in holes,
And hidden in prison houses.
They have become a spoil,
With none to rescue,
An object of plunder,
With none to say, Restore.

II. Spiritual Forces in Judaism. The political horizon furnished
little to inspire the disappointed and persecuted Jews. Their eyes were
still blinded by the brilliant hopes that had stirred them at the time
when the temple was rebuilt. The quenching of these hopes had left

them in deeper darkness than before. There seemed no rift in the clouds that overshadowed them. Even their priestly rulers were selfish and inconsiderate. For the faithful few who rose above the discouragements and obstacles that confronted them, however, this period of deepest gloom was lighted by a faith that shines through and glorifies most of the later books of the Old Testament. From the psalms and prophecies of the period it is evident that there were a few who in the midst of these discouraging circumstances found peace and joy. As they meditated upon the experiences of their race, and read and pondered the writings of the earlier prophets, they began to appreciate not only the real significance of their past history but the meaning of the present affliction. The chief spokesman of these immortal heroes of the faith was the prophetic author of Isaiah 40–66.

III. **Evidences That Isaiah 40-66 were Written in Palestine.** Only recently have careful students of Isaiah 40–66 begun to realize that the point of view in all of these chapters is not distant Babylon but Jerusalem. The repeated references in chapter 56 and following to conditions in Jerusalem have led all to recognize their Palestinian origin. The evidence, however, regarding chapters 40–55 is almost equally convincing. The vocabulary and literary figures employed throughout are those peculiar to the agricultural life of Palestine and not to the commercial civilization of Babylon. The problems also are those of the Judean community. The class to whom the prophet addresses his messages is evidently the same as that to which Haggai and Zechariah speak. Jerusalem, not a Jewish colony in Babylon, is the constant object of the prophet's appeal. Babylon is only one of the distant lands of the dispersion. It is from Jerusalem that the prophet ever views the world. Thus in $43^{5,6}$ he declares in the name of Jehovah:

> Fear not, for I am with thee.
> From the east I will bring thine offspring,
> And from the west I will gather them;
> I will say to the north, Give up!
> And to the south, Withhold not!
> Bring my sons from afar,
> And my daughters from the ends of the earth.

Interpreted in the light of their true geographical setting, these prophecies gain at once a new and clearer meaning.

IV. Their Probable Date. The reference in 43²³,²⁴ to the offerings brought by the people to Jehovah's temple clearly implies that it had already been built. Furthermore, the charges preferred against the Judean community are very similar to those in the book of Malachi, which is generally assigned to the period immediately preceding the arrival of Nehemiah in 445 B.C. (*cf.* § XCVII). From the parallels in chapter 48 and elsewhere it is evident that Jehovah's Messiah in 45¹ is not Cyrus but Israel, the messianic nation, to which Jehovah in earlier days under David and his successors gave repeated victories and far-extended authority. The presence of the name Cyrus seems without reasonable doubt to be due to a later scribe, who thus incorrectly identified the allusion. It is supported neither by the metrical structure nor the context of the passages in which it is found. Furthermore, the ideas in Isaiah 40–55 are almost without exception those which Zechariah had already voiced in germinal form, especially in his latest prophecies preserved in chapters 7 and 8. They are here more fully and far more gloriously expanded, indicating that their author lived perhaps a generation later than Zechariah. The years between 500 and 450 furnish the most satisfactory setting for these prophecies. In a very true sense, however, like many of the psalms, they are timeless. The question of their exact date is comparatively unimportant except as it throws light upon their interpretation.

V. Their Literary Characteristics. The prophecies in Isaiah 40–66 are psalms, sharing the characteristics of all lyric Hebrew poetry. Each is complete in itself and yet closely related to the others both in content and literary form. Their nobility of theme, their breadth of outlook, their wealth of rich and glowing figures, and their finished literary character give them an incontestable place among the greatest writings of the Old Testament. While there is a powerful argument running through them all, the logic is not cumulative but rather moves in a spiral, frequently returning to the same subject but having a gradual onward movement. It is the characteristic Oriental method of thinking, which is the opposite of that of the Western world. These poems are grouped into three cycles which apparently represent the prophet's thinking during succeeding periods. The first cycle is included in 40–48. Chapter 48 is a recapitulation of the thought of the preceding, and furnishes a natural conclusion to the first collection. The second group is in 49–55. The note of suffering is here more prominent, and the portrait of the ideal type of servant which Jehovah desires in order to realize his purpose in human history is

developed in greater detail (*cf.* § XCIX).   The third group, in 56–66, is by many assigned to another prophet and to a much later period. While the general theme of the group is different and implies a somewhat changed historical background, the characteristic ideas and literary forms of 40–55 also recur here.   From the study of Israel's past and future the prophet turns to the closer consideration of the problems in Palestine.   The historical allusions are for the most part in accord with the conditions which Nehemiah found in Jerusalem in 445 B.C.

VI. **Their Theme and Purpose.**   The poems deal with one theme, the destiny of the chosen people.   The prophet first reviews their past history to illustrate Jehovah's purpose that was being realized through Israel.   He notes the different ways in which Jehovah had trained and prepared them for their great task.   In the light of the new situation and his enlarged acquaintance with the world the prophet then proceeds to define the task that awaits his people.   While he does not break entirely away from the popular expectation that the scattered exiles would yet be restored to Jerusalem to participate in the universal kingdom that was there to be established, he fully appreciates the larger significance of Israel's mission.   He recognizes that it is worldwide.   He sees that the Jewish race is called not merely to receive honors and material blessings but also to serve suffering and needy mankind.   The disappointments and afflictions through which it is passing are but a part of the divine training for that nobler spiritual service.   The servant Israel is called to be a witness to all the nations, faithfully to set forth Jehovah's teachings until his law is established in all the earth.   Thus the prophet interprets Israel's past, present, and future in its vital relation to the universal life of humanity, and declares that Israel is destined to be a prophet nation and to reveal Jehovah's character to all mankind.

VII. **Reasons Why Jehovah Will Restore His People.**   The prophet opens with a declaration that Jerusalem's period of forced service is over, that she has paid double for the sins of the past, and that Jehovah is about to remove all obstacles and restore and exalt his oppressed people.   He then gives the reasons for his strong conviction: (1) Jehovah is incomparably superior to the forces of nature, to the nations that hold Israel in bondage, and to the heathen gods whose images are shaped by the hand of man.   All the powers of heaven and earth are under his control.   He is the creator and supreme ruler of the universe, able to remove all obstacles and to give strength and might to those who put their trust in him.   (2) Through his leadership of his people in the past, through their victories over their powerful foes, and in all the experiences of their national life he has shown his power to guide and deliver. (3) Toward Israel, his servant, he stands in a unique relation, for he has chosen and trained his people for a great service in behalf of all the world. Therefore he who is able and eager to deliver will not fail his people in their hour of need. (4) Their present affliction is but a part of that training which is essential before they can perform their task as Jehovah's servant; that task is tenderly to espouse the cause of those who are crushed, to open eyes that are blind, to bring captives out of their confinement, and, as a faithful teacher, to inspire all mankind with love for Israel's God.

The prophet's aim was clearly to encourage his despondent people, to show them the deeper meaning of their present afflictions, to open their eyes to Jehovah's gracious purpose, to give to the entire race a goal for which to live and strive, and, above all, to arouse them to effective action. Doubtless the prophet thought only of the problems of the men of his day, but in his interpretation of Jehovah's world-wide purpose and in the faith and devotion which his words inspire he gave to all mankind a universal, undying message.

§ XCVII. CONDITIONS AND PROBLEMS WITHIN THE JUDEAN COMMUNITY

1. The presentation of unworthy offerings (Mal. 1⁶⁻⁹)

A son honoreth his father, and a servant feareth his master;
If then I am a father, where is mine honor?
And if I am a master, where is the one who fears me?
Saith Jehovah to you, O ye priests, who despise my name.
But ye say, 'Wherein have we despised thy name?'
Ye offer upon mine altar bread that is polluted
And ye say, 'Wherein have we polluted it?'
In that ye say, 'The table of Jehovah is contemptible.'
And that when ye offer the blind for sacrifice, 'It is no harm!'
And that when ye offer the lame and the sick, 'It is no harm!'
Present it now to thy governor; will he be pleased with it?
Or will he receive thee favorably? saith Jehovah of hosts.
And now entreat the favor of God with such an offering, that he may be gracious to us,
Would I receive any of you favorably? saith Jehovah of hosts.

O that there were those among you who would shut the doors,
That ye might not kindle fire on mine altar in vain!
I have no pleasure in you, saith Jehovah of hosts,
Neither will I accept an offering at your hand.
For from the rising of the sun even to its setting my name is
    sacred among the nations,
And in every place they offer to my name a pure offering;
For my name is great among the nations, saith Jehovah of
    hosts.

2. Offerings of the heathen more acceptable to God (10, 11)

But ye profane it, in that ye say,
'The table of Jehovah is polluted, and its food is contemptible.'
Ye say also, 'Behold what a weariness is it!' and ye have
    scorned me;
And ye have brought the blind, the lame and the sick.
Should I accept this at your hand? saith Jehovah of hosts.
But cursed be the deceiver, who has in his flock a male,
And vows, and sacrifices to the Lord a blemished thing;
For I am a great King, and my name is feared among the
    nations.

3. His own people despise his service (12-14)

And now, O ye priests, this command is for you.
If ye will not hear, and if ye will not lay it to heart,
To give glory to my name, saith Jehovah of hosts,
Then I will send the curse upon you, and I will curse your
    blessings;
Behold, I will cut off your arm,
And will spread offal upon your faces, even the offal of your
    feasts,
And ye shall know that I have sent this command to you,
That my covenant with Levi may be preserved, saith Jehovah of hosts.

4. Penalty if the priests neglect their task (2¹⁻⁴)

    My covenant with him was to give life and peace;
    And I gave them to him that he might revere me;
    And he revered me, and stood in awe of my name.
    The true instruction was in his mouth,
    And unrighteousness was not found in his lips;
    He walked with me in peace and uprightness,

5. The ideal and fidelity of the earlier priests (5-7)

And turned many away from iniquity.
For the priest's lips should keep knowledge,
And men should seek the law at his mouth;
For he is the messenger of Jehovah of hosts.

6.
Degeneracy
and
shame
of the
later
priests
(8, 9)

But ye are turned aside out of the way;
Ye have caused many to stumble in the law;
Ye have corrupted the covenant of Levi,
Saith Jehovah of hosts.
Therefore have I also made you contemptible,
And base before all the people,
According as ye have not kept my ways,
And have had no respect for me in imparting the law.

7.
Divorce
contrary
to the
spirit of
Israel's
religion
(10, 13,14)

Have we not all one father?
Hath not one God created us?
Why do we deal faithlessly with one another,
Profaning the covenant of our fathers?
And this ye do also:
Ye cover the altar of Jehovah with tears,
So that he regardeth not the offering any more,
Neither receiveth it acceptably from your hand.
Yet ye say, Why?
Because Jehovah hath been witness between thee and
     the wife of thy youth,
Against whom thou hast dealt faithlessly,
Though she is thy companion, and the wife of thy covenant.

8.
Hateful
to Jehovah
(15, 16)

Therefore give heed to your spirit,
And let none deal faithlessly with the wife of his youth,
For I hate putting away,
Saith Jehovah, the God of Israel,
And him who covers his garment with violence;
Therefore take heed to your spirit, that ye deal not
     faithlessly.

9.
Doubt
of Jehovah's
justice
(17)

Ye have wearied Jehovah with your words.
Yet ye say, How have we wearied him?
In that ye say, Everyone that doeth evil

Is good in the sight of Jehovah,
And he delighteth in them;
Or where is the God of justice?

Behold, I am about to send my messenger,
And he shall prepare the way before me;
And the Lord, whom ye seek,
Will suddenly come to his temple;
But who can endure the day of his coming?
And who shall stand when he appeareth?
For he is like a refiner's fire,
And like fullers' lyes;
And he will sit as a refiner and purifier,
And he will purify the sons of Levi,
And refine them as gold and silver;
And they shall offer offerings in righteousness.
Then shall the offerings of Judah and Jerusalem be
    pleasant to Jehovah,
As in the days of old, and as in former years.

10. The advent of Jehovah to purify his people (3$^{1-4}$)

And I will come near to you to judgment;
And I will be a swift witness
Against the sorcerers, and against the adulterers,
And against those who sware to that which is false,
And against those who oppress the hireling, the widow,
    and the fatherless,
Who turn aside the resident alien from his right,
And fear not me, saith Jehovah of hosts.
For I, Jehovah, change not;
But ye have not ceased to be sons of Jac .

11. Those whom Jehovah will condemn ($^{5,\ 6}$)

From the days of thy fathers ye have turned aside from my
    statutes, and ye have not kept them.
Turn to me and I will turn to you, saith Jehovah.
But ye say, 'Wherein shall we turn?'
Will a man rob God? Yet ye robbed me.
But ye say, 'Wherein have we robbed thee?' In tithes and
    gifts.
Ye are cursed with a curse, ior ye rob me.

12. Robbing Jehovah

67

13. Rewards that will come from faithful service (10-13)

Bring ye the whole tithe into the store-house,
That there may be provision in mine house; and test me
    thereby,
If I will not open to you the windows of heaven,
And pour you out a blessing, until there is more than enough.
I will rebuke for your sakes the devourer that he destroy
    not the fruit of the ground,
Neither shall the vine fail to ripen its fruit in the field,
And all nations shall call you happy,
For ye shall be a delightsome land, saith Jehovah of hosts.

14. The cry of the suffering servants Jehovah (13-15)

Your words are hard upon me, saith Jehovah.
Ye say, 'What have we said against thee?'
Ye have said, 'It is useless to serve God,
And what gain is it to us to have kept his charge,
And that we have walked in funeral garb before him?
Even now we call the proud happy,
Yea, those who work iniquity thrive,
Yea, they tempt God and escape.'

15. Vindication of the faithful (16-18)

Such things those who feared Jehovah spoke to one another,
And Jehovah gave heed, and heard,
And a book of remembrance was written before him,
Regarding those who feared Jehovah,
And those who keep in mind his name;
And they shall be mine, saith Jehovah of hosts,
In the day that I make up mine especial treasure.
And I will spare them,
As a man spares his son who serves him.
Then shall ye return and discern between the righteous and
    the wicked,
Between him who serves God and him who serves him not.

16. The coming day of judgment and vindication (4¹⁻³)

For behold the day is coming that shall burn like a furnace,
And all the proud and those who work iniquity shall be
    stubble,
And the day that is coming shall burn them up, saith
    Jehovah of hosts,
So that there shall be left them neither root nor branch.
But to you who fear my name there shall arise

CONDITIONS AND PROBLEMS

The sun of righteousness with healing on his wings,
And ye shall go forth and leap like calves out of the stall.
And ye shall tread down the wicked,
For they shall be as ashes under the soles of your feet,
In the day in which I begin to execute, saith Jehovah of
    hosts.

My God, why dost thou forsake me,
Far from my salvation is my groaning
By day I call, but thou answerest not,
And by night there is no respite for me.
Yet thou, O my God, art the Holy One,
Enthroned on Israel's songs of praise.
In thee our fathers trusted,
They trusted, and thou didst deliver them;
To thee they cried, and were delivered,
In thee they trusted and were not ashamed.

17. Why does not Jehovah answer his servant as of old? (Ps. 22¹⁻⁵)

But I am a worm and no man,
Reproached by men and despised by the people.
Whoever sees me derideth me,
They sneer as they toss the head:
"He depended upon Jehovah, let him deliver him,
Let him save him, since he delighteth in him!"

18 And deliver him from reproach? (⁶⁻⁸)

Yet it was thou who took me from the womb,
Who made me safe on my mother's breast;
On thee was I cast from birth,
Thou art my God from my mother's womb.
Be not far from me, for there is distress,
Draw nigh, for there is no helper.

19. God alone can deliver (⁹⁻¹¹)

Many bulls encompass me,
Mighty ones of Bashan beset me round,
They open their mouths at me,
Like a ravening, roaring lion.
As water I am poured out,
Yea, all my bones are out of joint,
My heart hath become like wax,
It is melted within my body,

20 Pitiable condition of his servant (¹²⁻¹⁸)

69

My palate is dried up like a potsherd,
And my tongue cleaveth to my jaws;
In the dust of death thou dost lay me,
For dogs circle me about,
The assembly of evil-doers enclose me;
They pierce my hands and my feet,
I can count all my bones;
They stare, they gloat over me.
They divide my garments among them,
And for my clothing they cast lots!

I. Date of the Book of Malachi. Malachi in the Hebrew means My Messenger, and the word was apparently taken from the opening verse of the third chapter. Like many of the writings of the post-exilic period, the book, therefore, is anonymous. Its date, however, may be determined from its contents. The reference to the desolation of the land of the Edomites suggests that it was written late in the Persian period after the Edomites had been driven out from Mount Seir by the Nabateans and had found a home on the southern borders of Judah. The priests in the Judean community had become corrupt and the temple service was neglected, indicating that they had lost the early enthusiasm which followed the rebuilding of the sanctuary. The Judean community was discouraged and a spirit of doubt and questioning prevailed in the minds of those who were faithfully striving to serve Jehovah. The prophecy is an exact picture of conditions as Nehemiah found them, so that the book of Malachi may be dated not far from 445 B.C.

II. Neglect of the Temple Service. The prophet's method is kin to that of Zechariah. Evidently the early reverence for the word of the prophet has disappeared. Instead of bare assertions, each conclusion is supported by detailed arguments. The author of Malachi is also deeply interested in the ritual and regards the preservation of its purity as essential to the religious life of the Judean community. He charges the priests with failure to observe the ceremonial laws, especially in allowing the people to bring for sacrifice animals that are blind, lame, and sick. These acts are evidence of the religious apathy that had seized even the religious leaders of the people. The prophet declares boldly that under the guise of religion the priests are robbing Jehovah. Above all they are faithless to their responsibilities as the appointed teachers of the people. In 2^{5-7} he presents the clearest picture extant of the task of the priest as teacher. His duty was to instruct the people, to help them to overcome temptation, and to make very clear to them the way of duty. This ideal, the prophet declares, was realized by earlier priests, but now those who are the appointed religious guides are misleading the people.

III. **The Need of a Great Moral Awakening.** The evils which the prophet denounced were not confined to the priests. The old Semitic law regarding divorce was exceedingly lax. A husband could lead his wife to the door of his tent and tell her to be gone, thereby severing their marriage relation. The Deuteronomic law sought to relieve this injustice by providing that the husband must place in the hand of his wife, as she departs, a document stating the grounds on which he had divorced her. By the middle of the fifth century b.c. divorce had evidently become exceedingly common in Palestine. The prophet denounced it on the basis of its injustice and cruelty. He also maintained that marriage was a solemn covenant before Jehovah between man and wife, and that he who disregarded it dealt faithlessly and was the especial obj᠎t of divine displeasure.

Traces of the old heathenis᠎ ᠎ll remained in Judah, and the dependent, oppressed classes received little ᠎᠎ty from the selfish, heartless rulers. In the face of these evils the prophe᠎ ᠎eclared that Jehovah would surely send a messenger to punish and to ᠎ ᠎rm priest and people. The prophecy was evidently based on a clear rec᠎᠎ ᠎tion that Jehovah was ever working to train and uplift his people, and ᠎ ᠎t a period of degeneration must surely be followed by a period of refor᠎ In the work of Nehemiah the prophet's hopes were in part fulfilled, b᠎ ᠎he larger fulfilment of the underlying principle was realized in the thoroughgoing reformatory work of John the Baptist and in that of the Great Teacher. In a later appendix to the prophecy of Malachi this theme is still further developed. The promise is made that another prophet, with the zeal of the great reformer Elijah, would come and prepare the way for a new and nobler era.

IV. **The Lot of the Faithful.** In the prophecy of Malachi is first voiced the despairing cries and doubts of those of the faithful who failed to rise above the effect of the existing social and religious evils. They are the righteous or afflicted who also speak through certain of the earlier psalms of the Psalter (e. g., 10–17, 22). It was a period when the man who did right and was faithful to the demands of the law was thereby condemned to poverty and persecution at the hands of the corrupt priests and rulers. Worse than that, their poverty and wretchedness were interpreted, according to the current belief of the day, as convincing evidence of Jehovah's displeasure because of their sins. It was a time when wickedness triumphed and innocence suffered, and when the question whether or not a righteous God ruled the universe rose persistently in the minds of the faithful. The author of Malachi recognizes and seeks to meet these doubts:

> Ye have said, It is useless to serve God,
> And what gain is it to us to have kept his charge,
> And that we have walked in funeral garb before him?
> Even now we call the proud happy,
> Verily those who work iniquity thrive,
> Yea, they tempt God and escape.

Here the problem is the same as that of the book of Job. To these doubts the prophet could only reply that Jehovah will keep a record of the faithful and in his good time will reward them.

V. **The Problem of Suffering in the Literature of the Period.** As was natural, this problem of innocent suffering was prominent in the literature of the period. It became especially insistent at this time, because it had ceased to be the problem of the community, and had become that of individuals or of a class. While the nation rested under the shadow of misfortune, a solution of the problem was found in the consciousness of national guilt and in the hope that the affliction would be but temporary. The old dogma that virtue was always rewarded and wickedness punished continued to satisfy Israel's leaders. When, however, a considerable class in the community were conscious that they had committed no crimes worthy of the bitter persecutions and calamities that overtook them, and that it was often just because of their virtue and the steadfastness with which they clung to the nobler ideals of their race that they were thus assailed, the current interpretations of evil were no longer satisfactory. When in time many of them went down to the grave crushed by affliction and the objects of the taunts and revilings of their wicked pursuers, the insufficiency of the current explanation of misfortune was tragically demonstrated. To their minds Sheol or the grave offered no solution, for, as among all early Aryan and Semitic peoples, it was thought of as the dark, passionless, joyless abode of the shades.

In most of the psalms of this period the poets who speak in behalf of the afflicted class, like the author of Malachi, expressed the hope that Jehovah would speedily come to their deliverance and signally vindicate and reward them. The heroism and fidelity that they represent can only be fully appreciated in the light of this discouraging period when evil was regnant. It was apparently at this time that the great poet, who speaks through the book of Job, presented, with the spirit and method of a modern philosopher, the lot of these innocent sufferers. He also proved for all time that misfortune is not always the evidence of guilt, and that the current doctrine of proportionate rewards and the explanations that were adduced to support it were in certain cases absolutely untenable.

§ XCVIII. THE PROBLEM AND TEACHINGS OF THE BOOK OF JOB

There was a man in the land of Uz, whose name was Job. And that man was blameless and upright; he feared God and turned away from evil. And seven sons and three daughters were born to him. His possessions also included seven thousand sheep, three thousand camels, five hundred yoke of oxen, five hundred she asses, and an exceedingly large number of servants; so that this man was the greatest of all the peoples of Palestine. And his sons were accustomed to hold a feast in one another's house each on his day. And they were wont to send and invite their three sisters to eat and drink with them. And when the days of their feasting were over, Job used to send and sanctify them, and he rose up early in the morning, and offered burnt-offerings according to the number of them all; for Job said, Perhaps my sons have sinned, and renounced God in their hearts. Thus Job did continually. *1. Job's great prosperity and exemplary piety (Job 1¹⁻⁵)*

Now on a certain day when the sons of God came to present themselves before Jehovah, Satan also came among them. And Jehovah said to Satan, Whence comest thou? Then Satan answered Jehovah, and said, From going to and fro in the earth, and walking up and down on it. And Jehovah said to Satan, Hast thou considered my servant Job? for there is none like him on the earth, a blameless and upright man who fears God, and turns away from evil. Then Satan answered Jehovah, and said, Doth Job fear God for nought? Hast thou not made a hedge about him, and about his household, and about all that he hath, on every side? Thou hast blessed the work of his hands, and his possessions are increased in the land. But put forth *2. The charge that his piety is not disinterested (6-11)* thy hand now, and touch all that he hath, and he will curse thee to thy face.

Then Jehovah said to Satan, Behold all that he hath is in thy power; only put not forth thy hand upon him. So Satan went forth from the presence of Jehovah.

Now on a certain day when his sons and daughters were eating and drinking in their eldest brother's house, a messenger came to Job and said, The oxen were plowing and the asses were feeding beside them, when the Sabeans suddenly attacked and captured them, and they have slain the servants with the edge of the sword; and I alone have escaped to tell you. While that one was yet speaking, another came and said, The fire of God has fallen from heaven, and has burned up the sheep and the servants, and consumed them; and I alone have escaped to tell you. While that one was yet speaking, another came and said, The Chaldeans made three bands, and raided the camels and took them away, and they have slain the servants with the edge of the sword; I alone have escaped to tell you. While that one was yet speaking, another came and said, Your sons and your daughters were eating and drinking in their eldest brother's house, when there came a great wind from over the wilderness, and smote the four corners of the house, and it fell upon the young men, and they are dead. I alone have escaped to tell you.

Then Job arose, and tore his robe, and shaved his head, and fell upon the ground and worshipped; and he said:

> Naked I came from my mother's womb,
> And naked shall I return thither!
> Jehovah gave and he hath taken away;
> Blessed be the name of Jehovah!

In all this Job sinned not, nor reviled God.

And on a certain day when the sons of God came to present themselves before Jehovah, Satan came also to present himself before Jehovah. And Jehovah said to Satan, Whence comest thou? And Satan answered Jehovah, and said, From going to and fro in the earth, and from walking up and down on it. And Jehovah said to Satan, Hast thou considered my servant Job? for there is none like him in

the earth, a blameless and upright man, one who fears
God, and turns away from evil; and he still remains steadfast in his piety, although thou incitest me against him, to
destroy him without cause. And Satan answered Jehovah,
and said, Skin for skin, yea, all that a man hath will he
give for his life. But put forth thy hand now, and touch
his bone and his flesh; surely he will curse thee to thy face.
And Jehovah said to Satan, Behold, he is in thy power:
only spare his life.

So Satan went forth from the presence of Jehovah, and
smote Job with a malignant eruption from the sole of his
foot to his crown. And he took a potsherd with which to
scrape himself; and he sat among the ashes.

7 Af-
flicted
with
vile
leprosy
(7, 8)

Then said his wife to him, Do you still remain steadfast
in your piety? Curse God, and die. But he said to her,
You speak like one of the foolish women. We receive
good at the hand of God, shall we not also receive evil?
In all this did not Job sin with his lips.

8.
Tempt-
ed by
his wife
(9, 10)

Now when Job's three friends heard of all this evil that
was come upon him, they came each from his own place:
Eliphaz the Temanite, and Bildad the Shuhite, and Zophar
the Naamathite; and they made an appointment together
to come to show their sympathy for him and to comfort
him. And when they lifted up their eyes afar off and knew
him not, they raised their voice and wept; and all tore
their robes, and sprinkled dust upon their heads toward
heaven. So they sat down with him on the ground seven
days and seven nights, without any one speaking a word to
him, for they saw that his pain was very great.

9. Vis-
ited by
his
friends
(11-13)

Then Job began to speak and said:
　Why did I not die before birth?
　Why did I not expire when my mother bore me?
　For now would I have lain down and been quiet,
　I would have slept, then had I been at rest,
　With kings and counsellors of the earth,
　Who built up ruins for themselves;
　Or with princes who possessed gold,
　Who filled their houses with silver.
　There the wicked cease from raging,

10. His
lament
because
he was
not al-
lowed
to die
(3², 11,
12-16,
17-19)

And the weary are at rest.
There the prisoners have peace as well,
They hear not the voice of the taskmaster.
The small and the great are there,
And the servant is free from his master.

11. Injustice of his being compelled to live (20-22, 25, 26)

Why is light given to the suffering,
And life to those in anguish,
Who long for death but it comes not,
And search for it more than treasures,
Who rejoice with great exultation,
And are glad when they can find the grave?
For the thing which I feared has come upon me,
And that of which I was afraid has overtaken me.
No peace nor quiet, have I,
No rest, but trembling seizes me.

12. Eliphaz: Misfortune the inevitable consequence of sin, as he well knows (4 1-7)

Then answered Eliphaz the Temanite, and said:
If one tries to speak with you, will you be impatient,
But who can restrain himself from speaking?
Behold, you have instructed many,
And have strengthened feeble hands.
Your words have upheld him who was falling,
And you have made tottering knees strong.
But now, that it is come to you, you are impatient,
It touches yourself and you lose courage.
Is not your piety, your trust,
Your hope the integrity of your ways?
Remember now who, being innocent, perished?
Or where have the upright been destroyed?

13. No mortal can be wholly pure (17-19)

Can mortal man be righteous before God?
Can a man be pure before his maker?
Behold, he trusteth not in his own servants,
And his angels he chargeth with error;
How much more the dwellers in clay houses,
Whose foundation is laid in the dust?

76

Happy is the man whom God correcteth,
Therefore reject not the chastening of the Almighty.
For he causeth pain and bindeth up;
He woundeth and his hands heal.
He will deliver you out of six troubles,
Yea, in seven, no evil shall touch you,
In famine he will redeem you from death,
And in war from the power of the sword.
You shall be hid from the scourge of the tongue;
You shall not be afraid of destruction when it
    comes.
At destruction and want you shall laugh,
And you need not fear the beasts of the earth.
You shall come to your grave in a ripe old age,
As a sheaf garnered in its season.
Lo this, we have searched out, so it is;
Hear it and know it yourself.

14.
Submit
to
God's
dis-
cipline
and you
will
prosper
(5¹⁷⁻²²,
²⁶, ²⁷)

Then Job answered and said:
Oh, that my bitterness were weighed,
All my calamity laid in the scales!
Then would it be heavier than the sand of the seas;
For this reason my words are rash.
For the arrows of the Almighty are within me,
Their poison my spirit drinks up.

15. Job:
Crush-
ing
char-
acter
of his
afflic-
tion
(6¹⁻⁴ᵇ)

Oh that I might have my request,
And that God would grant that for which I long:
Even that it would please God to crush me,
And that he would let loose his hand and cut me off!
Then this would be my consolation,
I would exult in pain that spares not.

16. Sigh
for
deliver-
ance
(8-10)

What strength have I still to endure?
And what is mine end that I should be patient?
Is my strength the strength of stones?
Or is my body made of brass?
Behold there is no help in me,
And wisdom is driven quite from me.

17. Pa-
tience
impos-
sible
(11-13)

18.
Faith-
lessness
of his
friends
(14, 15,
20-23)

Kindness from his friend is due to one in despair,
Even though he forsakes the fear of the Almighty.
My brothers have been as deceptive as a brook,
As the channel of brooks that disappear.
For now you are nothing,
You see a terror and are afraid.
Did I say, 'Give to me?'
Or, 'Offer a present to me of your wealth?'
Or, 'Deliver me from a foeman's hand?'
Or, 'Redeem me from the oppressor's power?'

19.
Their
inabil-
ity to
bring a
valid
charge
(24-30)

Teach me and I will hold my peace,
And make plain to me wherein I have erred.
How agreeable are upright words!
But what does a reproof from you reprove?
Do you think to reprove mere words,
When the speeches of the desperate are as wind?
You fall upon a blameless man,
And you make merchandise of your friend.
Now therefore be pleased to look upon me;
For surely I will not lie to you.
Turn ere you let injustice be done,
Yea, turn again, my cause is righteous.
Is there injustice on my tongue?
Can not my taste discern what is evil?

20. Mis-
ery and
brevity
of life
(7¹⁻⁶)

Has not man a hard service on earth?
And are not his days like the days of a hireling?
As a slave who sighs for the shadows of the even-
ing,
And as a hireling who looks for his wages,
So am I given months of misery,
And wearisome nights are appointed me.
When I lie down, I say:
'When shall I arise, and the night be gone?'
And I am full of unrest until the dawn.
My flesh is clothed with worms and clods of dust;
My skin hardens, then breaks out again.
My days are swifter than a weaver's shuttle,
And are spent without hope.

As the cloud is consumed and vanishes away,
So he who goes down to Sheol shall come up no more,
He shall return no more to his house,
Nor shall his place know him any more.

Therefore I will not refrain my mouth;
I will speak in the bitterness of my spirit.
Am I a sea, or a sea-monster,
That thou shouldest set a watch over me?
When I say, "My bed shall comfort me,
My couch shall ease my complaint;"
Then thou frightest me with dreams,
And terrifiest me through visions:
So that I myself choose strangling,
And death rather than my pains.
I loath life, I would not live always,
Let me alone, for my days are as a breath,
What is man, that thou exaltest him,
That on him thou directest thy thought,
That thou visitest him each morning,
And testest him each moment?

22. God
piti-
lessly
perse-
cutes
man
(11-18)

If I have sinned, what have I done to thee, O watcher
of men?
Why hast thou set me as thy target?
And why am I a burden to thee?
And why dost thou not pardon my transgression and
take away mine iniquity?
For now I shall lie down in the dust,
When thou shalt seek me, I shall not be.

23. If
a man
has
sinned,
why
does
God not
pardon
(20, 21)

Then answered Bildad the Shuhite and said,
How long will you speak these things?
And the words of your mouth be like a mighty wind?
Doth God pervert justice?
Or doth the Almighty pervert righteousness?

24.
Bildad:
God
cannot
be un-
just
(8¹⁻²)

If your children sinned against him,
And he delivered them to the consequences of their
guilt;
You should earnestly seek God,

25. Re-
pent-
ance
will
bring
deliver-
ance
(3-6)

79

And make your supplication to the Almighty.
If you are pure and upright,
Then he will prosper your righteous habitation.

26. Job:
Impossible for
man to
prove
his innocence
before
God
(9¹-⁷)

Then Job answered and said:
Verily I know that it is so,
But how can a man be made just with God?
If he be pleased to contend with him,
He cannot answer him one of a thousand.
He is wise in mind and mighty in strength;
Who has defied him, and remained unharmed?
He who removeth mountains and they know it not,
And overturneth them in his anger,
Who shaketh the earth out of its place,
So that its pillars tremble,
Who commandeth the sun and it rises not,
And on the stars placeth his seal.

27.
Though
innocent he
is the
prey of
an unjust
Deity
(16-26, 24)

If I called and he answered me,
I would not believe that he had heard my voice.
He who crusheth me with a tempest,
And multiplieth my wounds without cause.
He will not permit me to take my breath,
But filleth me with bitterness,
If we speak of the strength of the mighty, lo it is he!
And if of justice, Who will summon him?
Though I am righteous, my own mouth condemns me,
Though I am perfect, it would prove me to be perverse.
The earth is given into the hand of the wicked;
He covereth the faces of its judges;
If not he, then who is it?

28. No
arbiter
before
whom
to
prove
his innocence
(21-35)

If I wash myself with snow,
And cleanse my hands with lye,
Yet wilt thou plunge me into the filth,
And mine own friends will abhor me.
For he is not a man as I am, that I should answer
    him,
That we should come together in judgment,
There is no arbiter betwixt us,
To lay his hand upon us both.

Let him take his rod away from me,
And let not his terror make me afraid,
Then would I speak and not fear him,
For in myself I am not thus fearful.

Remember that as clay thou hast fashioned me,
And wilt thou again turn me into dust?
Hast thou not poured me out as milk?
And curdled me like a cheese?
Thou hast clothed me with a skin and with flesh,
And knit me together with bones and with sinews.
Thou hast granted me life and favor,
And thy care hath preserved my breath.
Yet these things thou didst hide in thy heart;
I know that this is thy plan:
If I sin, then thou watchest me,
And if I be just, yet I cannot lift up my head!

29. Why God's care for man if but to destroy him (10⁹⁻¹⁵)

Are not the days of my life few enough?
Let me alone, that I may have a little cheer,
Before I go whence I shall not return,
To the land of darkness and of gloom,
The land dark as blackness,
Gloom without a gleam or ray of light.

30. Cry for at least temporary relief before death (²⁰⁻²²)

Then answered Zophar, the Naamathite, and said:
Shall the multitude of words be unanswered?
Can you find the depths of God?
Can you reach the perfection of the Almighty?
It is high as heaven; what canst thou do?
Deeper than Sheol; what can you know?
Its measure is longer than the earth,
And broader than the sea.

31. Zophar: Man cannot comprehend God (11¹,⁷⁻⁹)

If you set your heart aright,
And stretch out your hands toward him;
If iniquity be in thy hand, put it far away,
And let not unrighteousness dwell in your tent.
Then you shall lift up your face without spot;
And you shall be steadfast, and have no fear.

32. Repentance will again bring peace and honor (¹³⁻¹⁵)

33.
Job's
retort
(12¹⁻³)

Then Job answered and said:
No doubt but you are the people,
And wisdom shall die with you!
But I have a mind as well as you,
And who does not know these things?

34.
Folly of
trying
to dis-
tort
truth
in order
to vin-
dicate
God
(13⁷⁻¹²)

Will you speak what is wrong for God?
And will you talk deceitfully for him?
Will you show favor to him?
Will you contend for God?
Would it be well, should he search you out?
Or as one deceives a man, will you deceive him?
He will surely reprove you,
If secretly you show favor.
Shall not his majesty overawe you,
And dread of him fall upon you?
Your memorable sayings are proverbs of ashes,
Your defences are defences of clay!

35.
Bold
protes-
tation
of inno-
cence
(13-18)

Hold your peace that I may speak,
And let come to me what will.
I take my flesh in my teeth,
And put my life in my hand.
Behold he will slay me; I have no hope,
But I will defend my ways before him.
No godless man would come before him.
Give careful heed to my speech,
And let my declaration be in your ears.
Behold now, I have prepared my case,
I know that I shall be justified.

36. Ap-
peal to
God for
justice
(21-25)

Withdraw thy hand far from me;
And let not thy terror make me afraid.
Then call and I will answer,
Or let me speak, and answer thou me.
How many are my iniquities and sins?
Make me know my transgression and my sin.
Why dost thou hide thy face,
And regard me as thine enemy?
Wilt thou harass a wind blown leaf?
And wilt thou pursue the dry stubble?

THE PROBLEM OF THE BOOK OF JOB

For there is hope of a tree,
If it will be cut down, that it will sprout again,
And that its shoot will not cease.
Though its root grow old in the earth,
And its stock die in the ground;
By the scent of water it will bud,
And put forth its branches like a plant.
But man dies and is laid low:
Yea, a man expires, and where is he?

37. Man has no hope beyond this life (14⁷⁻ⁱ)

Oh, that thou wouldst hide me in Sheol,
That thou wouldst keep me in secret, until thy wrath
be past,
That thou wouldst appoint over me a time, and remem-
ber me!
If a man might die, shall he live again!
All the days of my hard service would I wait,
Until my release should come.
Thou wouldst call and I myself would answer thee;
Thou wouldst long for the work of thy hands.
But the mountain surely falls,
And the rock moves from its place,
The water wears away the stones,
Its floods wash away the dust of the earth.

38. Would that God might vindicate his servants after death (13-15, 18, 19)

Then answered Eliphaz the Temanite and said:
Verily, you do away with the fear of God,
And hinder devotion before God.
For your wickedness inspires your speech,
And you choose the tongue of the crafty.
Your own mouth condemns you, and not I;
And your own lips testify against you.

39. Eliphaz Job's words proclaim his guilt (15⁴⁻⁶)

Then answered Job and said:
I have heard many such things;
Troublesome comforters are you all.
Is there no end to vain words?
If you were only in my place,
I could join words together against you!

40. Job's retort (16¹⁻⁵, &b.)

83

41. He
is the
object
of
divine
perse-
cution
(11-13a)

God delivereth me to the ungodly,
And casteth me into the hands of the wicked.
I was at ease, and he shattered me,
He seized me by the neck and dashed me to pieces,
He hath also set me up as his target,
His arrows encompass me round about.

42. But
God
will yet
vindi-
cate
him
(18-21)

O earth, cover not my blood,
And let my cry have no resting place.
Even now behold my witness is in the heaven,
And he who voucheth for me is on high.
He will be found to be my friend,
To God my eye pours out its tears.
And he will maintain the right of a man with God,
And between a man and his neighbor!

43.
Bildad:
Fate
of the
wicked
(18¹, 5-7)

Then answered Bildad the Shuhite, and said:
The light of the wicked is put out,
And the flame of his fire does not shine,
The light is darkened in his tent,
And his light above him is put out.
The steps of his strength are shortened,
And his own counsel shall cast him down.

44. Job:
His
pitiable
fate
(19¹,
13-16)

Then Job answered and said:
My brothers keep far from me,
And my acquaintances are like strangers to me.
My kinsmen have ceased to know me,
Even the guests in my house have forgotten me.
My maids regard me as a stranger,
I am an alien in their sight.

45.
Firm
hope
that
even
after
death
he will
be vin-
dicated
by God
(23-27)

Oh, that my words were now written!
Oh, that they were inscribed in a book!
That with an iron pen and lead
They were engraved in a rock forever!
But I indeed know that my Vindicator liveth,
And at last he will stand upon the earth:
And after this, my skin, is destroyed,
Then I shall behold God,

Whom I myself shall see on my side,
Mine eyes shall behold, and not a stranger.

Then answered Zophar the Naamathite, and said:
    Not so do my thoughts give answer to me,
    Because of this my haste is mine!
    I have heard the reproof which puts me to shame;
    But with wind void of understanding you answer me.
    Have you not known this from of old,
    Since man was placed upon the earth,
    That the exulting of the wicked is short,
    And the joy of the godless but for a moment?

46. Zophar Prosperity of the wicked is brief (20[1-5])

Then answered Job and said:
    Why do the wicked live,
    Grow old, and attain great power?
    Their descendants are established in their sight,
    And their offspring before their eyes.
    Their households are secure from terror,
    And the rod of God is not upon them.

47. Job: Facts contradict the popular dogma (21[1, 7-9])

Then Eliphaz the Temanite answered, and said,
    Is a man of any account to God?
    Surely a wise man is of account to himself.
    Is it any pleasure to the Almighty that you are righteous?
    Or is it gain to him that you are upright?
    Is it because of your fear of him that he reproveth you,
    That he entereth into judgment with you?
    Is not your wickedness great?
    And there is no end to your iniquities.

48. Eliphaz: Sin the only explanation of Job's affliction (22[1-5])

If you return to the Almighty and humble yourself,
If you remove unrighteousness far from your tents.
You shall make your prayer to him, and he will hear
    you,
And you shall pay your vows.
You shall also decree a thing, and it shall be established
    for you.
And light shall shine upon your ways.

49. Repentance will yet bring deliverance (23, 27, 28)

THE PROBLEM OF THE BOOK OF JOB

50. Job:
If God could only be found, vindication is assured (23[1-8])

Then Job answered and said,
    Even now my complaint is bitter,
    My stroke is heavier than my groaning.
    Oh, that I knew where I might find him!
    That I might come even to his throne!
    I would set forth my cause before him,
    And fill my mouth with arguments.
    I would know the words which he would answer me,
    And understand what he would say to me.
    Would he contend with me in the greatness of his power?
    Verily he would give heed to me.

51. Bildad:
No man can be just with God (25[1-4])

Then answered Bildad the Shuhite, and said,
    Dominion and terror are with him;
    He maketh peace in his high places.
    Is there any number to his armies?
    And upon whom does not his light arise?
    How then can man be just with God?
    Or how can he be clean who is born of woman?

52. Job:
Protestation of innocence even though God has taken away his right (26[1], 27[2, 4, 5])

Then Job answered and said,
    As God liveth, who hath taken away my right,
    And the Almighty, who hath made my life bitter,
    Surely my lips do not speak unrighteousness,
    Nor does my tongue utter falsehood,
    Far be it from me that I should grant that you are right;
    Until I die I will not give up my innocence.

53. Zophar:
The wicked have no hope (7[-9])

[Then Zophar answered and said]:
    Let mine enemy be as the wicked,
    And let him who rises up against me be as the unrighteous.
    For what is the hope of the godless,
    When God requireth his life?
    Will God hear his cry,
    When trouble comes upon him?

And Job again took up his parable and said,
  Oh, that I were as in the months of old,
  As in the days when God watched over me,
  When his lamp shined upon my head,
  And by his light I walked through darkness;
  As I was in the prime of my life,
  When God put a covering over my tent,
  When the Almighty was yet with me,
  And my children were about me.

54. Job: Review of his former prosperity (29¹⁻⁶)

But now my soul is poured out within me;
Days of affliction have taken hold of me.
The night bores through my bones,
And my gnawing pains rest not.
By reason of great wasting my garment is crumpled
    together;
It binds me about as the collar of my coat.
He hath cast me into the mire,
And I am become like dust and ashes.
I cry to thee but thou dost not answer me.
I stand up, but thou dost not regard me.
Thou art turned to be cruel to me;
With the might of thy hand thou persecutest me.

55. Now wracked with pain and persecuted by God (30¹⁶⁻²¹)

If I have walked with falsehood,
And my foot has hasted to deceit;
Let me be weighed in a just balance,
That God may know my integrity.
If my step has turned out of the way,
And my heart followed my inclination,
And if any spot besmirches my hands;
Then let me sow, and let another eat,
And let the produce of my field be uprooted.

56. Innocent in thought and deed of deceitful dealings (31⁵⁻⁸)

Oh, that there was someone to hear me!
See, here is my signature, let the Almighty answer me!
And the indictment which my adversary has written!
Surely I would carry it on my shoulder;
I would bind it to me as a crown;
I would declare to him the number of my steps,
As a prince would I draw near to him.

57. His desire to confront the divine Judge with his innocence (35-37)

THE PROBLEM OF THE BOOK OF JOB

58. God's character, as revealed in the mighty works of creation, contrasted with that of finite man (38²⁻⁷)

Then Jehovah answered Job out of the storm, and
    said,
Who is this that darkeneth counsel
By words that lack knowledge?
Gird up thy loins now like a man,
And let me ask of thee and inform thou me.
Where wast thou when I laid the foundations of
    the earth?
Declare, if thou hast understanding.
Who determined its measures that thou knowest?
Or who stretched out the line upon it?
On what were its foundations fastened?
Or who laid its corner-stone,
When the morning stars sang together,
And all the sons of God shouted for joy?

59. As the ruler of nature (8-11)

Or who shut up the sea with doors,
When it broke forth, and issued out of the womb;
When I made clouds its garments,
And thick mists its swaddling-bands,
And marked out for it my bound,
And set bars and doors,
And said, Here shalt thou come, but no further;
And here shall thy proud waves stop?

60. As creator and ruler of animate creatures (39-41)

Canst thou hunt the prey for the lioness,
Or satisfy the appetite of the young lions,
When they couch in their dens,
And abide in the covert to lie in wait?
Who provideth at evening his prey,
When his young ones cry to God,
And wander to seek for food?

61. The absurdity of man's questioning God's justice (40², 8, 9)

Will the fault-finder contend with the Almighty?
He who argueth with God, let him answer it.
Wilt thou even annul my judgment?
Condemn me, that thou mayest be justified,
Or hast thou an arm like God?
And canst thou thunder with a voice like him?

88

Then Job answered Jehovah and said:
I know that thou canst do all things,
And that no purpose of thine can be restrained.
Therefore, I have uttered that which I did not understand;
Things too wonderful for me, which I knew not.
I have heard of thee by the hearing of the ear,
But now mine eye seeth thee,
Therefore I loath [my words],
And repent in dust and ashes.

**62
Job's
per-
sonal
realiza-
tion of
God's
real
char-
acter
(42¹, ², ³, ⁵, ⁶)**

I. The Structure of the Book of Job. Like most of the books of the Old Testament, Job is, without reasonable doubt, the work of several different writers. The prose introduction (1–2), with its corresponding conclusion (42⁷⁻¹⁷), was probably once an independent story. The words of Jehovah in the epilogue (42⁷) clearly implies that, as in 1 and 2, Job had endured the test and had meekly submitted to the afflictions which Satan, with the divine approval, had sent upon him, and that on the other hand his friends, like his wife, had urged him to curse God and die. The language and phrases of this prose story are radically different from those in the poem which constitutes the main body of the book. The unique explanation of why Job was afflicted that is given in the opening chapters is also completely ignored in the poetic dialogues (3–31). Likewise the problem of whether or not Job fears God for naught, raised in the prologue, is not taken up again except in the concluding prose epilogue. In the prose story Job's piety conforms to the popular standards, while in the poetic sections he is measured by the loftier ethical principles laid down by the pre-exilic prophets (*cf.* chap. 31). In form, therefore, in aim, and in content, the prose story differs fundamentally from the great dramatic poem which constitutes the real book of Job. The main body of the book is found in chapters 3–27, 29–31, 38¹–40¹⁴, and 42¹⁻⁶. At a few points the original order has apparently been disarranged and later hands have frequently supplemented the older sections, but the literary unity of the whole is obvious. In three cycles of speeches the problem of innocent suffering is fully developed and the current solutions presented. In conclusion the voice of Jehovah comes to Job calling him forth from himself to the contemplation of the larger universe which manifests the divine wisdom and rulership.

The Elihu speeches in 32–37 are evidently from a still later author or authors who wished to rebuke Job's seeming impiety and the failure of his friends to bring forth a satisfactory explanation of the suffering of the innocent. Its independence is shown by the presence of many Aramaic words, by the lack of literary vigor, and by the frequent repetitions, which distinguish it sharply from the writings of the author of the main body of the book. Elihu and his contributions are also completely ignored in the rest of the book and at points where, if they were original, certain references would be almost inevitable. These speeches, in fact, are simply a fuller development of the argument of Eliphaz found in the fifth chapter. They also incorporate many suggestions drawn from the speeches of Jehovah in chapters 38 and 39.

II. Dates of the Different Parts. The classic Hebrew style and the absence of Aramaic words indicate that the prose story is the oldest section of the book. It also reasserts in modified form the dogma current far down into the Persian period, that if the righteous but patiently bear affliction they will surely in the end be richly rewarded. It contains a message well adapted to the needs and beliefs of the Jewish people during the calamities of the Babylonian period. Its conception of Satan as the prosecuting attorney of heaven, and of Jehovah as a transcendental ruler surrounded by a hierarchy of angels, is closely akin to that which first appears in the second chapter of Zechariah. The references to Job in Ezekiel $14^{14, 20}$, as one of the three heroes of popular tradition famous for their piety, implies the existence during the exile of a story closely akin to if not identical with the one found in the prologue and epilogue of the book of Job. Such a story was probably current long before the days of Ezekiel, but in its present form it was not committed to writing until the latter part of the Babylonian or the beginning of the Persian period.

The first part of this story was evidently used by the author as an introduction to the great dramatic poem. He thereby deliberately protested against the solution of the problem of innocent suffering suggested by the ancient story. The poem itself cannot be dated earlier than the middle of the Persian period. In it the great ethical and social standards of the pre-exilic prophets are fully accepted. Its marvellous breadth of vision also implies an advanced stage in Israel's thinking. The problem of suffering with which it deals is not merely that of the nation but of the individual or of a class within the Judean community. It is precisely the problem that confronted the author of Malachi and to which he refers in 3^{13-16}. It is the same problem that bulks largely in the psalms of this period and finds its noblest solution in Isaiah 53. All its affinities, therefore, confirm the conclusion that it comes from the

90

middle of the fifth century B.C. and is probably slightly older than Isaiah 49–55, which presents a more fundamental treatment of the problem of human suffering. The author still holds the old, prophetic conception of the universe (38[4, 6]), and is unaffected by the priestly thought and tendencies which became especially prominent during the closing years of the Persian period.

The Elihu speeches and the supplemental poem in description of wisdom in 28, and of the behemoth and leviathan in 40[15]–41[34], probably come from the Greek period.

III. **The Prose Story.** In the prose story Job is pictured as a man of superlative piety and prosperity. According to the popular standards of the earlier day he lived a blameless life. His afflictions came simply as a means of demonstrating the unselfish character of his piety. In rapid succession he is stripped of all his possessions and afflicted by the vilest of all diseases, apparently the loathsome tubercular leprosy. Even his wife tempts him to curse God and die, but he fully meets the test, and, according to the testimony of the concluding epilogue, receives Jehovah's approval and is restored to the joys of family, reputation, and riches. It is obvious that, as in the stories found in the opening chapters of Genesis, this is a popular narrative freely adjusted to the ends which the story-teller wished to attain. The incidents recorded are not in keeping with the ordinary experiences of life, but belong rather to the realm of popular fancy. As a reference in Ezekiel implies, it was probably, like the similar stories regarding Noah and Daniel, a heritage from the common Semitic lore. In fact, a recently discovered Babylonian tablet tells of a famous king of Nippur, Ṭâbi-utul-Bêl by name, whose experiences and spirit corresponds closely to those of the hero of this prose story.

The message of the prose story of Job, as it was sent out to the Jewish race, was that it was not always possible to understand the reason why the righteous were afflicted, but that if they faithfully met the test restoration to Jehovah's approval, with the honor and reputation that necessarily follow, were assured. To the nation such a message was not without its practical application and value, but it failed completely to meet the individual problems that became pathetically insistent during the middle of the fifth century B.C.

IV. **The Poem of Job.** In the later poetic version of the story (which begins with the third chapter) Job himself is the embodiment of the problem of innocent suffering. His friends' suppositions and condemnations add still another burden to his weight of woe. More intolerable, however, than less of possessions, health, and reputation is his sense of being forsaken and condemned by Jehovah. Job cannot shake himself entirely free from the belief, which had been inculcated in his mind from earliest infancy, that calamity was a sign of divine displeasure, and therefore of sin on the part of the victim. In the series of monologues and dialogues between Job and his friends he voices every phase of the great problem and makes it concrete and objective. With marvellous psychological truth and insight the author has presented the different phases of feeling through which an innocent sufferer in Job's position naturally passes. At times Job is intemperate in his speech and at other times he yields to despondency; again his faith overleaps all obstacles and he holds for the moment a clear belief in the ultimate vindication not only of himself but of Jehovah's justice.

His friends, on the other hand, formulate at length the current explanation of suffering. Job in his sharp retorts makes clear the inapplicability of the arguments and the limitations of the dogmas which they constantly reassert. In the concluding speeches of Jehovah the author with masterly skill takes Job out of his little circle into the larger world of nature, and brings him face to face with the evidences of Jehovah's might, wisdom, and gracious rulership of the great universe and of the complex life of those who inhabit it. Above all, Job learns to know God, not through the testimony of others, but by direct personal experience, and this knowledge begets humility and trust.

V. Progress in Job's Thought. The thought of the book of Job is characteristically Oriental. Instead of moving straight on from premises to conclusion it constantly reverts to the same themes yet advances along independent, parallel lines. Its progress is not objective, as is usually the case in a drama, but almost entirely subjective. These parallel lines of progress are: (1) the conviction gradually crystallizing into certainty that the current explanations of suffering are in certain cases inadequate and false. While viewed from one point of view this conclusion is merely negative, it nevertheless opened the eyes of Job and his generation to a larger conception of Jehovah and a far broader interpretation of the universe and of the laws which regulate it. The second is that he is guilty of no crime commensurate with the calamity which had overtaken him. Overwhelmed by misfortune and the reiterated charges of his friends, only through a superhuman struggle did Job ultimately attain the unshaken conviction that he was indeed innocent in the sight of God and man. The third line of progress is that, if not in the present life, in that beyond the grave his reputation would not only be vindicated but he himself would be fully conscious of that vindication.

As is illustrated by the third chapter, Job in common with his race still shared the belief that for the ordinary individual life beyond the grave was a shadowy existence, far removed from Jehovah's presence. This conception of the life after death was inherited by the Israelites from their Semitic ancestors, and was held in common by most ancient peoples, both of the East and of the West. The Babylonians believed, however, that certain favored mortals, as, for example, the hero of the flood, were transported to the abode of the gods, there to enjoy blessed individual immortality. The same belief is the foundation of the Hebrew stories regarding Enoch and Elijah. This belief was apparently the germ which in time developed, as in the twelfth chapter of Daniel, into the widespread conviction that the grave would not hold those who had been loyal to Jehovah, but that he would surely raise them again to a glorious life. In the book of Job it is possible to trace the birth-pangs of this broader hope. Conscious of his innocence and confronted by the grave, Job repeatedly voices the deep conviction that God, because he is just, will raise his afflicted servant from the grave and accord to him that justice which seems excluded from his present life. This solution of the problem of innocent suffering is not given the central place by the author of the book of Job. It is safe, however, to conjecture that if the appearance of Jehovah had not furnished to the author's mind a more satisfactory conclusion, the vindication after death would have been the solution offered. At several points Job approaches very close to the belief in individual immortality which became a commonly accepted tenet in the trying days of the Maccabean struggle.

The fourth line of progress is that Jehovah, after all, must be just and that he will right the seeming wrongs of life. In his opening speeches Job gives free vent to the anguish and impatience that fills his tortured mind. With a boldness strangely foreign to Hebrew thought, he charges Jehovah with injustice and speaks of him as a cruel monster that watches man, his helpless prey, and takes cruel pleasure in the pain which he inflicts. As the discussion progresses Job's mind becomes calmer, and the conviction that God, after all, is just comes more clearly to expression. His strong utterances gradually yield to this quieter mood. Even before he hears the voice of Jehovah, Job has attained an attitude of trust, though he is still groping in darkness. Thus with marvellous fidelity to human nature and experience the author of the book of Job would have made a great contribution to the problem with

93

which he was dealing even had he not added the concluding speeches of Jehovah.

VI. Significance of the Speeches of Jehovah. To many Western readers the concluding speeches of Jehovah are unsatisfying. They lack the emphasis on Jehovah's love and that divine tenderness in addressing the heroic sufferer which to us would seem to have been a satisfactory conclusion to the great drama. This element is furnished in characteristically concrete form by the epilogue of the book, in which Job's prosperity is restored in double measure and he is personally assured of Jehovah's favor. The severe and realistic author of the great poem, however, knew that in ordinary life such solutions are rare. In the speeches of Jehovah he does not introduce an altogether new element, but emphasizes motifs already developed in the earlier dialogues. The effect of these speeches upon Job are threefold: (1) They rebuke his over-accentuated individualism. (2) They reveal the fundamental contrast between the infinite God and finite man. In the light of this revelation Job plainly recognizes his presumption and folly in attempting, with his limited outlook, to comprehend, much less to criticise, the mighty ruler of all the universe. (3) After Job had thus been led out of himself into personal companionship with God he was content to trust his all-wise guide, even though he recognized his own inability to fathom the mysteries of the universe or to solve the problem of innocent suffering.

Thus the great contributions of the book of Job to the problem of suffering are: (1) A clear and scientific presentation of the problem; (2) a bold sweeping aside of the insufficient current theological explanations; (3) a vastly enlarged conception of Jehovah's character and rule; and (4) that attitude of faith which comes from a personal experience of God and which trusts unreservedly, even though it cannot see or divine the reason why, and in that trust finds peace and joy.

Although the thought of the book of Job is profound, and it deals in a masterly manner with a fundamental human problem, it is more than a mere philosophical discussion. Its primary aim is to set forth the vital truth that God is not to be found through current theological dogmas or intellectual discussions, but through personal experience. This is the dominant note throughout the book. The greatest calamity that overtakes Job in his hour of deepest distress is the sense of being shut away from God's presence.

> Oh! that I knew where I might find him,
> That I might come even to his throne!

As he looks back fondly to the happy days of old the fact that **stands** forth above all others is that

> The Almighty was yet with me.

Looking forward to a possible vindication after death his hope **centres** in the belief that

> Thou wouldst call and I myself would answer thee;
> Thou wouldst long for the work of thy hands.

When at last Jehovah answered Job out of the storm, it was not so much the thought expressed as the fact that God had spoken directly to **him** that brought penitence and peace:

> I have heard of thee by the hearing of the ear,
> But now mine eye seeth thee.
> Therefore I loath my words,
> And repent in dust and ashes.

---

§ XCIX. THE TRAINING AND MISSION OF THE TRUE SERVANT OF JEHOVAH

Hearken to me, ye coastlands,
And listen, ye distant peoples:
Jehovah hath called me from the womb,
From my mother's lap made mention of my name.
He hath made my mouth like a sharp sword,
In the shadow of his hand he hid me,
He made me a polished arrow,
In his quiver he concealed me,
And he said to me, Thou art my servant,
Israel, in whom I will glorify myself.

1. Call and preparation of Jehovah's true servant (Isa. 49¹⁻³)

But I said, I have labored in vain,
I spent my strength for nothing and vanity,
Nevertheless my right is with Jehovah,
And my recompense with my God.

2. His confidence in Jehovah (⁴)

And now, thus saith Jehovah,
(He who formed from birth to be his servant,
To bring Jacob back to him,

3. His worldwide mission (⁵, ⁶)

And that Israel might be gathered to him;
For I was honored in the sight of Jehovah,
And my God became my strength):
It is too little a thing to be my servant,
To raise up the tribes of Jacob,
And to restore the survivors of Israel;
Therefore I will make thee the light of the nations,
That thy salvation may reach to the ends of the earth.

4.
Future
recog-
nition
of his
work
(7)

Thus saith Jehovah,
The Redeemer of Israel, his Holy One,
To him who is heartily despised,
To the one abhorred of the people, a servant of rulers:
Kings shall see and arise,
Princes and they shall do homage,
Because of Jehovah who is faithful,
The Holy One of Israel who hath chosen thy.

5. His
work of
restora-
tion
(8-9b)

Thus saith Jehovah,
In a time of favor I answer thee,
And in a day of deliverance I help thee,
And I make thee a pledge to the people,
To raise up the [ruined] land,
To reapportion the desolate heritages,
Saying to those who are bound, 'Go forth '
To those in darkness, 'Show yourselves!'

6. Re-
turn
of the
exiles
(9c-11)

They shall pasture along all ways,
Even on all the bare hills shall they graze.
They shall not be hungry nor thirsty,
Neither shall the glowing heat nor the sun smite them,
For he who hath pity on them shall lead them,
And to gushing fountains will he guide them.
And I will make all mountains a road,
And highways shall be built up.

7. Joy
over
the
restora-
tion
(12, 13)

Behold, these come from afar,
And these from the north and west,
And these from the land of the Syenites!
Shout with joy, O heavens, and exult, O earth!

Let the mountains break forth into shouts of joy!
For Jehovah hath had pity on his people,
And will show mercy to his afflicted ones.

The Lord Jehovah hath given me the tongue of a trained
    disciple?
To give to the fainting a word of help, he waketh me early,
Early he waketh me, that I may listen as a disciple.
The Lord Jehovah hath opened mine ear,
And I have not been wilful nor turned back rebelliously.

8. Training and attitude of the servant (50⁴, ⁵)

My back I gave to smiters and my cheek to those who
    plucked the beard,
My face I hid not from insult and spitting,
For my Lord Jehovah is my helper; so that I am not con-
    founded.
Therefore I have set my face like flint, and I know that I
    shall not be put to shame.

9. Faith and determination amidst persecution (⁶, ⁷)

He is near who justifieth me, who will contend with me?
    let us stand up together!
Who is the adversary to oppose my cause? let him draw
    near to me!
Behold the Lord Jehovah is my helper; who is he that can
    harm me?
Lo, they shall all fall to pieces like a garment, the moth shall
    consume them.

10. Assurance of ultimate vindication (⁸, ⁹)

Who among you feareth Jehovah, let him hearken to the
    voice of his servant?
Who walked in darkness, having no light,
Let him trust in the name of Jehovah and rely on his God?

11. Lesson of encouragement (¹⁰)

Behold, my servant shall prosper,
He shall be raised up and highly exalted.
Even as many were appalled at him,
So shall many nations tremble,
Kings will close their mouths before him,
When what has not been told them they see,
And what they have not heard they perceive.

12. Testimony of Jehovah to the work of his servant (52 ¹³-¹⁵)

13. Of his contemporaries: He seemed unpromising (53¹⁻²ᵇ)

Who believed what has been reported to us,
And to whom was Jehovah's might revealed?
For he grew up before us as a young shoot,
And as a root out of dry ground.

14. Unattractive (²ᵉ⁻ᶠ)

He had no form that we should regard him,
Nor appearance that we should delight in him.
His appearance was more disfigured than any man's,
And his form than any human being's.

15. Afflicted with diseases (³)

He was despised and forsaken of men,
A man of suffering and acquainted with sickness;
Like one for whom men hide their face,
He was despised so that we esteemed him not.

16. ...eemed ...ly st...cken ...ith a di...ne judgment

Surely our sickness he himself bore,
And our sufferings—he carried them,
Yet we ourselves esteemed him stricken,
Smitten of God and afflicted.

17. But it was all for our wellbeing (⁵)

But he was wounded for our transgressions,
Crushed because of our iniquities;
The chastisement for our wellbeing was upon him,
And through his stripes healing came to us.

18. Upon him rested our guilt (⁶)

All of us, like sheep, had gone astray,
We had turned each to his own way;
While Jehovah made to light upon him
The guilt of us all.

19. Prophet's testimony: He was submissive (⁷)

Yet when afflicted he opened not his mouth;
Like a lamb led to the slaughter,
And like a sheep dumb before her shearers,
So he opened not his mouth.

20. Unappreciated (⁸)

By an oppressive judgment was he taken away,
Yet who of his generation considered
That he had been cut off from the land of the living;
For our transgressions had been stricken to death?

And his grave was made with the wicked,
And among evil-doers his burial mound,
Although he had done no violence,
Neither was deceit in his mouth.

21. Victim of injustice (⁹)

Yet Jehovah was pleased to crush him;
Through giving himself as an offering for guilt,
He shall see posterity and length of days,
And the pleasure of Jehovah will be realized in his hands;
Out of his own suffering he shall see light,
He shall be satisfied with his knowledge.

22. Yet realizing Jehovah's purpose (10-11b)

My righteous servant shall make many righteous,
And himself will bear the burden of their iniquities.
Therefore I will give him a portion among the great,
And with the strong shall he divide spoil,
Because he poured out his life-blood,
And was numbered with transgressors,
And himself bore the sins of many,
And interposed for transgressors.

23. Jehovah's concluding testimony (11c-12)

I. The Different Portraits of Jehovah's Servant. Isaiah 49–54 contains three distinct portraits of the ideal servant of Jehovah. Each in turn develops characteristics suggested in the preceding. These descriptions are interspersed with exhortations addressed to Jehovah's servant Israel and assurances that God will fully restore Jerusalem and bring back her scattered children. These three portraits of the type of servant that Jehovah required to realize his purpose in human history, together with the earlier portrait in 42¹⁻⁷, supplement each other. In the first of these four (42¹⁻⁷) the prophetic qualities of the servant are especially emphasized. Like the earlier prophets, he will not fail nor be discouraged until he has established justice in the earth. His task is to open blind eyes and to deliver prisoners from the darkness of ignorance and sin in which they were sitting. In the second picture (49¹⁻⁹ᵃ) the world-wide mission of the servant is emphasized. He is called not only to gather the outcasts of Israel, but also as an apostle to bring light to all the nations of the earth. In this passage for the first time appears that note of suffering and ignominy which is the lot of the true servant of Jehovah. In the third portrait (50⁴⁻¹⁰) the servant is pictured as a disciple, attentively listening to the divine teachings, learning the les-

sons which will fit him in turn to become a teacher of men. The last and fullest picture (52^{13}–53^{12}) describes at length his suffering. A strong contrast is drawn between his present shame and ignominy and the future glory and victory which he will achieve through his voluntary and complete self-sacrifice. These pictures embody the prophet's ideal, and they can be fully understood only in the light of their historical background.

II. **The Prophet's Purpose.** In his earlier poems this great unknown prophet dealt largely with the interpretation of Israel's past history and the proclamation of the coming deliverance (40–48). His chief aims in chapters 49–55 may be briefly epitomized as follows: (1) to interpret the inner meaning of the period of adversity through which the Jewish race was then passing; (2) to make absolutely clear the character and quality of the service that Jehovah required of his chosen people, if they were to realize his purpose in human history; (3) to inspire them all to make the needed sacrifices and thus to prove themselves true servants of Jehovah; (4) especially to make plain to the innocent and faithful sufferers in the Judean community the real meaning and value of their present shame and suffering, if bravely and voluntarily borne.

III. **Character and Condition of Those to Whom the Prophet Appealed.** From the allusions in the prophecies themselves it is possible to determine the classes that the prophet had in mind. In 49^1 his address is to the coast lands and the distant peoples who lived at the extremities of Israel's horizon. It is not probable, however, that he anticipated that his message in its present form would go out as it has to all races and nations; rather his attention was fixed on the scattered members of his own race, those who lived in the north and the west and in the distant city of Syene, far up the Nile (49^{12}). In 49^3 he clearly identifies the nation Israel as Jehovah's servant, whom he makes declare:

> Jehovah said to me, Thou art my servant,
> Israel, in whom I will glorify myself.

It is evident, however, that the prophet has especially in mind the Judean community amidst which he lived and for which he worked. In 54, as elsewhere, he calls upon this group of discouraged Jews to enlarge their tent, for their period of punishment is over and their foundation and walls are about to be rebuilt. At last they shall cease to tremble at the fury of the oppressor. In 51^{13-20} he addresses Jerusalem

directly and gives a vivid picture of its condition before the appearance
of Nehemiah:

> Rouse thee! Rouse thee! stand up, O Jerusalem,
> Who hast drunk at Jehovah's hand the cup of his wrath!
> The bowl of reeling thou hast drunken, hast drained!
> There is none to guide thee of all the sons whom thou hast
> borne,
> And none to take thee by the hand of all the sons whom thou hast
> reared.
> These two things have befallen thee—who can condole with thee?
> Desolation and destruction, famine and the sword—who can com-
> fort thee?

IV. **The Task and Training of Jehovah's Servant.** The term
servant means literally slave, not in the Western sense, but in that of
the ancient East, where a slave was often a privileged member of society.
In many a Hebrew household the slaves, next to the children, enjoyed
the protection and consideration of the master of the household. He
was under obligation to guard their welfare and interests. On the other
hand, slaves, like Eleazar in the story of Abraham (Gen. 26) faithfully
cared for the interests of their master and spared no effort to carry out
his commands. Semitic usage had also given the term slave a significant
meaning. The faithful officials of all Oriental kings called themselves
his servants or slaves. It was the common term expressing, on the one
hand, confidence and protection, and on the other, devotion, loyalty, and
service. Most of Israel's patriarchs, kings, and prophets are spoken
of as the servants or slaves of Jehovah. Haggai, in his address to
Zerubbabel, called him Jehovah's servant. In Deuteronomy 32[36, 43] the
people of Israel are called the servants of Jehovah, and, as has been
noted, in the prophecies of the II Isaiah they are frequently referred to
as the servant of Jehovah. The term, therefore, was well chosen to express that complete devotion and loyalty to Jehovah which the prophet
aimed to evoke from his fellow-countrymen. It was also free from the
kingly associations and material interpretation that were connected with
the word Messiah.

The prophet's aim was to present so vividly the task and methods of
the true servant of Jehovah that all would recognize a personal call to
duty. He emphasizes three distinct yet related elements in the mission
of the servant. They were: (1) To free the prisoners from their cap-

tivity, whether imprisoned by walls of stone or brick or under the tyranny of fears and false ideas. (2) To restore the scattered tribes of Israel and thus to lay the foundations for a renewed national life that would furnish concrete evidence to all the world of Jehovah's power to deliver. (3) To go beyond the narrow bounds of their race and to bring to the nations that were groping in the darkness of heathenism the knowledge and truth that had been imparted to Israel. Thus the unknown prophet laid the foundations for that Kingdom of God, that dominion of God in nature and in the minds of men that was the guide and inspiration of all later prophets and the goal for whose realization the Great Teacher and Prophet of Nazareth labored and died.

The prophet places great emphasis upon the training of Jehovah's servant. He declares that from birth Jehovah formed him to be his servant. In 50^{4-7} he is spoken of as a trained disciple attentively listening to the words of his divine teacher, never rebelling at the bitterness of the needful discipline, but ever seeking to prepare himself to give to the fainting a word of help. The steadfastness with which he endures shame and bitter wrongs is the evidence of his ability as a disciple and an essential part in his preparation for his exalted mission.

V. Methods of Jehovah's Servant. In accomplishing his task the servant is to use definite instruction, but his teaching is to be illustrated by his own character and attitude. By the voluntary, uncomplaining endurance of ignominy and suffering he is to do Jehovah's work and win the grateful recognition, not only of his divine Master, but of all succeeding generations. Through a keen analysis of life the prophet had attained to a clear appreciation of the inestimable value of voluntary self-sacrifice. He saw that it was the most effective means of uplifting the race and leading mankind to accept God's mastery over their minds and lives. The truth here presented is illustrated in human experience as clearly to-day as in the past. The self-denying service of parents is absolutely essential if their children are to attain to the noblest manhood and womanhood. Only through the self-sacrificing labors of those who love their fellow-men can social evils be removed and society attain its highest development. The low standards in the business and professional world can be raised only as certain men, with the spirit and courage of the ancient prophets, make their own personal interests and popularity subservient to the rigorous demands of justice. It is the law of life that he who would elevate the standards of his associates and thus lead men to the fullest realization of the divine ideals must ordinarily do it in the face of opposition, ignominy, and seeming failure. It is this quiet, heroic self-sacrifice—the heroism of the commonplace—that the great prophet proclaims is the absolutely essential characteristic of Jehovah's servant. Despised by his contemporaries, the victim of persecution and calamity, he must do his task, leaving the reward and the appreciation to Jehovah and to the enlightened sense of later generations.

VI. **Realization of the Ideal of Service.** The portrait is so concrete that the question naturally arises, Who was the servant of whom the prophet was speaking? Undoubtedly the tragic experiences of such prophets as Jeremiah suggested many elements in the picture. For half a century that faithful servant of Jehovah suffered, often shrinkingly, yet voluntarily, a constant martyrdom. Upon him fell the persecutions of his countrymen. Yet in the life of later Judaism those principles for which he lived and died gained acceptance and application. Of him it may be truly said:

> He was numbered with trangressors,
> And himself bore the sins of many,
> And interposed for transgressors.

The unknown author of these immortal poems spoke out of the depth of his own painful experience and doubtless in a large degree realized the ideals of service which he thus effectively set forth. Those of his contemporaries who, amidst persecution and insults, in their lives embodied the ideals of the earlier prophets were crushed like Jeremiah because of the iniquities of others; but by thus pouring out their lifeblood they brought healing to their race. Nehemiah, in responding to the call of service and in turning his back upon the allurements of the Persian court in order to rebuild the city of his fathers, proved himself a faithful servant of Jehovah. With true insight the Christian Church has always recognized that in the character and life of Jesus is found the only complete realization of this ancient ideal of service. With the immortal chapters of the II Isaiah he was clearly familiar, and from them he doubtless received many suggestions regarding his divine mission and the methods by which it was to be accomplished. Their author was clearly speaking to his contemporaries; but in portraying the way in which Jehovah's purpose in human history could alone be realized he presented an ideal which has a permanent significance in the thought of the human race. Paul rightly recognized that the same responsibility to make this ideal a reality rested upon him, and all who would serve God, when he quoted the words of 49⁸ (*cf.* Acts 13⁴⁷):

"I have set thee for a light of the Gentiles
That thou shouldst be for salvation to the uttermost parts of the earth."

§ C. NEHEMIAH'S WORK IN REBUILDING THE WALLS OF JERUSALEM

1. Report of the deputation from Jerusalem (Neh. 1¹⁻³)

Now in the month of Chislev [November-December, 446 B.C.], I was in Shushan the royal palace, when Hanani, one of my kinsmen came, together with certain men from Judah, and I asked them concerning the Jews who had escaped, who were left from the captivity, and concerning Jerusalem. And they said to me, The survivors who are left from the captivity there in the provinces are in great misfortune and reproach, and the wall of Jerusalem is broken down and its gates have been destroyed by fire.

2. Nehemiah's prayer for his race and for God's help (4-11b)

Now when I heard these statements I sat down and wept and mourned certain days; and I fasted and made supplication before the God of heaven, and I said, 'I beseech thee, O Jehovah, the God of heaven, the great and terrible God, who keepeth the covenant and showeth kindness to them who love and keep his commands; let thine ears now be attentive and thine eyes open, to hear the supplication of thy servant, which I am now making before thee, day and night, for the Israelites thy servants, while I confess the sins of the Israelites, which we have sinned against thee, as I also and my father's house have sinned. We have dealt very wickedly against thee, and have not kept the commandments, nor the statutes, nor the ordinances, which thou didst command thy servant Moses. Remember, I beseech thee, the word which thou didst command thy servant Moses, saying, "If ye trespass I will scatter you abroad among the peoples; but if ye return to me, and keep my commands and do them, then, though your outcasts were at the ends of the earth, yet will I gather them thence and will bring them to the place that I have chosen, there to cause my name to dwell." Now these are thy servants and thy people, whom thou hast redeemed by thy great power and by thy strong hand. O Lord, I beseech thee, let thine ear be attentive to the supplication of thy servant, and to the supplications of thy servants, who delight to fear thy name; and give success to thy servant this day, and grant him mercy in the sight of this man.

Now I was cupbearer to the king. And it came to pass in the month of Nisan, in the twentieth year of Artaxerxes the king, when I had charge of the wine, that I took up the wine and gave it to the king, and I had not beforetime been sad. And the king said to me, 'Why is your countenance sad, since you are not sick? This is nothing else but sorrow of heart.' Then I was greatly afraid, and I said to the king, 'Let the king live forever: why should not my countenance be sad, when the city, the place of my fathers' sepulchres, lies in ruins, and its gates have been destroyed by fire?' And then the king said to me, 'For what do you make request?' So I prayed to the God of heaven. And I said to the king, 'If it please the king, and if your servant has found favor in your sight, that you would send me to Judah, to the city of my fathers' sepulchres, that I may rebuild it.' And the king said to me (and the queen was also sitting by him), 'For how long will your journey be? And when will you return?' Then it pleased the king to send me; for I set him a time. Moreover I said to the king, 'If it please the king, let official letters be given me to the governors of the province beyond the River, that they may let me pass through until I come to Judah, and a letter to Asaph the keeper of the king's park, that he may give me the timber to make beams for the gates of the castle, which belongs to the temple, and for the wall of the city, and for the house that I shall enter. And the king granted me this, according to the hand of my God which kindly cared for me.

3. His request and the king's response (1¹¹e-2⁸)

Then I came to the governors of the province beyond the River, and gave them the king's official letters. Now the king had sent with me military officers and horsemen. And when Sanballat, the Horonite, and Tobiah, the Ammonite slave, heard of it, it troubled them exceedingly, that one had come to seek the welfare of the Israelites. So I came to Jerusalem and was there three days. And I arose in the night, together with a few of my followers, and I told

4. His arrival in Jerusalem and inspection of conditions (9-16)

no man what my God had put into my heart to do for Jerusalem, neither was there any beast with me, except the
beast upon which I rode. And I went out by night through
the Valley Gate, toward the Dragon's Well and to the
Dung Gate, and investigated carefully the walls of Jerusalem, which were broken down, and where its gates had been
destroyed by fire. Then I went on to the Fountain Gate
and to the King's Pool, but there was no place for the beast
that was under me to pass. Then I went up in the night
by the Brook Kidron and investigated carefully the wall;
then I turned back and entered by the Valley Gate, and so
returned. And the rulers did not know where I went or
what I did, neither had I as yet told it to the Jews nor to the
priests nor to the nobles nor to the rulers nor to the rest
who did the work.

5. Response of the people to his call and the jeers of their foes (17-20)

Then I said to them, 'You see the bad condition in which
we are, how Jerusalem lies in ruins and its gates are destroyed by fire. Come and let us rebuild the wall of Jerusalem, that we be no more an object of reproach.' And I
told them of the hand of my God, which had kindly cared
for me, as also of the king's words that he had spoken to
me. And they said, 'Let us rise up and build.' So they
strengthened their hands for the good work. But when
Sanballat, the Horonite, and Tobiah, the Ammonite slave,
and Geshem the Arabian heard it, they jeered at us and
despised us, and said, 'What is this thing that you are
doing? Will you rebel against the king?' Then I answered
and said to them, 'The God of heaven, he will give us
success, for we his servants will proceed to build; but you
shall have no portion nor right nor memorial in Jerusalem.'

6. Builders of the northern wall and gate (3¹, ²)

Then Eliashib the high priest rose up with his kinsmen
the priests and built the Sheep Gate; they laid its beams
and set up the doors, even to the Tower of the Hundred,
and to the Tower of Hananel. And next to him the men
of Jericho built. And next to them Zaccur the son of
Imri built.

7. Northwestern wall and gate (3-5)

And the Fish Gate the sons of Hassenaah built; they
laid its beams, and set up its doors, its bolts, and its bars.
And next to them Meremoth and Meshullam and Zadok
and the Tekoites repaired the wall; but their nobles did not
bend their necks in the service of their lord.

106

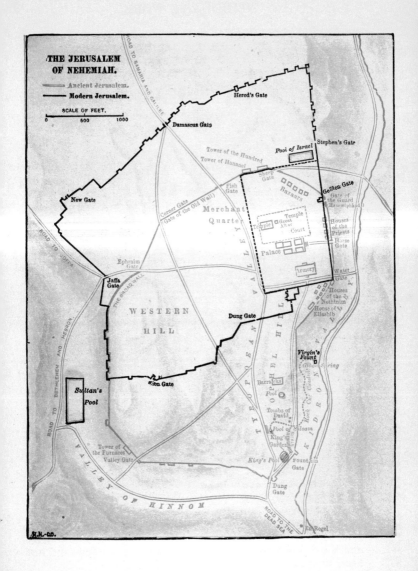

THE JERUSALEM
OF NEHEMIAH.

Ancient Jerusalem.
Modern Jerusalem.

SCALE OF FEET.
0   500   1000

ROAD TO SAMARIA AND GALILEE

Herod's Gate

Damascus Gate

Tower of the Hundred

Pool of Israel

Stephen's Gate

Tower of Hananel

Sheep Gate

Golden Gate

Fish Gate

Bazaars

Gate of the Guard (Hammiphkad)

New Gate

Corner Gate
Gate of the Old Wall

Merchant Quarter

Temple   Great Altar   Temple
Court

Houses of the Priests

ROAD TO JOPPA

Ephraim Gate

Palace

Horse Gate

Jaffa Gate

THE BROAD WALL

Water Gate

Armory

Houses of the Nethinim

House of Eliashib

ROAD TO BETHLEHEM AND HEBRON

WESTERN HILL

Dung Gate

Virgin's Fount

TYROPEAN VALLEY

Gihon Spring

Rock Cut Conduit

KIDRON VALLEY

Zion Gate

Sultan's Pool

Barra...
Pool

OPHEL HILL

Tombs of David

Pool of Siloam

King's Garden

Tower of the Furnaces

Valley Gate

King's Pool

Fountain Gate

VALLEY   OF   HINNOM

Dung Gate

ROAD TO THE DEAD SEA

En Rogel

H.H.-CO.

And the Old Gate Joida repaired; they laid its beams, and set up its doors, its bolts, and its bars. And next to them Melatiah the Gibeonite and Jadon the Meronothite, the men of Gibeon and of Mizpah, which belongs to the jurisdiction of the governor of the province beyond the River, repaired. Next to him Uzziel, one of the goldsmiths, repaired. And next to him Hananiah, one of those who prepare sweet ointments, repaired. And they fortified Jerusalem even to the broad wall. And next to them Rephaiah, the ruler of half the district of Jerusalem, repaired. And next to them Jedaiah repaired opposite his house. And next to him Hattush and Malchijah and Hasshub repaired another section, even to the Tower of the Furnaces. And next to him Shallum, the ruler of half the district of Jerusalem, together with its dependencies, repaired. _{8.Western wall (6-12)}

The Valley Gate Hanun and the inhabitants of Zanoah repaired; they built it, and set up its doors, its bolts, and its bars, and also built a thousand cubits of the wall to the Dung Gate. And the Dung Gate Malchijah, the ruler of the district of Beth-haccherem, together with his sons, repaired. _{9. Southern wall and gates (13, 14)}

And the Fountain Gate Shallun, the ruler of the district of Mizpah, repaired; and he built it, and covered it, and set up its doors, its bolts, and its bars, and he also built the wall of the Pool of Siloam by the King's Garden, even to the stairs that go down from the city of David. After him Nehemiah, the ruler of half the district of Bethzur, repaired to the place opposite the Sepulchres of David, even to the pool that was made and to the House of the Warriors. After him Rehum the son of Bani repaired. Next to him Hashabiah, the ruler of half the district of Keilah, repaired for his district. After him their kinsmen Bennui, the ruler of half the district of Keilah, repaired. And next to him Ezer, the ruler of Mizpah, repaired another section opposite the ascent to the armory at the bend in the wall. After him Baruch repaired from the bend in the wall to the door of the house of Eliashib the high priest. After him Meremoth repaired another section, from the entrance to the house of Eliashib even to the end of the house of Eliashib. And after him the priests, the men of the Plain of the _{10. Southeastern wall and gates (15-27)}

Jordan, repaired. After them Benjamin and Hasshub repaired opposite their house. After them Azariah repaired beside his own house. After him Binnui repaired another section, from the house of Azariah to the bend in the wall and to the corner. After him Palal repaired opposite the bend and the upper tower that stands out from the royal palace of the king, which is toward the court of the guard. After him Pedaiah repaired, to the place opposite the Water Gate toward the east and the tower that stands out. After him the Tekoites repaired another section, opposite the great tower that stands out and to the wall of Ophel. And the temple servants dwelt in Ophel.

11. Eastern and northeastern wall and gates (28-32)

Above the Horse Gate the priests repaired, each one opposite his own house. After them Zadok the son of Immer repaired opposite his own house. After him Shemaiah the son of Shechaniah, the keeper of the East Gate, repaired. After him Hananiah the son of Shelemiah and Hanum the sixth son of Zalaph repaired another section. After him Meshullam the son of Berschiah repaired opposite his chamber. After him Malchijah, one of the goldsmiths, repaired as far as the house of the temple servants and of the merchants, opposite the Gate of the Watch Tower and to the ascent of the corner. And between the ascent of the corner and the Sheep Gate the goldsmiths and the merchants repaired.

12. Taunts of the heathen foes of the Jewish community (4¹-⁵)

Now when Sanballat heard that we were rebuilding the wall, his anger was aroused and he was very indignant, and mocked the Jews. And he spoke before his kinsmen and the army of Samaria and said, 'What are these feeble Jews doing? Will they leave it to God? Will they sacrifice? Will they complete it in a day? Will they revive the stones out of the heaps of rubbish, although they are burned? Now Tobiah the Ammonite was with him, and he said, 'Even that which they are building, if a fox should go up on it, he would break down their stone wall!' Hear, O our God—for we are despised—and turn back their reproach upon their own head and give them up as an object of spoil in a land of captivity, and cover not their iniquity and let not their sin be blotted out from thy sight, for they have provoked thee to anger before the builders.

103

So we built the wall; and all the wall was joined together to half its height, for the people were eager to work. But when Sanballat and Tobiah and the Arabians and the Ammonites and the Ashdodites, heard that the restoration of the walls of Jerusalem was progressing, so that the breaches began to be stopped, they were very angry. And they all conspired together to come and fight against Jerusalem and to produce a panic therein. 13.
Their plots to stop the work (6-8)

But we made supplication to our God, and set a watch as a protection against them day and night. Then the Judean community said, 'The strength of the burden-bearers is broken, for there is much rubbish; so that we shall not be able to rebuild the wall. And our adversaries have said, "They shall neither know nor see, until we come into their midst and slay them and bring the work to a standstill."' And it came to pass that when the Jews who dwelt by them came, they said to us ten times, 'From all the places where they dwell they will come up against us.' Therefore I stationed in the lowest parts of the space behind the wall, in the protected places, I set there the people by their families with their swords, their spears, and their bows. And when I saw their fear, I rose up and said to the nobles and to the rulers and to the rest of the people, 'Be not afraid of them. Remember the Lord, who is great and terrible, and fight for your kinsmen, your sons and your daughters, your wives and your homes.' 14.
Fears of the builders and Nehemiah's plan of work (9-14)

And when our enemies heard that their plan was known to us and God had brought it to nought, we all of us returned to the wall, each to his own work. And from that time on, while half of my servants were engaged in the work, half of them held the lances, the shields, the bows, and the coats of mail; and the rulers stood behind all the house of Judah. Those who built the wall and those who bore burdens were also armed, each with one of his hands engaged in the work, and with the other was ready to grasp his spear; and each of the builders had his sword girded by his side, and so builded. And he who sounded the trumpet was by me. And I said to the nobles and to the rulers and to the rest of the people, 'The work is great and extensive, and we are separated upon the wall far from each other. In 15.
Rapid progress of the work and the method of defence (15-23)

whatever place you hear the sound of the trumpet, gather there to us; our God will fight for us.' So we were active in the work, while half of them held the lances from the gray of morning until the stars came out. Also I said at that time to the people, Let each man with his servant lodge in Jerusalem, that they may be a guard to us by night and may labor by day. So neither I, nor my kinsmen, nor my servants, nor the men of the guard who accompanied me, not one of us took off our clothes, each had his spear in his hand.

16. Charge that Nehemiah was plotting a rebellion (6¹⁻⁹)

Now when it was reported to Sanballat and to Tobiah and to Geshem the Arabian and to the rest of our enemies, that I had rebuilt the wall and that there was no breach left in it—though even to that time I had not set up the doors in the gates—Sanballat and Geshem sent to me, saying, 'Come, let us meet together in one of the villages on the plain of Ono.' But they planned to do me injury. So I sent messengers to them, saying, 'I am doing a great work, so that I cannot come down; why should the work cease, while I leave it and come down to you?' And they sent to me in this way four times, and I gave them the same answer. Then Sanballat sent his servant to me in the same way the fifth time with an open letter in his hand, in which was written, 'It is reported among the nations, and Gashmu confirms it, that you and the Jews plan to rebel, and that this is the reason you are building the wall, and that you would be their king, and that you also have appointed prophets to preach of you at Jerusalem, saying, "There is a king in Judah." And now it will be reported to the king to this effect. Come now, therefore, and let us take counsel together.' Then I sent to him, saying, 'No such things have been done as you say, but you have devised them in your own mind.' For they all would have made us afraid, thinking, 'Their hands shall be weakened from the work, that it may not be done.' But now, O God, strengthen thou my hands.

17. Shemaiah's attempt to frighten Nehemiah (10⁻¹⁴)

And when I went to the house of Shemaiah the son of Delaiah, the son of Mehetabel, who was shut up at home, he said, 'Let us meet together in the house of God, within the temple, and let us shut the doors of the temple: for they

110

are coming to slay you in the night; yes, in the night they are coming to slay you!' And I said, 'Should such a man as I flee? And how could anyone like me [a layman] enter the chief room of the temple and still live? I will not enter.' Then I perceived and it was clear that God had not sent him; but he pronounced this prophecy against me, because Tobiah and Sanballat had hired him, that I should be alarmed and act accordingly and sin; and it would have given them occasion for an evil report, that they might reproach me. Remember, O my God, Tobiah and Sanballat according to these their acts, and also the prophetess Noadiah and the rest of the prophets who would have made me afraid.

So the wall was finished in the twenty-fifth day of the month Elul, in fifty-two days. And when all our enemies heard, all the surrounding nations feared and fell in their own esteem, for they perceived that this work had been done by our God. **18. Completion of the walls (15, 16)**

Moreover in those days the nobles of Judah sent many letters to Tobiah, and those of Tobiah came to them. For many in Judah had taken oath to him, because he was the son-in-law of Shechaniah the son of Arah and his son Jehohanan had taken the daughter of Meshullam, the son of Berechiah, as wife. Also they praised his good deeds before me and reported my words to him. Then Tobiah sent letters to make me afraid. **19. Conspiracies of the friends of Tobiah (17-19)**

Now when the wall had been built and I had set up the doors, and the porters and the singers and the Levites had been appointed, I placed my brother Hanani and Hananiah the commander of the castle in charge of Jerusalem; for he was a faithful man, and more God-fearing than many. And I said to them, 'Let not the gates of Jerusalem be opened until the sun is hot; and while watchmen are still on guard, let them shut the doors and bar them. Also appoint watches consisting of the inhabitants of Jerusalem, every one in his watch and each opposite his own house.' **20. The guarding of the city gates (7¹-³)**

Now the city was wide and large; but there were few people in it, and the households were not large. Therefore my God put it into my mind to gather together the nobles and the rulers and the people. **21. Need of more citizens (4, 5a)**

111

22. Dedica-
tion of
the
walls
(12²¹,
³², ³⁷-
⁴⁰)Then I had the rulers of Judah take their position upon the wall, and I appointed two great companies that gave thanks, and the first went to the right hand upon the wall toward the Dung Gate. And behind them went Hoshaiah and half of the nobles of Judah. And by the Fountain Gate, they went straight up the stairs of the city of David, at the ascent of the wall, above the house of David, even to the Water Gate on the east. And the other company of those who gave thanks went to the left, and I after them, with the half of the nobles of the people, upon the wall, above the Tower of the Furnaces, even to the broad wall, and above the Gate of Ephraim and by the Old Gate and by the Fish Gate and the Tower of Hananel and the Tower of the Hundred, even to the Sheep Gate; and they stood in the Gate of the Guard. So the two companies of those who gave thanks in the house of God took their position, and I, and the half of the rulers with me.

I. Nehemiah's Memoirs. Fortunately the author of the books of Ezra and Nehemiah has quoted at length in the opening chapters of Nehemiah from the personal memoirs of the noble patriot through whose activity the walls of Jerusalem were restored. They are the best historical records in the Old Testament and they shed clear, contemporary light upon this most important period in the evolution of Judaism. The narrative is straightforward and vivid. It lights up the otherwise dark period that precedes Nehemiah and enables the historian to bridge with assurance the century that intervened before the apocryphal book of I Maccabees throws its light upon the course of Israel's troubled history. The detailed description of the rebuilding of the walls in Nehemiah 3 is probably from the Chronicler, but it reveals an intimate acquaintance with the topography and the later history of Judah's capital.

II. Nehemiah's Response to the Call to Service. The presence of a deputation from Jerusalem (including Nehemiah's kinsman Hanani) in the distant Persian capital of Susa was not a mere accident. Nehemiah's response to their appeal and the epoch-making movement which he inaugurated reveal the presence of an impelling force. Probably back of all this movement was the work of the great prophet who speaks in Isaiah 40–66. In all that Nehemiah did that influence may be seen. In the fervent and patriotic prayer that he uttered on learning of conditions in Jerusalem he used the term servant or servants of Jehovah eight times in six short verses. It also echoes the phraseology and thought of the II Isaiah.

The king under whom Nehemiah served was evidently Artaxerxes I. In Nehemiah 12[10, 11] the Chronicler states that Eliashib, the high priest in the days of Nehemiah, was the grandson of Joshua, who shared in the rebuilding of the temple in 520 B.C. Eliashib was also the great-grandfather of Jaddua, who was high priest in Jerusalem in 332 B.C., when Alexander conquered Palestine. References in the recently discovered Elephantine letters, as well as in the history of Josephus, confirm the conclusion that Nehemiah set out upon his expedition in the spring of 445 B.C. Like all those who ministered personally to the Persian kings, he was probably a eunuch and still a young man. The true piety which is revealed in his prayer, the courage shown by his daring to appear with sad face in the presence of the absolute tyrant who ruled the Eastern world, and his tact in winning the king's consent to his departure indicate that he was a man of rare energy and ability. Artaxerxes I was famous for his susceptibility to the influence of court favorites. The queen referred to in 1[6] was probably the queen-mother Amestris, who exercised commanding authority in the Persian court. Without the royal consent and the resources and authority granted him, Nehemiah could hardly have accomplished the large task which he undertook. The arduous journey of fifteen hundred miles over mountains and barren deserts was enough to daunt a man reared in the luxury of an Oriental court, but Nehemiah was inspired by an ideal of service which recognized no obstacles.

III. Obstacles that Confronted Him. The high-priestly rulers do not appear to have welcomed Nehemiah with enthusiasm. Some of them, at least, later sought to undermine his work. It is not difficult to infer the reason for their apathy. Intrenched wealth and authority are usually conservative, especially if conscious that their position is easily assailable. As the sequel proved, these leaders of the community were simply intent upon self-aggrandizement, even at the expense of the dependent members of the community. A revolutionizing work like that proposed by Nehemiah was certain to affect their vested interests and to reveal their cruel selfishness. Certain of their families had also intermarried with neighboring chieftains; and they were quite content with the existing conditions. A second obstacle was the opposition of the hostile peoples who surrounded the little Judean community. On the east the Ammonites had apparently pressed in and occupied the ancient

Hebrew territory as far as the Jordan. Tobiah, the Ammonite, who figures prominently in Nehemiah's narrative, was probably one of their local chiefs. Gashmu, the Arabian, represented the half-civilized Bedouin tribes that had invaded the territory of Judea from the south and east during the period of weakness following the destruction of Jerusalem. Possibly he belonged to the Edomites who then held Hebron and all of the southern part of Judea. Nehemiah also refers to the descendents of Israel's ancient foes, the Philistines, living in the city of Ashdod. On the north the superior resources of Samaria had asserted themselves, and these survivors of the ancient Israelites who lived among the hills of Ephraim had grown into a powerful nation that overshadowed the struggling Judean community. These northerners, however, still worshipped at Jerusalem and were closely allied with the Jews. At their head was Sanballat, the Horonite, who probably came from Bethhoron, in southwestern Samaria. Each of these peoples inherited the feeling of hostility with which their fathers had regarded the people of Judah, and looked with suspicion upon any movement to re-establish Jerusalem's former strength and prestige. Furthermore, the men of the Judean community itself lacked courage and training. With inefficient helpers and with opponents within and without the community, Nehemiah's task seemed wellnigh impossible. That he succeeded in the face of all these obstacles in rebuilding the walls in the incredibly short period of fifty-two days is only explained by his superlative skill, devotion, and energy.

IV. **Nehemiah's Plan of Work.** Fortunately Nehemiah possessed resources as well as tact. He quickly disarmed the opposition and won at least the nominal support of the leaders by entertaining one hundred and fifty of them as his guests. Thus he was able to place them under personal obligation to him, to keep them under close surveillance, and to command their co-operation. In the second place he appealed to them and to the people by means of eloquent addresses which reveal his enthusiasm and devotion. Furthermore, he did not depend upon the reports of others, but personally studied the situation. His secret midnight ride down through the Valley Gate to the southwest of Jerusalem and thence eastward along the Hinnom Valley to the point where it joins the Kidron, and from there up the valley, gave him most accurate information regarding conditions. In most cases the ancient foundations of the city walls still remained. The first need was to remove the rubbish and where stones had fallen to replace them. The towers required certain timbers, which were cut probably from the royal domains to the south of the city. Nehemiah enlisted all members of the community both within and without Jerusalem. He organized them under their local leaders and set them to the task in which each was most interested. Thus the heads of the different villages, the elders of the leading families, the guilds of workmen, and even the priests, were all put to work and inspired by the spirit of natural rivalry as well as common loyalty. Nehemiah himself with his immediate followers directed the work, and instituted a strict military rule which secured both efficiency and protection.

V. The Restored Walls. In the light of recent excavations at Jerusalem it is possible to follow Nehemiah's work in detail. In the destruction of the walls by the Chaldeans the city had suffered most on the north where it was nearly level and protected by no descending valleys. Just north of the temple area a little valley ran up from the Kidron, leaving but a narrow neck of land connected directly with the plateau on the north. Here two great towers were restored that probably occupied the site of the later Roman tower of Antonia. Thence the wall ran westward across the upper Tyropœan Valley, which was here comparatively level. Numerous bands of workmen were assigned to this part of the work. The gate of the old wall was probably identical with the corner gate at the northwestern end of the city. The Ephraim Gate a little further to the southwest apparently corresponded to the modern Joppa Gate. From this point a broad wall ran to the western side of the city where the hill descended rapidly into the Valley of Hinnom, making its defence easy. At the southwestern end of the city stood the Tower of the Furnaces and the Valley Gate of which the foundations have recently been laid bare. The gate itself was narrow, being only eight feet wide, but the wall was here nine feet in thickness. The eighteen hundred or two thousand feet of wall along the Valley of Hinnom was evidently practically intact, for its repair was intrusted to but one group of workmen. Across the southern end of the Tyropœan Valley the ground was almost level, so that a strong wall was required. Excavations have shown that it was twenty feet thick at its base and supported by six strong buttresses. The Fountain Gate, through which ran the main street down the Tyropœan Valley out into the valley of the Kidron, was the chief southern gate of the city. It was nine feet wide and defended by a tower about forty-five feet square. Portions of this ancient thoroughfare, with its stones, worn smooth by the feet of the inhabitants of the ancient city, have here been uncovered. Just above the Pool of Siloam, which was within the city walls, was the King's Garden.

Thence the Hill of Ophel ascended rapidly making necessary the stairs mentioned in Nehemiah 3. The wall on the southeast was readily repaired, for it ran along the sloping western side of the Kidron Valley. The Water Gate probably led down to the Virgin's Fount, and the Horse Gate further to the north opened directly from the Kidron Valley to the public buildings that occupied the site of Solomon's palace immediately to the south of the temple. It is the space to-day occupied by the southern end of the temple area, which was thus extended in the days of Herod. Opposite the northeastern end of the temple area the wall curved westward until it reached the great towers that guarded the northern end of the city.

VI. Completion and Dedication of the Walls. Under the inspiration of Nehemiah's leadership, and as a result of the constant fear of attack, the building of the walls proceeded rapidly and without interruption. To the threats of hostile foes Nehemiah paid little heed. Trained in the Persian court, he saw at once their murderous purpose when they requested a conference in southwestern Samaria on the border of the Plain of Ono. Through the treacherous prophets in the Judean community they sought to play upon his fears and to lead him to compromise himself by taking refuge in the sacred precincts of the temple, but his courage, as well as his high respect for the sanctuary, delivered him from the plot. The cry that he was himself aspiring to the kingship and that his acts were treason against Persia did not daunt him, and when, in response to their malicious reports, the order finally came from the Persian king to cease working, the walls were already rebuilt.

Apparently Nehemiah's original leave of absence was for but a short period. His kinsman Hanani, who had headed the original deputation to Susa, and a certain Hananiah were by him placed in charge of the city. To protect it against sudden attack its gates were closed at night and not opened until the middle of the following forenoon. Effective measures were also instituted to increase its population. When the work of rebuilding the walls was complete, Nehemiah arranged for their public dedication. Starting from the Valley Gate on the southwestern side of the city, one half of the nobles and the people marched along the southern and eastern wall, while Nehemiah with the other half of the people proceeded along the western and northern wall. Finally meeting on the northern side of the temple area, the two companies blended their voices in thanksgiving to Jehovah who at last had made it possible for them to worship him in his sanctuary secure from attack.

Nehemiah had reorganized the Judean community, rebuilt their walls, and inspired them with a new sense of self-respect; thus he made possible that genuine revival of the Judean state that took place during the succeeding centuries. He, like Ezekiel, Haggai, Zechariah, and the II Isaiah, was indeed one of the makers of Judaism. Ben Sira with true insight declared (49¹³):

> The memorial of Nehemiah is great,
> Who raised up for us the walls that were fallen,
> And set up the gates and bars,
> And raised up our homes again.

§ CI. NEHEMIAH'S SOCIAL AND RELIGIOUS REFORMS

Thus saith Jehovah, Guard justice and practice righteousness;
For my deliverance is near at hand, and my righteousness is soon to be revealed.
Happy the man who practices, the mortal who holds fast to it,
Keeping the sabbath so as not to profane it, and keeping his hand from evil.

1. Exhortation to persevere in right doing (Is. 56¹, ²)

Let not the foreigner who hath joined himself to Jehovah say,
'Jehovah will surely separate me from his people.'
And let not the eunuch say, 'Behold I am a dry tree.'
For thus saith Jehovah to the eunuchs, 'Those who keep my sabbaths,
And choose that in which I delight, and hold fast to my covenant,
I will give them in my house and walls a monument,
And a name better than sons and daughters,
An everlasting name will I give them which cannot be cut off.

2. Eunuchs to have full rights in Jehovah's temple (³⁻⁵)

And the foreigners who join themselves to Jehovah to minister to him,
And to love the name of Jehovah, to be his servants,
Every one who keeps the sabbath so as not to pollute it and faithfully abides by my covenant—
Them will I bring to my holy mountain and make joyful in my house of prayer;

3. To all foreigners who keep Jehovah's commands (⁶⁻⁸)

117

Their burnt-offerings and sacrifices will be accepted upon
my altar;
For my house shall be called a house of prayer for all
peoples.
It is the oracle of Jehovah, who gathereth the outcasts of
Israel,
'I will gather still others to him in addition to those already
gathered.'

4. The neglect and greed of the rulers (9-12)

O all ye wild beasts of the field come to devour, all ye wild
beasts of the forest!
My watchmen are all blind, they know not how to give
heed,
They are all dumb dogs which cannot bark,
Dreaming, lying down, loving to slumber.
And the dogs are greedy, they know not how to be satis-
fied,
They all turn to their own way, each for his own profit
[saying],
Come, I will get wine, and we will drink our fill of strong
drink,
And to-morrow shall be as to-day, an exceedingly great
day!

5. Israel's worship merely formal, not life and service (58²⁻⁴)

Cry with full throat, be not silent!
Like a trumpet lift up thy voice,
Make known to my people their transgression,
And to the house of Jacob their sin.
Me indeed they consult daily,
And to know my ways is their delight.
As a nation that hath done righteousness,
And hath not forsaken the law of its God!
They ask me regarding righteous judgments,
To draw near to God is their delight!
'Why have we fasted and thou seest not,
Mortified ourselves and thou dost not notice?'
Behold, on your fast day ye follow your own pleasure,
And ye exact all money lent on pledge.
Behold ye fast for strife and contention,
And to smite the poor with the fist.

Your fasting to-day is not such
As to make your voice heard on high.

Can such be the fast which I choose,
A day when a man mortifies himself?
To droop one's head like a bulrush,
And to lie down in sackcloth and ashes?
Wilt thou call this a fast,
And a day acceptable to Jehovah?
Is not this the fast that I choose:
To loose the fetters of injustice,
To untie the bands of violence,
To set free those who are crushed,
To tear apart every yoke?

6. Jehovah desires mercy not sacrifice (⁴⁻⁷)

Is it not to share thy bread with the hungry,
And to bring the wanderers to thy home?
When thou seest the naked, to cover him,
And not hide thyself from thine own flesh?
Then shall thy light break forth as the dawn,
Thy restoration quickly spring forth,
And thy righteousness shall go before thee,
The glory of Jehovah shall be thy reward;
Then when thou callest Jehovah will answer,
When thou criest out he will say, Here am I.
If from thy midst thou remove the yoke,
The finger of scorn, and mischievous speech,
And bestow thy bread upon the hungry,
And satisfy the soul that is afflicted;
Then shall thy light shine forth in darkness,
And thy gloom shall be as noonday,
Jehovah will lead thee continually,
And will satisfy thy soul in parched lands,
And thy strength will he renew,
Thou shalt be like a watered garden,
As a fountain whose waters fail not.
Thy sons shall rebuild the ancient ruins,
Thou shalt rear again the foundations of olden **days**;
And men shall call thee, Repairer of Ruins,
Restorer of Ruined Places for Inhabiting.

7. The rewards of mercy (⁸⁻¹²)

8. Complaints of the poor because of the greed of the rich and ruling class (Neh. 51-5)

Then there was a loud complaint from the common people and their wives against their fellow-countrymen the Jews. For there were those who were saying, 'We must give our sons and our daughters in pledge to secure grain that we may eat and live.' Some also there were who were saying, 'We must mortgage our fields and our vineyards and our houses, that we may get grain because of the dearth.' There were also those who were saying, 'We have borrowed money for the king's tribute. Yet now our flesh is as the flesh of our brothers, our children as their children; but now, we must bring our sons and our daughters into slavery, and some of our daughters have already thus been brought into bondage, neither is it in our power to help it, for our fields and our vineyards belong to the nobles.'

9. Nehemiah's remonstrance and commands (6-11)

Then I was very angry when I heard their complaint and these statements. And I took counsel with myself, and contended with the nobles and rulers, and said to them, 'You exact usury each of his brother.' And I held a great assembly against them. And I said to them, 'We ourselves have, according to our ability, redeemed our fellow-countrymen the Jews, who have been sold to the heathen; and would you yourselves sell your fellow-countrymen, and should they sell themselves to us?' Then they were silent and could not find a word to say. Therefore I said, 'The thing that you are doing is not good. Ought you not to walk in the fear of our God, because of the reproach of the heathen our enemies? For I also, my kinsmen and my servants, lend them money and grain. Let us, therefore, leave off this usury. Restore to them this day their fields, their vineyards, their oliveyards, and their houses, also the usury of the money and of the grain, of the new wine, and of the oil, that you exact from them.'

0. Response and promise of those who were guilty (12, 13)

Then they said, 'We will restore them and will demand nothing from them; we will do just as you say.' Then I called the priests and took an oath of them, that they would do according to this promise. Also I shook out the fold of my garment, and said, 'So may God shake out every man from his house and from the fruit of his labor, who does not fulfil this promise; even thus may he be shaken out and emptied.' And all the assembly said, 'So may it be.' And they praised Jehovah. And the people did according to this promise.

Moreover from the time that I was appointed to be their governor in the land of Judah, from the twentieth year (445 B.C.) even to the thirty-second year (432) of Artaxerxes the king, that is for twelve years, I and my kinsmen had not eaten the bread which was due me as governor. But the former governors who were before me were a source of expense to the people, and took of them bread and wine, and also forty shekels of silver each day; and furthermore their servants oppressed the people. But I did not so, because of the fear of God. I also devoted myself to this work on the wall, and we did not buy any land; and all my servants were gathered there for the work. Also the Jews and the rulers, a hundred and fifty men, besides those who came to us from among the surrounding nations, were at my table. Now that which was prepared for each day was one ox and six choice sheep and fowls. These were prepared at my expense, and once in ten days wine in abundance for all the people. Yet with all this I did not demand the bread which was due me as governor, because the public service rested heavily upon this people. Remember to my credit, O my God, all that I have done for this people.

11. Nehemiah's generosity while governor (14-19)

Now before my return from the king, Eliashib the priest, who was appointed over the chambers of the house of our God, being related to Tobiah, had prepared for him a great chamber, where formerly they had stored the cereal-offerings, the incense, the vessels, and the tithes of grain, the new wine, and the oil. But during this time I had not been at Jerusalem; for in the thirty-second year of Artaxerxes king of Babylon I went to the king. Then after some time I asked leave of the king, and I came to Jerusalem and discovered the crime that Eliashib had committed for the sake of Tobiah, in preparing him a chamber in the court of the house of God. And it displeased me greatly; therefore I cast all the household possessions of Tobiah out of the chamber. Then I gave command that they should cleanse the chambers, and I brought there again the vessels of the house of God, with the cereal-offerings and the incense.

12. Ejection of Tobiah's possessions from the temple chamber (13 4-9)

13. Providing for the support of the Levites (10-14) And I perceived that the portions of the Levites had not been given them; so that the Levites and the singers, who performed the service had each fled to his field. Then I contended with the rulers and said, 'Why is the house of God forsaken?' And I gathered them together and placed them at their posts. And all Judah brought the tithe of the grain and the new wine and the oil into the store-rooms. And I appointed in charge of the store-rooms: Shelemiah the priest and Zadok the scribe, and Pedaiah the Levite; for they were considered faithful, and their business was to distribute to their kinsmen. Remember me, O my God, concerning this and forget not all my good deeds that I have done for the house of my God, and for its services.

14. Provisions to guard the observation of the sabbath (15-22) At that time I saw in Judah some men treading wine-presses on the sabbath and bringing in heaps of grain and loading asses, as also wine, grapes, figs, and all kinds of burdens, and that they were bringing them into Jerusalem on the sabbath; and I warned them when they sold provisions. Tyrians also dwelt therein, who brought in fish and all kinds of wares, and sold on the sabbath to the inhabitants of Judah and in Jerusalem. Then I contended with the nobles of Judah and said to them, 'What evil thing is this that you are doing, and thereby profaning the sabbath? Did not your fathers do thus and did not our God bring all this calamity upon them and upon us and upon this city? Yet you bring more wrath upon Israel by profaning the sabbath.' Accordingly, when it began to be dark, the gates of Jerusalem were shut before the sabbath; and I gave command that they should not be opened until after the sabbath. And I placed some of my servants in charge of the gates, and commanded that no burden should be brought in on the sabbath. So the merchants and sellers of all kinds of wares spent the night without Jerusalem once or twice. Then I warned them and said to them, 'Why do you spend the night before the wall? If ye do so again, I will lay hands on you.' From that time forth they came no more on the sabbath. Remember, O my God, this also to my credit and show me mercy according to the greatness of thy loving-kindness.

At that time also I saw the Jews who had married women of Ashdod, of Ammon, and of Moab. And their children spoke half in the language of Ashdod, but none of them could speak in the Jews' language, but according to the language of each people. And I contended with them and cursed them and struck some of them and pulled out their hair and made them swear by God, saying, 'You shall not give your daughters to their sons nor take their daughters as wives for your sons or for yourselves. Did not Solomon king of Israel sin by these acts? Yet among many nations there was no king like him, and he was beloved by his God, and God made him king over all Israel; nevertheless foreign women led him into sin. Shall it also be reported of you that you do all this great evil, to trespass against our God in marrying foreign women?' *15. Energetic protest against mixed marriages (23–27)*

And one of the sons of Joiada, the son of Eliashib the high priest, was the son-in-law of Sanballat the Horonite; therefore I chased him from me. Remember them, O my God, because they have defiled the covenant of the priesthood and of the Levites. *16. Ejection of a guilty priest (28, 29)*

Thus I cleansed them from all foreigners and fixed the duties for the priests and the Levites, each for his appointed task, and the bringing of wood for the service at appointed times, and the first-fruits. Remember it, O my God, to my credit. *17. Résumé of Nehemiah's reforms (30, 31)*

I. Cruelty and Hypocrisy of the Jewish Leaders. The fifty-sixth chapter of Isaiah presents a sharp contrast: on the one hand a high ideal of justice toward the oppressed and tolerance toward all foreigners who sincerely desired to unite in Jehovah's worship; on the other the sordid selfishness of the Jewish leaders, who disregarded their responsibilities and thought of religion only as a round of ceremonial observances. The situation is very similar to that in Northern Israel in the days of Amos. The II Isaiah stands on the same platform as did his predecessors of the Assyrian period. He strips fearlessly from the rulers of the community the mantle of hypocrisy with which they sought to cover their shame. In clearest terms he declares that their first duty to God is to loose the fetters of injustice and to share their bread with the hungry. This stirring prophetic message is the natural introduction to the reformatory work of Nehemiah.

II. Nehemiah's Method of Correcting the Social Evils in the Community. Nehemiah's address recorded in the fifth chapter of his memoirs completes the picture suggested in Isaiah 56 and 58. The poor had been compelled by their poverty to sell their children into slavery to the rich and ruling class. In order to pay their personal taxes they had also mortgaged their inherited fields, vineyards, and houses. Doubtless much of the tax thus raised went into the pockets of their rulers, who preyed mercilessly upon the helpless and needy. These crimes directly violated the laws of Deuteronomy (*cf.* Deut. 23⁹· ²⁰), as well as those in the older Book of the Covenant (Ex. 21–23). Nehemiah's position, therefore, when he demanded that these evils be righted, was unassailable. In the spirit and with the methods of the earlier prophets he gathered together the people, probably within the precincts of the temple court, and plainly and unsparingly denounced their acts. There is much in common between this later Jewish layman and the shepherd Amos. Each spoke on the basis of close personal observation and experience; but Nehemiah possessed many advantages over the prophets who had preceded him. His own personal example lent force to his words. Although it was his right as governor, he had exacted no tribute from the Judean community. Even though the opportunity had probably offered itself, he steadily refused to take their hereditary land from the poor who applied to him for loans of money or grain. Instead of enslaving his countrymen, he had lost no opportunity to free those who had been forced by misfortune or poverty into slavery. He had also entertained lavishly rich and poor alike, and thus given to all an example of practical charity. His authority as Persian governor doubtless carried great weight with the cringing, greedy leaders at Jerusalem. Above all, the force of his personality was irresistible. It is easy to imagine the powerful impression which his words made upon them. The restoration of their lands and the freeing of their children were undoubtedly mighty factors in arousing the men of Jerusalem to those herculean efforts which alone made possible the rebuilding of the walls in the brief period of fifty-two days.

III. The Historical Value of Nehemiah 13. In his *Composition of Ezra-Nehemiah* (pp. 44–49) Professor Torrey, of Yale, maintains that this chapter is a pure creation of the Chronicler. Certainly its phraseology and the subjects with which it deals are characteristic of the Chronicler, but on the whole it is probable that he has here simply recast what was originally an extract from the memoirs of Nehemiah. Some of the phrases peculiar to the Chronicler are loosely connected with the context. The nucleus which remains has the vigorous style of Nehemiah and many of his peculiar idioms. Its courageous, assertive spirit is very different from that of the other writings of the Chronicler. It is also doubtful whether this later writer, with his strong, priestly interests, would have made Nehemiah, the layman, a religious reformer and therefore in a sense the rival of Ezra. Above all, the work attributed to Nehemiah in this chapter is in harmony with his spirit and attitude, as revealed in the unquestioned extracts from his memoirs. Already, as stated in 1²⁰, he had told Sanballat and Tobiah that they should have no portion or memorial in Jerusalem. He had already shown himself keen in righting wrongs within the community. Zeal in preserving the sanctity of the sabbath and in opposing heathen marriages was characteristic rather of the Jews of the dispersion than of those of Palestine. It is probable, therefore, that this chapter records Nehemiah's work when he revisited Jerusalem some time after 432 B.C., although it must be frankly confessed that the historical evidence is far from conclusive and that the entire account of this second visit, including the chronological data in 5¹⁴ and the reference to the expulsion of Sanballat in 1²⁰, may possibly be due to the Chronicler's desire to discredit the Samaritans and to enlist the authority of Nehemiah in support of the later priestly laws and customs.

IV. **Regulations Regarding the Temple Service.** The expulsion of Tobiah the Ammonite from the room which had been assigned him in the temple by Eliashib, the high priest, was apparently due to two reasons, first because Tobiah was *persona non grata* to Nehemiah and had already shown himself a dangerous foe to the Jews. The second and chief reason was because the room was needed for storing the offerings that were brought in for the support of the temple officials. These offerings were presented in accordance with the demands of the Deuteronomic regulation, which at this time was the code acknowledged by the Judean community (Deut. 18⁴ 14²³, ²⁷, ²⁸). The narrative adds that, with his practical knowledge of affairs, Nehemiah appointed a representative committee consisting of a priest, a scribe, and a Levite, and to them he intrusted the task of receiving and distributing the temple tithes to their kinsmen.

V. **Provisions Regarding Sabbath Observation and Foreign Marriages.** Far away from the temple, and therefore unable to participate in the distinctive feasts and ceremonials that distinguished the religious life of their race, and confronted by the constant danger of being absorbed by the heathen among whom they found themselves, the Jews of the dispersion placed strong emphasis on two institutions.

The one was the observation of the sabbath and the other was the preservation of the purity of their blood by abstaining from all marriage alliances with their Gentile neighbors. In Palestine, where they were able to revive the ancient feasts in connection with the temple, and where the danger of absorption was not so imminent, their practices in these regards appear to have been much more lax. Not only had the priests set the example by contracting foreign marriages, but apparently about this time the author of the beautiful story of Ruth, by citing the tradition regarding the Moabite ancestry of their illustrious King David, voiced the belief of many in the community that such marriages were permissible. Nehemiah, however, rigorously opposed this tendency. He also appreciated the menace to the dignity and character of the temple service, if the commercial pursuits of ordinary days were carried into the sabbath. His measure, therefore, in closing the gates and thus excluding all traders, was both sane and effective. In setting his face strongly against foreign marriages he was simply enforcing the laws found in Deuteronomy 7$^{1, 3}$ and 33^3, which forbade the Hebrews to intermarry with the people of the land.

VI. **Significance of Nehemiah's Work.** In rebuilding the walls of Jerusalem Nehemiah prepared the way for that revival of the Jewish state which characterized the closing years of the Persian period. More important still was his work in re-establishing a close relation between the Jews of the dispersion and those of Palestine. He himself was the connecting link between them, and his activity prepared the minds of the Palestinian Jews for the acceptance of those new principles that were strongly held by leaders like himself. He also enforced the ethical and social ideals of the earlier prophets, and ably advocated the principles that are fundamental in the late priestly laws. Above all, in his own personality as a prophetic layman, he held up before his race an example of patriotism, self-sacrifice, efficiency, and devotion to the service of Jehovah which made a profound and lasting impression upon his own and later generations.

§ CII. THE TRADITIONAL ACCOUNT OF THE ADOPTION OF THE PRIESTLY LAW

1. The return of Ezra and his band to Jerusalem (Ezra 7^1, 6-10)

In the reign of Artaxerxes king of Persia, Ezra, a descendant of Aaron, went up from Babylon; and he was a scribe skilled in the law of Moses, which Jehovah, the God of Israel, had given. And the king granted him all his request, inasmuch as the hand of Jehovah his God was upon him. And some of the Israelites, and of the priests, the Levites, the singers, the porters, and the temple servants went up to Jerusalem [with him]. And he came to Jerusalem in the fifth month, which was in the seventh year of the king. For on the first day of the first month he began the journey from Babylon, and on the first day of the fifth month he came to Jerusalem, since the good hand of God was with him. For Ezra had set his heart to seek the law of Jehovah, and to observe it and to teach in Israel statutes and ordinances.

And when the seventh month drew near, all the people gathered themselves together as one man to the broad place that was before the Water Gate. And they spoke to Ezra the priest and scribe to bring the book of the law of Moses, which Jehovah had commanded Israel. And Ezra the priest brought the law before the assembly of men and women, and all who could hear with understanding, upon the first day of the seventh month. And he read from it before the open place that was before the Water Gate, from early morning until mid-day, in the presence of the men and women and of those who could understand; and all the people were attentive to the book of the law. And Ezra the priest and scribe stood upon a wooden pulpit, which they made for the purpose and opened the book in the sight of all the people—for he was above all the people—and when he opened it all the people stood up. And Ezra blessed Jehovah, the great God. And all the people answered, Amen, Amen, while they lifted up their hands and bowed their heads and worshipped Jehovah with their faces to the ground.

2. Reading and explanation of the law to the people (Neh. 7⁷³ᵇ, 8¹⁻⁶)

Then Ezra the priest, the scribe, and the Levites who taught the people said to all the people, This day is holy to Jehovah your God; mourn not, nor weep; for all the people wept when they heard the words of the law. Then he said to them, Go away, eat the fat, and drink the sweet, and send portions to him for whom nothing is prepared, for this day is holy to our Lord; and do not be troubled, for the joy of Jehovah is your bulwark. So the Levites quieted all the people, saying, Be still, for the day is holy, and do not be troubled. And all the people went away to eat and drink and to send portions and to make a great rejoicing, for they had understood the words which had been made known to them.

3. Command to rejoice and give gifts to each other (⁹⁻¹²)

4. Celebration of the feast of tabernacles according to the new law (13-18)

And on the second day the heads of fathers' houses of all the people, the priests and the Levites were gathered together to Ezra the scribe, in order to gain an insight into the words of the law. And they found written in the law, how Jehovah had commanded by Moses that the Israelites should dwell in booths at the feast in the seventh month; and that they should proclaim aloud in all their cities and in Jerusalem: Go forth to the mount and bring olive branches and branches of wild olive and myrtle and palm branches and branches of thick trees to make booths, as it is prescribed. So the people went out and brought them, and made themselves booths, each man upon the roof of his house and in their courts and in the courts of the house of God and in the open space at the Water Gate and in the open space at the Ephraim Gate. And all the assembly of those who had come back from the captivity made booths and lived in the booths; for since the days of Joshua the son of Nun to that day the Israelites had not done so. And there was very great gladness. And day by day, from the first to the last day, he read in the book of the law of God. And they celebrated the feast seven days, and on the eighth day, as was the custom, there was a concluding solemn assembly.

5. Confession of the people (91-3)

Now in the twenty-fourth day of this month the Israelites were assembled with fasting, and with sackcloth and earth upon their heads. And the children of Israel had separated themselves from all foreigners, and stood and confessed their sins and the iniquities of their fathers. And they stood up in their place and read in the book of the law of Jehovah their God a fourth part of the day; and another fourth part they confessed and worshipped Jehovah their God.

6. Ezra's prayer: Jehovah's supreme rule and promises to Abraham (6-8)

And Ezra said, Thou art Jehovah, even thou alone; thou hast made heaven and the heaven of heavens with all their host, the earth and all things that are on it, the seas and all that is in them, and thou preservest them all and the host of heaven worshippeth thee. Thou art Jehovah the God, who didst choose Abraham and bring him forth out of Ur of the Chaldees, and didst give him the name Abraham, and find his heart faithful before thee and make a cove-

128

nant with him to give the land of the Canaanites to his descendants, and hast performed thy words, for thou art righteous.

Now therefore, our God, the great, the mighty, and the terrible God, who keepest covenant and kindness, let not all the affliction seem little before thee, that hath come on us, on our kings, our nobles, our priests, our prophets, our fathers, and on all thy people, since the days of the kings of Assyria to this day. However thou art just in all that has come upon us; for thou hast done right, but we have done wickedly, neither have our kings, our nobles, our priests, nor our fathers, kept thy law nor heeded thy commands and thy testimonies with which thou didst testify against them. For they have not served thee in the time of their kingly rule, and in spite of thy great goodness that thou gavest them, they have not turned from their wicked deeds. Behold, we this day are slaves, and as for the land that thou gavest to our fathers to eat its fruit and enjoy its good gifts, see we are only slaves in it. And it yieldeth a great income to the kings whom thou hast set over us because of our sin; also they have power over our bodies and over our cattle, at their pleasure, and we are in great distress.

7. Petition to avert the merited judgment that rests upon the race (32-37)

Moreover in addition to all this we made a fixed covenant and wrote it out, and our nobles, our Levites, and our priests were enrolled upon the sealed document.

8. Signers of the written covenant (38)

And all those who had separated themselves from the peoples of the lands to the law of God, their wives, their sons, and their daughters, every one who had knowledge and insight, strongly supported their kinsmen, their nobles, and entered into a solemn obligation and took oath to walk in God's law, which was given by Moses the servant of God, and to observe and do all the commands of Jehovah our Lord, and his ordinances and his statutes; and that we would neither give our daughters to the peoples of the land nor take their daughters as wives for our sons; and that, if the peoples of the land should bring wares or any grain on the sabbath day to sell, we would not buy of them on the sabbath or on a holy day; and that on the seventh year we would leave the land uncultivated and would refrain from the exaction of any debt.

9. Regulations adopted by the community (10²⁸⁻³¹ʰ)

129

10.
Obligations assumed for the support of the temple and ritual
(32-39)

We also imposed upon ourselves the obligation to give yearly the third part of a shekel for the service of the house of our God, for the bread that was set forth, and for the continual burnt-offering, for the sabbaths, the new moons, the fixed feasts, and the holy things, and for the sin-offerings to make atonement for Israel, and for all the work of the house of our God. And we cast lots, the priests, the Levites, and the people, for the wood-offering, to bring it into the house of our God, according to our father's houses, at appointed times year by year, to burn upon the altar of Jehovah our God, as it is prescribed in the law; and to bring the earliest products of our ground, and the first of all fruit of every kind of tree year by year, to the temple of Jehovah; also the first-born of our sons and of our cattle, as is prescribed in the law, and the firstlings of our herds and of our flocks, to bring to the house of God to the priests who minister in the house of our God; and that we should bring the first bread baked of our dough, the fruit of every kind of tree, the new wine and the oil, to the priests, in the chambers of the house of our God; and the tithes of our ground to the Levites; and that they, the Levites, should receive the tithes in all the cities of our agricultural districts. And that the priest the son of Aaron should be with the Levites, when the Levites shall bring up the tithe of the tithes to the house of our God, to the chambers, into the store-house. For the Israelites and the sons of Levi shall bring the gifts of grain, of new wine, and of oil, into the chambers, where are the vessels of the sanctuary, and the priests who minister and the porters and the singers, and that we would not neglect the house of our God.

I. **The Ezra Tradition.** The tradition regarding Ezra and his work presents many difficult problems. Part of it is found in the heart of the book of Nehemiah; while another part is now found in the second half of the book of Ezra. It is not entirely clear whether this dislocation is due to the Chronicler, who desired to give Ezra, the priest and scribe, the precedence before Nehemiah, the layman, or to the mistake of a scribe. A recent writer (Professor Torrey, in *Composition of Ezra-Neh.*) has shown convincingly that the Ezra story in its present form is at least from the school to which the Chronicler belonged, if not from his own pen.   Not only does it abound in the characteristic phrases of this voluminous editor, but it also reflects at many points his peculiar conception of the history of this period.   Ezra is described as a descendant of Aaron and "a scribe skilled in the law of Moses."   His work as interpreter of the law, which he is represented as bringing in his hand, is typical of the scribes, who were becoming the chief teachers of Judaism in the days of the Chronicler (the Greek period).   The decree of Artaxerxes found in the seventh chapter of Ezra suggests at every point its late Jewish origin.   It confers upon Ezra, the scribe, royal authority far eclipsing that given by Artaxerxes to Nehemiah, his favorite.   A sum representing more than three million dollars is placed at Ezra's disposal.   At his summons seventeen hundred priests, Levites, singers, and servants of the temple rally about the standard of the faithful scribe. He is represented as going under the royal protection to Palestine to instruct the Judean community, to reform its abuses, and to institute the rule of the law of Moses which he bore in his hand.

He first holds a great synagogue service in which the law is read and interpreted to the people.   They are then bidden to observe the Feast of Booths or Tabernacles in accordance with its regulations.   Later, when he discovers that the people of the land have entered into foreign marriages, he tears his clothes and hair and sits for hours overwhelmed by the great crime that rests upon the community.   When the people are gathered about him, he upbraids them for their laxness and secures the appointment of a commission with himself at the head to investigate and put an end to these evil practices.   When after three months the community has been purified from this foreign element, the people are again assembled to listen to the reading of the law.   Then Ezra utters a fervent prayer in which he sets forth Jehovah's leadership of his people in the past and the disasters which have come as a result of their sins. After this public petition for Jehovah's forgiveness, the people through their nobles, Levites, and priests subscribe in writing to the regulations imposed by the lawbook that Ezra had brought.   Its more important regulations are also recapitulated.   They are to refrain from foreign marriages, to observe strictly the sabbath laws, and also the requirements of the seventh year of release, to bring to the temple the annual tax of one-tenth of a shekel and the other dues required for its support and for the maintenance of the priests and Levites.

II. **The Historical Value of the Ezra Tradition.** Recognizing that the Ezra tradition comes from the hand of the Chronicler, certain Old Testament scholars are inclined to regard it as entirely unhistorical.

131

It can no longer be regarded as a strictly historical record. Like II Chronicles 31, it is shot through with the ideas current during the Greek period. With no desire to deceive, but with nothing of the modern historical spirit, the Chronicler freely projects the institutions, ideas, and traditions of his own day into these earlier periods. The result is that he has given not an exact or reliable historical record, but his own conception of the way in which the course of history should have unfolded. The Ezra tradition also lacks the support not only of contemporary testimony, but also of all the Jews who wrote during the next few centuries. Ben Sira in his review of Israel's heroes speaks in highest terms of Nehemiah, but knows nothing of Ezra's work. Even the comparatively late Jewish tradition reflected in the opening chapters of II Maccabees attributes to Nehemiah the re-establishment of the temple service and the collection of the sacred writings of his race. At many points the Ezra tradition is also inconsistent with the straightforward contemporary record contained in Nehemiah's memoirs. The real question is whether or not there is a historical nucleus in the Ezra story, and if so, what are the facts which it reflects.

III. **The Facts Underlying the Ezra Tradition.** The later records make it clear that during the latter part of the Persian period the attitude of the Jews in Palestine toward their neighbors became more and more exclusive. Nehemiah appears to have given a great impetus to the movement which ultimately resulted in the Samaritan schism and the high wall that henceforth separated Jew and Gentile. The emphasis on the strict observation of the sabbath grew stronger and stronger, until at the beginning of the Greek period the Jews of Jerusalem preferred to fall before the sword of their foes rather than fight on the sabbath day (*cf.* § CIII). The ritual of the temple became even more elaborate, and its income was greatly increased during the latter part of the Persian period. The extension of the territory of the Judean community implied that its numbers were increased by the return of loyal Jews attracted by the security offered by its walls and by the new spirit that animated the Jews of Palestine. The priestly laws which were formulated to meet the new needs of the Judean community appear to have been written in Palestine and by those closely connected with the temple service, but in the emphasis upon the sabbath and in their endeavor to prevent marriage with foreigners they suggest the presence and influence of Jews who had returned from the land of the dispersion. It is possible that among those who thus returned was the priest Ezra, and he may have been at the head of one of these groups of returning exiles. In the days of Josiah the code contained in the newly discovered Book of the Covenant was presented to the people in a public assembly and adopted and enforced by the king, who acted as the representative of the people (§ LXXXIII[iii]). It is probable that in the small Judean community new regulations gained acceptance in the same way, except that the people were represented by their nobles and priests rather than by a king. The tradition of Ezra, therefore, is typical of the great movement that shaped the life of Judaism in the century immediately following the work of Nehemiah.

IV. Origin and Aims of the Priestly Laws. The late priestly laws which moulded the life of Judaism are found in the books of Exodus, Leviticus, and Numbers. They do not constitute a unified code, but rather are made up of a series of smaller groups of laws, the older nucleus being the Holiness Code found in chapters 17–26 of Leviticus (*cf.* § XCIII[iii]). In some cases variants of the same law are found in different groups. Certain of these laws simply reiterate in slightly different form those already found in the primitive and Deuteronomic codes; but in general they supplement these earlier codes. The formulation, collection, and codification of these later laws apparently continued until toward the latter part of the Persian period when the Samaritan schism (§ CIII) fixed them in their present form.

To these laws was prefixed, as an introduction, the priestly history that opens with the account of creation in the first chapter of Genesis and briefly traces Israel's history to the settlement in Canaan. The interest of these late priestly historians is, like that of the Chronicler, in the origin of institutions. Thus the object of the first chapter of Genesis is to give the traditional origin and authority of the sabbath. The account of the flood culminates in a covenant embodying the command that man shall not eat of the blood of sacrificial animals; the priestly stories regarding Abraham aim to give the origin of the rite of circumcision Israel's early experiences in the wilderness furnish the setting for the giving of the law at Sinai. In this way the late editors of these opening books of the Old Testament connect all of Israel's legislation with Moses and aim to establish its divine authority.

V. Their Important Regulations. The central aim in all these late priestly laws was similar to that of Ezekiel: it was to make Israel a holy people and to prevent them from falling again into the sins to which were attributed the overwhelming disasters that had overtaken them. This aim they sought to accomplish: (1) by making the temple and its services the centre of the life of the people and through ceremonial barriers and regulations to shield it from everything that might pollute it;

(2) by rendering the temple service attractive; (3) by insuring through rigid ceremonial laws the purity of its priesthood; (4) by preserving the ceremonial cleanliness of the people through strict laws regarding the food which they ate and elaborate provisions for their purification in case they were contaminated by contact with that which was regarded as unclean; (5) by prohibiting absolutely all marriages with the heathen; and (6) by emphasizing the rigid observation of the sabbath and other distinctive institutions. In general these late priestly laws represented a return to the older and more primitive conception of religion, and defined duty in terms of ceremonial rather than moral acts.

VI. Their Practical Effects. Later Judaism represents to a great extent the result of the rigid enforcement of these regulations. Its life was centralized more and more about the temple. In its services the people found their chief interest and joy. The numbers of the priests and Levites were also greatly increased. To the older temple dues many new ones were added. Thus each man brought to the temple the first-born of his flock. Even his oldest son must be redeemed within a month after his birth by a gift of five shekels (which represented in modern currency between three and four dollars). Of every animal slain the shoulder, two joints, and the stomach went to the priests. Of the vintage and oil and grain they received about one-fiftieth. In addition a tithe was turned over to the Levites. Part of the wool in every sheep-shearing, as well as a part of the bread which they baked, found its way to the temple. In addition a large income came through the vows made by the people or the conscience money which was paid either in currency or gifts. Although the priests had no temporal authority by which to enforce these laws, it is evident that the people bore their heavy burdens gladly and brought willingly their offerings, that they might thereby win a definite assurance of Jehovah's favor. The law was to them a source of joy rather than a burden. Their love for it steadily grew until two centuries later during the Maccabean persecutions there were many who were ready to lay down their lives for it.

§ CIII. THE JEWISH STATE DURING THE LAST CENTURY OF PERSIAN RULE

1. Thanks-giving for Je-hovah's protect-ing care (Ps. 36⁵⁻¹⁰)

Thy loving-kindness, O Jehovah, is in the heavens,
Thy faithfulness reacheth to the skies,
Thy righteousness is like the mighty mountains,
Thy judgments are like the great deep;
Thou preservest man and beast.

How precious is thy loving-kindness, O God!
And the sons of men put their trust in the shadow of thy
     wings.
They are fully satisfied with the rich things of thy house,
And thou makest them drink of thy river of delights.
For with thee is the fountain of life,
And in thy light shall we see light.
O continue thy loving-kindness to those who know thee,
And thy righteousness to the upright in heart.

The word of Jehovah, which came to Joel, the son of Pethuel:
     Blow a horn in Zion,
     Sound an alarm in my holy mountain,
     Let all the inhabitants of the land tremble,
     For the day of Jehovah comes,
     For near is the day of darkness and gloom,
     The day of cloud and thick darkness!

2. Jehovah's judgment at hand (Joel 2¹, 2b)

     Like the light of dawn scattered over the mountains,
     A people great and powerful;
     Its like has not been from of old,
     Neither shall be any more after it,
     Even to the years of coming ages.
     Before them the fire devours,
     And behind them a flame burns;
     Like the garden of Eden is the land before them,
     And after them it is a desolate desert,
     Yea, nothing escapes them.
     Their appearance is as the appearance of horses,
     And like horsemen they run.
     Like the sound of chariots on the tops of the mountains
          they leap,
     Like the crackle of flames devouring stubble,
     Like a mighty people preparing for battle.
     Peoples are in anguish before them,
     All faces glow with excitement.

3. Advance of his dread agents (²ᶜ⁻⁶)

     Like mighty men they run,
     Like warriors they mount up a wall,
     They march each by himself,

4. Their attack (⁷⁻⁹)

135

They break not their ranks,
None jostles the other,
They march each in his path,
They fall upon the weapons without breaking,
They scour the city, they run on the wall,
They climb up into the houses,
Like a thief they enter the windows.

5.
Effect
upon
nature
and
mankind
(10, 11)

Earth trembles before them,
Heaven quakes,
The sun and the moon become dark,
And the stars withdraw their shining;
And Jehovah uttereth his voice before his army,
For his host is exceedingly great,
Yea, mighty is he who performs his word,
For great is the day of Jehovah,
It is very terrible, who can abide it?

6 True
repentance
the one
hope
(12-14)

But now this is the oracle of Jehovah:
Turn ye to me with all your heart,
And with fasting and weeping and mourning.
Rend your hearts and not your garments,
And turn to Jehovah your God;
For he indeed is gracious and merciful,
Slow to anger and plenteous in love,
And relenteth of the evil.
Who knows but he will turn and relent,
And leave a blessing behind him,
A cereal and drink-offering for Jehovah your God?

7. Call
to a
general
assembly and
united
supplication
(15-17)

Blow a horn in Zion,
Sanctify a fast, summon an assembly,
Gather the people, make holy the congregation,
Assemble the old men,
Gather the children, and the infants at the breast,
Let the bridegroom come forth from his chamber,
And the bride from her bridal tent.
Between the porch and the altar,
Let the priests, the ministers of Jehovah, weep aloud,
Let them say, Spare, O Jehovah, thy people,

136

And make not thine heritage an object of reproach,
For the heathen to mock them.
Why should it be said among the nations, Where is
  their God?

Then Jehovah became jealous for his land, and took pity
  upon his people,
And Jehovah answered and said to his people,
Behold, I will send you corn, and wine, and oil,
And ye shall be satisfied therewith;
I will not make you again an object of reproach among the
  nations,
I will remove far from you the northern foe,
And I will drive him into a land barren and desolate,
His van to the eastern sea,
And his rear to the western sea,
And a stench from him shall arise.

8. Jehovah's response to the petitions of his people (18-20)

Fear not, O land, exult,
And rejoice for Jehovah hath done great things.
Fear not, O beasts of the field,
For the pastures of the wilderness are putting forth new
  grass,
For the trees bear their fruit,
Fig tree and vine yield their strength.
Be glad, then, ye sons of Zion,
And rejoice in Jehovah your God,
For he hath given you the early rain in just measure,
And poured down upon you the winter rain,
And sent the latter rain as before.
The threshing floors shall be full of grain,
And the vats shall overflow with new wine and oil.

9. His promises that the fields shall again be fruitful (21-24)

I will make restoration to you for the years which the
  swarmer hath eaten,
The devourer, the destroyer, and the shearer,
My great army which I sent among you,
And ye shall eat your food and be satisfied,
And praise the name of Jehovah your God,
Who hath dealt so wonderfully by you,

10. Renewed prosperity and the sense of Jehovah's presence (25-27)

And ye shall know that I am in the midst of Israel,
That I am Jehovah your God and none else,
And my people shall nevermore be abashed.

11. Universal spiritual blessings (28, 29)

And it shall come to pass afterwards,
That I will pour out my spirit upon all flesh,
And your sons and your daughters shall prophesy,
Your old men shall dream dreams,
Your young men shall see visions,
And even upon thy male and female slaves,
In those days I will pour out my spirit.

12. Effects of the murder of the high priest's brother (Josephus, Ant. XI, 7¹)

When Eliashib the high priest was dead, his son Judas succeeded him in the high priesthood. Then, when he was dead, his son Johanan assumed that dignity. It was on his account that Bagoses, the general of Artaxerxes [Mnemon], desecrated the temple and imposed tribute on the Jews, that at public expense they should pay for every lamb fifty shekels. The reason for this was as follows: Jeshua was the brother of Johanan. Bagoses, who was Jeshua's friend, promised to secure for him the high priesthood. Trusting, therefore, in this support, Jeshua quarrelled with Johanan in the temple and so provoked his brother that, in his anger, Johanan slew him. On this account the people were enslaved and the temple desecrated by the Persians. For when Bagoses, the general of Artaxerxes, knew that Johanan, the high priest of the Jews had slain his own brother Jeshua in the temple, he immediately came against the Jews and began in anger to say to them, Have you dared commit a murder in your temple! And when he attempted to go into the temple they tried to prevent him doing so; but he said to them, Am I not purer than he who was slain in the temple? And when he had said these words, he went into the temple. Thus Bagoses made use of this pretext and punished the Jews seven years for the murder of Jeshua.

13. Marriage of Manasseh to Sanballat's daughter (²)

Now when Johanan had departed this life, his son Jaddua succeeded to the high priesthood. He had a brother whose name was Manasseh. And there was a certain Sanballat who was sent to Samaria by Darius, the last king of Persia. This man, knowing that Jerusalem was a famous city and that its kings had given great trouble to the Assyrians and the people of Cœle-Syria, willingly gave his daughter, whose name was Nicaso, in marriage to Manasseh, thinking that this marriage alliance would be a pledge that the nation of the Jews would continue their good will toward him.

The elders of Jerusalem, complaining loudly that the brother of Jaddua, the high priest, though married to a foreigner, was sharing with him the high priesthood, took sides against Jaddua; for they regarded this man's marriage as an encouragement to those who were eager to transgress by marrying foreign wives and that this would be the beginning of a closer association with foreigners. Therefore they commanded Manasseh to divorce his wife or else not to approach the altar. The high priest himself joined with the people in their indignation and drove his brother from the altar.

14. His expulsion from Jerusalem (8²ᵃ⁻ᶜ)

Then Manasseh went to his father-in-law, Sanballat, and told him that, although he loved his daughter, Nicaso, he was not willing to be deprived on her account of his priestly dignity, since it was the greatest dignity in their nation and had always continued in the same family. Thereupon Sanballat promised him not only to preserve for him the honor of his priesthood but also to procure for him the power and dignity of a high priest and to make him governor of all the places which he himself ruled, if he would retain his daughter as his wife. He also told him that he would build him a temple like that at Jerusalem upon Mount Gerizim, which is the highest of all the mountains in Samaria. Moreover he promised that he would do this with the approval of Darius, the king. Manasseh, being elated with these promises, remained with Sanballat, thinking that he would gain a high priesthood as the gift from Darius, for Sanballat was then well advanced in years. Now there was a great disturbance among the people of Jerusalem because many of the priests and Levites were entangled in such marriages, for they all revolted to Manasseh, and Sanballat offered them money and distributed among them land for cultivation and dwelling places also. He did all this in order in every way to gratify his son-in-law.

15. Origin of the Samaritan temple and priesthood (2ᵈ⁻ᵍ)

THE LAST CENTURY OF PERSIAN RULE

I. Prosperity of the Judean Community. Behind their restored walls the Jews of Jerusalem enjoyed a sense of security and peace that had not been theirs since the days of Josiah. At last they were free to develop the limited resources of little Judah and gradually to extend their territory northwestward over the fertile plain of Sharon. At the most their numbers and territory were small. The memories of their glorious past and their hopes for the future were their chief inspiration. The belief that in supporting faithfully the service of the temple and in conforming to the definite demands of the ritual they were winning Jehovah's favor was to them an unfailing source of comfort and thankfulness. In the rich services of the temple and in the contemplation of Jehovah's character and deeds they found true joy. These feelings are expressed in certain of the psalms, as, for example, Psalm 36, which probably comes from this period. In their weakness they looked up in confidence and gratitude to Jehovah who ruled supreme in the heavens, and who was able and eager to preserve those who "put their trust in the shadow of his wings." Their one prayer was that his loving-kindness would continue to protect them.

II. The Growth of the Psalter. Nehemiah's work apparently gave an impulse not only to the development of the law and the temple ritual, but also inspired poets to voice their own feelings and those of the community in certain of the psalms now found in the Psalter. It also encouraged them to collect the earlier religious songs of their race. The result of their work is the first edition of the Hebrew Psalter. In its present form the Psalter, like the Pentateuch, is divided into five books with a general introduction consisting of Psalms 1 and 2 and a concluding doxology (Ps. 150). At the end of each of these divisions are shorter doxologies or brief epilogues (*e. g.*, 41^{13} 72^{19} 89^{52} 106^{48}). The Psalter itself is a library containing a great variety of poems written at different periods, from many different points of view and by many different poets. Like the Priestly Code and the book of Proverbs, it consists of a collection of smaller collections. Thus many psalms in the first half of the Psalter are repeated wholly or in part in later psalms. Psalm 14, for example, is identical with Psalm 73, except that in 14 Jehovah is used as the designation of the Deity and in 73 Elohim (or God).

The problem of determining the date of the individual psalms and of the different collections is exceedingly difficult, both because the superscriptions were clearly added by later editors who thought thereby to connect the psalm with an earlier writer or historic incident, and because the psalms themselves contain few historical allusions. A great

140

majority of them reflect the teachings of the pre-exilic prophets or, like the book of Proverbs, come from the lips of the sages and deal with universal human problems. Some were written by priests or Levites for use in connection with the song service of the temple. Because of this timeless quality, however, an appreciation of them does not depend upon an exact knowledge of their authorship or historical background. It is possible that a few of the psalms in the first part of the Psalter come from the pre-exilic period, but the great majority reflect the problems, the hopes, the fears, and the trials of the faithful who lived under the shadow of the second temple. While the superscriptions clearly do not come from the original psalmists themselves, they do record the conclusions of the editors who made the earliest collections. The oft-recurring title "Psalm to David" either means that by the editor it was attributed to David as the author, or is a general designation of psalms that were recognized to be comparatively early. The two great Davidic collections, 3–41 and 51–72, were apparently collected not long after the rebuilding of the walls of Jerusalem. They are deeply influenced by the inspiring teachings of the II Isaiah. They are remarkably free from that ceremonialism which became a powerful force in Judaism during the last century of the Persian rule. Psalm 51$^{16, 17}$, for example, echoes the noble ethical teachings of the great prophets:

> Thou desirest not sacrifice, else would I give it,
> Thou delightest not in burnt offering,
> The sacrifice of God is a broken heart,
> A broken and a contrite heart, O God, thou wilt not despise.

They represent, therefore, the oldest edition of the Psalter and the songs which were probably sung by the temple singers and the people as they went up to the temple on the great feast days during the closing years of the Persian period.

III. **The Prophecy of Joel.** For a brief moment the clear light of contemporary prophecy is turned upon the Judean community by the little book of Joel. The immediate occasion was the invasion of a great swarm of locusts which swept into Judea either from the desert or from the mountains in the north. It contains in 3^6 the first Old Testament reference to the Greeks. From 3^2 it is evident that the Jewish race has already been widely scattered. In 3^2 the hope is expressed that the time will soon come when strangers shall no longer pass through Jerusalem. The temple, however, and the city walls (2^9) have already been rebuilt, indicating that the prophecy followed the work of Nehemiah.

The priests are exceedingly prominent in the life of the community, and Joel, though a prophet, places great emphasis upon the importance of the ritual. When the community is threatened by the swarms of locusts, whose advance he describes with dramatic imagery, he calls upon the people to sanctify a fast and to summon an assembly, and commands the priests to cry aloud to Jehovah for deliverance.

IV. Hopes of the Jews. In his prophecy Joel has given a very complete description of the hopes which the people entertained regarding the coming day of Jehovah. It is the same day of Jehovah that Zephaniah described (§ LXXXI^v) and yet the portrait is very different. A divine judgment is to be pronounced, not upon Jehovah's people, but upon their foes. Here Joel reveals the influence of Ezekiel's graphic descriptions found in the thirty-eighth and thirty-ninth chapters of his prophecy. Vividly he describes the advance of Israel's hereditary foes. With full panoply of war they are pictured as advancing to the Valley of Jehoshaphat, the valley of judgment (popularly identified with the Kidron), where Jehovah is to pass sentence upon them. Then suddenly, as the harvester puts the sickle in the grain, they shall be cut down and utterly destroyed. Also in the prophet's imagination above this carnage rises Jerusalem, an impregnable fortress for the people of Israel, holy and no longer polluted by the presence of heathen invaders. Peace and prosperity shall then be the lot of Jehovah's people. Above all he will pour out his purifying, enlightening spirit upon all classes, so that young and old, slave and free, shall be inspired by the consciousness of his message and presence in their hearts.

V. Rule of the High Priests. The few facts that have been preserved regarding the external history of the Judean community during the last century of the Persian rule are in striking contrast to the inner life and hopes of the people. At their head were the high priests, whose names we know, Eliashib, Johanan, and Jaddua. They constituted a hereditary aristocracy intrenched in the temple, which controlled not only the religious but also the civil life of the Jews. Like all hierarchies it lacked the corrective influence of a superior civil authority. The one safeguard of popular liberties, however, was the written law, which was fast becoming the absolute authority in the life of the community. To it the people could appeal even against the decisions of the priests. It therefore kept alive that inherited democratic spirit which had been the priceless possession of Israel through all its history.

There is every reason for accepting the detailed account which Josephus has given of the quarrel between the high priest Johanan and his brother Joshua which resulted in the murder of the latter within the sacred temple precincts. Such an opportunity would naturally be improved by the greedy Persian official to impose an onerous tax upon the Jews. The Elephantine letter establishes the fact that Johanan was high priest in 411 B.C. and that Baghohi (of which Bagoses is the Jewish equivalent) was the Persian satrap. It thus directly confirms the testimony of Josephus. References in late Greek writings (Solinus XXXV, 6; Syncellus I, 486) suggest that the Jews about 350 B.C. were involved with the Phœnicians in the rebellion against Persia. These historians state that at this time Jericho was captured and destroyed and that a part of the Jewish people were transported to the province of Hyrcania at the south of the Caspian Sea. The rebellion was instigated by Tachos, the ruler of Egypt, who about 362 not only shook off the rule of Persia, but invaded Syria and stirred up the Phœnicians to defy the Persian king. Artaxerxes III, popularly known as Ochus, proved, however, the last ruler who was able to revive the waning power of the Persian Empire. At his accession he slew all the members of the royal family, and throughout his reign (358–337 B.C.) he trusted chiefly to the unsheathed sword to maintain his authority. In 346 B.C. he finally succeeded in collecting a huge army with which he invaded Syria and besieged Sidon. Its king betrayed his city into the hands of the Persians, only to be murdered by the treacherous Ochus. The citizens of Sidon, recognizing that they would receive no mercy from the hands of their conqueror, shut themselves up in their homes and then burned them over their heads. According to the Greek historians forty thousand Phœnicians perished in this revolt.

VI. **The Date of the Samaritan Schism.** Josephus has given an unusually full and detailed account of the final schism between the Jews and Samaritans. He dates it under the high priesthood of Jaddua, who died shortly after the close of the Persian period. He implies, therefore, that the schism took place not long before 332 B.C., when Alexander the Great conquered Palestine. This is also in keeping with the fact that the Elephantine letter written in 411 B.C. knows nothing of a division between Jew and Gentile. The fact that at the time of the division the defecting priests took from Jerusalem the Pentateuch in its final form strongly confirms the conclusion (as Professor Torrey has pointed out in his *Ezra Studies*, pp. 324–330) that the Sanballat who ruled over the Samaritan community was not the contemporary of Nehemiah, but his grandson, who as an old man was ruling in Samaria at the time when Alexander conquered the East.

VII. The Nature and Consequences of the Schism. The schism between Jew and Samaritan was but a revival of the ancient rivalry which dated from the days when the Israelites had first settled in Canaan. The destruction of Samaria in 722 and the strong policy of Josiah had apparently led the Samaritans to look to the temple at Jerusalem as the chief sanctuary of the land. Shechem, however, and Mount Gerizim, which rises abruptly on the south, enjoyed traditions which dated from the earliest days of Israel's history. The sacred oak and altar at Shechem figured even in the patriarchal period. At the temple of Baal-berith in Shechem apparently both Canaanites and Israelites worshipped during the days of the settlement. According to the Samaritan version of Deuteronomy 24[4], Mount Gerizim, not Ebal or Jerusalem, was the place where the Israelites, after entering Canaan, were first commanded to rear an altar to Jehovah, and to inscribe upon it the laws given to Moses. Even in the Jewish version of Deuteronomy 11[29] and 27[12] Mount Gerizim is the mountain of blessing. In the light of these passages such commands as, for example, that in Deuteronomy 12[4, 5] would naturally be interpreted by the Samaritans as a reference to Gerizim rather than to Jerusalem. The destruction of the Judean capital and temple gave a great incentive to the revival of these ancient traditions and a new prestige to the northern sanctuary. Until the close of the Persian period, however, the Samaritans evidently regarded Jerusalem as an important shrine and worshipped there side by side with the Jews. The ultimate schism appears to have come as a result of the growing jealousy with which certain of the Jews regarded foreign marriages. The marriage of Manasseh, the brother of Jaddua the high priest, to Nicaso, the daughter of Sanballat II, and his ultimate expulsion by the Jews blew into a flame the smouldering jealousy and opposition that had long existed between the two communities. As Josephus recounts, Sanballat, in order to satisfy his son-in-law, ceded lands and special rights to him and to the other Jerusalem priests, who were attracted by these offers, and ultimately built the famous temple on Mount Gerizim over which Manasseh and his descendants presided. In many ways the temple and service on Mount Gerizim appear to have been duplicates of those at Jerusalem. The same law was recognized by both communities; they shared together the same traditions and the same ideals; and yet their subsequent history illustrates the psychological truth that of all forms of hatred that between brothers is the most venomous and lasting. The bitter rivalry and growing hatred that resulted from this act are reflected even in the wisdom teachings of Ben

Sira (B. Sir. 47[21, 24, 25]). They also fundamentally color the writings of the Chronicler. The strenuous efforts that he made to discountenance the claims of the Samaritans reveals the intensity of the feud even in the Greek period (*cf.* II Chron. 11[13-16]). His zeal in trying to prove that the rebuilders of the Jerusalem temple were of Jewish extraction was doubtless inspired by the Samaritan charge that during the Babylonian and Persian periods they had freely intermarried with the heathen population of the land. He was compelled to admit that even the high priestly families had been guilty of this sin, but asserted that the foreign wives were later divorced or else the offenders were expelled from Jerusalem. In the light of the oldest records it appears that the Samaritans were able to establish almost as pure a lineage as the Jews. Naturally during the succeeding years the ancient breach continued to widen until it was beyond all healing.

THE GREEK AND MACCABEAN AGE

§ CIV. THE JEWS UNDER THEIR GREEK RULERS

1.
Alex-
ander's
con-
quests
(I Mac.
1¹⁻⁴)

Now after Alexander the Macedonian, the son of Philip, who came from the land of the Greeks, had smitten Darius king of the Persians and Medes, he reigned in his place as the first ruler of the Syrian kingdom.

> He fought many battles,
> And won many strongholds,
> And slew the kings of the earth;
> He went on to the ends of the earth;
> And took spoils from a multitude of nations.
> And when the earth was at peace before him,
> He was exalted and his heart was lifted up;
> He gathered an exceedingly great army,
> And ruled over countries and peoples and principalities;
> And they became tributary to him.

2.
Death
of Jad-
dua
(Jos.
Ant.
XI,
8⁷ᵃˑ c)

Now when Alexander was dead, the government was divided among his successors. It was about this time that Jaddua the high priest died and Onias, his son, took the high priesthood.

3.
Egypt
and
Syria
under
Alex-
ander's
suc-
cessors
(XII,
1¹ᵇ⁻ᵈ)

Alexander's empire was divided among many: Antigonus gained possession of the province of Asia; Seleucus of Babylon and the surrounding nations; Lysimachus governed the Hellespont, and Cassander held Macedonia; Ptolemy, the son of Lagus, got Egypt. While these princes ambitiously contended with one another, each for his own kingdom, there were continual and protracted wars. And the cities suffered and lost many of their inhabitants in these days of distress, so that all Syria experienced at the hands of Ptolemy, the son of Lagus, the opposite of what is implied by his title of saviour. He also captured Jerusalem by means of deceit and treachery; for, coming into the city on a sabbath day, as if to offer sacrifices, he without difficulty gained pos-

146

session of the city, since the Jews did not oppose him, for they did not suspect him to be their enemy, and that day they always spent in rest and quietness. And when he had gained possession of it, he ruled over it in a cruel manner.

And when Ptolemy had taken many captives both from the mountainous parts of Judea and the places about Jerusalem and Samaria and Mount Gerizim, he led them all into Egypt and settled them there. And since he knew that the people of Jerusalem were most faithful in keeping their oaths and convenants, he distributed many of them among garrisons. At Alexandria he gave them equal privileges as citizens with the Macedonians themselves. He also required them to take oath that they would be faithful to his descendants. And not a few other Jews went into Egypt of their own accord, attracted both by the goodness of the soil and Ptolemy's generosity. However, there were disorders between their descendants and the Samaritans because of their resolve to preserve that manner of life which was transmitted to them by their forefathers. They accordingly contended with each other; those from Jerusalem said that their temple was holy and they resolved to send their sacrifices there, but the Samaritans were determined that they should be sent to Mount Gerizim.

4. Fortunes of the Jews in Egypt under Ptolemy Soter (1g-i)

When Alexander had reigned twelve years and after him Ptolemy Soter forty years, Ptolemy Philadelphus next had the kingdom of Egypt and held it thirty-nine years.

5. The rulers of Egypt (2ia)

Now when Onias I. the high priest died, his son Simon succeeded him. When he died and left only a young son called Onias, Simon's brother Eleazer took the high priesthood. After Eleazar's death, his uncle Manasseh assumed the priesthood, and after he died, Onias II. received that honor. This Onia was lacking in sense and was a great lover of money; for that reason he did not pay the tax of twenty talents of silver for the people, which his forefathers had paid out of their own estates to the kings of Egypt. Thus he aroused the anger of King Ptolemy Euergetes, the father of Philopator. Euergetes sent an ambassador to Jerusalem and complained that Onias did not pay the taxes and threatened that if he did not receive them, he would parcel out their land and send soldiers to live upon it. When the Jews heard this message

6. Rule of the Jewish high priests (2³ᵈ, e 4ⁱᵈ-f)

147

of the king they were filled with dismay, but Onias was so avaricious that nothing of this kind made him ashamed.

7. Rise of Joseph the tax-collector (2a-f)

There was a certain Joseph, young in years, but of great reputation among the people of Jerusalem for dignity and exact foresight. His father's name was Tobias and his mother was the sister of Onias the high priest. She informed him of the coming of Ptolemy's ambassador. Thereupon Joseph came to Jerusalem and reproved Onias for not taking thought for the security of his countrymen and for bringing the nation into dangers by not paying this money. Onias's answer was that he did not care for his authority, that he was ready, if it were possible, to lay down his high priesthood, and that he would not go to the king, for he cared nothing at all about these matters. Joseph then asked him if he would give him leave to go as ambassador on behalf of the nation. He replied that he would. So Joseph went down from the temple and treated Ptolemy's ambassador in a hospitable manner. He also presented him with rich gifts and feasted him magnificently for many days and then sent him to the king before him and told him that he would soon follow him.

8. The reward of his audacity (3b, 4a-e)

Now it happened that at this time all the principal men and rulers of the cities of Syria and Phœnicia went up to bid for the taxes; for every year the king sold them to the most powerful men of each city. And when the day came on which the king was to let the farming of the taxes of the cities, the taxes of Cœle-Syria, Phœnicia, Judea and Samaria amounted altogether to eight thousand talents. Thereupon Joseph accused the bidders of having agreed together to estimate the value of the taxes at too low a rate and he promised that he would give twice as much for them, and for those who did not pay he would send the king their entire possessions, for this privilege was sold together with the taxes. The king was pleased to hear this offer, and because it increased his revenues he said he would confirm the sale of the taxes to him.

9. Establishment of his authority (5a-c, 6, 6a)

And Joseph took with him two thousand soldiers from the king, for he desired to have assistance in order to compel those who refused in the city to pay. And when the people of Askelon refused to pay anything, he seized about twenty of their principal men and slew them, and gathered what they had and sent it all to the king and informed him what he had done. Ptolemy admired the spirit of the man, commended him for what he had done and gave him permission to do as he pleased. By these means he amassed great wealth and made vast profits by this farming of taxes. And he made use of the wealth he had thus secured in order to support his authority. This good fortune he enjoyed for twenty-two years; and he became the father of seven sons by one wife. He had also another son whose name was Hyrcanus.

Now in the reign of Antiochus the Great, who ruled over all Asia, the Jews, as well as the inhabitants of Cœle-Syria, suffered greatly, and their land was sorely harassed, for while Antiochus was at war with Ptolemy Philopator and his son Ptolemy, who was called Epiphanes, these nations suffered equally both when he was defeated and when he was victorious. So they were like a ship in the storm which is tossed by the waves on both sides. 10 Misfortunes of the Judean community (3³ᵃ, b)

But at length when Antiochus had beaten Ptolemy he seized Judea. And when Philopator was dead, his son sent out against the inhabitants of Cœle-Syria a great army under Scopas, general of his forces, and took many of their cities and especially our people, who, when he attacked them, went over to him. But soon afterwards Antiochus overcame Scopas in a battle fought at the fountains of the Jordan and destroyed a great part of his army. And afterwards, when Antiochus subdued those cities of Cœle-Syria which Scopas had captured, and Samaria among them, the Jews of their own accord went over to him and received him into Jerusalem and gave plentiful provisions to all his army and readily assisted him when he besieged the garrison which was in the citadel at Jerusalem. 11. Capture of Palestine by the Syrian king (3³ᶜ⁻ᵉ)

I. Josephus's Histories. The Greek period began with Alexander's conquest of Palestine in 332 and extended to the Maccabean uprising in 168 B.C. For the external history of this period the writings of the historian Josephus are the chief sources. This famous Jewish writer was born in 37 A.D., and apparently lived till about the close of the reign of Domitian in 96. According to his own testimony he was the son of a priest named Mattathiah. Until he was sixteen he studied under the Jewish rabbis. He then spent three years with the Jewish sect known as the Essenes. At the age of nineteen he joined the party of the Pharisees. His point of view in general is that of this dominant popular party. He was able to read Latin, but wrote his histories in Greek. At the age of twenty-six he went to Rome where he spent three years. Returning to Palestine at the beginning of the great rebellion against Rome, he was appointed revolutionary governor of the important province of Galilee. The appointment was unfortunate, for he proved both incompetent and unreliable. In 67 A.D. he and his followers were shut up by Vespasian in the Galilean city, Jotapata. During the siege he vainly tried to desert to the enemy. At the fall of the city he was captured, but his life was spared by Vespasian. In time he ingratiated himself with Titus and also incurred the hostility of his countrymen by trying to persuade them to lay down their arms. He spent the latter part of his life in Rome, devoting himself to study and writing. As a result of his long residence at Rome under the patronage of the Roman emperors, he was powerfully influenced by the Greek and Roman philosophical schools.

Josephus was the great apologist of his race. His chief aims in writing his histories were: (1) to excuse his own acts in connection with the great rebellion; (2) to show why the overwhelming calamity had overtaken his race; and (3) to answer the attack of their Gentile foes by tracing the remarkable history of his people, and by presenting in attractive form their beliefs, institutions, and laws. Of his two great historical works the one entitled *The Jewish War* was issued probably between 75 and 79 A.D. It opens with the beginnings of the Maccabean struggle, and traces the history, with increasing detail, to the destruction of Jerusalem and the suppression of the Jewish revolt at Cyrene, two or three years before the book was written. His second great work was issued in 93 A.D. under the title of *The Antiquities of the Jews*. In twenty books it traces Israel's history from the earliest beginnings to the opening years of the Jewish war (68 A.D.). The first half of this extensive history is based on the author's free paraphrase of the Greek version of the Old Testament. For the latter half he draws largely from the apocryphal book of I Maccabees and from the writings of contemporary Greek and Jewish historians. Chief among these are Polybius, Nicolaus of Damascus, and Strabo. At certain points, where earlier sources fail him, he employs popular romances and late traditions. The result is that the different parts of his history are of widely varying values. All must be carefully tested by the canons of historical criticism. After due allowance has been made for his apologetic purpose and his well-known tendencies, a large and valuable body of historical facts remain with which it is possible at many otherwise obscure points to reconstruct the course of Israel's history.

II. **Alexander's Conquests.** In many ways Alexander's conquest was the most significant and far-reaching event in the history of Asia. The causes of this great movement were, first, the fact that the limited territory of Greece and Macedonia gave to the powerful Hellenic civilization little opportunity for local expansion. Compelled, therefore, to break these narrow bonds, it naturally spread in the direction of least resistance. In the second place the decadent Persian Empire, with its fabulous riches and almost limitless plains, was a loadstone that lured on Greek adventurers to attempt feats that seemed incredible. The third reason was Alexander's inherited lust for conquest. His father, Philip of Macedon, had long been accumulating the resources which made it possible for his son to realize his ambitious dreams. The fourth reason was Alexander's desire to make the world more glorious by the diffusion of Hellenic culture, ideas, and institutions and by binding all races together into one great, harmonious family. His brilliant conquests are a familiar chapter in the world's history. At Issus, at the northeastern end of the Mediterranean, he won, in 333 B.C., the decisive battle which left him in possession of the western part of the huge Persian Empire. By 332 he was master of Palestine. Tyre, the commercial mistress of the eastern Mediterranean, and Gaza, the key to Egypt, alone offered resistance. The Persian kings by their onerous taxation and cruel policy had completely destroyed the loyalty of their western subjects. In the symbolic pictures of the book of Daniel Alexander is regarded as the "fourth beast, terrible and fearful and exceedingly strong. And it had great iron teeth. It devoured and broke in pieces, and stamped the rest with its feet" ($7^{17, 23}$, 8^{5-8}). Josephus has preserved a popular tradition regarding the meeting between Alexander and the white-robed Jerusalem priests and the homage paid by the conqueror to the God of the Jews. It bears on its face evidence of its unhistorical character. As a matter of fact, the first goal of Alexander's conquest was the rich land of Egypt. Not being possessed of a navy, he entered it through its one vulnerable point, the Wady Tumilat, that ran from the Isthmus of Suez to the Nile Delta. By 331 B.C. he was master of the Nile Valley, and thence turned eastward, conquering in succession the different provinces of the great empire, until before his death in 323 B.C.

his empire extended from the Mediterranean to the Indus, and in the northeast far up toward central Asia.

Alexander's conquests were significant because they represented the victory of Greek ideas and culture as well as of arms. In each country conquered he usually succeeded in Hellenizing the native peoples. Greek cities, settled by his veterans and the horde of migratory Greeks that followed in his wake, were founded at strategic points throughout the vast empire. As recent excavations have shown, Greek art and ideas continued even after the death of Alexander to sweep eastward across Asia, until they profoundly influenced the culture and ideas in such distant nations as China and Japan.

III. **The Jews in Egypt and Alexandria.** The crown of Alexander's constructive work was the building of Alexandria in Egypt. Selecting a narrow strip of coast, protected on the south by the low-lying lake Mareotis and on the north by the Mediterranean, he built there a magnificent Greek city. On the south it was connected by canal with the Canopic arm of the Nile. Alexander thus diverted to this new metropolis the rich trade of the Red Sea and the Nile. A mile distant was the island of Pharos, which was connected with the mainland by a great mole. On either side, protected from the storms, were the eastern and western harbors, large enough to accommodate the merchant-men and navies of the ancient world. On the west was the native Egyptian quarter. In the centre, opposite the island of Pharos, was the Greek and official quarter. In the northeastern part of the city was the Jewish quarter. Here the Jews lived together under the rule of their law; they were also represented in the civic council by their own leaders. When Ptolemy, the son of Lagus, became governor of Egypt and, after the death of Alexander, subjected Palestine, he carried back to Alexandria many Jewish captives, and attracted others by the special privileges which he granted them. In them he recognized valuable allies in developing the commercial resources of Alexandria and in maintaining his rule over the native Egyptians. Here in time the Jews became wealthy and powerful and developed a unique civilization. From the beginning of the Greek period the number of the Jews in Egypt equalled, if it did not surpass, that of the Jews in Palestine. While they maintained close connection with the Jews in Palestine and remained true to their Scriptures, they were profoundly influenced by their close contact with the civilization and ideas of the Greek world.

IV. **The Rule of the Ptolemies.** The long-continued rule of the Ptolemies in Egypt is one of the most astonishing phenomena in this

THE RULE OF THE PTOLEMIES

remarkable period in human history. Far outnumbered by the native population, involved in almost constant war with their fellow-Greeks, they succeeded by sheer audacity and vigilance in maintaining their authority during the many crises through which they passed. Egypt's natural defences also made its conquest by outside powers exceedingly difficult. Alexandria with its fleet commanded Egypt's one entrance by the sea. In order to protect its eastern gateway, the Isthmus of Suez, it was essential that the Ptolemies should control Palestine. Southern Palestine also commanded the great commercial highway that led southward and eastward to Arabia and Babylonia. Alexandria's ancient rivals, Tyre and Sidon, also lay on the borders of Palestine, and it was essential that they be under the control of Egypt, if Alexandria was to remain the mistress of the eastern Mediterranean. Furthermore, Palestine and the Lebanons (known to Josephus as Cœle-Syria, that is, Hollow Syria), alone of the countries adjacent to Egypt, possessed the timber required for the building of Alexandria's navies and merchantmen. Hence Ptolemy, the son of Lagus, and his successors spared no effort to maintain their control over the lands lying along the eastern Mediterranean.

In the division of the empire which followed the death of Alexander three rivals struggled in turn for this coveted territory: Ptolemy, in the south; Antigonus, who soon became master of Asia Minor and northern Syria; and Seleucus, to whom fell the Tigris-Euphrates Valley and the more distant eastern provinces. In the decisive battle of Ipsus in 301 B.C. the overshadowing power of Antigonus was broken and the control of southwestern Asia was divided between Seleucus and Ptolemy. By the treaty that was made after the battle, Cœle-Syria was given to Ptolemy; but Seleucus and his descendants, who were known as the Seleucids or the Seleucidæ, soon attempted to wrest it from Egypt, and during the following century frequently, with varying success, renewed the attempt. In 295 and again in 219 they were for a brief period masters of Palestine, but during most of this period it was held by the Ptolemies.

V. Fortunes of the Jews of Palestine. Josephus's figure of a ship in a storm, smitten by the waves on either side, well describes the lot of the Jews of Palestine during the Greek period. They were in turn victimized and courted by the rival kings of Egypt and Syria. The Jews, on the whole, favored the rule of the Ptolemies, who had made many concessions to their kinsmen in Egypt. The presence of many Jews in Egypt also made this relation more natural. As a rule the

153

Ptolemies during the intervals of peace left the Jews of Palestine largely to themselves, as long as they paid the heavy tribute that was exacted. It was, however, one of the most corrupt periods in human history. The Ptolemaic court was rich, profligate, and constantly degenerating. The popular story of Joseph the tax-collector (which Josephus recounts at length), while largely fanciful, vividly reflects the conditions and spirit of the age. Joseph, who evidently belonged to one of the leading families of Jerusalem, by his energy and effrontery secured the valuable right of farming the taxes of Palestine. By the iniquitous methods then in vogue, he succeeded in amassing a great fortune. The splendid ruins of Arak el-Emir on the heights of southern Gilead, east of the Jordan, represent the huge castle and town built by his son Hyrcanus and testify to the wealth of this Jewish adventurer. The stories that Josephus relates regarding Joseph indicate that the materialism and sensuality which were regnant in Alexandria had penetrated even into the province of Judea.

The one bright spot in the political history of this period is the reign of the high priest Simon, known as the Just. He appears to have devoted himself to developing, so far as was in his power, the interests and resources of the Palestinian Jews and to have lifted the temple service to a state of magnificence that received the unqualified commendation of Jesus, the son of Sirach.

VI. Conquest of Palestine by the Seleucids in 311 B.C. Seleucus Nikanor transferred the western capital of his empire, known as Syria (a shortened form of the ancient name Assyria), to Antioch, near the northeastern end of the Mediterranean. This city was situated at the point where the Orontes breaks through the Lebanons and where the great roads from the Euphrates and Cœle-Syria converge and run westward to its seaport, Seleucia. It was built in the midst of a fertile valley, partly on an island in the river and partly on its northern bank. Not having natural defences, the city depended for protection upon its broad, encompassing walls. To this new capital was attracted a diverse native, Greek, and Jewish population. By virtue of its strategic position and its commercial and political importance, it soon became one of the great cities of the eastern Mediterranean. It occupied the natural site on the eastern Mediterranean seaboard for the capital of a great empire. Shut in by the sea on the west and the desert on the east, Syria's natural line of expansion was north and south. Not until 198 B.C., however, under the rule of Antiochus the Great, did it secure permanent control of Palestine. The degenerate house of the Ptolemies made several ineffectual attempts to win back their lost province, but henceforth Palestine remained under the rule of Syria. The personal attractions of Antiochus the Great, the specious promises which he made, and disgust because of the corrupt rule of Egypt inclined the Jews of Palestine to welcome this change of rulers. The court at Antioch, however, soon became almost as corrupt as that of Egypt, and the Jews were the victims of the greed and caprice of the Syrian despots. Meantime the insidious Greek culture and vices were influencing and largely undermining the character of the Jewish rulers. Judaism was unconsciously facing a supreme crisis in its history.

§ CV. THE WISE AND THEIR TEACHINGS

That men may learn wisdom and instruction,
May understand intelligent discourses,
May receive instruction in wise conduct,
In justice, judgment and equity;
That discretion may be given to the inexperienced,
To the youth knowledge and a purpose;
That the wise man may hear and increase in learning,
And the intelligent man may receive counsel,
That he may understand proverb and parable,
The words of the wise and their riddles.

1. Aims of the wise (Pr. 1²⁻⁶)

Does not Wisdom call?
And Understanding raise her voice?
On the top of high places by the way,
In the midst of the street she stands,
Beside the gateways in front of the city,
At the entrance of the gates she cries aloud:
To you, O men, I call,
And my appeal is to the sons of men.
O inexperienced, acquire discretion,
And ye stupid, gain understanding.
Hear, for I speak true things,
And the utterance of my lips is right.

2. Their appeal to men (8¹⁻⁶)

Pride and arrogance and evil conduct
And false speech do I hate.

3. Antagonistic to evil (¹³)

155

4. Indispensable to rulers (14-16)

With me is counsel and practical knowledge;
With me understanding and might.
By me kings do reign,
And rulers decree justice.
By me princes rule,
And nobles judge the land.

5. Easily found (17)

I love those who love me,
Those who seek me diligently shall find me.

6. Inestimable value of their teachings (18-21)

Riches and honor are with me,
Lordly wealth and prosperity.
My fruit is better than gold, yea, than fine gold,
And my increase than choice silver.
I walk in the way of righteousness,
In the midst of the paths of justice,
That I may endow those who love me with wealth,
And that I may fill their treasuries.

7. Place of wisdom in the universe: first of God's creation (22-26)

Jehovah formed me as the beginning of his creation,
The first of his works of old,
In the primeval past was I formed,
In the beginning, before the earth was,
When there were no depths, I was brought forth,
When there were no fountains full of water.
Before the mountains were settled,
Before the hills were brought forth,
When he had not as yet made the earth,
Nor the first of the dust of the world.

8. Present and active at the creation (27, 29, 30)

When he established the heavens, I was there,
When he marked off the vault on the face of the deep,
Made fast the fountains of the deep,
When he set to the sea its bound,
When he marked out the foundations of the earth,
Then I was at his side as a foster-child;
And I was daily full of delight,
Sporting in his presence continually,
Sporting in his habitable earth.

And my delight is with the sons of men;
Now therefore, my sons, hearken to me,
Hear instruction that you may be wise,
And reject it not.
Happy is the man who hearkens to me,
Happy are they who walk in my ways,
Watching daily at my gates,
Waiting at the posts of my doors.
For he who finds me finds life,
And obtains favor from Jehovah.

9. Able
to guide
men
(31-35)

The teaching of the wise is a fountain of life
That man may avoid the ways of death.
Walk with the wise and you will become wise,
But he who associates with fools shall smart for it.
A wise man is better than a strong man,
And a man who has knowledge than he who has
    strength.

10.
Practical
value of
learning
from
the wise
(13¹⁴, ²⁰
24⁵)

A wise man has regard for the well-being of his beast,
But the heart of the wicked is cruel.

11.
Man's
duty to
animals
(12¹⁰)

Love not sleep lest you come to poverty;
Open your eyes and you shall have plenty.

12.
Temperance
in
sleeping
(20¹³)

If you find honey, eat what is sufficient for you,
Lest you be surfeited with it and vomit it up.

13. In
eating
(25¹⁶)

Who cries, Woe? who, Alas?
Who has contentions?   Who, complaining?
Who has dullness of eyes?
They who linger long over wine,
They who go about tasting mixed wine.
Look not upon the wine when it is red,
When it sparkles in the cup.
At last it bites like a serpent,
And stings like an adder.
Your eyes shall see strange things,
And your mind shall suggest queer things.

14. In
drinking
(23⁹⁻³⁵)

157

You shall be like one sleeping at sea,
Like one asleep in a great storm.
" They have struck me, but I feel no pain;
They have beaten me, but I feel it not;
I will seek it yet again.   When shall I awake from my
   wine?"

15. In speech (29²⁰ 15²³)

Do you see a man hasty in his words?
There is more hope for a fool than for him.
A man has joy from the utterance of his mouth,
And a word in due season, how good it is!

16. Restraint of anger (19¹¹ 16³²)

A man's wisdom makes him slow to anger,
And it is his glory to pass over transgression.
He who is slow to anger is better than the mighty,
And he who rules his spirit than he who takes a
   city.

17. Sensual passions (23²⁶⁻²⁸)

My son, give me your attention,
And let your eyes give careful heed to my ways.
For a harlot is a deep well,
And an adultress is a narrow pit.
Yea, she lies in wait as a robber,
And increases the faithless among men.

18. Duty to resist temptation (4²⁵⁻²⁷)

Let your eyes look right straight forward,
And let your gaze be straight before you.
Let the path of your feet be level,
And let all your ways be stable.
Turn not to the right hand nor to the left,
Keep your foot away from evil.

19. To be prudent (14¹⁵)

The simpleton believes everything,
But the prudent man looks well to where he walks.

20. To be modest (26¹² 27²)

Do you see a man wise in his own conceit?
There is more hope of a fool than him.
Let another man praise you and not your own mouth;
Some other, and not your own lips.

Keep your heart above all that you guard,
For out of it are the issues of life.
The righteousness of the upright shall save them,
But the treacherous are caught by their own desire.

21. To be pure in purpose (4²², 11⁶)

To do what is just and right
Is more acceptable to Jehovah than sacrifice.

22. To do what is right (21³)

A soft answer turns away wrath;
But a harsh word stirs up anger.

23. To strive for peace (15¹)

Withhold not good from your neighbor,
When it is in your power to do it.
Say not to your neighbor, "Go, and come again,
And to-morrow I will give," when you have it by you.

24. To be generous (3²⁷)

He who despises his neighbor, sins,
But he who has pity on the poor, happy is he.
He who has pity on the poor, lends to Jehovah,
And his good deed will yet pay him.

25. To be merciful (14²¹, 19¹⁷)

If your enemy be hungry, give him bread to eat,
And if he be thirsty, give him water to drink;
For you will heap coals of fire upon his head,
And Jehovah will reward you.

26. To be kind to an enemy (25²¹, ²²)

My son, reject not the instruction of Jehovah,
And do not grow weary of his reproof,
For whom Jehovah loveth he reproveth,
Even as a father the son in whom he delights.

27. To heed divine instruction (3¹¹, ¹²)

Trust in Jehovah with all your heart,
And depend not upon your own understanding.
In all your ways know him well,
And he will make plain your path.

28. To trust and seek God's guidance (5, 6)

I. Structure and Authorship of the Book of Proverbs. The book of Proverbs is in reality a collection of originally independent groups of proverbs. In its present form it consists of nine general divisions: (1) The preface defining the aims of the book, 1^{1-6}. (2) A general introduction describing the characteristics and value of the wisdom teaching, 1^7-9^{18}. (3) A large collection designated as the Proverbs of Solomon, 10^1-22^{16}. The fact that ten proverbs are repeated in practically the same words indicates that it, like the book of Proverbs as a whole, is made up of smaller collections. In chapters 10–15 the prevailing type of the poetic parallelism is antithetic or contrasting, while in the remainder of the book the synonymous or repeating parallelism prevails. (4) A supplemental collection, $22^{17}-24^{22}$. This is introduced by the suggestive superscription, "Incline your ear and hear the words of the wise." (5) A shorter appendix, 24^{23-34}, with the superscription, "These also are from the wise." (6) The second large collection of proverbs, 25–29. This bears the superscription, "These also are the proverbs of Solomon which the men of Hezekiah, king of Judah, transcribed." It contains several proverbs found in the first large collection, and evidently represents later gleanings from the same field. (7) The words of Agur, 30. Of Agur nothing is known beyond his name, which may be simply typical. The latter part of the chapter contains a collection of numerical enigmas which may or may not have been associated at first with the opening section. (8) The words of King Lemuel, 31^{1-9}. (9) A description of the ideal Hebrew housewife, 31^{10-31}. The contents of these collections as well as their superscriptions clearly indicate that these proverbs represent the work of many different wise men, living at different periods and writing from different points of view. Few, if any, can be confidently attributed to Solomon. Even the proverbs in the large collection, 10^1-22^{16}, which are definitely designated as the Proverbs of Solomon, emphasize monogamy and denounce rulers who oppress their subjects. Many of the proverbs in these larger Solomonic collections give practical advice regarding the bearing of a subject in the presence of the king, and few of them fit in the mouth of the splendor-loving monarch, who by his foreign marriages and grinding taxation exerted a baleful influence upon the political and religious life of Israel. The great majority of the proverbs reflect the noble ethical teachings of the prophets. Clearly the term Proverbs of Solomon is simply a late designation of early proverbs the authorship of which, like that of most popular maxims, had long since been forgotten.

II. **Date of the Different Collections.** The preface and general introduction to the book of Proverbs reflect the immorality and evils that characterized both the Persian and Greek periods. Their background is the corrupt life of the city. The tendency to personify wisdom is also one of the marks of later Jewish thought. It is probable, therefore, that this part of the book of Proverbs was added by a late editor who lived during the Greek period. The oldest collection in the book is clearly to be found in 10^1–22^{16}. The evils which it describes, the oppression of the poor and dependent by the rich and powerful, existed throughout most of Israel's history, but were especially prominent in the days of the divided kingdom immediately before the destruction of Jerusalem. The references to the king imply that the proverb writers had in mind Hebrew rulers. In general their rule is just and they enjoy the respect of their subjects. The prevailing occupation of the people is agriculture. Commerce is just beginning to develop. The exile has not yet cast its shadow over Hebrew life and thought. The majority of these proverbs clearly represent the fruitage of the teachings of the pre-exilic prophets, and many of them come from the days immediately before the final destruction of Jerusalem. From the occasional references to the scoffers, the absence of allusions to idolatry, and the fact that monogamy is here assumed, we may infer that some of them at least come from the Persian or even the Greek periods. It is probable that this large collection was not made until the latter part of the Persian or the early part of the Greek period.

The appendices in 22^{17}–24^{34} contain many repetitions of proverbs found in the larger collection. The prevalence of intemperance, the existence of a merchant class, and the allusions to exiled Jews (e. g., 24^{11}) point rather clearly to the dissolute Greek period as the age when these small collections were made. The word meaning "transcribe," that is found in the superscription to the second large collection (25–29), is peculiar to the late Hebrew, and implies that this superscription, like those of the Psalms, was added by a late Jewish scribe. The literary form of these proverbs is more complex than those of the other large collection. The kings are feared by their subjects, but figure now as oppressors rather than champions of the people. While this collection may contain a few proverbs coming from the period before the final destruction of Jerusalem, it is probable that, like the smaller appendices to the first large collection, they were not gathered until the early part of the Greek period. The long appendices in chapters 30–31 are clearly late. The note of doubt in the opening section of 30 is closely akin to that which recurs in the book of Ecclesiastes. It is also based on Isaiah 44^5 and 45^4. Aramaisms and the acrostic form in 31^{10-31} imply that the background was the late Persian or early Greek period.

The history of the book of Proverbs is therefore reasonably clear. Its

THE WISE AND THEIR TEACHINGS

original nucleus was probably a small group of popular proverbs that had been transmitted orally from the days before the final destruction of Jerusalem. These, together with proverbs which first became current during the Persian period, were collected some time in the days following the work of Nehemiah. To these was added in the Greek period the smaller appendices in 22^{17}–24^{34}. Possibly the same editor joined to them the large collection found in 25–29. He or some wise man in the Greek period prefixed the elaborate introduction in chapters 1–9. To the whole was added the appendices in chapters 30 and 31. It is probable that by the middle of the Greek period, or at least before 200 B.C., the book of Proverbs was complete in its present form.

III. **The Wise in Israel's Early History.** Long before 2000 B.C. the scribes of ancient Egypt were busy collecting "the words of counsel of the men of olden time." Many of these ancient maxims still survive. The best-known is that which bears the title "The Wisdom of Ptah-hotep." The desire to preserve and transmit the results of practical experience is the common motive that underlies the work of the wise. It is that which inspires the teachers of all ages. The ancients were keenly alive to the importance of instruction and training. All that is significant in the civilizations of the past is, in a sense, the result of this teaching motif.

In early Israel there were many men and women famous for their ability to give wise counsel. In his stormy career Joab, David's valiant commander, frequently profited by the counsel of certain wise women (§ LIII$^{8-11}$ LIX^{35}). David's friend Hushai, by his wily counsel at the time of Absalom's rebellion, saved the king's life. The narrative in II Samuel declares that the counsel of Ahithophel was esteemed almost as highly as the divine oracle. For his keen insight and acute decisions, as well as for his witty utterances, Solomon gained a reputation which made him in the thought of later generations the father of all wisdom literature. In a significant passage found in Jeremiah 18^{18} the three classes of Israel's teachers are brought into sharp contrast. In urging that the prophet be put to death his foes declared: "Teaching will not perish from the priest, nor counsel from the wise, nor the word from the prophet." From references in Isaiah and Jeremiah it is evident that before the final destruction of the Hebrew state the counsel of the wise was chiefly political and secular, and often not in accord with the higher ideals of the great pre-exilic prophets.

IV. **Their Prominence in the Greek Period.** The transformation of the wise into religious as well as secular teachers apparently came

162

after the destruction of Jerusalem. It was the result of a variety of forces which have already been studied. The destruction of the Hebrew state and the resulting prominence of the individual led the wise to turn their attention from questions of political to those of personal import. The result is that the word "Israel" is found nowhere in the book of Proverbs. The teachings there found are both individual and universal and apply to Gentile as well as Jew, to the present as well as the past. The gradual disappearance of the prophets during the latter part of the Persian period, and the fact that the priests ever devoted themselves more and more to the ritual and less to teaching, left a great need in the life of Judaism which called to the front the wise. At the same time the problems of the individual became more and more complex and insistent. Especially was this true during the Greek period when Hellenic civilization, with its corrupting influences, swept over Palestine and the lands of the dispersion. It was a period when the principles enunciated by the earlier prophets had been in general adopted by the Jewish race. The task, however, of interpreting these principles simply and practically into the every-day life of the people was left to these lovers and teachers of men, the wise. The evidence of the voluminous writings of Ben Sira, as well as of the books of Proverbs and Ecclesiastes, makes it quite clear that it was during the Greek period, and possibly in part under the intellectual stimulus of Greek thought, that the wise attained their greatest prominence and influence.

V. **The Aims of the Wise.** The aims of the wise are in part defined in the remarkable preface to the book of Proverbs, which was intended primarily to describe the purpose of the collection of proverbs which embodies their teachings. Four distinct classes commanded their attention: (1) The ignorant, those who were unacquainted with the moral, religious, and practical heritage received from preceding generations. (2) The inexperienced, those who had not yet learned in the school of life the art of adjusting themselves successfully to their environment. (3) The scoffers, who openly rejected the counsel of the sages. And (4) the disciples who were eager to learn and profit by the teachings of the wise.

The definite aims of the wise must be inferred from their teachings. They were concerned with the development of the individual, not the nation. Their first aim was to instruct the ignorant in the fundamental moral and religious principles already laid down by earlier priests and prophets. In the words of the preface to the book of Proverbs they taught,

> That men may learn wisdom and instruction,
> May understand intelligent discourses,
> May receive instruction in wise dealing,
> In justice, judgment, and equity.

Their second aim was to point out the pitfalls that lay in the path of the inexperienced, and to save them from moral wreck by inspiring within them right ideals and ambitions. This aim is also well stated in the preface to the book of Proverbs:

> That discretion may be given to the inexperienced,
> To the youth knowledge and a purpose.

The third aim of the wise was to educate the receptive and all who came to them in the attitude of disciples. This aim corresponded very closely to that of the modern educator. Again the preface to the book of Proverbs clearly expresses this educational ideal:

> That the wise man may hear and increase in learning,
> And the intelligent man may receive counsel.
> That he may understand a proverb and parable,
> The words of the wise and their riddles.

The wise, therefore, sought not merely to instruct, but to educate; that is, to develop sane, happy, and efficient men and women. They sought to train those who would have not only knowledge and experience, but also the ability to apply these successfully in the varied relations of life. Above all, they endeavored to educate not parts of a man, but the whole man. Hence their interest and the subjects that they treat are as broad as human experience.

The wise were keenly alive to the importance of youthful education. The proverb:

> Train up a child in the way in which he should go,
> And even when he is old he will not depart from it,

voices the fundamental principle upon which all effective education is based. They recognized that in the plastic days of childhood and youth ideals and character and efficiency could best be developed, and that education was not the work of a moment, but a gradual, progressive development.

Primary education, however, they intrusted to parents, and in many proverbs emphasized the responsibility which every parent owed to his child. They also counselled parents regarding the training of their children. The maxims:

> The rod of correction gives wisdom,
> But a child left to himself brings disgrace to his mother.
> Chastise your son while there is still hope,
> And set not your heart on his destruction.
> He who spares his rod hates his son,
> But he who loves him chastises him,

express their appreciation of the importance of discipline in the early training of the child. It is not clear at what age the wise took up the instruction of the young. Possibly it was at about the age of twelve, when the individual passed from childhood to adolescence, with its increasing dangers and possibilities. Many of their teachings are especially adapted to the problems of this tempestuous period.

VI. The Methods of the Wise. In attaining their aims the wise men of Israel employed a variety of methods. Proverbs such as,

> Every purpose is established by counsel,
> And by wise guidance make thou war,

suggest that, as in the days before the exile, they were still active in connection with the civic, social, and national life of the people, and that by influencing public policies they conserved the moral welfare of the individual as well as the state. Many references to "wisdom's voice crying aloud in the public places" suggest that, like the earlier prophets, the wise men at times taught in public, in the market-places, in the open spaces within the city gates, or wherever men were gathered together. They appear also to have taught in private, by wise counsel delivering the individual disciple who resorted to them from the perils that beset his path, or aiding him by prudent advice in solving successfully his individual problems.

In 6^{32-37} Ben Sira has given a vivid sketch of the schools of the wise, which are clearly the forerunners of the later rabbinical schools:

> My son, if you wish, you will be instructed,
> And if you pay attention, you will become prudent.
> If you are willing to hear, you will receive,

And if you listen attentively, you will be wise.
Stand in the assembly of the elders,
And whoever is wise, stick close to him.
Be willing to listen to every discourse,
And let no illuminating proverbs escape you.
If you see a man of insight, hasten to him,
And let your foot wear out his threshold.
Let your mind dwell upon the law of the Most High,
And meditate continually on his commands.
Thus he will enlighten your mind,
And teach you the wisdom you desire.

It requires little imagination to picture these ancient prototypes of our modern universities. Like all Oriental teachers, the wise doubtless sat cross-legged, with their disciples in a circle about them. They trusted largely to question and answer, and poured out from their own and their inherited experience wise maxims such as would guide the simple and inexperienced and develop efficient manhood.

VIII. **Their Important Teachings.** In the opening chapters of Proverbs the wise describe the character and value of that wisdom which represents their teaching as a whole. In chapters 8 and 9 "Wisdom" is personified. Inasmuch as the Hebrew word for "wisdom" is feminine, it is spoken of as a woman. Chapter 9 describes, in a form intended to arrest the attention of the most inattentive, the feast that Wisdom offers to her guests. This is contrasted with Folly's banquet, and the consequences to those who participated in these rival banquets are clearly presented.

In the practical teachings of the wise no question that vitally concerned the individual man was considered beneath their attention. Like the wise modern teacher they made no distinction between the religious and the secular. Everything that influenced man's acts and ideals possessed for them profound religious import. While the proverbial epigrammatic form of their teaching was not conducive to a logical or complete treatment of their theme, yet in a series of concise, dramatic maxims they dealt with almost every phase of man's domestic, economic, legal, and social life. They presented clearly man's duty to animals, to himself, to his fellow-men, and to God. If utilitarian motives were urged in the great majority of cases, it is because they sought to reach their pupils on their own level. Although their ideals sometimes fell below those of the great prophets, and especially those of the Great Teacher

166

of Nazareth, the importance of their work in establishing individual standards of right and wrong, in keeping alive in concrete form the principles of the earlier prophets, and in preparing their race for the crises through which it was soon to pass cannot be overestimated. As effective teachers of the individual they have an intensely practical and significant message for all men in the stream of life to-day as well as in the past.

§ CVI. THE DIFFERENT CURRENTS OF THOUGHT IN JUDAISM DURING THE GREEK PERIOD

The law of Jehovah is perfect, restoring the soul;

The testimony of Jehovah is trustworthy, making wise the simple,

The precepts of Jehovah are right, rejoicing the heart,

The commandment of Jehovah is pure, enlightening the eyes.

The fear of Jehovah is clean, enduring forever,

The judgments of Jehovah are true and altogether just,

They are of more value than gold, yea, than much fine gold,

Sweeter than honey and the droppings from the honey-comb.

By them is thy servant warned; in keeping them is great reward.

Who can discern his errors; cleanse thou me from secret faults,

Also from the presumptuous restrain thy servant; let them not have dominion over me.

Then shall I be perfect and cleared from great transgression.

Let the words of my mouth be acceptable and the meditation of my heart,

In thy sight, O Jehovah, my Rock and my Redeemer.

1. True character of Jehovah's law (Ps. 19⁷⁻¹⁴)

Jehovah is our refuge and strength,

An ever present help in trouble.

Therefore we fear not, though the earth be moved,

And though the mountains totter into the heart of the sea;

The seas roar, their waters foam,

Mountains shake with the swelling of its stream.

Jehovah of hosts is with us,

The God of Jacob is our refuge.

2. Jehovah's protecting care in time of trouble (46¹⁻²)

167

3. His guardianship of Jerusalem (4-7)

His brooks make glad the city of Jehovah,
The holy dwelling place of the Most High.
Jehovah is in the midst of her, she cannot totter;
Jehovah will help her at the turn of the morn.
Nations raged, kingdoms tottered,
When he uttered his voice the earth melted.
> Jehovah of hosts is with us,
> The God of Jacob is our refuge.

4. His ability to break the power of hostile nations (8-11)

Come, behold the works of Jehovah,
What desolations he hath made in the earth.
He is about to make wars to cease unto the end of the earth.
The bow he breaketh, and dasheth the spear in pieces;
He burneth the chariots with fire.
Be still, and know that I am Jehovah;
I shall be exalted among the nations, I shall be exalted on the earth.
> Jehovah of hosts is with us,
> The God of Jacob is our refuge.

5. His universal dominion (22²⁷⁻³⁰)

All the ends of the earth will remember and will turn to Jehovah,
And all the families of the nations will worship in his presence;
For the dominion belongs to Jehovah and he rules over the nations.
Verily, him alone will all the prosperous of the earth worship.
Before him all those about to go down to the dust will bow,
A seed will serve him, it will be told to a generation to come;
And they will declare his righteousness that he hath accomplished to a people yet to be born.

6. Jonah's commission and his refusal to act (Jonah 1¹⁻³)

Now this word of Jehovah came to Jonah the son of Amittai:

Arise, go to that great city, Nineveh, and preach against it; for their wickedness has come up before me. But Jonah rose up to flee to Tarshish from the presence of Jehovah. And he went down to Joppa and found a ship going to Tarshish; so he paid the fare and embarked to go with them to Tarshish from the presence of Jehovah.

But Jehovah sent a furious wind upon the sea, and there was a mighty tempest, so that the ship threatened to break in pieces. Then the sailors were afraid and cried, each to his own god; and they cast into the sea the wares that were in the ship, in order to lighten it. But Jonah had gone down into the bottom of the ship; and he lay fast asleep. And the captain of the ship came and said to him: What are you doing asleep? Call on your God, perhaps that God will think on us that we perish not. And they said to one another, Come, let us cast lots, that we may know for whose sake this evil has come upon us. So they cast lots and the lot fell upon Jonah. *7. Discovery of his guilt (4-7)*

Then they said to him, Tell us, what is your occupation, and whence do you come? what is your country and of what people are you? And he said to them, I am a Hebrew, and a worshipper of Jehovah, the God of heaven, who hath made the sea and the dry land. Then the men were exceedingly afraid, and said to him, What is this you have done? For they knew that he was fleeing from the presence of Jehovah, for he had told them. *8. Disclosure of his identity (8-10)*

Then they said to him, What shall we do to thee, that the sea may be calm for us? for the sea grew more and more stormy. And he said to them, Take me up and throw me into the sea; so shall the sea be calm for you, for I know that for my sake this great storm has overtaken you. But the men rowed hard to get back to the land; but they could not, for the sea grew more and more stormy against them. *9. Courage of Jonah and the sailors (11-13)*

Therefore they cried to Jehovah, and said, We beseech thee, O Jehovah, we beseech thee, let us not perish for this man's life, neither bring innocent blood upon us, for thou art Jehovah; thou hast done as it pleaseth thee. So they took up Jonah, and threw him into the sea; and the sea ceased from its raging. Then the men feared Jehovah exceedingly, and they offered a sacrifice to Jehovah, and made vows. *10. Conversion of the heathen sailors (14, 15)*

Then Jehovah prepared a great fish to swallow Jonah and Jonah was in the belly of this fish three days and three nights. Thereupon Jonah prayed to Jehovah his God, out of the belly of the fish. And Jehovah spoke to the fish, and it threw up Jonah upon the dry land. *11. Jonah's deliverance (1 17— 2 1, 10)*

12. His message to the Ninevites (3¹⁻⁴) And the word of Jehovah came to Jonah the second time, saying, Arise, go to that great city, Nineveh, and preach to it what I shall tell thee. So Jonah rose and went to Nineveh, as Jehovah said. Now Nineveh was a great city before God, of three days' journey. And Jonah began by going through the city a day's journey, and he cried, and said, Forty days more and Nineveh shall be overthrown.

13. Their repentance (⁵⁻⁹) And the people of Nineveh believed God; and they proclaimed a fast, and put on sackcloth, from the greatest of them to the least of them. And when word came to the king of Nineveh, he rose from his throne, and took off his robe, and dressed in sackcloth, and sat in the dust. And he made proclamation and published in Nineveh: By the decree of the king and his nobles: Man, beast, herd, and flock shall not taste anything; let them neither eat nor drink water; But let them clothe themselves with sackcloth, both man and beast, and let them cry mightily to God, and turn each from his evil way, and from the act of violence which they have in hand. Who knows but that God may relent, and turn from his fierce anger, that we perish not?

14. Their pardon (¹⁰) And God saw their works, how they turned from their evil way; and God relented of the evil which he said he would do to them, and did it not.

15. Jonah's anger because of God's mercy to the heathen (4¹⁻⁵) But it displeased Jonah greatly, and he was angry. And he prayed to Jehovah, and said, Ah now, Jehovah, was not this what I said when I was yet in mine own country? Therefore I hastened to flee to Tarshish; for I knew that thou art a God, gracious and merciful, slow to anger, and abounding in love, and relenting of evil. Therefore, O Jehovah, take now, I beseech thee, my life from me; for it is better for me to die than to live! And Jehovah said, Doest thou well to be angry? Then Jonah went out of the city, and sat down before the city, and there made him a booth, and sat under it, until he might see what would become of the city.

16. His selfishness contrasted with God's infinite love (⁶⁻¹¹) And Jehovah God prepared a gourd, and made it to come up over Jonah, that it might be a shade over his head. So Jonah rejoiced exceedingly over the gourd. But as the dawn appeared the next day God prepared a worm and it injured the gourd, so that it withered. And when the sun arose, God prepared a sultry east wind. And the sun beat

upon the head of Jonah, so that he was faint, and begged for himself that he might die saying, It is better for me to die than to live. And God said to Jonah, Is it well for thee to be angry about the gourd? And he said, It is well for me to be angry, even to death! And Jehovah said, Thou carest for a gourd, for which thou hast not troubled thyself, nor hast thou brought it up—a thing that came in a night and hath perished in a night. Shall I, indeed, not care for the great city, Nineveh, in which there are one hundred and twenty thousand human beings who know not their right hand from their left; besides much cattle?

I, Koheleth, was king over Israel in Jerusalem. And I applied my mind to searching out and exploring wisdom, all that is done under heaven: it is an evil task that God hath given the children of men at which to toil. I have seen all the works that are done under the sun; and behold, the whole is vanity and a striving after wind. The crooked cannot be made straight; and the wanting cannot be numbered. I communed with myself, saying, Behold, I have increased and gathered wisdom more than all who were before me in Jerusalem, and my mind has abundantly beheld wisdom and knowledge. And I applied my mind to know wisdom and knowledge, madness and folly: I know that this also is a striving after wind. For in much wisdom is much trouble, and he who increases knowledge, increases pain.

17. Experience teaches the folly of striving after knowledge and wisdom (Eccles. 1¹²⁻¹⁸)

I said in my mind, Come now, I will test you with pleasure; so look upon what is attractive; and, behold, this also is vanity. I said of laughter, It is mad; and of pleasure, What does it do? I searched in my mind, how to stimulate my flesh with wine, while my mind was guiding with wisdom, and how to lay hold on folly, until I should see what is good for the children of men to do under the heavens all the days of their life. I did great works: I built for myself houses; I planted for myself vineyards; I made for myself gardens and parks, and I planted trees in them, every kind of fruit-tree. I made for myself pools of water, to water a grove springing up with trees. I bought male and female slaves

18. Enduring satisfaction not found in gratification of the appetite nor in wealth and possessions (2¹⁻¹¹)

and had slaves born in my house; also I had great possessions of herds and flocks, more than all who had been before me in Jerusalem. I also gathered for myself silver and gold, and the treasure of kings and of provinces. I secured for myself male and female singers, and the delights of the sons of men, mistresses of all kinds. And I grew more wealthy than all who were before in Jerusalem; also my wisdom remained with me. And nothing that my eyes craved did I keep from them; I did not deny my heart any joy, for my heart rejoiced because of all my labor. Then I looked on all the works that my hands had wrought, and on the labor that I had labored to do; and, behold, all was vanity and a striving after wind, and there was no gain under the sun.

19. A like fate awaits the wise man and the fool (12-17)

And I turned to behold wisdom and madness, and folly; for what can the man do who comes after the king? Even that which has been done already. Then I saw that wisdom excels folly, as far as light excels darkness. The wise man's eyes are in his head, but the fool walks in darkness: yet I know that the same fate overtakes them all. Then I said in my heart, As is the fate of a fool so will be my fate; so why have I then been more wise? Then I said in my heart that this also is vanity. For of the wise man, even as of the fool, there is no remembrance for ever, inasmuch as in the days to come all will have been already forgotten. And how the wise man dies even as the fool! So I hated life, because the work that is done under the sun is evil to me; for all is vanity and a striving after wind.

20. Nothing better than to enjoy the good things of life (24-26b)

There is nothing better for a man than that he should eat and drink, and find his pleasure in his labor. This also I saw that it is from the hand of God. For who can eat, or who can have enjoyment without him? This is also vanity and a striving after wind.

I. The Ritualists. Liberty of thought as well as speech was from the first characteristic of Israel's life and thought. It was one of the many valuable heritages that the Hebrews brought with them from the free life of the desert. Their close contact with the outside world, and especially with Hellenic life and thought during the Greek period, increased this sense of freedom. The result is that many different currents of thought are reflected in the Old Testament writings that come from this age. Most familiar and easiest understood is the ritualistic type. It is represented by the Chronicler, who lived and wrote some time between 300 and 250 B.C. For him all life and interest centred about the temple and its services. In general the vision of the ritualists was turned toward the past rather than the present and the future. In the traditions regarding the origin of the temple and its institutions, in keeping the ceremonial law, in participating in the formal ritual, and in joining their songs with those of the temple singers they found an escape from the pettiness of the age and attained that peace and joy which is expressed in many of the psalms of the Psalter.

II. **The Legalists.** Closely related to the ritualists were those whose interests were all fixed in the study of the law and the teachings of the earlier priests. They regarded the written laws as a complete guide to conduct and the embodiment of Jehovah's supreme message to his race. Psalms like the fragment found in 19[7-14] voice their convictions:

> The law of Jehovah is perfect, restoring the soul,
> The judgments of Jehovah are true and altogether just.
> By them is thy servant warned; in keeping them is great reward.

They emphasized not merely external acts and words, but inner motives. In character and in conduct they were noble products of that religion which Israel had inherited from the past. By them were probably treasured stories such as are found in the first chapters of the book of Daniel. The detailed references in chapter 2 to the marriage of Antiochus Theos and the daughter of Ptolemy Philadelphus in 248 B.C. and to the murder of Antiochus by his former wife Laodicea, together with the absence of allusions to subsequent events, indicate that these stories were probably committed to writing somewhere between 255 and 245 B.C. Their aim was clearly to emphasize the supreme importance of fulfilling faithfully the demands of the law, even in the face of bitter opposition and persecution, and the certainty that Jehovah would deliver those who were loyal to him. Their teachings were especially adapted to inspire the tried and tempted Jews of the dispersion, who were sorely persecuted by the heathen among whom they lived. The dramatic picture of men who dared face the fiery furnace or the hungry lions rather than depart from the demands of the law undoubtedly proved a great inspiration to the Jews of the Greek period.

III. **The Disciples of the Prophets.** Throughout the centuries that followed the destruction of Jerusalem the great ethical prophets of the pre-exilic period had never been without spiritual disciples. They faithfully studied and applied in their own lives the principles laid down by their earlier guides. Although the influence of the contemporary prophets constantly waned, yet the spirit of those earlier champions of the faith lived in the hearts of their followers. In many of the psalms of the Psalter Amos and Isaiah and Jeremiah speak in terms adapted to the changed problems of the Jews of the Greek period. In Psalm 46 the trust in Jehovah which Isaiah advocated has become a living force in the life of the Psalmist and of the class in behalf of which he spoke. In the background one hears the march of the multitude armed by Alexander for world-conquest and the din of conflict as army met army; but over all stands Jehovah, protecting his sanctuary and people, supreme in the lives of men and nations. The narrow, nationalistic, messianic hopes have long since been abandoned, and instead Jehovah is recognized as the one supreme being whose kingdom or dominion includes all the nations of the earth. In imagination these disciples of the prophets saw the time when rich and poor, Jew and Gentile, should bow before Jehovah and be united in loyalty to him. Thus arose that highest conception of the kingdom of God which is the foundation of Jesus' teaching.

IV. **The Date and Character of the Book of Jonah.** From those who sat at the feet of the earlier prophets came one of the most remarkable books of the Old Testament. In literary form the little book of Jonah is closely akin to the stories in the opening chapters of Genesis and the first half of the book of Daniel. Its many Aramaic words, its quotations from the late book of Joel, its universalism, and its missionary spirit all indicate that it comes either from the closing years of the Persian or from the earlier part of the Greek period. The story of Jonah, like many similar stories in the Old Testament, was probably known to the Semites centuries before it was employed by the author of the book to point his great prophetic teaching. In the familiar Greek story of Hercules, Hesione, the daughter of the Trojan king, is rescued by the hero from a sea-monster which held her in its stomach three days. An old Egyptian tale coming from the third millennium B.C. tells of an Egyptian who was shipwrecked and after floating three days was swallowed by a great sea-monster and thus carried to the land. From India comes the tradition of a man who went to sea contrary to the commands of his mother. While on the way the ship was seized by an unknown power and not allowed to proceed until the offender was three times selected by lot and then cast overboard.

174

V. Teachings of the Book of Jonah. The value and message of the book of Jonah have in the past been largely overlooked because the true literary character of the book has been misunderstood. It was never intended by its author to be regarded as a historical narrative. Its hero Jonah, the son of Amittai, according to II Kings 14^{25}, lived during the reign of Jeroboam II (780–740 B.C.), and predicted the wide extension of the territory of southern Israel; but the Jonah of the story is evidently a type of the Jew of the Persian and Greek periods. By showing the pettiness of his attitude toward the heathen the author sought to broaden the vision and quicken the conscience of his fellow-Jews. The portrait is remarkably vivid and suggestive. Jonah fled from Jehovah's land and took refuge in the sea, not because he feared the Ninevites, but, as he plainly declares later, because he feared that, if he did preach to the Assyrian foes of his race, Jehovah would repent and spare them. In the scene in the midst of the raging tempest the piety of the heathen sailors and their zeal in sparing the guilty Israelite stand forth in favorable contrast to Jonah's action in refusing to carry out Jehovah's command. The Ninevites, clad in sackcloth, repenting for their sins, and craving Jehovah's forgiveness, are far more attractive than the sullen prophet, complaining because Jehovah has spared the heathen foes of his race and later upbraiding Jehovah because of the destruction of the gourd that for a time had protected his head from the burning sun. Jehovah's concluding remonstrance voices the message of the book. Like the New Testament parable of the Prodigal Son, the story of Jonah presents in graphic form the unbounded love of the heavenly father and contrasts it sharply with the petty jealousies and hatred of his favored people. It was a call to Israel to go forth and become a missionary to all the world and a protest against the nation's failure to perform its God-given task.

VI. The Book of Ecclesiastes. Very different is the spirit and purpose of the book of Ecclesiastes. It evidently comes from one of the many wisdom teachers who flourished during the Greek period and it speaks in the name of Solomon. It is an essay on the value of life. In its original form its thought was so pessimistic that it has been supplemented at many points by later editors. These insertions include (1) proverbs commending wisdom and praising the current wisdom teachings, and (2) the work of a pious scribe, a forerunner of the later Pharisees, who sought to correct the utterances of the original writer (who is commonly designated as Koheleth) and to bring them into accord with current orthodoxy. The language and style of the book are closely

175

akin to those of the Chronicler and the author of the book of Esther. It also contains several Persian and possibly one Greek word. The book in its earlier form was evidently known to Ben Sira, the author of Ecclesiasticus, who lived about 180 B.C. In 4^{13-16} and 10^{16-17} there are apparent references to the reign of Ptolemy Epiphanes, who came to the throne of Egypt at the age of five, and whose court was famous for its dissoluteness and profligacy. The book, therefore, may be dated with considerable confidence a little before 200 B.C. It was a corrupt, barren period. Crime was rampant in the temple as well as at the court in Alexandria (3^{16}). The people were crushed by the powerful and were without means of redress (4^1). A despot sat on the throne (10^{5-7}) and spies lurked everywhere (10^{20}).

VII. **Koheleth's Philosophy of Life.** The author of the original book of Ecclesiastes is the spokesman of that class in Judaism who were oppressed and crushed by this dreary outlook. He evidently lived in Jerusalem and probably near the temple (5^1 8^{10}). From the allusions in $7^{26, 28}$ it is evident that he was unhappily married. From the classic description of old age found in 11^9-12^7 it would appear that when he wrote he was well advanced in years, and spoke out of the depths of his own painful personal experience, having been left without son or close kinsman (4^8). From his teachings it is clear that he had broken away from the orthodox wisdom school. Before his enfeebled vision rose the seamy, dreary side of life, and yet back of the lament of this ancient pessimist is revealed a man of high ideals, impelled by a spirit of scientific thoroughness. Though he was intense and eager in his quest for true happiness and in his analysis of the meaning of life, he found no abiding joy, for his outlook was sadly circumscribed. Life beyond the grave offered to him no hope or compensation. He was, however, by no means an agnostic. He believed in God's rulership of the world; but the God of his faith was inscrutable, far removed from the life of men. Hence, unlike many of his contemporaries, as for example the psalmists, he found little joy or inspiration in his religion. According to the conclusion, which he proclaimed in the beginning of his essay and held consistently throughout, all human striving and ambition, even life itself, are but superlative vanity, nor can man attain any permanent or complete satisfaction. The one positive teaching which Koheleth reiterates is that it is man's highest privilege to extract from passing experiences the small measure of joy and happiness that they offer, and therewith to be content. Compared with many other Old Testament books, the religious value of Ecclesiastes is slight indeed.

Its chief value, however, is historical: it presents one phase of thought in the Judaism of this period, and shows how sorely the Jewish people needed the spur of a great crisis to rouse them to noble and unselfish action. The book of Ecclesiastes also furnishes the darker background which brings out in clear relief the inspiring messages of the great prophets that had gone before, and of the greater Prophet who was to set before the human race a worthy goal and a fresh and true interpretation of the value of life.

§ CVII. THE TEACHINGS OF JESUS THE SON OF SIRACH

All wisdom is from the Lord,
And is with him forever.
The sand of the seas, and the drops of rain,
And the days of eternity—who shall number?
The height of the heaven, and the breadth of the earth,
And the depths of the abyss—who shall search them out?
Wisdom hath been created before all things,
And keen insight from everlasting.
To whom hath the root of wisdom been revealed?
And who hath known her shrewd counsels?
There is one wise, greatly to be feared,
The Lord sitting upon his throne,
He created her, and saw and numbered her,
And poured her out over all his works.
She is with all flesh according to his gift,
And he giveth her freely to those who love him.

1. Wisdom the creation and gift of God to man (B. Sir. 1¹⁻¹⁰)

My son, if you would serve the Lord,
Prepare your soul for temptation.
Set your heart aright, and be steadfast,
That you may not be dismayed in the time of calamity.
Cleave to him, and depart not,
That you may prove yourself wise at the last.
Accept whatever comes to you,
And be patient in sickness and affliction,
For gold is tried by the fire,
And acceptable men in the furnace of affliction.

2. Affliction, nobly met, tempers a man's soul (2¹⁻⁵)

177

3.
Trust
and
hope
will
surely
be re-
warded
(6-9)

Put your trust in the Lord, and he will help you,
Hope in him, and he will make smooth your way.
You who fear the Lord, wait for his mercy,
And turn not aside lest you fall.
You who fear the Lord trust in him,
And your reward shall not fail.
You who fear the Lord, hope for good things,
And for eternal gladness and deliverance?

4.
Value
of
meek-
ness
(3¹⁷⁻²⁰)

My son, if you are rich, walk in humility,
That you will be more beloved than a generous man.
The greater you are, humble yourself the more,
And you shall find favor before the Lord.
For great is the might of the Lord,
And he is glorified by those who are meek.

5.
Avoid-
ance of
futile
theories
(3²¹⁻²⁵)

Seek not the things that are too hard for you,
And search not out things that are beyond you.
That over which power has been given you, think
        thereon,
For you have no business with the things that are
    hidden.
With that which is out of your field have nothing
    to do,
For more things are shown to you than you can un-
    derstand.
For men have many speculations,
And evil theories have led them astray.
Where there is no pupil to the eye, the light fails,
And where there is no understanding, wisdom fails.

6. Im-
por-
tance
of the
recep-
tive
mind
(3²⁶⁻³⁰)

A stubborn heart fares ill at the last,
But he who loves the good finds it.
A stubborn heart has many troubles,
And the overbearing heap sin upon sin.
For the wound of the scorner there is no healing,
Since he is a plant of an evil kind.
A wise mind understands the proverbs of the wise,
And an ear attentive to wisdom is a joy.

178

Water quenches flaming fire,
And right acts make atonement for sins.
He who does a favor—it meets him on his way,
And when he falls he shall find support.
My son, deprive not the poor of his living,
And let not the eyes of the needy grow weary.
Make not a hungry soul groan,
And do not stir up the feelings of him who is smitten.
Deliver the oppressed from the oppressor,
And be not faint-hearted in giving judgment.
Be as a father to the fatherless,
And instead of a husband to the widow;
So will God call you his son,
And be gracious to you and save you from destruc-
tion.

7.
Help-
fulness
toward
the
poor
and op-
pressed
(3^{30}—4^2,
9, 10)

Observe the opportunity and beware of evil,
And be not ashamed of yourself.
For there is a shame that brings sin,
And another shame, glory and grace.
Do not be obsequious to your own shame,
And do not humiliate yourself until it is a sin against
yourself.

8.
Proper
mod-
esty
and
self-
respect
(4^{20-22})

Hold not back speech, in its proper time,
And hide not your wisdom.
For by speech wisdom shall be known,
And instruction by the word of the tongue.
Speak not against the truth,
But be humble because of your own ignorance.
Strive for the right even to death,
And the Lord will fight for you.
Be not boastful with your tongue,
And slack and remiss in your work.

9.
Proper
speech
(4^{23-25},
28, 29)

Be not as a lion in your house,
Nor arrogant and suspicious among your servants.
Let not your hand be stretched out to receive,
And closed when you should repay.

10. Up
right-
ness in
home
and
busi-
ness
(4^{30}, 31)

11. Evil
of self-
suffi-
ciency
(5^1, ^{2a})

Set not your mind upon your possessions,
And say not, They are sufficient for me.
Follow not your own mind and strength,
To walk in the desires of your heart.

12.
Evil of
yielding
to pas-
sion
(6^2, ^{4})

Do not give yourself up to your passion,
Lest it like a bull eat up your strength.
For a wild passion destroys its possessor,
And makes him the laughing-stock of his enemies.

13.
Making
friends
(6^{5-8})

Well ordered speech makes friends,
And a gracious tongue wins kindly greetings.
Let those who are friendly toward you be many,
But your confidant one of a thousand.
If you would get a friend, get him by testing,
And do not give him your confidence too quickly.
For there is many a fair-weather friend,
But he does not remain in the day of need.

14.
Value
of a
faithful
friend
($^{14-16}$)

A faithful friend is a strong defence,
And he who finds him finds a treasure.
There is nothing equal to a faithful friend,
And his worth is beyond price.
A faithful friend is a source of life,
And he who fears the Lord finds him.
He who fears the Lord directs his friendship aright,
For as he is, so is his friend.

15. Not
to
speak
what
is not
true
(7^{12}, ^{13})

Devise not a lie against your brother,
Nor do the like to a friend or associate.
Never take pleasure in speaking a falsehood.
For its outcome is not good.

16.
Duties
to ser-
vants
(^{20}, ^{21})

Do not treat badly a servant who serves you faithfully,
Nor a hired servant who gives to you his best.
Love a sensible servant as your own self,
Defraud him not of liberty.

17. To
parents
(^{22}, ^{23})

Honor your father with your whole heart,
And forget not the pangs of your mother.

Remember that of them you were born,
And now you can recompense them for what they have
    done for you.

Fear the Lord with all your soul,
And regard his priests with reverence.
Love your Creator with all your strength,
And do not neglect his ministers.

18. To
God
and his
min-
isters
(29, 30)

I. Date and Character of Jesus, the Son of Sirach. Out of the large number of anonymous books that come from the Persian and Greek periods one stands forth unique. It is the Wisdom of Ben Sira. With the exception of the Psalter and Isaiah, it is the largest book that has come to us from ancient Israel. Fortunately, its date and authorship may be determined with reasonable certainty. In the prologue to the Greek translation, its translator describes himself as the grandson of Jesus, the son of Sirach, and states that he went to Egypt in 132 B.C. Hence it is probable that his grandfather wrote some time during the early part of the second century B.C. The appreciative description of Simon the high priest in the fiftieth chapter of Ben Sira indicates that its author was a contemporary as well as an admirer of that famous head of the Judean community. From the references in the rabbinical writings, as well as from the definite statement of Eusebius, it is reasonably certain that this Simon lived between 200 and 175 B.C. Furthermore, the quotations in the writings of Ben Sira from Ecclesiastes in its original form imply that he wrote during the latter part of the Greek period. The complete absence of any reference to the Maccabean struggle also proves beyond question that he lived before 168 B.C. These facts indicate that the date of his writing was somewhere between 190 and 175 B.C.

In the Hebrew version the name of this famous sage appears as Jesus, the son of Eleazar, the son of Sira. In the Greek version, however, he is known simply as Jesus, the son of Sirach. Ben Sira, or Sirach, was apparently his family name, while Jesus is the Greek equivalent of Jeshua or Joshua. From his writings it may be inferred that he belonged to a well-known Jerusalemite family. It is also not improbable that he was connected with the high-priestly line. His references to Simon the high priest reveals his deep sympathies with the ecclesiastical rulers of Jerusalem. The closing words in the Hebrew version of 51¹² are equally significant: "Give thanks to him who chose the sons of Sadok to be priests." In his teachings Ben Sira is in some respects a forerunner of the later Sadducees. Evidently he was a man of influence in the Judean community. His fame as a wise man doubtless attracted many disciples. He was deeply interested in every phase of life. While his point of view was somewhat similar to that of Koheleth, his outlook was thoroughly optimistic. His teachings were positive rather than negative. His faith was that of the fathers, and his purpose constructive. Out of the wealth of teachings inherited from the past, and also out of his own personal experience and observation, he sought to inspire right ideals in the young and to develop them into happy and efficient servants of God and of their fellow-men. In this respect he was a worthy representative of the wise who during this period moulded the life of Judaism.

II. **His Writings.** The prologue to the Greek version of the wisdom of Sirach states that he was a devoted student of the earlier scriptures of his race. In 33^{16} he acknowledges, in all modesty, his indebtedness to the past:

I awakened last of all as one who gathers after the great gatherers,
By the blessing of the Lord I profited and filled my wine-press as one
    who gathers grapes.

It was natural, therefore, that he should write down his teachings in the language of his fathers. Unlike most of his contemporaries, he possessed a classical Hebrew style. Like the wise men whose teachings are preserved in the book of Proverbs, he put his thought into poetic, proverbial form. In his book there is a definite, logical arrangement of ideas. The first part consists of a series of essays on various topics. The same subject is often dealt with in many different settings (*e. g.*, choice of friends, 6^{5-17} 7^{18} 12^{8-12} 37^{1-6}). These brief essays are grouped together, and each group is provided with a brief introduction, usually in commendation of wisdom. Apparently the first half of the book consists of notes based on Ben Sira's early teachings. Each group of sayings may well represent his teachings on a given occasion. In 31^{21} through 50^{24} is found the roll call of Israel's spiritual heroes, beginning with a psalm in praise of Jehovah's majesty and power and concluding with the description of Simon the high priest. This latter part of the book is clearly a pure literary creation, and was probably added by him as a conclusion to the collection of his wisdom teachings.

III. **History of the Book.** The book containing the writings of Ben Sira was known under a variety of titles. The Latin Church followed the

Greek in calling it Ecclesiasticus. This term was applied to those books which were not in the canon, but were held to be edifying and proper for public use in the churches. The Hebrew text of Ben Sira enjoyed wide currency, was frequently quoted by the later rabbis, and was often referred to by later Jewish and Christian writers. It was almost completely supplanted in time, however, by the Greek version. Jerome was acquainted with the Hebrew version, but most of the Church fathers followed the Greek. Ben Sira was apparently quoted by Jesus, by Paul, and by the authors of the Epistle of James and of the Epistle to the Hebrews. Twenty or thirty such references or allusions are found in the New Testament. It was also a great favorite with the Church fathers, who quoted from it even more frequently than from the other Old Testament writings. It was adopted in the canon of the Greek and Latin Church; but, in common with the other apocryphal books, was given a secondary place by the Protestant reformers. Unfortunately, during the earlier part of the last century it ceased to be printed in the standard editions of the Bible. The modern revival of interest in the apocryphal books, both in Europe and America, is tending to restore this book, in common with I Maccabees, to the position which they certainly deserve in the practical working canon of the Old Testament. The discovery in 1896 of a fragment of the original Hebrew manuscript of Ben Sira, and the subsequent recovery of many other parts, have also tended to arouse wide interest in this hitherto much-neglected book. Hebrew portions of thirty-nine out of the fifty-one chapters have thus far been discovered. Most of them come from about the eleventh Christian century and are of widely differing values. By means of these, however, and the quotations by the Jewish rabbis and Christian fathers and in the Greek, Syriac, and Latin versions, it is now possible to restore most of the original Hebrew text, and the resulting translation is far superior to those based on the Greek text.

IV. **Its Picture of Jewish Life.** Ben Sira has given a vivid picture of the domestic, economic, and social life of the Jews of his age. The debased, Oriental conception of marriage had corrupted the atmosphere of the home. Wives were regarded as the possessions of their husbands, and the immoral influence of Hellenism still further undermined the purity and integrity of many a Jewish home. Greek customs and usages were pervading Palestine more and more. Ben Sira refers to banquets with their accompaniments of music and wine. Even these meet with his approval. Agriculture and commerce are the chief occupations of the people. In general Ben Sira voices the wholesome Jewish attitude toward labor:

> Hate not laborious work;
> Neither agriculture that the Most High hath ordained.

He is especially strong in his commendation of physicians:

> Be a friend to the physician, for one has need of him,
> For verily God hath appointed him.
> A physician receives his wisdom from God,
> And from the king he receives presents.
> The knowledge of a physician causes him to lift up his head,
> And before the princes may he enter.
> God created medicines out of the earth,
> And a prudent man will not be disgusted with them.

The following proverb has a universal application:

> He who sins before his maker,
> Let him fall into the hands of his physician!

V. Rise of the Scribes. The writings of Ben Sira reveal the close connection between the earlier wise and the later scribes. He lived at the period when the wise man was turning scribe. He himself had a profound respect for the law:

> A man of understanding will put his trust in the law,
> The law is faithful to him as when one asks at the oracle.

One of his fundamental teachings is formulated in the proverb:

> Fear the Lord and glorify his priests,
> And give him his portion even as it is commanded.

Elsewhere he declares:

> The leisure of the scribe increases his wisdom,
> And he who has no business becomes wise.

In his famous description of the typical wise man in 39^{1-11} may be recognized many of the traits of the later scribes. As the law and the ritual gained greater prominence in the life of Judaism, it was inevitable that it should command the attention of the practical teachers of the people. Thus gradually the wise devoted themselves to its study and interpretation, ever emphasizing, however, thought and conduct as well as conformity to the ritual. Scribism was greatly enriched by its lineal inheritance through the earlier wise, and long retained the proverbial, epigrammatic form of teaching and that personal attitude toward the individual and his problems which was one of their greatest sources of strength. The honor which the early scribes enjoyed was well deserved. Their methods were free from the casuistry that characterized many of the later scribes. They not only copied and guarded the law, but were its interpreters, applying it practically to the every-day problems of the people as well as to their duties in connection with the temple service. Their influence upon the Jews in this early period was on the whole exceedingly wholesome, and from their ranks rose the martyrs that a generation later were ready to die for the law.

VI. **The Teachings of Ben Sira.** Ben Sira was acquainted with Greek culture and shows at several points familiarity with Greek ideals and methods of thinking, but his point of view in general was distinctly Jewish. He gathered together all that was best in the earlier teachings of his race. In many ways he represents an advance beyond all that had gone before and a close approximation to the spirit and teachings of Jesus of Nazareth. The God of his faith was omnipotent, majestic, omniscient, just, and merciful. He was the God of all mankind, although it was through Israel that he especially revealed himself. Ben Sira did not, like Ezekiel, think of God as far removed from the life of men and as communicating with them only through angels, but as directly and personally interested in the experiences and life of the individual. In 23[1, 4] he addresses him as Lord, Father, and Master of my life. Thus he employs in the personal sense the term Father, which was most often on the lips of the Great Teacher of Nazareth. In Ben Sira's stalwart faith and simple trust there is also much that reminds us of the Greater than Solomon. Like the teachers who had preceded him, he had, however, no clear belief in individual immortality (*cf.* 41[3-4], 38[16, 23]). The only reward after death that he could hold up before a good man was his reputation:

> A good life has its number of days,
> But a good name continues forever.

Consistent with the orthodox wisdom school, he taught that rewards for right living came in this life:

Delight not in the delights of the wicked;
Remember they shall not go unpunished to the grave.

Even though he lacked the inspiration of future hope, Ben Sira taught loyalty to God and fidelity to every duty. Justice toward all, consideration for the needs of the suffering and dependent, and generosity to the poor are constantly urged by this noblest Jew of the age.

§ CVIII. THE CAUSES OF THE MACCABEAN STRUGGLE

1. Antiochus Epiphanes and the apostate Jews (I Mac. 1 10-15)

Now there came forth from [Alexander's successors] a sinful root, Antiochus Epiphanes, son of Antiochus the king, who had been a hostage at Rome, and he began to reign in the one hundred and thirty-seventh year of the Syrian rule (175 B.C.). In those days there appeared certain lawless Israelites who persuaded many, saying, Let us go and make a covenant with the heathen about us; for since we have stood aloof from them many evils have befallen us. And the proposal met with approval. And certain of the people were ready to do it, and went to the king who gave them the right to do as the heathen. Then they built a place for gymnastic exercise in Jerusalem according to the customs of the heathen. They also made themselves uncircumcised, and, forsaking the holy covenant, fraternized with the heathen, and sold themselves to do evil.

2. Antiochus's successful invasion of Egypt (16-19)

Now when Antiochus saw that his authority was well established, he thought to reign over Egypt, that he might reign over the two kingdoms. So he invaded Egypt with a great multitude, with chariots and elephants and horsemen, and with a great navy. And he made war against Ptolemy, king of Egypt. And Ptolemy was defeated by him and fled, and many fell mortally wounded. And they seized the strong cities in the land of Egypt, and he took the spoils of Egypt.

3. His plunder of the temple at Jerusalem (20-22, 24-28)

Then after Antiochus had conquered Egypt he returned in the hundred and forty-third year (169 B.C.) and went up against Israel and Jerusalem with a great multitude. And he insolently went into the sanctuary, and took the golden altar, and the candelabrum, and all that belonged to the table of the showbread, and the cups for libations, and the bowls, and the golden censers, and the curtain and the gar-

lands; and the decorations which were on the front of the temple—he scaled them all off. And taking all, he went away into his own land, after he had made a great slaughter, and had spoken very insolently. Thus a great mourning came to the Israelites wherever they were.

> And the rulers and elders groaned,
> The virgins and young men were made feeble.
> And the beauty of the women was changed.
> Every bridegroom took up a lamentation,
> She that sat in the marriage chamber was in heaviness.
> And the land was shaken because of its inhabitants,
> And all the house of Jacob was clothed with shame.

After two years the king sent a chief collector of tribute to the cities of Judah, who came to Jerusalem with a great multitude. And he spoke words of peace to deceive them, and they trusted him. Then he attacked the city suddenly, and inflicted a severe blow on it, and destroyed many Israelites. And he took the spoils of the city, and set it on fire, and pulled down its houses and walls on every side. They took captive the women and the children, and gained possession of the cattle. Then they walled in the city of David with a great and strong wall, with strong towers, and it served as a citadel. And they put there sinful people, lawless men. And they fortified themselves in it. And they stored up weapons and food and, gathering together the spoils of Jerusalem, they stowed them away there.

4. Later plundering and dismantling of Jerusalem (29-40)

> And the citadel became a great trap,
> And served as a place of ambush against the sanctuary,
> And an evil adversary to Israel continually.
> And they shed innocent blood on every side of the sanctuary
> And polluted the sanctuary.
> Then the inhabitants of Jerusalem fled because of this,
> And she became the habitation of foreigners.
> And she became strange to those who were born in her,
> And her children forsook her.
> Her sanctuary was laid waste like a wilderness,

187

> Her feasts were turned into mourning,
> Her sabbaths into a reproach,
> Her honor into contempt,
> So great as was once her glory, so now was her dishonor,
> And her exaltation was turned into mourning.

5. Antiochus's command to cease worshipping Jehovah (41-63)

Then King Antiochus wrote to his whole kingdom commanding that all should be one people, and that each should give up his own laws. And all the heathen nations yielded to the demand of the king. Many Israelites too consented to worship him and sacrificed to the idols, and profaned the sabbath. And the king sent letters by messengers to Jerusalem and the cities of Judah commanding them to follow customs foreign to the land, and to prevent the making of whole burnt-offerings and sacrifices and libations in the sanctuary, and to profane the sabbaths and feasts, and pollute the sanctuary and the holy things, to build altars, temples, and shrines for idols, and to sacrifice swine's flesh and unclean beasts; also to leave their sons uncircumcised, to stain their souls with all manner of uncleanness and profanation, so that they might forget the law, and change all the customs. And that whoever would not do as the king commanded should die. Thus he wrote to his whole kingdom; and appointed overseers over all the people, who commanded the cities of Judah to sacrifice city by city. Then many of the people, every one who had forsaken the law, gathered about them. And they did evil things in the land, and caused the Israelites to hide themselves in all their places of refuge.

6. Pollution of the temple and destruction of the books of the law (54-58)

On the twenty-fifth day of Chislev, in the one hundred and forty-fifth year, they built an abomination of desolation upon the altar; and in the cities of Judah on every side they built idol altars. And at the doors of the houses and in the streets they burnt incense. And tearing in pieces the books of the law which they found, they set fire to them. And wherever a book of the covenant was found in the possession of anyone, or if anyone obeyed the law, the king's decree sentenced him to death. Thus they did in their might month by month to the Israelites who were found in the cities.

188

And on the twenty-fifth day of the month they sa
upon the idol altar which was upon Jehovah's sac
altar. And the women who had circumcised their ch
they put to death according to the command. And
hanged their babies about their necks, and destroyed their
households with those who had circumcised them. But
many in Israel made strong resolutions not to eat unclean things, choosing to die that they might not be defiled
with the meats, and might not profane the holy covenant.
So they died. And exceedingly great woe came upon
Israel.

(59-63)

I. **Character and Contents of I Maccabees.** The first book of
Maccabees is in many ways the best history that has come down from
ancient Israel. Luther's conclusion that it was more deserving of a
place in the Old Testament canon than, for example, the book of Esther
is now being widely accepted both in theory and practice. The religious
spirit in which it is written, the importance of the events with which it
deals, and the faithfulness with which they are recorded, all confirm this
conclusion. It is the work of a devoted patriot, who appears to have
been personally acquainted with the events which he records. He was
an ardent admirer of Judas Maccabeus, and may well have been one
of the many valiant Jews who rallied about this sturdy champion.
The author was familiar with the early histories of his race, for he has
adopted many of the phrases peculiar to the books of Samuel and Kings.
His idioms leave no doubt that he wrote in Hebrew, although this version has been lost.

The first book of Maccabees opens with a brief reference to Alexander
the Great and to the Greek rulers who succeeded him. The detailed
history, however, begins with Antiochus Epiphanes and continues to
the death of Simon in 135 B.C. The references in the prologue to the
rebuilding of the walls of Jerusalem by Simon's son, John Hyrcanus,
between 135 and 125 B.C., and the absence of any allusions to the more
important events in the latter part of his reign, indicate that his history
was probably completed by 125 B.C. It was written, therefore, less than
half a century after all the events which it records took place. While
the author is a true patriot and keenly interested in the history of his
race, he does not allow his patriotism to carry him into exaggeration.
He reveals the true historical spirit and a splendid reserve in recounting
the epoch-making events that he records.

189

II. **Character and Contents of II Maccabees.** In marked contrast with I Maccabees is the second book which bears this name. The author states in 2^{19-32} that it was based on an earlier five-volume history written by Jason, of Cyrene, in northern Africa. The final epitomizer of this earlier work probably lived not long after 50 B.C. Jason himself appears to have lived somewhere between 160 and 140 B.C. and to have written from northern Syria. The language of the original was evidently Greek. The aim of the author was didactic rather than historical, and he drew freely from popular tradition. In general character it corresponds closely to the work of the Chronicler, who compiled the Old Testament books of Chronicles and Ezra-Nehemiah. The miraculous element is prominent, numbers are frequently enlarged, and Israel's disasters are minimized. Notwithstanding all of its obvious faults, II Maccabees has preserved many important historical facts. Where its testimony differs from that of I Maccabees, the latter in general should be followed, but its account of the events which led to the Maccabean uprising are much more detailed than those of I Maccabees, which it supplements at many important points. With the aid of these two histories it is possible to gain a remarkably vivid and detailed conception of the half-century that witnessed the reawakening of Judaism and the birth of a new national spirit.

III. **Aggressive Character of Hellenic Culture.** Jewish life and religion were at times almost uprooted, but never fundamentally transformed by the Babylonian and Persian conquerors. Alexander, however, and those who followed in his wake introduced an entirely new and aggressive force into the life and thought of Palestine. The centuries that began with 332 B.C. witnessed the most important struggle that the world has ever seen. It was fought not on the open battle-field, but wherever in Palestine and the lands of the dispersion the currents of that ancient life and commerce met and mingled. It was the age-long conflict between Hellenism and Judaism, those two mighty forces that had long been maturing in the coast lands of the northern and eastern Mediterranean. The outcome of this contest was destined to affect the civilization and faith of all the world throughout the ages.

Judaism represented the life and faith of a peasant people, while Hellenism was born in the city. Wherever Hellenism went, it found expression in civic life. The heathen races of Palestine, the Phœnicians and Philistines on the coast, and the east-Jordan peoples readily welcomed the superior civilization of the conquerors. It appealed powerfully to their intellectual, social, and æsthetic sense, and, in the debased form that it assumed in the East, to their passions. Even the Samaritans readily accepted it; and the city of Samaria was settled by a colony of Macedonian soldiers. The ancient cities of Gaza, Askelon, Accho under the name of Ptolemais, Tyre, Sidon, Damascus, Bethshean under its new name Scythopolis, Rabbath-ammon under the name of Philadelphia, and most of the important east-Jordan cities were soon transformed into active centres of Hellenic culture. Civic pride and patriotism took possession of their inhabitants. Most of the cities had a senate and magistrates elected each year by popular vote. Many of them were adorned by magnificent public buildings, including a forum, theatre, stadium, hippodrome, and gymnasium. Civic patriotism took the place of the old despotism and selfish individualism. Each Hellenic city gave to its citizens new ideals and opportunities. The discussions of the forum, the agora, and the gymnasium inspired them with political, social, and intellectual interests. The plays in the theatres, the races in the hippodrome and stadium amazed and fascinated them. Many of the youths were enlisted in the clubs that were formed in connection with the gymnasium, and all classes participated in the public festivities.

IV. **Contrast Between Hellenism and Judaism.** In the broad perspective of history it is clear that both Hellenism and Judaism were essential to the upbuilding and broadening of the human character and ideals. Hellenism in its nobler form brought what Judaism lacked, and Judaism was fitted to correct the evils and fatal weaknesses of Hellenism. Ben Sira vaguely recognized this, and sought to reconcile these two types of civilization; but in the second century B.C. men were chiefly aware of the glaring contrasts. Compared with the splendor of the life in the Greek cities that of the orthodox Jews seemed crude and barbarous. The intense horror with which the Jews viewed every form of idolatry led them to reject all forms of art. Their hatred of sensuality and immorality led them to regard with aversion the sports and exercises of the gymnasium and the attendant licentiousness. The practical teachers of Israel looked with suspicion upon the subtleties of the different Greek philosophical schools. On the other hand, the homely, domestic joys of the average Jew and his intense devotion to the service of the temple and to the faith of his fathers seemed contemptible to those familiar with the brilliant, voluptuous life of the Hellenic cities. Hellenism protested against the narrowness, barrenness, and intolerance of Judaism; Judaism protested against the godlessness and immorality of Hellenism. Both were right in their protests, and yet each in a sense needed the other.

THE CAUSES OF THE MACCABEAN STRUGGLE

V. Apostasy of the Jews and the Perfidy of the High Priests.
At the beginning of the second century B.C. the Judean state was closely
encircled by a ring of Hellenic cities and subjected on every side to the
seductions of that debased Greek culture which had taken firm root in
the soil of Palestine. As was almost inevitable, many of the Jewish
youth yielded to its attractions. Distaste for the narrowness and austere
customs of their fathers begat in their minds a growing contempt for
their race and its religion. Even some of the younger priests forsook
the temple for the gymnasium. Unconsciously but surely Judaism was
drifting from its old moorings toward Hellenism, until the perfidy of
its high priests and the persecutions of Antiochus Epiphanes aroused
it to a full realization of its peril. The apostates in Jerusalem found a
leader in Jeshua, who had assumed the Greek name of Jason. He was
the brother of Onias III, the reigning high priest, and had been sent to
represent him at the Syrian court. There he improved the opportunity
by promising greater tribute to secure his appointment as high priest.
He was soon outbid, however, by a certain renegade named Menelaus,
who with the aid of Syrian soldiers drove Jason from Jerusalem and
took his place as head of the hellenizing party. The first cause, therefore, of the Maccabean struggle was the apostasy of certain of the Jews
themselves. Apparently in large numbers they abandoned the traditions of their race, and assumed the Greek garb and customs, thus leading their Syrian rulers to believe that the hellenizing of the entire race
would be comparatively easy.

VI. Character of Antiochus Epiphanes. The ruler who by his injustice and persecutions fanned the smouldering flame of Jewish patriotism into a mighty conflagration was Antiochus Epiphanes. As a
youth he had been educated at Rome with the profligate sons of those
who ruled the Imperial City. The Greek and Roman historians, especially Polybius, give vivid portraits of this tyrannical king. In him
the prevailing passion for Hellenism found extreme expression. To
dazzle his contemporaries by the splendor of his building enterprises
and by his dramatic display was his chief ambition. In gratifying thus
his selfish ambition he drained the resources of his kingdom, and was
therefore obliged to resort to extreme measures to replenish his treasury.
In 170 B.C. he made a successful campaign into Egypt. Two years
later he again invaded the rich land of the Nile, only to find himself confronted by a Roman general, who peremptorily ordered him to retreat.
Rome was already the chief power in the eastern Mediterranean, and
Antiochus, although in a rage, wisely decided to retire. It was at this

192

inopportune moment that he found Jerusalem in revolt, misled by a false report and by the renegade high priest Jason. Antiochus not only improved this opportunity to loot the temple and slay many of the inhabitants, but from this time on conceived a bitter antipathy to the Jewish race. This antipathy he shared in common with all the Greek world, for already, as a result of the peculiar religion and customs of the Jews and their success in commercial pursuits, that which is known to-day as the anti-Semitic spirit was fully developed. One of Antiochus's chief ambitions was also to hellenize all his subjects, and the Jews alone offered opposition to the realization of this ambition. Hence they could expect no mercy at the hands of this selfish, capricious despot.

VII. Antiochus's Policy toward the Jews. The measures which Antiochus employed to crush the faith of Judaism were relentlessly thorough. He began with the seizure of Jerusalem, the tearing down of its walls, the fortifying and garrisoning of its citadel with Syrian soldiers and apostate Jews, and the slaughter of all who refused to accede to his demands. Not only was the temple service stopped, but the altar was torn down and desecrated and a heathen altar to Zeus—the abominable desolation of the book of Daniel—was reared in its place. On this swine's flesh was sacrificed, and the presence of harlots in the sacred precincts completed its ceremonial and moral pollution. All the surviving inhabitants of Jerusalem were compelled to sacrifice and pay homage to the heathen gods. Those who retained copies of their laws or persisted in maintaining the customs of their fathers were slain. When many fled to the outlying towns, emissaries of Antiochus pursued them, demanding of each citizen public recognition of the Greek gods. A majority of the Jews apparently yielded to these drastic measures and joined the ranks of the apostates. Of the many crises through which Israel passed this was in many ways the most severe; but then it gave to the world some of the noblest martyrs. The early Christians who perished for their faith were inspired by the example of their Master and by the hope of blessed, individual immortality. To the Jews of the Greek period, however, the great calamity that overtook them came as a sudden and unexpected blow. No clear hope of immortality at first inspired them, for, like Ben Sira and the earlier teachers of the race, the majority of them probably regarded the life beyond death as a passionless existence in the land of darkness. Even the expectation of family or racial immortality seemed denied by the dark outlook. They died as did Eleazar, the aged scribe, simply because of their devotion to the God and laws of their fathers, and because that loyalty meant more to them than life.

§ CIX. THE EFFECT OF PERSECUTION ON THE JEWS

1. Family of Mattathias (I Mac. 2¹⁻⁴)

At that time arose Mattathias the son of John the son of Simeon, a priest of the sons of Joarib, from Jerusalem; and he dwelt in Modein. And he had five sons, John, who was surnamed Gaddis, Simon, who was called Thassi, Judas, who was called Maccabeus, Eleazar, who was called Avaran, Jonathan, who was called Apphus.

When he saw the sacrilegious acts that were being committed in Judah and in Jerusalem, he said,

2. His lament over the fate of city and people (6-14)

> Woe to me! Why was I born
> To see the ruin of my people,
> And the ruin of the holy city,
> And to dwell there while it was being given into the
>   hands of the foe,
> The sanctuary into the hands of foreigners?
> The temple has become as though it had no glory,
> Its splendid vessels have been carried into captivity.
> Her children have been slain in the streets,
> Her young men by the sword of the enemy.
> What people has not taken possession of her palace,
> And seized upon her spoils?
> All her adornments have been taken away,
> From freedom she has been reduced to slavery.
> And now our holy things, our beauty and our glory have
>   been laid waste,
> And the heathen have polluted them.
> Why should we still live?

And Mattathias and his son tore their clothes, and put on sackcloth, and mourned bitterly.

3. His refusal to follow the commands of Antiochus (15-22)

Now the king's officers who were enforcing the apostasy, came into the city of Modein to sacrifice. And many of Israel went over to them, but Mattathias and his sons offered resistance. Then the king's officers said to Mattathias, You are a ruler and a man honored in this city and strengthened by sons and brothers. Now therefore come first and do what the king commands, as all the nations have done, the men of Judah too, with those who remain in Jerusalem. Then you and your house shall be in the number of the king's

MAP OF
PALESTINE,
CONTAINING PLACES FOR
MACCABEAN PERIOD.

0   5   10   20   30
Scale of Miles.

Mt. Hermon
9,166 ft. Damascus

Tyre

Sarepta

Ecdippa

Ptolemais

Jotapata
Cana

Sepphoris

Nazareth

Geba

Dora

Megiddo

Taanach

Straton's Tower

Ginnea

Bethulia

Geba

Samaria

Capharsaba

Shechem

Antipatris

Joppa

Shiloh

Thamnatha

Adida

Lydda

Modein

Eleasa

Lower
Bethhoron

Gophna

Ephraim

Bethel

Upper
Bethhoron

Michmash

Jamnia Gazera

Gibeon

Adasa

Emmaus

Ajalon

Mizpah

Jericho

Jerusalem
2,593

Bethlehem

Ascalon

Bethzacharias

Herodium

Anthedon

Eleutheropolis

Adullam

Bethsur

Tekoa

Mareshah

Halhul

Gaza

Hebron
3,040

Adora

Raphia

Beersheba

Masada

Dan

Kadesh

Gischala

Hazor

Safed

Ramah

Magdala

Capernaum

Sea of Galilee

Amatha

*Mount
Tabor*
1,843

Jezreel

Bethshan

Remtheh

Pella

Dium

Gerasa

Sychar

Gibeah

Amathus

River Jordan

Philadelphia

Heshbon

Medeba

Machaerus

Dibon

MEDITERRANEAN SEA

DEAD SEA

THE M.-N. CO., BUFFALO, N.Y.

friends, and you and your sons shall be honored with silver and gold and many gifts. But Mattathias replied with a loud voice, If all the nations included in the king's dominion obey him, in that each is untrue to the worship of his fathers and chooses to follow his command, yet I and my sons and my brothers will walk in the covenant made with our fathers. Heaven forbid that we should forsake the law and the ordinances. We will not listen to the king's words, to go aside from our worship, either to the right hand or to the left.

And when he had finished saying these things a Jew came in sight of all to sacrifice on the altar that was in Modein according to the king's command. When Mattathias saw it, his zeal was kindled and he trembled inwardly. And he let his anger take possession of him, as was right, and he ran and slew the Jew upon the altar. Also he killed at that time the king's officer, who was compelling men to sacrifice, and pulled down the altar. Thus he showed his zeal for the law, just as Phinehas did in the case of Zimri the son of Salu. Then Mattathias cried out in the city with a loud voice, saying, Whoever is zealous for the law and will maintain the covenant, let him follow me. And he and his sons fled into the mountains, and left behind all that they had in the city. *4. His hot indignation and open resistance (23-28)*

Then many who sought justice and right went down into the wilderness, to dwell there with their sons and wives and cattle, because the evils were becoming ever harder for them to bear. And it was reported to the king's officers and to the forces that were in Jerusalem, the city of David, that certain men who had broken the king's command had gone down into the hiding places in the wilderness. So many pursued after them, and having overtaken them encamped against them, and drew up the line of battle against them on the sabbath day. And they said to them, Things have gone far enough, now come forth and obey the command of the king and you shall live. But they said, We will not come forth, neither will we do as the king commands, to profane the sabbath day. Then they at once offered them battle. But they made no resistance, neither did they cast a stone at them, nor stop up the places of concealment, for they said, *5. Hardships and slaughter of the fugitives (29-38)*

Let us all die in our innocency: let heaven and earth bear witness for us, that you put us to death unjustly. Then they rose up against them in battle on the sabbath, and thus they died with their wives and children and cattle, to the number of a thousand souls.

6.
Their
later
success-
ful
armed
resist-
ance
(39-48)

When Mattathias and his friends knew it they mourned bitterly over them. And they said to each other, If we all do as our brothers have done, and do not fight against the heathen for our lives and our customs, they will now quickly destroy us from off the earth. So they took counsel that day, saying, Whoever shall come against us for battle on the sabbath day, let us fight against him, and we will by no means all die, as our brothers died in the hiding places. Then there gathered together to them a company of Hasideans, brave men of Israel, every one who offered himself willingly for the law. And all who fled from the evils were added to them, and strengthened them. And they mustered a host.

> And smote the sinners in their anger
> And the lawless in their wrath.

And the rest fled to the heathen for safety. Also Mattathias and his friends went about and pulled down the altars, and circumcised by force the children who were uncircumcised, as many as they found in the territory of Israel. Thus they pursued the sons of arrogance, and the work prospered in their hand. They took the direction of affairs out of the hands of the heathen and of the kings, nor did they yield ground to the sinner.

7.
Fare-
well
exhor-
tation
of
Matta-
thias
(49-64)

When the time approached for Mattathias to die he said to his sons, Now insolence and insult have grown strong, and a period of reversals has come, with flaming wrath.

> Now, my sons, be zealous for the law,
> And give your lives for the covenant of your fathers.
> And remember the deeds which your forefathers did in their
>   generations;
> And win great glory and everlasting fame.
> Was not Abraham found faithful when tested?
>   And it was counted to him as righteousness.

Joseph in the time of his distress kept the commandment,
   And became lord of Egypt.
Phinehas our father, because he was so zealous,
   Received the covenant of an everlasting priesthood.
Joshua for carrying out the word of God,
   Became a ruler in Israel.
Caleb for bearing witness in the congregation,
   Obtained a heritage in the land.
David for being merciful,
   Inherited a kingly throne for ever and ever.
Elijah because he was so zealous for the law,
   Was taken up into heaven.
Hananiah, Azariah, Mishael believed,
   And were rescued from the flame.
Daniel because of his innocence,
   Was delivered from the mouth of lions.
And thus consider from generation to generation:
None who put their trust in him ever want strength.
Then be not afraid of the words of a sinful man;
For his glory shall be dung and worms.
To-day he is exalted, but to-morrow he cannot be found,
Because he has returned to dust, and the memory of him
   has perished.
Then my sons be strong, and show yourselves men in behalf
   of the law;
By so doing you shall obtain glory.

And, behold, Simon your brother, I know that he is a man 8. His
   of counsel; appointment of
Obey him always; let him be your adviser. Simon
Judas Maccabeus, too, has been a man of war from his and
   youth; Judas
He shall be your captain, and fight the battle of the people. (65-68)
And take to yourselves all law-abiding men,
And avenge the wrong of your people.
Render a recompense to the heathen,
And give heed to the commands of the law.

                                         9. His
                                         death
   Thus he blessed them and was gathered to his fathers. and
And he died in the one hundred and forty-sixth year, and burial
                                           (69, 70)

his sons buried him in the sepulchres of his fathers at Modein, and all Israel made a great lamentation for him.

10. Daniel's vision of the four beasts (Dan. 7¹⁻⁵) In the first year of Belshazzar king of Babylon Daniel had a dream and visions of his head upon his bed. Then he wrote down the dream: I saw in my vision by night, and behold, the four winds of heaven broke forth upon the great sea. And four great beasts came up from the sea, each different from the other. The first was like a lion and had eagle's wings. I looked until its wings were stripped off, and it was lifted up from the earth, and made to stand upon two feet as a man; and a man's heart was given to it. And behold, a second beast, like a bear; and it was raised up on one side, and three ribs were in its mouth, between its teeth; and they said thus to it: Arise, devour much flesh. After this I beheld, and lo, another like a leopard, which had upon its sides four wings of a bird; and the beast had also four heads, and dominion was given to it. After this I saw in the night visions, and behold, a fourth beast, terrible and fearful, and exceedingly strong; and it had great iron teeth; it devoured and broke in pieces and stamped the rest with its feet; and it differed from all the beasts that were before it; and it had ten horns. I gave attention to the horns, and behold another little horn came up amongst them, before which three of the first horns were plucked up by the roots; and behold, in this horn were eyes, like the eyes of a man, and a mouth speaking great things.

11. The celestial court (9, 10) I waited until thrones were set up, and an aged one took his seat; his clothing was white as snow, and his hair like spotless wool, his throne was fiery flames, its wheels burning fire. A fiery stream issued and came forth before him; thousands of thousands ministered to him, and ten thousand times ten thousand stood before him; the judgment was set and the books were opened.

12. Overthrow of the beasts (11, 12) I looked at that time because of the sound of the great words which the horn spoke—I looked even until the beast was slain, and its body destroyed, and given to be fuel for the fire. Also the rule of the rest of the beasts was taken away; but their lives were prolonged for a fixed time and season.

I saw in the night visions, and behold, there came with the clouds of heaven one like to a son of man, and he came even to the Aged One, and was brought near before him. And there was given him dominion and glory, and sovereignty, that all the peoples, nations, and languages should serve him; his dominion is an everlasting dominion which shall not pass away, and his sovereignty one which shall not be destroyed.

13 Establishment of an eternal worldwide dominion (13, 14)

As for me, Daniel, my spirit was grieved by reason of this, and the visions of my head troubled me. I came near to one of those who stood by, and asked him the truth concerning all this. So he told me and made me know the interpretation of the things. These four great beasts are four kings who shall arise out of the earth. But the saints of the Most High shall receive the sovereignty, and possess the sovereignty forever, even for ever and ever.

14. Interpretation of the vision (15-18)

Then I desired to know the truth concerning the fourth beast, which was different from all of them, exceeding terrible, whose teeth were of iron, and its nails of brass; which devoured, broke in pieces, and stamped the rest with its feet; and concerning the ten horns that were on its head, and the other horn which came up, and before which three horns fell—it that had eyes, and a mouth that spoke great things, and it appeared to be greater than the rest. I looked, and the same horn made war with the saints, and prevailed against them, until the Aged One came, and judgment was given to the saints of the Most High, and the fixed time came that the saints possessed the sovereignty.

15. Question regarding the fourth beast and the conquering horn (19-22)

Thus he said, The fourth beast shall be a fourth kingdom upon earth, which shall be different from all the kingdoms; and shall devour the whole earth, and shall tread it down, and break it in pieces. And as for the ten horns, out of this kingdom shall ten kings arise; and another shall arise after them; and he shall be different from the former, and he shall put down three kings. And he shall speak words against the Most High, and shall continually harass the saints of the Most High; and he shall think to change the fixed times and the law; and they shall be given into his hand until a time and times and half a time. But the judgment shall be set, and they shall take away his kingdom, to

16. Alexander's empire and the rule of Antiochus Epiphanes (23-27)

199

consume and to destroy finally. And the sovereignty, and
the dominion, and the greatness of the kingdoms under the
whole heaven, shall surely be given to the people of the saints
of the Most High; his sovereignty is an everlasting sovereignty, and all dominions shall serve and obey him.

17. Ul-
timate
resur-
rection
of the
loyal
patri-
ots
(12¹⁻³)

And at that time Michael shall stand up, the great prince
who stands for the children of my people; and there shall
be a time of affliction such as there never was since there
was a nation, even to that time; and at that time thy people
shall be delivered, every one who shall be found written in
the book. And many of those who sleep in the dust of the
earth shall awake, some to everlasting life, and some to
shame and everlasting contempt. And they who are wise
shall shine as the brightness of the firmament; and they
who turn many to righteousness as the stars forever and ever.

I. The Uprising Led by Mattathias. The persecutions of Antiochus Epiphanes had at last reached the point where patient submission
and even martyrdom ceased to be a virtue. His agents had successfully
carried the merciless, hellenizing campaign throughout practically all
the territory of Judea. It was not until they reached its extreme northwestern border that they met the first open opposition. The little town
of Modein lay out on the edge of the great plain where the central hills
of Palestine break down into low foot-hills. These are intersected by
rushing brooks and clear, crystal streams that descend from the heights
above. The town lay on a rounded hill about one-third of a mile in
diameter that rises abruptly in a series of steep terraces. The Wady
Malakeh encircled it on the south and west. On the northeastern side,
where lies the modern town, was a broad shoulder of land slightly lower
and larger than the acropolis. In ancient times it was probably the site
of the lower city. Deep, encircling valleys on the north and east completed the natural defences of this border village that became the altar of
Jewish freedom. To-day the scattered ruins of the acropolis are covered in spring-time with a luxuriant growth of grain and olive trees,
making it one of the most picturesque mounds in Palestine.

It is surprising that the revolt against the cruel tyranny of Antiochus
was led by an aged priest. Like many priests, his home was outside
Jerusalem. Evidently he was one of the chief men of Modein. He
was descended from the family of Hasmon, hence his descendants, who
ultimately became the independent rulers of their race, are sometimes

called the Hasmonians. In Mattathias the long-suppressed, hot indignation of the Jewish race at last found expression. In slaying the apostate Jew and Syrian official, Mattathias evoked that warlike spirit which had in earlier days given Israel a home and a place among the nations. His impulsive act inaugurated a new chapter in Israel's life and thought. In its far-reaching consequences it was comparable only to Moses' impulsive slaying of the Egyptian taskmaster.

II. **Party of the Hasideans or Pious.** It was fortunate that Mattathias had five able, mature sons to support him. Simon, the eldest, was already famous in council. Judas, who bore the surname Maccabeus (whence the word Maccabees), soon proved himself a great military leader. Jonathan combined the qualities of Simon and Judas with a certain craftiness that makes him the least attractive of the three. Eleazar later proved on the battle-field that he had the qualities that make heroes and martyrs. Among the Judean hills, and especially in the barren, almost inaccessible fastnesses that descend in a series of terraces from the central plateau to the Dead Sea, Mattathias and his followers found refuge. Hither many patriotic Jews had already fled. The Syrian mercenaries, however, led by the relentless, apostate Jews, pursued them, and, knowing their scruples, attacked them on the sabbath day and pitilessly slaughtered them. Learning from this awful example, Mattathias and his sons wisely decided that it was more important to fight for their lives than to die for a mere institution. They soon attracted to their standard all who were still faithful to the law. Chief among these were those known as the Hasideans or Pious. They were the spiritual successors of the pious or afflicted, whose woes are voiced in the earlier psalms of the Psalter (§ XLVII^v). They were also the forerunners of the party of the Pharisees, which was one of the products of the Maccabean struggle. In them faith and patriotism were so blended that, like Cromwell's Ironsides, they were daunted by no odds. At first they depended upon the guerilla type of warfare, to which the hills of Judea were especially adapted. By enforcing the law of circumcision, by punishing the apostates, and by attacking straggling Syrian bands, they encouraged the faltering Jews, and intimidated the agents of Antiochus. Mattathias soon died, leaving the leadership to his third son, Judas. The poem recording his dying injunctions voices the inspiration that came at this time to Israel's patriots from their nation's past, and that supreme devotion to the law and dauntless courage that animated the leaders in this great movement.

III. **Date of the Visions in Daniel 7-12.** A parallel but different type of character and hope is reflected in the latter part of the book of

Daniel. In the form of visions or predictions, these chapters interpret the meaning of the great world movements from the beginning of the Babylonian to the end of the Greek period. Each vision culminates in a symbolic but detailed description of the rule and persecutions of Antiochus Epiphanes. Several passages describe the destructive policies of this Syrian ruler almost as vividly as the books of Maccabees (Dan. $8^{11,\ 12}$): "It (Antiochus) magnified itself even to the Prince of the Host (Jehovah), and took away from him the daily sacrifice, and cast down the place of his sanctuary, and set up the sacrilegious thing over the daily sacrifice, and cast down truth to the ground, and did it and prospered."

Daniel 11^{20-44} contains a review of the chief events of Antiochus's reign. This description closes with the prediction: "He shall plant his palace between the Mediterranean and the glorious holy mountain; so he shall come to his end and none shall help him." Contemporary records indicate, however, that Antiochus died while engaged in a campaign in distant Persia and not in western Palestine as the author of Daniel anticipated. In the other visions, after the description of Antiochus's persecutions, the details suddenly give place to general predictions, implying that at this point the author turned from the contemplation of past and present events to that which was to him future. The great victories of Judas and his followers that led to the restoration of the temple in 165 B.C. are nowhere mentioned. In 11^{34} is found an allusion to the Maccabean uprising: "Now when they are falling they shall be helped with a little help; but many shall join themselves to them with false protestations." This movement, clearly, is not regarded by the author as significant. The date of these visions, therefore, may be fixed with great confidence between the years 168 and 166 B.C.

IV. **Their Real Character and Aim.** In interpreting these visions it is important to note that they belong to the so-called apocalyptic type of literature. Already Ezekiel and Zechariah had employed the complex symbolism of the apocalypse to stir the imagination and strengthen the faith of their discouraged countrymen. The aim of the author of the closing chapters of Daniel was primarily to present a religious philosophy of history. Through the rise and fall of nations Jehovah's purpose was slowly but surely being realized. They are the expression of the eternal optimism of the prophets. They voice their deathless hope that "the best is yet to be." They were intended to encourage those in the midst of persecution with the assurance that God was still in his heaven, and that all would yet be right with his world.

V. **The Four Heathen Kingdoms and the Kingdom of God.** In the symbolism of the prophet the four beasts of Daniel 7 represented the Chaldean, Medean, Persian, and Greek Empires. The fourth beast with iron teeth that devoured and broke in pieces the rest was clearly the empire of Alexander, and the little horn that sprang up was the little horn which gored and mangled the helpless people of Jehovah. Opposed to the four beasts which represented the angels, or demons, the champions of each of the great heathen kingdoms, was Israel's patron angel Michael. It is this angel that is apparently referred to in 7[13] as coming from heaven, and in appearance like to a son of man. At Jehovah's direction he was to establish a glorious, universal kingdom, the citizens of which were to be the saints, the faithful Jews who remained loyal to Jehovah during the long, cruel persecutions. Not only those who survived but the martyrs sleeping in the dust of the earth were to awake and receive their glorious reward. The apostates were to be sentenced to everlasting shame and contempt. The wise teachers and martyrs who by word and example had striven to keep their race loyal to Jehovah were to be exalted in the coming messianic kingdom. Thus these visions reveal the hopes that inspired certain of the Jewish race in its period of supreme trial: the belief that Jehovah through his angel would speedily overthrow the power of the heathen persecutor, that he would establish a universal kingdom in which his own people should have chief place, and finally that even the bonds of death would not hold those who had died for the law. Thus at last out of this struggle Judaism emerged with a new-found faith in individual immortality. It was still bound up in the belief in the bodily resurrection, but at last the imperishable worth of the individual had become one of the cornerstones of Israel's religion.

§ CX. THE VICTORIES THAT GAVE THE JEWS RELIGIOUS LIBERTY

Then his son Judas, who was called Maccabeus, rose up in his place. And all his brothers helped him, as did all those who had supported his father, and they fought with gladness the battle of Israel.

1. Courage, prowess, and valiant deeds of Judas (I Mac. 3¹⁻⁹)

> He spread far and wide the fame of his glory
> And put on his breastplate like a giant,
> And girded on his weapons of war,
> And set battles in array,
> Protecting the army with his sword.

He was like a lion in his deeds,
And as a lion's whelp roaring for prey.
He pursued the lawless, seeking them out,
And he burnt up those who troubled his people.
The lawless shrunk for fear of him,
And all the workers of lawlessness were greatly terrified;
And deliverance was attained through him.
He angered many kings,
And made Jacob glad with his acts;
And his memory is blessed forever.
He went about among the cities of Judah,
And destroyed the godless from the land,
And turned away the wrath of God from Israel.
And he was renowned to the ends of the earth.

2. Defeat and death of Apollonius (10-12) Then Apollonius gathered the heathen together and a great army from Samaria to fight against Israel. And when Judas learned of it, he went out to meet him, and defeated and slew him; and many fell mortally wounded, while the rest fled. And they captured their spoils, and Judas took the sword of Apollonius, with which he fought all his days.

3. Seron's advance against Judas (13-15) When Seron, the commander of the army of Syria, heard that Judas had gathered a large force of faithful men about him, who went with him to war, he said, I will make myself famous and gain renown in the kingdom; for I will fight with Judas and those with him, who are defying the command of the king. And there went up with him also a mighty army of the godless to help him, to take vengeance on the Israelites.

4. Judas's address before the battle (16-22) As he approached the ascent of Bethhoron, Judas went forth to meet him with a small company. But when they saw the army coming to meet them, they said to Judas, How shall we, few as we are, be able to battle against so great a multitude? and we are faint also, having tasted no food to-day. Then Judas said, It is an easy thing for many to be shut up in the hands of a few; and with Heaven it is equally easy to save by many or by few; for victory in battle does not depend upon the size of an army, but from Heaven comes the strength. They come to us full of insolence and lawlessness, to destroy us with our wives and children and to plunder us; but, as for us, we are fighting for our lives and our laws. And he himself will crush them before our face; so do not be afraid of them.

Now when he had finished speaking, he leaped suddenly upon them, and Seron and his army were put to flight before him. And they pursued them by the descent of Bethhoron to the plain, and there fell of them about eight hundred men; but the rest fled into the land of the Philistines.

5. Defeat and flight of the Syrians (23, 24)

Now the fear of Judas and his brothers and the dread of them began to fall upon the nations round about them. And his reputation reached the king, for every nation was telling of the battles of Judas. But when King Antiochus heard these things, he was filled with indignation and sent and gathered together all the forces of his realm, a very strong army. And he opened his treasury and gave his forces pay for a year, and commanded them to be ready for every emergency. And seeing that money was scarce in his treasury and that the tributes of the country were small, because of the dissension and calamity which he had brought upon the land, for the purpose of taking away the laws which had been in force from the earliest days, he feared that he should not have enough, as at other times, for the expenses and the gifts which he had formerly given with a liberal hand, in which he had surpassed the kings who had been before him. And he was exceedingly perplexed in his mind, and determined to go into Persia and to take the tributes of the countries and to gather much money.

6. Measures to subdue the Jews and to refill the depleted Syrian treasury (25-31)

So he left Lysias, an honorable man and one of the royal family, in charge of the affairs of the king from the River Euphrates to the borders of Egypt and to bring up his son Antiochus, until he returned. And he delivered to him the half of his forces and the elephants, and gave him charge of all the things that he wished to have done and concerning those who dwelt in Judea and in Jerusalem, that he should send a force against them, to root out and destroy the strength of Israel and the remnant of Jerusalem, and to take away their memory from the place, and that he should make foreigners dwell in all their territory and should divide their land to them by lot. Then the king took the remaining half

7. Division of the military forces (32-37)

of the forces and set out from Antioch his capital, in the one hundred and forty-seventh year, and, crossing the Euphrates, he went through the upper countries.

8. The invading Syrian army (38-41)

Now Lysias chose Ptolemy the son of Dorymenes, and Nicanor, and Gorgias, influential men among the king's Friends, and with them sent forty thousand footmen and seven thousand horsemen to go into the land of Judah to destroy it, as the king had ordered. And they set out with all their army and pitched their camp near Emmaus in the plain. And the merchants of the country heard the rumors about them, and taking silver and gold in large quantities, and shackles, they came into the camp to get the Israelites for slaves. There were added to them the forces of Syria and of the Philistines.

9. Attitude of the Jews (42, 43, 46-54)

Then Judas and his brothers saw that evils were increasing and that the forces were encamping in their territory, and when they learned of the commands which the king had given to destroy the people and make an end of them, they said to each other,

Let us raise up the ruin of our people
And let us fight for our people and the sanctuary.

So they gathered together and came to Mizpeh, opposite Jerusalem; for in Mizpeh there was a place of prayer for Israel. And they fasted that day, and put sackcloth and ashes on their heads and tore their clothes, and spread out the book of the law—one of those in which the heathen had been painting images of their idols. And they brought the priests' garments with the first-fruits, and the tithes, and they cut the hair of the Nazirites who had accomplished their days. And they cried aloud toward Heaven, saying, What shall we do with these and whither shall we carry them away? For thy sanctuary is trodden down and profaned, and thy priests are in sorrow and humiliation. And now the heathen have assembled together against us to destroy us. Thou knowest what plans they are making against us. How shall we be able to stand before them, except thou be our help? And they sounded with the trumpets, and cried with a loud voice.

And after this Judas appointed leaders of the people, commanders over thousands, over hundreds, over fifties, and over tens. And he told those who were building houses and those who were planting vineyards and those who were afraid, to return, each to his own house, as the law commanded. Then the army removed and encamped upon the south side of Emmaus. And Judas said, Gird yourselves and be valiant men; and be ready in the morning to fight with these heathen who are assembled together against us to destroy us and our sanctuary. For it is better for us to die in battle than to see the misfortunes of our nation and of the sanctuary. Nevertheless, let Heaven do whatever be his will. 10. Preparations for the battle (55-60)

And Gorgias took five thousand footmen, and a thousand chosen horsemen, and the army set out by night, that it might fall upon the army of the Jews and attack them suddenly. And the men of the citadel were his guides. But when Judas heard of it, he broke camp with his valiant men, that he might attack the king's army which was at Emmaus, while as yet the forces were dispersed from the camp. And when Gorgias came to the camp of Judas by night, he found no one. Then he looked for them in the mountains, thinking that the men were fleeing from him. 11. Gorgias's futile night march (41-6a)

But as soon as it was day, Judas appeared in the plain with three thousand men; only they had neither armor nor swords as they wished. When now they saw the camp of the heathen strongly fortified and cavalry about it and experienced warriors there, Judas said to the men who were with him, Fear not their multitude neither be afraid of their attack. Remember how our fathers were saved in the Red Sea, when Pharaoh pursued them with a host. And now let us cry to Heaven, if he will show favor to us and will remember the covenant made with our fathers and destroy this army before our face to-day, that all the heathen may know that there is one who redeemeth and saveth Israel. 12. Judas's exhortation to his men (6b-11)

Then when the foreigners lifted up their eyes and saw them coming toward them, they went from their camp to battle. And those who were with Judas sounded their trumpets and joined battle; and the heathen were defeated and fled into the plain. But all who were in the rear fell by the 13. Defeat and pursuit of the Greeks (12-15)

207

sword, and they pursued them to Gazara and to the plains of Idumea and Azotus and Jamnia, and there fell of them about three thousand men.

14. Flight of the forces under Gorgias (16-25)

When Judas and his army returned from pursuing them, he said to the people, Do not be greedy for the spoils, since there is a battle before us, and Gorgias and his army are near us in the mountain. But stand now against our enemies and fight them, and afterward you may openly take the spoils. While Judas was still speaking there appeared a part of them, looking out from the mountain; and these saw that their army had been put to flight and that the Jews were burning their camp, for the smoke that was seen showed what had been done. And when they perceived these things, they were thrown into a panic, and seeing the army of Judas also in the plain ready for battle, they all retreated into the land of the Philistines. And Judas returned to sack the camp, and they took much gold and silver and blue and sea-purple and great riches. Then they returned home and sang a song of thanksgiving and gave praise to Heaven, because he is good, because his mercy endureth forever. Thus Israel had a great deliverance that day.

15. Discouragement of Lysias (26, 27)

But the foreigners, as many as had escaped, came and told Lysias all the things that had happened. And when he heard it he was astonished and discouraged, because neither had Israel met with reverses as he wished nor had what the king commanded been realized.

16. Bravery of the Jews in meeting the huge army of Lysias (28-34)

Now in the next year [Lysias] gathered together sixty thousand picked footmen and five thousand horsemen, that he might subdue [the Jews]. When they came to Idumea and encamped at Bethsura, Judas met them with ten thousand men. As he saw that the army was strong, he prayed and said, Blessed art thou, O Saviour of Israel, who didst shatter the attacking power of the mighty man by the hand of thy servant David, and didst deliver the army of the heathen into the hands of Jonathan the son of Saul, and of his armorbearer.

Shut up this army in the hand of thy people Israel,
And let them be ashamed of their army and their horsemen.
Give them faintness of heart,

208

And let their bold courage melt away,
And let them tremble at their destruction.
Cast them down by the sword of those who love thee,
So that all may know thy name who praise thee with
thanksgiving.

Then they joined battle; and there fell of the army of
Lysias about five thousand men, and they fell on the spot
before them.

But when Lysias saw that his army was retreating, and
the boldness that had come upon those who were with Judas,
and how they were ready either to live or to die nobly, he
removed to Antioch and gathered together hired soldiers,
that he might come again into Judea with a still greater
force.

17. Lysias's retreat to prepare for another attack (35)

Then Judas and his brothers said, Now that our enemies
have been defeated, let us go up to cleanse the sanctuary and
to dedicate it again; so they went up to Mount Zion. And
all the army was gathered together and went up to Mount
Zion. And when they saw the sanctuary laid desolate, the
altar profaned, the gates burnt, and shrubs growing in the
courts, as in a forest or as on one of the mountains, and the
priests' chambers pulled down, they tore their garments and
made great lamentation, and putting ashes upon their heads,
they fell prone upon the ground. Then they blew a signal
on the trumpets and cried to Heaven. And Judas appointed
certain men to fight against those who were in the citadel,
until he should have cleansed the sanctuary. And he chose
priests who were unimpeachable observers of the law, who
cleansed the sanctuary and carried out the polluted stones
to an unclean place. And they deliberated as to what they
should do with the altar of burnt-offerings which had been
profaned. They finally reached this wise decision: to pull
it down lest it should be a reproach to them, because the
heathen had defiled it. So they pulled down the altar and
laid the stones on the temple mount in a convenient place,
until there should come a prophet to give an oracle concerning them. Then they took whole stones as the law required
and built a new altar after the design of the former. They
also rebuilt the sanctuary and the inner parts of the temple

18. Ceremonial cleansing and restoration of the temple (36-51)

209

and consecrated the courts. They also made the holy vessels new and brought the candlestick and the altar for burnt-offerings and for incense and the table into the temple. And they burned incense on the altar and lighted the lamps that were on the candlestick, and they gave light in the temple. Then they set loaves upon the table and spread out the veils. So they finished all the work they had undertaken.

19. Institution of the feast of dedication (52-61)

And they arose early in the morning of the twenty-fifth day of the ninth month, which is the month Chislev, in the one hundred and forty-eighth year (165 B.C.) and offered sacrifice according to the law upon the new altar of burnt-offering which they had made. About the same time and on the same day, in which the heathen had profaned it, was it dedicated again with songs and harps and lutes and with cymbals. And all the people prostrated themselves and worshipped and gave praise to Heaven, who had given them good success. And they celebrated the dedication of the altar eight days, and offered burnt-offerings with gladness and sacrificed a sacrifice of deliverance and praise. And they decorated the front of the temple with crowns of gold and small shields and rededicated the gates and the priests' chambers and made doors for them. And great joy reigned among the people, because the reproach of the heathen had been removed. And Judas and his brothers and the whole congregation of Israel decreed that the days of the dedication of the altar should be kept in their seasons from year to year for the period of eight days, from the twenty-fifth day of the month Chislev, with gladness and joy. At that time also they fortified Mount Zion with high walls and strong towers all round, lest by any chance the heathen should come and tread them down, as they had done before. And he stationed there a force to keep it, and they fortified Bethsura, that the people might have a stronghold in Idumea.

I. The Character of Judas. Judas Maccabeus was a man of un-questioned courage. In the many battles which he fought he was always found at the forefront in the most desperate engagement. More than that he was able to arouse courage in a people that for centuries had learned only to bow unresistingly before their conquerors. All the evidence found in the two books of Maccabees indicates that he was inspired by the noblest patriotism. The motive power in his patriotism was devotion to the law and customs of his race. In this respect he was a leader supremely acceptable to the Hasideans or Pious, who rallied about his standard. In any other age or setting his devotion would have seemed but fanaticism. The situation, however, was extremely critical. Disloyalty to the law and the distinctive rites of Judaism was treason. If ever in the world's history it was justifiable to meet force by force and to unshield the sword in behalf of religion, this certainly was the occasion. In his military tactics Judas revealed the cunning that characterizes the hunted. He developed great skill in choosing a strategic position and in launching his followers against a vulnerable point in the enemy's line. In this respect he showed himself a disciple of David's able general Joab. They were the same tactics that Napoleon employed so effectively in later days and on larger battle-fields. Judas resembled in many ways Israel's first king, Saul. He was impetuous, patriotic, intense, and energetic. He was especially skilled in leading a sudden attack. His task also was strikingly similar to that of Israel's first king, and like Saul in his later days he showed the same inability to organize and hold his followers in a time of comparative peace.

II. **Obstacles against Which Judas Contended.** When Judas was called to champion the cause of the Jews, they were hated by the rest of the world. It was a disorganized band of fugitives that rallied about him, without homes, resources, or arms. Opposed to him were the large armies of a powerful empire. The Greek mercenaries that fought in the Syrian ranks were armed with coats of mail and the best weapons known to the ancient world. They were also thoroughly trained in the art of war and under the direction of experienced generals. On every battle-field the Syrians outnumbered the Jews almost six to one. Pitted against Judas and his followers were apostates of his own race, who knew the land, were able to spy out the movements of the Jews, and were inspired by the bitterest hatred. The few advantages on the side of Judas were: first, his followers were aroused to heroic deeds by the peril of the situation. In the second place they were inspired by an intense religious zeal. The one force throughout Semitic history that has bound together tribes and nations and made the Semite an almost invincible fighting power has been religion. The familiar illustrations are the Mohammedan conquests that swept victoriously across the Bosporus and conquered Constantinople, also across northern Africa, and surged into southern Europe over the Straits of Gibraltar and threatened for a time completely to engulf the Western civilization. Familiar modern illustrations are the Mahdist insurrections that have from time to time taxed the resources of the English in northern Africa. In the third place the land of Judea, with its narrow western passes rapidly ascending to the heights above, enabled Judas to choose his battle-field at a point where only a few of the enemy could be brought into action and where a handful of valiant men could keep an army at bay.

III. **Defeat of Apollonius and Seron.** At first Judas wisely confined himself to guerilla warfare. This enabled him in time to clothe and arm his followers with the garments and weapons taken from the enemy. The most important of these smaller engagments took place north of Jerusalem. As Apollonius, the Syrian governor of Samaria, was advancing into Judea, Judas suddenly fell upon the Syrians and slew their leader. Henceforth the sword of the Syrian governor was effectively wielded by Judas in behalf of religious liberty.

News of the victory soon brought Seron, the governor of Cœle-Syria, with a large army. He advanced from the coast plain by the most direct road to Jerusalem over the famous pass of the Bethhorons. Within a distance of two miles the road ascended nearly fifteen hundred feet. At points it was merely a steep, rocky pass, so that an invading army was forced to march single file and to pull themselves up over the rocks. Here on the heights that looked out toward his home at Modein Judas, appealing to the faith and patriotism of his men, swept down upon the enemy and won his first great victory.

IV. **The Battle of Emmaus.** The first great Jewish victory was a severe blow to the power of Antiochus Epiphanes, for at that time he was confronted by a depleted treasury. He therefore left his kingdom in charge of Lysias, one of his nobles, and set out on a campaign into Persia from which he never returned. Three generals with a large army were sent by Lysias against the Jews. So confident were they of a Syrian victory that a horde of slave merchants accompanied the army that they might purchase the Jewish captives. This time the Syrians avoided the difficult pass of Bethhoron and chose the Wady Ali, along which the modern carriage road winds up from the coast to Jerusalem. The main camp was pitched at Emmaus at the southeastern side of the Plain of Ajalon under the Judean hills. Meantime Judas had selected as his head-quarters the lofty hill of Mizpah, associated by earlier tradition with Samuel and the scene of the short-lived rule of Gedaliah. It was well chosen, for it commanded a view of the territory to the north, south, and west. While the army of the Syrians, sent by night to surprise Judas, were marching up the northern valley, the Jewish patriots were led westward toward the plain along one of the parallel valleys that penetrated the Judean hills. Having appealed to the patriotic memories and the religious zeal of his followers, Judas led them in a sudden early morning attack against the Syrians encamped near Emmaus. Soon the Syrians were in wild flight across the plain to the Philistine cities, and Judas and his followers were left in possession of the camp and its rich spoil. Panic also seized his pursuers when they saw their camp in possession of the enemy, and Judas was left for the moment undisputed master of the land of his fathers. This victory in the year 166 B.C. was in many ways the most sweeping and significant in early Maccabean history.

V. The Battle at Bethsura. The next year Lysias himself gathered a huge army of sixty thousand infantry and five thousand cavalry and led them against the Jews. This time the Syrians advanced through the broad valley of Elah where David had fought against the Philistine giant. Thence they followed the Wady Sur, turned southward and then eastward, penetrating to the top of the Judean plateau a little north of Hebron. Approaching from this point the Syrians were protected in their rear by the Idumeans, the descendants of the Edomites. They succeeded in reaching the point where the road from the west joins the central highway from Hebron to Jerusalem. There on a sloping hill crowned with the border town of Bethsura, Judas was able to rally ten thousand followers to meet the huge Syrian army. From the parallel account in II Maccabees it is clear that he did not succeed in winning a decisive victory, but a crisis in Antioch suddenly compelled Lysias to return, leaving the Jews in possession of the battle-field.

VI. Restoration of the Temple Service. With mingled sadness and rejoicing Judas proceeded at once to Jerusalem and with his followers took up the task of restoring the desecrated temple and its service. The citadel of Acra, which appears to have been situated on the Hill of Ophel to the south of the temple, was still strongly garrisoned by apostate Jews and Syrian soldiers. For nearly a quarter of a century, until the days of Simon, it continued to be held by Syrian forces, and remained a constant menace to the peace of Jerusalem. The vivid account of the purification of the temple reveals the intense devotion of the Jews to this ancient sanctuary, and throws clear light upon the nature of its service. This epoch-making act is commemorated even to-day by the Jews throughout the world and is known as the Feast of Lights. It is a memorial of that successful struggle for religious freedom in which principles were established that have affected the thought and action of all succeeding generations. Through all their many vicissitudes and under their many Gentile rulers, with few exceptions, the Jews have enjoyed uninterruptedly the right of worshipping in accordance with the dictates of their law and the customs of their fathers.

VII. **The New Spirit in Judaism.** Henceforth the law for which their fathers had poured out their life-blood and for which the Jews had fought so valiantly was regarded with new and deeper veneration and its commands gained a new authority. Again the Jews had enjoyed a taste of freedom and had learned that by united and courageous action they could shake off the hated heathen yoke. This new warlike note is sounded in many of the later psalms of the Psalter. Chapters 9–14, appended to the older books of Zechariah, apparently come from this same period and voice the thought of the conquerors. The words of the ninth chapter express their joy and exultation:

> For I have bent Judah to me,
> As a bow which I have filled with Ephraim;
> I will urge thy sons against the sons of Greece,
> And I will make thee like the sword of a hero.
> Then Jehovah shall be seen above them,
> And his shaft shall go forth like lightning.
> Jehovah shall blow a blast upon a trumpet,
> And travel on the whirlwinds of the south.
> Jehovah of hosts shall defend them;
> And they shall devour and tread down the slingstones,
> They shall drink their blood like wine,
> They shall be filled with it like the crevices of an altar.
> And Jehovah their God shall give them victory in that day.
> Like sheep he shall feed them in his land.
> Yea, how good and how beautiful shall it be!
> Corn shall make the young men flourish, and new wine the
> maidens.

The victories of Judas in all probability also inspired the messianic hope expressed in 9^{9-10}:

> Rejoice greatly, O daughter of Zion!
> Shout aloud, O daughter of Jerusalem!
> Behold thy king will come to thee;

Vindicated and victorious is he,
Humble, and riding upon an ass.
Upon the foal of an ass.
He shall cut off chariots from Ephraim,
And horses from Jerusalem;
The battle-bow shall also be cut off,
And he shall speak to the nations;
His rule shall be from sea to sea,
From the river to the ends of the earth.

§ CXI. THE LONG CONTEST FOR POLITICAL INDEPENDENCE

Now when the heathen round about heard that the altar had been built and the sanctuary dedicated as it was formerly, they were very angry and concluded to destroy the race of Jacob that was in the midst of them, and they began to slay and destroy among the people. Judas, however, fought against the people of Esau in Idumea at Akrabattine, because they besieged Israel, and he defeated them with a great slaughter and humbled their pride and took their spoils. He remembered the wickedness of the inhabitants of Baean, who were a source of annoyance and of danger, lying in ambush for them along the roads. And they were shut up by him in the towers, and he besieged them and destroyed them utterly and burned the towers of the place, with all who were in them. *1. Slaughter of the Idumeans (I Mac. 5¹⁻⁵)*

Then he passed over to the Ammonites and found a strong force and many people, with Timotheus as their leader. And he fought many battles with them, and they were defeated before him, and he conquered them. Then when he had gained possession of Jazer and its villages, he returned again into Judea. *2. Defeat of the Ammonites (6-8)*

Then the heathen who were in Gilead gathered together against the Israelites who were on the borders to destroy them. And they fled to the stronghold of Dathema and sent letters to Judas and his brothers, saying, The heathen who are about us have gathered together against us to destroy us, and they are preparing to come and get possession of the *3. Reports of outrages in Gilead and Galilee (9-15)*

215

stronghold to which we have fled for refuge, and Timotheus
is the leader of their forces. Now therefore come and rescue
us from their power, for many of our men have fallen; and
all our countrymen who dwell in the land of Tob, have been
put to death, and they have carried into captivity their wives
and children and their possessions. And they destroyed
there about a thousand men. While the letters were being
read, there came other messengers from Galilee with their
garments torn, bringing a message of similar import, saying,
That there were gathered together against them men of
Ptolemais, of Tyre, of Sidon, and from all heathen Galilee
to destroy them completely.

**4.
Prepa-
rations
for the
cam-
paign
in
Gilead
and
Galilee
(16-20)**

Now when Judas and the people heard these things, a
great assembly came together to consult what they should
do for their kinsmen who were in distress and being attacked
by the heathen. And Judas said to Simon his brother,
Choose men, and go, rescue your countrymen who are in
Galilee, but Jonathan my brother and I will go into the land
of Gilead. And he left Joseph the son of Zacharias and
Azarias, as leaders of the people, with the rest of the army in
Judea, in order to guard it. And he gave orders to them,
saying, Take charge of the heathen until we return. And to
Simon were assigned three thousand men to go to Galilee
and to Judas eight thousand men to go into the land of
Gilead.

**5.
Simon's
suc-
cesses
in Gal-
ilee
(21-23)**

Then Simon went into Galilee and fought many battles
with the heathen, and the heathen were defeated by him.
And he pursued them to the gate of Ptolemais. And there
fell of the heathen about three thousand men, and he took
the spoils from them. They took with them those who were
in Galilee and in Arbatta, with their wives and their children
and all that they had, and brought them into Judea with
great rejoicing.

**6. Re-
turn to
Jeru-
salem
(45, 54)**

Then Judas gathered all the Israelites who were in the
land of Gilead, from the least to the greatest, with their
wives and children and their household possessions, a very
great host, that they might go into the land of Judah. And
they went up to Mount Zion with gladness and joy and offered
whole burnt-offerings, because not one of them had been
slain, but they had returned safe and sound.

Then Judas and his brothers went out and fought against the people of Esau in the land toward the south. And he smote Hebron and the villages belonging to it and pulled down its citadel and burned the surrounding towers. Then he set out to go into the land of the Philistines; and he went through Marissa. On that day certain priests, desiring to do exploits there, were slain in battle, when they unwisely went out to fight. Then Judas turned aside to Azotus, to the land of the Philistines, and pulled down their altars and burned the carved images of their gods and, taking the spoil of their cities, he returned to the land of Judah. And the hero Judas and his brothers were greatly honored by all Israel and by all the heathen wherever their name was heard.

7. Judas's success-ful wars against the Idu-means and Philis-tines (65-68, 62)

Now those who were in the citadel were hindering Israel round about the sanctuary and were always seeking to do them harm and were a support to the heathen. But Judas determined to destroy them and called all the people together to besiege them. And they were gathered together and besieged them in the hundred and fiftieth year, and he made mounds from which to shoot and engines of war. Then some of those who were shut up came out and certain apostate Israelites joined them. And they went to the king and said, When will you finally satisfy justice and avenge our brothers? We were willing to serve your father and to live as he enjoined, and to obey his commands; but because of this our own people besieged us in the citadel and were alienated from us; and as many of us as they could find, they killed and despoiled our inheritances. And not against us only have they stretched out their hand, but also against all that bordered on them. And now they are to-day encamped against the citadel at Jerusalem, to take it, and they have fortified the sanctuary and Bethsura. And if you do not quickly anticipate them, they will do greater things than these, and you will not be able to check them.

8. Siege of the citadel and the appeal of the apos-tates to the Syrian king (6:18-27)

When the king had heard this, he was angry, and gathered together all his Friends, the officers of his army, and those who commanded the cavalry. There came to him also from other kingdoms and from isles of the sea, bands of hired soldiers. So the number of his forces was a hundred thousand footmen and twenty thousand horsemen and thirty-two ele-

9. Advance of a power-ful Syrian army (28-41)

phants trained for war. Then they went through Idumea
and encamped against Bethsura and carried on the siege a
long time and made engines of war. The besieged, however,
sallied out and burned them and fought valiantly. And
Judas departed from the citadel and encamped at Beth-
zacharias, opposite the king's camp. Then the king rose
early in the morning and had his army set out at full speed
along the road to Beth-zacharias and his forces prepared for
battle and the trumpets were sounded. And they showed
the elephants the blood of grapes and mulberries, in order to
excite them for the battle. Then they distributed the beasts
among the phalanxes and stationed by each elephant a thousand men armed with coats of mail and helmets, with brass
on their heads; and to each beast five hundred chosen
horsemen were appointed. These were already there,
wherever the beast was, and wherever the beast went, they
went with him and did not separate themselves from him.
And upon them were towers of wood, strong, covered, one
girded upon each beast. Upon them were engines and two
or three men, who fought upon them, besides the Indian
who guided the elephant. The rest of the horsemen he
stationed on both sides of the two wings of the army to inspire terror and to protect the phalanxes. And when the
sun struck the golden and bronze shields, the mountain
shone with them and blazed like torches of fire. And a part
of the king's army was spread out on the heights, and some
on the low ground, and they moved firmly and in good order.
And all who heard the noise of their multitude, and the
marching of the great numbers, and the rattling of the arms,
trembled because the army was very great and strong.

10.
Brave
but
futile
attack
of the
Jews
(42-47)

Then Judas and his army approached for battle, and there
fell of the king's army six hundred men. Now when Eleazar,
who was called Avaran, saw one of the beasts armed with
royal breastplates, which was higher than all the beasts,
and it looked as though the king was upon it, he gave himself to save his people and to gain for himself an everlasting
fame; and he ran upon him courageously in the midst of
the phalanx and slew on the right hand and on the left, and
they scattered from before him on either side. Then he
crept under the elephant, thrust him from beneath, and slew

218

him. And the elephant fell to the earth upon him, and he died there. But when they saw the strength of the king and the fierce onset of the armies, they turned away from them.

But those who were in the king's army went up to Jerusalem to meet them, and the king encamped for a struggle with Judea and Mount Zion. And he made peace with those in Bethsura; for they surrendered the city, because they had no food there to endure the siege, because the land had a sabbath. So the king took Bethsura and stationed a garrison there to keep it. Then he encamped against the sanctuary for a long time; and he set there mounds from which to shoot and engines of war and instruments for casting stones and fire, and pieces to cast darts and slings. And they also erected engines against those of the besiegers and fought for a long time. But since there was no food in the sanctuary, because it was the seventh year and those who had fled for safety into Judea from among the heathen had eaten up what remained of the store of provisions, there were but a few left in the sanctuary, because the famine became so severe upon them, and they scattered, each man to his own home.

11. Surrender of Bethsura and the extremities of the Jews in Jerusalem (48-54)

Now Lysias heard that Philip, whom Antiochus the king, had appointed during his lifetime to bring up his son Antiochus that he might be king, had returned from Persia and Media and with him the forces that went with the king, and that he was trying to get control of the government, he hastily decided to depart. And he said to the king, and to the officers of the army and to the men, We are growing weaker every day, our supplies are scanty, and the place which we are besieging is strong, and the welfare of the kingdom depends upon us; now therefore let us give the right hand to these men and make peace with them and with all their nation, and covenant with them that they may live according to their own customs as formerly; for because of their laws, which we abolished, they were angered and did all these things. This counsel pleased the king and the princes, and he sent to them to make peace. They accepted it, and when the king and the princes took oath to them, they came out of the stronghold. But when the king en-

12. Complications at Antioch and the rights guaranteed to the Jews (55-63)

tered Mount Zion and saw the strength of the place, he broke the oath which he had sworn and gave orders to pull down the wall round about. Then he set out in haste and returned to Antioch and found Philip master of the city; and he fought against him and took the city by force.

13. Accession of Demetrius I (7¹⁻⁴) In the one hundred and fiftieth year, Demetrius the son of Seleucus escaped from Rome and went up with a few men to a city by the sea, and there proclaimed himself king. And when he entered the palace of his fathers, the army seized Antiochus and Lysias, to bring them to him. But when the fact was made known to him, he said, Do not show me their faces. And the army slew them. So Demetrius sat upon the throne of his kingdom.

14. Deceitful claims and charges of Alcimus (5-18) And there came to him all the lawless and the apostate men of Israel, with Alcimus, their leader, desiring to be high priest. And they accused the people before the king, saying, Judas and his brothers have destroyed all your friends, and have scattered us from our own land. Now therefore send a man whom you trust, and let him go and see all the havoc which he has made of us and of the king's country, and how he has punished them and all who helped them. So the king chose Bacchides, one of the king's Friends, who was ruler in the province beyond the River Euphrates, and was a great man in the kingdom, and faithful to the king. He sent him and also that godless Alcimus, and confirmed him in the high priesthood, and commanded him to take vengeance upon the Israelites. So they set out and came with a great army into the land of Judah, and he sent messengers to Judas and his brothers with words of peace, deceitfully. But they paid no attention to their words for they saw that these men had come with a great army. Then there were gathered together to Alcimus and Bacchides a company of scribes, to seek for justice. And the Hasideans were the first among the Israelites who sought peace with them; for they said, One who is a descendant of Aaron has come with the forces and he will do us no wrong. And he spoke words of peace to them, and took oath to them, saying, We will seek the hurt neither of you nor of your friends. And they put confidence in him. But he seized sixty of them, and slew them in one day, as it is written in the Scriptures,

The flesh of thy saints . . .
And their blood they poured out round about Jerusalem;
And there was no man to bury them.

And the fear and hatred of them fell upon all the people, for they said, There is neither truth nor justice in them; for they have broken the covenant and the oaths which they made.

And when Judas saw that Alcimus and his company had done more mischief among the Israelites than the heathen, he went out into the whole territory of Judea round about and took vengeance on the men who had deserted from him, and they were restrained from going forth into the country. But when Alcimus saw that Judas and his company were growing strong and knew that he was not able to withstand them, he returned to the king and brought evil charges against them. So the king sent Nicanor, one of his honored princes, a man who hated Israel and was their enemy, and commanded him to destroy the people. _{15. Judas's policy and its effect (23-26)}

When Nicanor came to Jerusalem with a great army, he sent to Judas and his brother a message of peaceful words with deceitful intent, saying, Let there be no battle between us. I will come with a few men, that I may see your faces in peace. And he came to Judas, and they saluted one another peaceably. But the enemies were prepared to take away Judas, by violence. And when the fact was clear to Judas, that he had come to him with deceit, he was very much afraid of him and would see his face no more. So Nicanor knew that his plan was discovered, and he went out to meet Judas in battle near Capharsalama. And there fell of those with Nicanor about five hundred men. Then they fled into the city of David. _{16. Nicanor's treachery (27-32)}

Now after these things Nicanor went to Zion. And when some of the priests came out of the sanctuary, and some of the elders of the people, to salute him peaceably and to show him the whole burnt-offering that was being offered for the king, he mocked them, and laughed at them, and abused them, and talked insolently. He also swore in a rage, saying, Unless Judas and his army are now delivered into my hands, if I come again in peace, I will burn up this temple. _{17. His outrages (33-38)}

221

He went out in a great rage. Then the priests went in and stood before the altar and the temple; and they wept and said, Thou didst choose this temple to be called by thy name, to be a house of prayer and supplication for thy people. Take vengeance on this man and his army, and let him fall by the sword. Remember their blasphemies, and let them live no longer.

18. Judas's prayer and great victory over Nicanor (39-46)

And Nicanor set forth from Jerusalem and encamped in Bethhoron, and there the army of Syria met him. But Judas encamped in Adasa with three thousand men. Then Judas prayed and said, When they who came from the king blasphemed, thine angel went out and smote among them an hundred and sixty-five thousand. Even so destroy thou this army before us to-day, and let all the rest know that he hath spoken wickedly against thy sanctuary, and judge thou him according to his wickedness. So on the thirteenth day of the month Adar the armies joined battle; and Nicanor's army was defeated, and he himself was the first to fall in the battle. And when his army saw that Nicanor had fallen, they threw away their weapons and fled. And [the Jews] pursued them a day's journey from Adasa as far as Gazara when they sounded the trumpet-signal for the return. Then they came out from all the villages of Judea on every hand and outflanked them; and the one turned them back on the other army, and they all fell by the sword, so that none of them was left.

19. Exultation over the death of Nicanor (47-50)

And they took the spoils and the booty, and they struck off Nicanor's head and his right hand, which he had stretched out so haughtily, and brought them and hung them up in the citadel of Jerusalem. And the people were very glad. They also enacted an ordinance for the celebration of this day year by year, the thirteenth day of Adar. So the land of Judah had rest for a brief period.

20. Advance of the Syrian army and the desertion of Judas by the Jews (91-6)

When Demetrius heard that Nicanor had fallen with his forces in battle, he sent Bacchides and Alcimus again into the land of Judah a second time, and the southern wing of his army with them. And they went by that way that leads to Gilgal, and encamped against Masaloth, which is in Arbela, and gained possession of it and destroyed many people. And the first month of the hundred and fifty-second year

222

they encamped against Jerusalem. Then they set out and went to Berea with twenty thousand footmen and two thousand horsemen. And Judas was encamped at Elasa, and three thousand chosen men with him. And when they saw the multitude of the forces, that they were many, they were greatly frightened, and many slipped away from the army, so that there were left of them not more than eight hundred men.

And when Judas saw that his army had dispersed, he was deeply troubled, because he had no time to gather them together, and he grew discouraged. And he said to those who were left, Let us arise and go up against our adversaries, if perhaps we may be able to fight with them. And they would have dissuaded him, saying, We shall not be able; but let us rather save our lives now; let us return again with our fellow-countrymen and fight against them, for we are few. But Judas said, Far be it from me so to do, that I should flee from them. For if our time has come, let us die manfully for the sake of our fellow-countrymen and not leave a cause of reproach against our honor.

21. His determination to fight (7-10)

Then the army set out from the camp and drew up to meet them; and the cavalry drew up into two companies, and the slingers and the archers went before the army, with all the strong, foremost warriors. But Bacchides was in the rear wing. Then the phalanx advanced on both sides, and they sounded their trumpets. And Judas's men also sounded their trumpets, and the earth shook with the shout of the armies; so the battle was begun and continued from morning until evening. And when Judas saw that Bacchides and the strength of his army were on the right side, all who were brave in heart went with him, and the right wing was defeated by them, and he pursued them to the slope of the mountains. And they who were on the left wing, when they saw that the right wing was defeated, turned and followed upon the footsteps of Judas and of those who were with him. And the battle grew fierce, and many on both sides fell mortally wounded. Then Judas fell and the rest fled.

22. The battle and death of Judas (11-18)

And Jonathan and Simon took Judas their brother and buried him in the sepulchre of his fathers at Modein. And

23. Burial of Judas (19, 20)

they bewailed him, and all Israel made great lamentation for him and mourned many days, and said,

> How is the hero fallen,
> The saviour of Israel!

24. His unrecorded deeds (22)

And the rest of the valiant acts of Judas, and his wars and the valiant deeds which he did, and his greatness—they have not been recorded, for they were very many.

25. Persecution of the followers of Judas (23-27)

Now after the death of Judas, the apostates showed themselves in all the territory of Israel, and all who practised injustice flourished. About the same time there was a very severe famine, and the whole people sided with them. Then Bacchides selected the godless men and made them rulers of the country. And they conducted a thorough search for the friends of Judas and brought them to Bacchides, and he took vengeance on them and tortured them cruelly. Then great tribulation came upon Israel, such as had not been since the time that prophets had ceased to appear among them.

26. Choice of Jonathan as leader (28-36)

Thereupon all the friends of Judas assembled and said to Jonathan, Since your brother Judas has died, we have no one like him to go out against our enemies and Bacchides and against those of our own kin who hate us. Now therefore we have chosen you this day to be our prince and leader in his place that you may fight our battles. So Jonathan assumed the leadership at that time and took the place of his brother Judas.

27. Authority conferred upon Jonathan by Demetrius (10¹⁻⁶)

Now in the one hundred and sixtieth year, Alexander the son of Antiochus Epiphanes went up and took possession of Ptolemais, and they received him, and he reigned there. When King Demetrius heard of it, he gathered very large forces and went out to meet him in battle. Demetrius also sent letters to Jonathan with words of peace, so as to honor him greatly. For he said, Let us get the start in making peace with them before he makes a compact with Alexander against us. For he will remember all the wrongs that we have done to him, and to his brothers and his nation. And he gave him authority to collect forces and to provide arms and to be his ally. Also he commanded that they should deliver up to him the hostages who were in the citadel.

Then Jonathan came to Jerusalem, and read the letters in the hearing of all the people, and of those who were in the citadel. And they were greatly afraid when they heard that the king had given him authority to collect an army. And the garrison delivered up the hostages to Jonathan, and he restored them to their parents. And Jonathan took up his residence in Jerusalem and began to rebuild and renew the city. And he commanded those who did the work to build the walls and Mount Zion round about with square stones for defence; and they did so. Then the foreigners, who were in the strongholds which Bacchides had built, fled, and each man left his place and went into his own land. Only some of those who had forsaken the law and the commandments were left at Bethsura, because it was an asylum for them. 28. Restoration of hostages and the rebuilding of Jerusalem (7-14)

And when King Alexander heard all the promises which Demetrius had made to Jonathan and had been told of the battles which he and his brothers had fought and the valiant deeds that they had done and of the hardships which they had endured, he said, Shall we find such another man? Now therefore let us make him our friend and ally. So he wrote letters and sent them to him with contents like these: 29. Jonathan's appointment as high priest by Alexander Balas (15-17)

King Alexander to his brother Jonathan, greeting: We have heard of you that you are a valiant man and fit to be our friend. And now we have appointed you to-day to be high priest of your nation and to be called the king's Friend (and he sent to him a purple robe and a crown of gold), and to take our part and to remain on friendly terms with us.

And Jonathan put on the holy garments in the seventh month of the hundred and sixtieth year at the feast of tabernacles, and he gathered together forces, and provided arms in abundance. 30. His assumption of his honors (21)

Now in the one hundred and sixty-fifth year, Demetrius son of Demetrius, came from Crete into the land of his fathers. Then King Alexander heard of it, and he was exceedingly troubled and returned to Antioch. And Demetrius appointed Apollonius, who was over Coele-Syria, and he collected a great army and encamped in Jamnia, and sent to Jonathan the high priest this message: 31. Apollonius's challenge to Jonathan (67-71)

You alone are hostile to us, and I have become a laughing-stock and butt of ridicule on account of you. Now why do you flaunt your power against us in the mountains? If, indeed, you trust your forces, come down to us in the plain, and there let us try the matter together, because with me is the power of the cities.

32. The battle and defeat of Apollonius (74-76) Now when Jonathan heard the words of Apollonius, he was stirred to anger, and he chose ten thousand men and went forth from Jerusalem, and Simon his brother met him to help him. And he encamped against Joppa. The people of the city, however, shut him out, because Apollonius had a garrison in Joppa. So they fought against it. Then the people of the city were afraid and opened to him, and Jonathan became master of Joppa.

33. Confirmation of Jonathan's authority (11²⁰⁻²⁷) At that time Jonathan gathered together the people of Judea to take the citadel that was at Jerusalem, and he erected many engines of war against it. Some, however, who hated their own nation, apostates, went to the king, and reported to him that Jonathan was besieging the citadel. And when he heard it, he was angry, and immediately after he heard of it he set out and came to Ptolemais, and wrote to Jonathan that he should not besiege it, and that he should meet him and confer with him at Ptolemais with all speed. But when Jonathan heard this, he gave orders to proceed with the siege, while he chose certain of the elders of Israel and of the priests, and putting himself in peril, and taking silver and gold and garments, and various presents besides, he went to the king at Ptolemais. And he was favorably received; and although some apostates of the nation made complaints against him, the king treated him just as his predecessors had done and exalted him in the presence of all his Friends, both confirming to him the high priesthood, and all the other honors that he had before, and giving him pre-eminence among his Chief Friends.

34. Demetrius's concessions (28, 29) And Jonathan requested the king to make Judea free from tribute, together with the three districts of Samaria, and he promised him three hundred talents. And the king consented and wrote letters to Jonathan concerning all these things.

I. **The Political Situation.** The position of the Jewish patriots was both perilous and tragic. A ring of hostile peoples pressed them closely

226

on every side. The Jews were the victims of centuries of wrong and hatred. Those residing in the neighboring lands also suffered from this widespread and bitter hostility. Among all the peoples of south-western Asia they had no allies except the Nabateans, an Arabian people that had driven the Edomites from their home on Mount Seir. The only bond that bound them to this ambitious heathen race was the common hatred of the Syrians. It was natural, therefore, that Judas a little later should send an embassy with the object of securing the moral support, if not the direct intervention, of the distant Roman power whose influence was beginning to be felt throughout all the Mediterranean coast lands. For the present, however, Judas was dependent simply upon the sword for defence. He also had no time for permanent conquest, for he must prepare himself for the heavier blow that the court of Antioch was preparing to deliver. All that he could do, therefore, was to make sudden attacks upon his foes on every side and rescue the persecuted Jews by bringing them back with him to Judea.

II. **The Jewish Attitude toward the Heathen Reflected in the Book of Esther.** In these perilous circumstances it is not strange that the Jews gravitated far from the position of broad tolerance advocated by the II Isaiah and the authors of the prophecy of Malachi and in the stories of Ruth and Jonah. In the stress of conflict they completely lost sight of their mission as Jehovah's witnesses to all the world. The destruction of the heathen seemed to them absolutely necessary if Jehovah's justice was to be vindicated. The spirit of this warlike, bloodthirsty age is most clearly formulated in the book of Esther. The presence of Aramaic and Persian words testify to its late date. It is closely allied to the midrashim or didactic stories that were a characteristic literary product of later Judaism. Like the stories of Daniel, the book of Esther contains many historical inconsistencies. For example, Mordecai, carried as a captive to Babylon in 597 B.C., is made Xerxes's prime-minister in 474 B.C. Its pictures of Persian customs are also characteristic of popular tradition rather than of contemporary history. Its basis is apparently an old Babylonian tradition of a great victory of the Babylonians over their ancient foes, the Elamites. Mordecai is a modificaton of the name of the Babylonian god Marduk. Estra, which appears in the Hebrew Esther, was the late Babylonian form of the name of the Semitic goddess Ishtar. Vashti and Hamman, the biblical Haman, were names of Elamite deities. Like the story of creation, this tale has been hebraized and adapted to the story-teller's purpose. His aim is evidently to trace the origin of the late Jewish feast of Purim. It is probable that this feast was an adaptation of the Babylonian New-Year's feast which commemorated the ancient victory. The story in its present form is strongly Jewish. It exalts loyalty to the race, but its morality is far removed from that of Amos and Isaiah. Its exultation over the slaughter of thousands of the heathen is displeasing even in a romance, although it can easily be understood in the light of the Maccabean age in which it was written.

III. **Campaigns against the Neighboring Peoples.** The first book of Maccabees records in detail the repeated blows that Judas struck against his heathen foes. At Akrabattine, probably identical with the Scorpion Pass at the southwestern end of the Dead Sea, he fought and won a signal victory over his hereditary foes, the Idumeans. His chief enemy on the east was Timotheus, the leader of the Ammonites against whom Judas was successful in the preliminary skirmishes. Angered by these defeats, the heathen east of the Jordan attacked the resident Jews, who fled to one of the towns, where they were besieged. Judas, assembling six thousand of his picked warriors, made a rapid march of three days out into the wilderness. He apparently carried few supplies, but depended rather upon the spoil of the captured towns for support. Bosra, far out on the borders of the desert, was seized and looted. Thence returning westward, he rescued the Jews from the town of Damethah, or, as it appears in the Syriac, Rametha. This is probably identical with the modern town of Remtheh a little south of the Yarmuk on the great pilgrim highway from Damascus to Mecca. After making a détour to the south he crossed the Yarmuk and captured a series of towns lying to the north and northeast of this river. Returning he apparently met his Ammonite foe, who had succeeded in rallying an army, at the point where the pilgrim highway crosses the headwaters of the Yarmuk. Here Judas won a sweeping victory. Then collecting the many Jews of the dispersion who had settled near these upper waters of the Yarmuk, he returned victoriously to Jerusalem. His brother Simon, who had been despatched on a similar mission to Galilee, likewise came back bringing many fellow-Jews and laden with spoils.

Anticipating a renewal of the Syrian attack, Judas next made a rapid campaign into the territory of the Idumeans, capturing the old Hebrew capital of Hebron and carrying his victories as far as Ashdod on the western borders of the Philistine plain. Within a few months he had overrun and partially conquered a territory larger than the kingdom of David. In an incredibly short time this peasant warrior had won more victories against greater odds than any other leader in Israel's history.

The results of these victories were necessarily ephemeral. They accomplished, however, three things: (1) Judas intimidated his foes and established his prestige; (2) he was able to rescue thousands of Jews from the hands of the heathen; and (3) by bringing them back to Judea he increased its population and laid the foundations of that kingdom which rose as the result of his patriotic achievements.

IV. **The Battle of Beth=zacharias.** There was still a Syrian outpost in the heart of Judea: it was the citadel at Jerusalem, which looked down upon the temple area. This Judas attempted to capture, but in so doing incited to action the Syrian king, Antiochus Eupator, who had succeeded to the throne after the death of his father Antiochus Epiphanes. Under the direction of his prime-minister Lysias he collected a huge army of one hundred thousand infantry and twenty thousand cavalry. To this was added thirty-two elephants with full military equipment— the heavy ordinance used in the warfare of the period. The approach from the plain was along the valley of Elah and up past Bethsura, as in the last Syrian campaign. Judas, who was able at this time to rally an army of ten thousand men, met the Syrian host near the town of Beth-zacharias, a little north of Bethsura on the central highway from Hebron to Jerusalem. This time the natural advantages were with the Syrians, one wing of whose army rested upon a declining hill and the other on the level plain. Thus they were able to utilize their entire fighting force and to launch against the valiant Jews their elephants against which the heroism of an Eleazar was fruitless. For the first time during this struggle Judas was defeated and fell back upon Jerusalem, where he was closely besieged. Soon the Jews were obliged to surrender, and the Maccabean cause would have been lost had not complications at Antioch compelled the Syrians to retire.

V. **Victories Over Nicanor.** In the treaty which followed the surrender of Jerusalem the religious liberty of the Jews was assured. This concession satisfied the majority of the Hasideans, so that henceforth Judas found himself deserted by a great body of his followers. The apostate high priest who was placed in control of the temple was supported by Syrian soldiery and Judas was obliged to resort again to outlaw life. He succeeded, however, in winning two signal victories over Nicanor, the Syrian general. The one at Capharsalama was probably fought near the modern town of Kefr Silwan, across the Kidron Valley from the City of David on the southern slope of Jerusalem. In the latter victory Nicanor was slain, and Judas was left for the moment in control of Judea.

VI. The Death of Judas. Soon another Syrian army invaded the land. The advance was from the northwest up over the pass of Beth-horon. A little east of the road that ascends from Lower to Upper Bethhoron, near where he won his first great battle and in sight of his home at Modein, the intrepid Jewish champion fought his last battle. Terror at the approach of the enemy had thinned his ranks until he was obliged to meet them with only eight hundred men at his back. Even against these great odds he was on the eve of victory when he was slain. At the sight of their fallen leader his followers fled. This disastrous ending of his career as a warrior obscured to a great extent the character and quality of Judas's services for his people. In brief (1) he taught them to fight for their rights; (2) he helped them to save their law and traditions; (3) he secured for them religious freedom; (4) he restored many of the Jews of the dispersion and thus prepared the way for the consolidated kingdom which later rose with Jerusalem as the centre; (5) he inspired his countrymen with ambitions for political independence; and (6) he set them a noble example of courage, patriotism, and practical piety. While measured by the higher standards of a later day Judas is not without his faults, yet he is unquestionably one of the great heroes of Israel's history and an example to all of unselfish and devoted patriotism.

VII. The Dissensions in the Syrian Court. The Jews ultimately attained political independence not primarily through their own efforts, but because the protracted contests between the rival claimants for the Syrian throne gave them opportunities which they quickly improved. In 152 B.C. a youth known as Alexander Balas, who claimed to be a son of Antiochus Epiphanes, raised the standard of revolt against the reigning Syrian king, Demetrius I. The kings of southwestern Asia and Egypt at first lent their support to this impostor. By 150 B.C. he had succeeded in defeating and putting to death Demetrius I. Two years later, however, Demetrius II, the son of the deposed king, appeared with a large body of Cretan mercenaries to contest the throne of his father. Many of the Syrian cities at once espoused his cause. Ptolemy Philometor, of Egypt, finally turned against Alexander Balas; and in 145 B.C. this strange adventurer was slain near Antioch by his own followers Soon after his death, however, one of his generals, Tryphon, appeared with an infant son of Alexander whom he sought to place on the Syrian throne, thus perpetuating the feud that was constantly undermining the power of the Seleucid kingdom.

VIII. Concessions to Jonathan. The Jews profited by each turn in these tortuous politics. In 158 B.C., after a period of outlawry in the wilderness east of Judea, Jonathan and his followers were allowed by Demetrius I to settle again within the bounds of Judea. Jonathan established his head-quarters at Michmash, the fortress famous for the achievement of Saul's valiant son Jonathan. Here he ruled over the Jews as a vassal of Demetrius, who retained immediate control over the citadel at Jerusalem and the fortified cities that had been built along the borders of Judea. On the appearance of Alexander Balas in 152 B.C. Demetrius I, in order to retain the loyalty of the Jews, permitted Jonathan to maintain a small standing army and to rebuild the fortifications of Jerusalem. To outbid his rival the impostor Alexander Balas conferred upon Jonathan the coveted honor of the high priesthood, thus making him both the civil and religious head of the Jewish state. Disregarding his promises to Demetrius and the contemptible character of Alexander, Jonathan at once proceeded to establish his new authority. He was doubtless more acceptable to the majority of the Jews than the apostate high priests whom he succeeded, but the stricter Hasideans naturally regarded it as a sacrilege that a man whose hands were stained with war and bloodshed should perform the holiest duties in the temple service.

Under Alexander Balas Jonathan's power rapidly increased. He was made governor of Judea, and, under pretence of supporting the waning fortunes of Alexander, he captured in succession the Philistine cities of Joppa, Azotus (Ashdod), Ascalon, and Akron. When Demetrius II became master of Syria, Jonathan succeeded by rich gifts and diplomacy in so far gaining the support of the new king that part of the territory of Samaria was joined to Judea. In return for three hundred talents they were also promised exemption from taxation. Furthermore, membership in one of the royal orders was conferred upon the Maccabean leader. Thus by good fortune and by often questionable diplomacy the Jews finally secured in the days of Jonathan that freedom for which they had fought and which they had partially won under the valiant Judas.

§ CXII.   PEACE AND PROSPERITY UNDER SIMON

1. Tryphon's plans to place the son of Alexander on the throne. (I Mac. 11[38-43])

And when King Demetrius saw that the land was quiet before him and that no resistance was made to him, he sent away all his forces, each one to his own home, except the foreign mercenaries, whom he had enlisted from the isles of the heathen. All the troops, however, who had served his

231

father hated him. Now Tryphon was one of those who had formerly belonged to Alexander's party, and when he saw that all the troops were murmuring against Demetrius, he went to Yamliku, the Arabian who was bringing up Antiochus, the young child of Alexander, and importuned him that he should deliver him to him, that he might reign in his father's place. And he told him all that Demetrius had done, and the hatred which his troops bore him. And he stayed there a long time.

2. Antiochus as king (54-56)

Now after this Tryphon returned, and with him the young child Antiochus, and he assumed the sovereignty and put on the diadem. And there were gathered to him all the forces which Demetrius had sent away in disgrace, and they fought against him, and he fled and was defeated. And Tryphon took the elephants and became master of Antioch.

3. Tryphon's false promises and plot to disarm Jonathan (12³⁹⁻⁴⁷)

Then Tryphon tried to get the sovereignty over Asia and to put on the diadem and to engage in hostilities against Antiochus the king. But he was afraid lest perhaps Jonathan might not allow him, and that he might fight against him. So he sought a way to take him, that he might destroy him. And he set out and came to Bethshan. Then Jonathan went out to meet him with forty thousand picked soldiers and came to Bethshan. And when Tryphon saw that he came with a great army, he was afraid to attack him, and he received him honorably and commended him to all his Friends and gave him gifts, and commanded his forces to be obedient to him as to himself. And he said to Jonathan, Why have you put all this people to trouble, since that there is no war between us? Now therefore send them away to their homes, retaining for yourself only a few men who shall be with you, and come with me to Ptolemais, and I will give it to you with the rest of the strongholds and the rest of the forces and all the king's officers, and I will set out on my way back, for this is the cause of my coming. Then he trusted him and did even as he said, and sent away his forces so that they departed into the land of Judah. But he reserved for himself three thousand men, of whom he left two thousand in Galilee, while one thousand went with him.

Now as soon as Jonathan entered Ptolemais, the people of Ptolemais shut the gates and laid hands on him, and they slew with the sword all who came in with him. And Tryphon sent forces and horsemen into Galilee, and into the great plain, to destroy all of Jonathan's men. But they perceived that he had been taken and had perished, and those who were with him, and they encouraged one another and marched in closed ranks, prepared to fight. And when those who were pursuing them saw that they were ready to fight for their lives, they turned back again. Thus they all came safely into the land of Judah, and they mourned for Jonathan and those who were with him, and they were greatly afraid. And all Israel mourned bitterly. Then all the heathen who were round about them sought to destroy them utterly, for they said, They have no ruler nor any to help them, now therefore let us fight against them and wipe out the memory of them from among men.

Now when Simon heard that Tryphon had collected a vast army to come into the land of Judah to destroy it utterly, and saw that the people trembled and were greatly afraid, he went up to Jerusalem and gathered the people together, and encouraged them and said to them, You yourselves know all the things that I and my brothers, and my father's house, have done for the laws and the sanctuary, and the battles and times of distress through which we have passed. In this cause all my brothers have perished for Israel's sake, and I alone am left. And now be it far from me that I should spare my own life, in any time of affliction; for I am not better than my brothers. Rather I will take revenge for my nation, and for the sanctuary, and for our wives and children, because all the heathen are gathered to destroy us out of pure hatred. And the courage of the people rose as they heard these words. And they answered with a loud voice, saying, You are our leader instead of Judas and Jonathan your brothers. Fight our battles, and we will do all that you command. So he gathered together all the warriors and made haste to finish the walls of Jerusalem, and fortified the entire length of it. And he sent Jonathan the son of Absalom at the head of a large army to Joppa, and he drove out those who were in it, and stayed there in it.

**6.
Failure
to in-
vade
Judea
(20-22)**

And after this Tryphon came to invade the land and destroy it, and he went round about by the way that goes to Adora; and Simon and his army marched opposite and abreast of him to every place wherever he went. And the people of the citadel sent to Tryphon ambassadors urging him to come by forced marches through the wilderness to them and to send them supplies. So Tryphon made ready all his cavalry to go. But that night a very deep snow fell, so that he did not come because of the snow.

**7.
Murder
and
burial
of Jon-
athan
(23-30)**

Then he set out and came to the country of Gilead, and when he came near to Bascama, he slew Jonathan, and he was buried there. But when Tryphon went back into his own land, Simon sent and took the bones of Jonathan his brother, and buried them at Modein, his ancestral city. And all Israel made great lamentation over him and mourned for him for many days. And Simon built a monument upon the sepulchre of his father and his brothers, and raised it aloft to the sight, with polished stone on the back and front sides. He also set up seven pyramids, one opposite another, for his father and his mother and his four brothers. And for these he made artistic designs, setting about them great pillars, and upon the pillars he fashioned different kinds of arms as an everlasting memorial, and beside the arms ships carved, that they should be seen by all who sail on the sea. This is the sepulchre which he made at Modein, which stands there at the present time.

**8.
Siege
and
capture
of Ga-
zara
(33, 43-48)**

Then Simon built the strongholds of Judea and fenced them about with high towers and great walls and gates and bars, and laid up stores in the strongholds. In those days he laid siege to Gazara, and surrounded it with armies, and made an engine of siege and brought it up to the city, and smote a tower and captured it. And those who were in the engine leaped forth into the city, and there was a great tumult in the city. And the people of the city tore their garments, and went up on the walls with their wives and children, and cried with a loud voice, requesting Simon to make peace with them. And they said, Do not deal with us according to our wickednesses but according to your mercy. So Simon was reconciled to them and did not fight against them. But he expelled them from the city and cleansed the houses in which the idols were, and so entered into it with singing and praise. And when he had put all uncleanness out of it, he placed in it such men as would keep the law and made it stronger than it was before, and built a dwelling place for himself in it.

But those who were in the citadel at Jerusalem were prevented from going out and from going into the country, and from buying and selling, so that they suffered exceedingly from hunger, and a great number of them perished through famine. Then they cried out to Simon to make peace with them. He did so, but put them out from there, and cleansed the citadel from its pollutions. And he entered it on the twenty-third day of the second month in the one hundred and seventy-first year, with praise and palm branches, with harps, with cymbals, with viols, with hymns, and with songs, because a great enemy was destroyed out of Israel. And he ordained that they should observe that day each year with gladness. And the temple mount, which was beside the citadel, he made stronger than before, and there he dwelt with his men. And Simon saw that John his son had grown to manhood, and so he made him commander of all his forces. And he lived in Gazara.

9. Capture and fortification of the citadel at Jerusalem (49-53)

Now when they heard at Rome and at Sparta that Jonathan was dead, they were very sorry. But as soon as they learned that his brother Simon had been made high priest in his place and ruled the country and its cities, they wrote to him on brass tablets, to renew with him the friendship and the treaty which they had made with Judas and Jonathan his brothers.

10. Renewal of alliances with Rome and Sparta (14:16-18)

Moreover King Demetrius confirmed to him the high priesthood according to these things, and made him one of his Friends, and bestowed great honor upon him, for he had heard that the Jews had been called friends and allies and brothers by the Romans, and that they had met the ambassadors of Simon with honor, and that the Jews and the priests were well pleased that Simon should be their governor and high priest forever, until there should arise a faithful prophet; and that he should be commander over them, and should take charge of the sanctuary, to appoint men on his own authority over their works and over the country and

11. Confirmation of his authority by Demetrius and the Jewish people (38-47)

235

over the arms and over the forts, and that he should be obeyed by all, and that all documents drawn up in the country should be written in his name, and that he should be clothed in purple, and wear gold; and that it should not be lawful for any of the people or of the priests to nullify any of these things, or to resist the commands that he should issue, or to gather an assembly in the country without his permission, or to be clothed in purple or to wear a golden buckle. But whoever should do otherwise, or act in defiance of any of these things, should be liable to punishment. All the people agreed to ordain that Simon should act according to these regulations. And Simon accepted and consented to be high priest and to be general and governor of the Jews and of the priests and to be protector of all.

12. The public record (48, 49)

And they gave orders to put this writing on brass tablets and to set them up within the precinct of the sanctuary in a conspicuous place, and also to put the copies of it in the treasury in order that Simon and his sons might have them.

13. Benign policy and conquests of Simon (4-8)

So the land had rest all the days of Simon,
And he sought the good of his nation.
His authority and his glory were well-pleasing to them
    all his days.
And amid all his glory he took Joppa for a haven,
And made it a way to the isles of the sea,
And he enlarged the boundaries of his nation,
And became master of the land.
He also brought many captives together,
And made himself master of Gazara and Bethsura, and
    the citadel.
Moreover he took away from it its uncleannesses;
And there was none who resisted him.
And they tilled their land in peace,
And the earth gave her increase,
And the trees of the plains their fruit.

14. Universal peace and prosperity under his rule (9-15)

The old men sat in the streets,
They talked together of the common good,
And the young men put on glorious, fine apparel.
He provided food for the cities,

And furnished them with means of fortification,
Until his famous name was known to the end of the
    earth.
He made peace in the land,
And Israel rejoiced with great joy,
Everyone sat under his own vine and fig tree,
And there was no one to make them afraid,
And none who warred against them was left upon the
    earth,
For the kings were utterly crushed in those days.
And he strengthened all the distressed of his people,
He was full of zeal for the law,
And every lawless and wicked person he banished.
He made the sanctuary glorious,
And multiplied the vessels of the temple.

I. **Capture and Death of Jonathan.** It was not strange in that corrupt age that Jonathan, who had risen to power largely by intrigue, should himself in the end fall a prey to treachery. Tryphon, the general who secretly aspired to the Syrian throne, by lies succeeded in misleading even the wily Jewish leader. His object was to gain possession of southern Palestine, and he evidently believed that by capturing Jonathan he would easily realize his ambition. He overlooked the fact, however, that Simon, next to Judas the ablest of the sons of Mattathias, still remained to rally and lead the Jewish patriots. The natural barriers of Judea again proved insurmountable, for when Tryphon tried repeatedly on the west, south, and east to invade the central uplands, he found the passes guarded by Simon and his experienced warriors. Thus baffled, the treacherous Tryphon vented his disappointment upon Jonathan, whom he slew in Gilead. As the would-be usurper advanced northward, where he ultimately met the fate which he richly deserved, Simon and his followers bore the body of Jonathan back to Modein, and there they reared over it the fourth of those tombs which testified to the warlike spirit and devotion of the sons of Mattathias.

II. **Character and Policy of Simon.** Simon, who was at this crisis called to the leadership of the Jewish race, had been famed from the first for his moderation and wise counsel. In many campaigns he had also shown the military skill and courage that had characterized his younger brothers. In him the noble spirit of Judas lived again. He was devoted to the law, intent upon building up the state, and at the same time was deeply and genuinely interested in all members of his race, whether in Judea or in distant nations. Like David and Josiah, he was a true father of his people and set an example which unfortunately his descendants failed to follow. He still recognized the authority of Demetrius II, but the Syrian kingdom was so weak that Simon succeeded in securing a definite promise of the remission of all taxes, and ruled practically as an independent sovereign. To strengthen his position he sent an embassy laden with rich gifts to Rome. During a later crisis in his rule its prestige proved of great value, but Simon in following the example of his brothers gave to Rome that claim upon Judea that was destined within less than a century to put an end to Jewish independence. In still further consolidating and developing the resources of his people and in preparing for future expansion, Simon laid the foundations for the later Jewish kingdom. His policy also brought to Palestine that peace and prosperity which made his rule one of the few bright spots in Israel's troubled history.

III. **His Conquests.** The chief conquest of Simon was the capture of Gazara, the ancient Gezer. This lay on the western side of the plain of Ajalon. It guarded the approaches to Judea from the west, and above all the highway that ran from Joppa and along which passed the commerce of the Mediterranean. After a stubborn resistance he captured the town, deported part of its heathen population, and settled Jewish colonists in their place. Joppa also was under Simon's control. Thus he also prepared the way for that commercial expansion which was necessary if the Jewish state was to survive in the midst of its many powerful foes. Early in his reign Simon laid siege to the Syrian garrison in Jerusalem, and finally, amidst the rejoicing of the people, captured this stronghold and delivered Judea from the presence of the hated foreigners. The temple area was also fortified. Simon's victories, and especially his conquest of the Greek cities on the plain, aroused the Syrian king, Antiochus Sidetes, the son of Demetrius I, to demand heavy indemnity. When Simon refused to pay the tribute a Syrian army was sent to enforce the claim, but were defeated by a Jewish force under John Hyrcanus. This victory left Simon during the remainder of his reign practically independent of outside authority.

IV. **Simon's Authority.** Simon, with commendable moderation, refrained from attempting to secure for himself the title of king. He did, however, issue coins in his own name, although that right was ordinarily the prerogative only of kings. Upon him was conferred by the grateful people the authority that had first been given Jonathan by the shameless Alexander Balas. In return for Simon's many services and as a tribute to the achievements of his family he was proclaimed by the Jews not only civil governor and military leader, but also high priest. He thus became their rightful leader both in peace and war, and the representative of the nation in the sacred services of the temple. In all but name he was king, and Jewish history would have doubtless flowed in calmer channels had his descendants been contented with these substantial honors.

V. Completion of the Psalter. The reign of Simon probably witnessed the completion of the Psalter. Many of the psalms, especially those in the latter half of the book, bear the unmistakable marks of the Maccabean struggle. In Psalms 74 and 89, for example, there are clear references to the desecration of the temple and the bitter persecutions of Antiochus. They voice the wails of despair which then rose from the lips of many Jews. Many other psalms, as, for example, the one hundred and eighteenth, express that intense love and devotion to the law which was from this time on in many ways the most prominent characteristic of Judaism. The prevailingly prominent liturgical element that characterizes the concluding psalms of the Psalter suggest their original adaptation to the song services of the temple. Under the reign of Simon the temple choir was probably extended and greater prominence given to this form of the temple service. The peace and prosperity in the days of Simon gave the opportunity and the incentive to put in final form the earlier collections of psalms and probably to add the introduction found in Psalms 1-2 and the concluding doxology in Psalm 150. The Psalter appears to have been the last to be completed of all the Old Testament books, so that probably before the close of Simon's reign all of the present Old Testament books were written. Discussions regarding the value of such books as Ecclesiastes, Song of Solomon, and Esther continued until nearly the close of the first Christian century, when at last the canon of the Old Testament was completed.

VI. The Religious Life Reflected in the Later Psalms. The prevailing note in the psalms found in the latter part of the Psalter is joyous. A deep sense of gratitude to Jehovah for deliverance pervades them. The Jews felt that Jehovah had indeed delivered them "as a bird from the snare of the fowler" (Psalm 124). In the near background were the dark days of persecution. Hostile foes still encircled Israel, but trust in Jehovah's power and willingness to deliver triumphed over all fear.

> Oh, give thanks to Jehovah for he is good,
> For his mercy endureth forever.
> He hath delivered us from our enemies;
> Oh, give thanks to the God of heaven,
> For his mercy endureth forever,

was the oft-repeated refrain that was sung in the temple service by the warriors when they returned victorious from battle and by the people as they went about their tasks. The sense of constant danger and of great achievement bound together the Jews of this period as perhaps never before since the days of the exile. The same experiences developed a powerful religious consciousness. Jehovah had repeatedly and signally demonstrated that he was in their midst. Without his strong hand they were helpless against their foes. The apostates had been expelled, and the classes that remained were bound closely together by their desire to preserve their hard-won liberties, by their devotion to the temple and its services and by a profound respect for the authority of their scriptures. The voice of the living prophet was silent. The priests had ceased to teach and were simply ministers at the altar, and in the turmoil of the Maccabean struggle the teaching of the wise had practically come to an end. Instead the Jews became in every sense the people of the book. It was at this time and as a result of the forces at work in this age that the scribes attained their place as the chief teachers of the people. It was natural that they who copied, edited, and above all interpreted the revered Law and the Prophets should have the ear of the masses and should be regarded more and more as the authorized teachers of the Jewish race. Judaism had at last attained its maturity.

§ CXIII. THE RULE OF JOHN HYRCANUS AND ARISTOBULUS

1. Ptolemy's dastardly plot (I Mac. 16¹¹⁻¹⁷)

Now Ptolemy the son of Abubus had been appointed commander over the plain of Jericho. He possessed much silver and gold, for he was the high priest's son-in-law. Then he grew ambitious and determined to make himself master of the country. So he formed treacherous plots against Simon and his sons, to make away with them. Now Simon was visiting the cities that were in the country and providing for their good management. And he went down to Jericho

240

with Mattathias and Judas his sons, in the one hundred and seventy-seventh year, in the eleventh month, that is the month Sebat. Then the son of Abubus received them treacherously in a little stronghold that is called Dok, which he had built, and made them a great banquet, and his men were there. And when Simon and his sons were drunk, Ptolemy and his men rose up and took their weapons, and rushing in upon Simon in the banquet hall, they slew him and his two sons, and some of his servants. Thus he committed a great act of treachery and paid back evil for good.

Then Ptolemy wrote what had happened, and asked the king to send forces to aid him, and promised to hand over to him their country and the cities. And he sent others to Gazara to make away with John. And to the officers commanding thousands he sent letters to come to him, that he might give them silver and gold and gifts. And others he sent to take possession of Jerusalem and the temple-mount. But some ran before to Gazara and told John that his father and brothers had perished, and they said, He has sent to slay you too. And when he heard, he was dumb with amazement, but he seized the men who came to destroy him, and slew them, for he saw that they were seeking to destroy him. *2. His failure to murder John Hyrcanus (18-22)*

Now when Hyrcanus had received the high priesthood which his father had held before him and had offered sacrifice to God, he made haste to attack Ptolemy, that he might relieve his mother and brothers. So he laid siege to the fortress and was superior to Ptolemy in other respects; but he was defeated through his natural affection. For when Ptolemy was distressed, he brought Hyrcanus's mother and his brothers and set them upon the wall and beat them with rods in the sight of all and threatened that unless Hyrcanus went away immediately, he would throw them down headlong. At this sight Hyrcanus's pity and concern overcame his anger. *3. Hyrcanus's attempt to save his kinsmen (Jos. Jew. War, I, 2^{8c-4b})*

And since the siege was delayed in this way, the year of rest came on, during which the Jews rest every seventh year as they do on every seventh day. In this year, therefore, Ptolemy was freed from being besieged. He also slew the brothers of Hyrcanus with their mother, and fled to Zeno, who was the tyrant of Philadelphia. *4. Ptolemy's escape (4d)*

5. Invasion of Judea by the Syrian king (5)

And now Antiochus [Sidetes] was so angry at what he had suffered from Simon that he made an expedition into Judea and laid siege to Jerusalem and shut up Hyrcanus. But Hyrcanus opened the tomb of David, who was the richest of all kings, took from there more than three thousand talents of money and induced Antiochus upon the promise of three thousand talents to raise the siege. Moreover he was the first of the Jews who had plenty of money, and so began to hire foreign mercenaries.

6. Capture of east-Jordan and Samaritan cities by Hyrcanus (6)

At another time, when Antiochus had gone upon an expedition against the Medes and thus given Hyrcanus an opportunity to be revenged upon him, Hyrcanus made an attack upon the cities of Syria, thinking, as proved to be the case, that he would find them empty of good troops. So he took Medeba and Samaga with their surrounding towns; likewise Shechem and Mount Gerizim.

7. Conquest and Judaizing of the Idumeans (Ant. XIII, 9ld, e)

Hyrcanus also took Dora and Marissa, cities of Idumea, and subdued all the Idumeans. He permitted them to stay in their country, if they would undergo circumcision and conform to the Jewish laws. They were so desirous of living in the country of their fathers that they submitted to circumcision and the other Jewish ways of living. From this time on, therefore, they were none other than Jews.

8. Capture of Samaria (Jew. War, I, 27a, b)

Hyrcanus also proceeded as far as Samaria and invested it on all sides with a wall, and placed his sons, Aristobulus and Antigonus in charge of the siege. They pushed it with such vigor that a famine prevailed within the city, so that the inhabitants were forced to eat what was never before regarded as food. They also invited Antiochus to come to their assistance and he readily responded to their invitation, but he was beaten by Aristobulus and Antigonus, and he was pursued as far as Scythopolis by these brothers and fled away from them. So they returned to Samaria and shut up the multitude within the wall again, and when they had taken the city, they tore it down and made slaves of its inhabitants.

9. The opposition of the Pharisees to Hyrcanus (Ant. XIII, 10⁵)

However the prosperity of Hyrcanus caused the Jews to envy him; and they who were worst disposed to him were the Pharisees. Now Hyrcanus was one of their disciples and had been greatly beloved by them. But once when he invited

them to a feast and entertained them kindly and saw them
in a good humor, he began to say to them that they knew
that he desired to be a righteous man and do all things by
which he might please God and them, for the Pharisees are
philosophers.   However, he desired, if they observed him
offending in any respect or departing from the right way,
that they would call him back and correct him.   When they
testified that he was entirely virtuous he was well pleased
with their approval.   But one of his guests, Eleazar by name,
was a man malignant by nature, who delighted in dissension.
This man said: "Since you wish to know the truth, if you
really desire to do what is right, lay down the high priesthood and content yourself with the civil government of the
people."   And when Hyrcanus desired to know for what
cause he ought to lay down the high priesthood, the other
replied: "We have heard from old men that your mother
was a captive in the reign of Antiochus Epiphanes."   This
story was false, and Hyrcanus was provoked against him.
All the Pharisees likewise were very indignant with him.

Now there was a certain Jonathan, a great friend of Hyrcanus, but of the sect of the Sadducees, whose ideas are the
opposite of those of the Pharisees.   He told Hyrcanus that
Eleazar had cast that slur upon him according to the common opinion of all the Pharisees and that this would be
made clear if he would ask them the question, What punishment they thought this man deserved?   For in this way he
might be sure that the slur was not laid on him with their
approval, if they advised punishing him as the crime deserved.   Therefore when Hyrcanus asked this question, the
Pharisees answered that the man deserved stripes and im-
prisonment, but it did not seem right to punish a slur with
death.   And indeed the Pharisees ordinarily are not apt to
be severe in punishment.   At this mild sentence Hyrcanus
was very angry and thought that this man reproved him
with their approval.   It was this Jonathan who influenced
him so far that he made him join the Sadducees and leave
the party of the Pharisees and abolish the decrees that they
had thus imposed on the people and punish those who obeyed
them.   This was the source of the hatred with which he and
his sons were regarded by the multitude.

10. The
result-
ing
antag-
onism
(6a-e)

11. The rule of Hyrcanus (7)

But when Hyrcanus had put an end to this sedition, he afterward lived happily and administered the government in the best manner for thirty-one years and then died, leaving behind him five sons. He was esteemed by God worthy of the three highest honors, the rulership of his nation, the high priesthood, and prophecy, for God was with him and enabled him to predict the future.

12. Assumption of the kingship by Aristobulus (II^1a-e, 2a)

Now when Hyrcanus was dead, his eldest son Aristobulus, intent upon changing the government into a monarchy, was the first to put a diadem on his head. This Aristobulus loved his next brother Antigonus and treated him as an equal, but the others he kept in bonds. He also cast his mother into prison because she disputed the government with him, for Hyrcanus had left her in control of everything. He also proceeded to that degree of barbarity that he killed her in prison with hunger. Moreover he was estranged from his brother Antigonus by false charges and also slew him, although he seemed to have a great affection for him and had shared the kingdom with him. But Aristobulus immediately repented of the slaughter of his brother; on which account his disease grew upon him.

His conquest of Galilee (3e)

Then Aristobulus died, after having reigned a year. He was called a lover of the Greeks and conferred many benefits on his country. He also made a war against Iturea [Galilee], and added a great part of it to Judea and compelled the inhabitants, if they wished to remain in that country, to be circumcised and to live according to the Jewish laws.

I. **Murder of Simon.** Even his moderation and kindly rule did not deliver Simon from the violent death that overtook all the sons of Mattathias. His murderer was his son-in-law, a certain Ptolemy, who was governor of the Jordan Valley, the resources of which had been developed under Simon. Ptolemy trusted to the support of the Syrian court, but he failed to reckon with two things: (1) the loyalty of the people to their Maccabean leaders; and (2) the ability of Simon's son, John Hyrcanus. Instead of falling a victim to Ptolemy's plot, John at once went to Jerusalem where he was made the high priest and governor by the people. Ptolemy, who was besieged in the castle of Dok, saved his miserable life only by shameless perfidy.

THE SYRIAN INVASION

II. The Syrian Invasion. Antiochus Sidetes proved the ablest Syrian king of this period. Although his first attack had been repelled by Simon, he again attempted, on the accession of Hyrcanus, to re-establish his authority in Palestine. Josephus, in his account, obscures this humiliating chapter in Jewish history. The statement that Hyrcanus took from the tomb of David vast wealth and thus purchased immunity from Syrian attack has all the characteristics of an Oriental tale. Instead, Antiochus Sidetes not only besieged but captured Jerusalem, and doubtless compelled the Jews to pay heavy tribute. Preferring, however, to retain their loyalty rather than to crush them, he left John Hyrcanus in control of Judea, and Jerusalem escaped destruction. In the disastrous campaign against the Parthians in which Antiochus lost his life John Hyrcanus accompanied him with a following of Jewish soldiers. The death of Antiochus Sidetes in 129 B.C. at last left the Jews free to develop their kingdom without further fear of Syrian interference. This event marks for the Jews the attainment of absolute political freedom—a privilege which they continued to enjoy for a little over half a century.

III. John's Military Policy and Conquests. John possessed the characteristic ambitions and energy of his family. In his policy he also seems to have been strongly influenced by the achievements of Israel's early conquering king, David. His aim was to build up a small empire, and by crushing the ancient foes of Israel to secure immunity from further attack. In employing foreign mercenaries he also followed the example of King David. Doubtless he was influenced in doing so by his experiences in the Parthian campaign. This policy, however, was far removed from the spirit of the early Maccabean leaders who had unsheathed the sword in behalf of their principles. John's first campaign was against the cities to the east of the Jordan, and resulted in the conquest of the towns of Medeba and Samaga and the territory subject to them. The conquest of Shechem and southern Samaria was undoubtedly prompted both by hereditary hatred toward the Samaritans and by the desire to provide an outlet for the growing Jewish population. After standing for two centuries, the Samaritan temple on Mount Gerizim was destroyed by the Jews. This sacrilegious act naturally intensified that hatred between Jew and Samaritan which burned so fiercely during the early part of the first Christian century. Marissa and Dora, the chief cities of the Idumeans, were next conquered. With strange inconsistency, John Hyrcanus, whose ancestors had first taken up the sword in defence of religious liberty, compelled the descendants of their old foes,

245

the Edomites, to give up their national religion or else go into exile. This policy was fraught with far-reaching consequences, for among those appointed to rule over the conquered Edomites was Antipater, the ancestor of Herod, who was destined to rule the Jews and to initiate that long series of disasters that culminated in the destruction of the Jewish state. Last of all, John Hyrcanus advanced to the conquest of the Greek city of Samaria. Because of its natural strength and formidable defences a year was required for the siege, and it was ultimately captured only through famine. The sons of John Hyrcanus succeeded in holding at bay the Syrian armies that were sent to relieve the besieged. The conquered inhabitants were sold as slaves, and the city was left for a time in complete ruins. The conquest of Scythopolis, the ancient Bethshean, extended the bounds of John's kingdom to the southern hills of Galilee. Thus he became master of a small empire extending out toward the desert on the east, to the South Country on the south, touching the sea at Joppa, and including the entire territory of ancient Samaria on the north. While not as large as the kingdom of David, it was a more perfect political unit, and offered superior opportunities for commerce and internal developemnt.

IV. **The Break with the Pharisees.** The successes of John Hyrcanus blinded the majority of the nation to the real issues at stake. But a powerful group, which during the Maccabean period appeared for the first time under the name of Pharisees, began to withdraw their allegiance and silently, at least, to protest against a high priest whose chief ambition was conquest. The story which Josephus tells to explain the defection of the Pharisees may be simply a popular tradition, but it is indicative of that division within Judaism which ultimately wrecked the Maccabean state. From the days of John Hyrcanus, the Maccabean rulers, with only one exception, were compelled to meet the silent but strong opposition of the Pharisees. As a result they turned to the rising party of the Sadducees which henceforth identified itself with the interests of the reigning family. Thus in the year of its greatest triumph the Jewish state became a house divided against itself. Estranged from the better-minded religious leaders of the nation, John Hyrcanus and his successors followed an increasingly secular, selfish policy until they completely forgot the noble ideals for which their fathers had striven.

V. **The Reign of Aristobulus.** The accession of Aristobulus marks a triumph of that Hellenism against which Judas and Simon had unsheathed the sword. Like many an Oriental monarch, he established his position on the throne by the murder of all members of his family who might contest his power. His inhuman cruelty to his mother and the suspicions which led him to murder his brother reveal a barbarous spirit that can only be explained as a result of the wrong ambitions that had already taken possession of Israel's rulers. Aristobulus's brief reign of one year is marked by two significant acts. The first is the assumption of the title of king. On his own initiative, and apparently without the consent of the people, he placed the diadem upon his head. The other important act was the conquest of part of the territory of Iturea, which was known in later times as Galilee. He found it occupied by a mixed Syrian and Greek population in which were probably a few descendants of the ancient Israelites. Following the policy of his family, he doubtless at once inaugurated a system of colonization which carried to Galilee a strong Jewish population. Henceforth, by virtue of race, language, and religion, Galilee was closely bound to Judea.

§ CXIV. THE PHARISEES, SADDUCEES, AND ESSENES

The Jews have three sects of philosophy: the Essenes, the Sadducees, and those called Pharisees. The Pharisees do not yield to luxury but despise that kind of life; and they follow the guidance of reason, and what that prescribes to them as good, they do. They also pay respect to those advanced in years nor are they so bold as to contradict them in anything which they have introduced. While they believe that all things are done by predestination, they do not take away from a man the choice of acting as he deems proper, for they believe that it is God's will that an event be decided for good or evil both by the divine counsel and by the man who is willing to accede to it. They also believe that souls possess immortal power and that under the earth there will be rewards or punishments according as men have lived virtuously or viciously in this life, and that the vicious are to be detained in an everlasting prison and that the virtuous shall have the power to live again. *1. Beliefs of the Pharisees (Jos. Ant. XVIII, 1², 1a-c)*

On account of this doctrine they have great influence with the people, and whatsoever they do in connection with the divine worship, prayers and sacrifices, they perform in accordance with the direction of the Pharisees. *2. Their influence over the people (3d)*

3. Beliefs of the Sadducees (4a, Jew. War, II, 8^14c)

But the doctrine of the Sadducees is that souls die with the bodies, nor do they give heed to anything beyond these things which the law enjoins. They deny predestination entirely and assert that God exercises no oversight over any evil doing and they say that good or evil lies before man to choose, and, according to each man's inclination, he chooses the one or the other.

4. Their unpopularity (Ant. XVIII, 1^4b)

They also think it virtuous to dispute with those teachers of philosophy which they follow. This doctrine, however, is accepted by only a few, but these are of the highest rank. They are able to accomplish almost nothing by themselves; for when they come to power, unwillingly but perforce, they accede to the Pharisaic doctrine, for otherwise they would not be tolerated by the multitude.

5. Beliefs and ceremonial usages of the Essenes (5a, b)

The doctrine of the Essenes is that all things are best left to God. They teach the immortality of souls and think that the rewards of righteousness are to be earnestly striven for; and when they send what they have dedicated to God to the temple, they offer their sacrifices in accordance with the special law of purity which they observe. On this account they are excluded from the common court of the temple but themselves offer their sacrifices. Yet their course of life is far better than that of other men and they devote themselves wholly to agriculture.

6. Their self-restraint and celibacy (Jew. War, II, 8^2, 13a)

The Essenes seem to have a greater affection for each other than do the other sects. They reject pleasure as an evil, but regard self-restraint and the conquest of passions as a virtue. They despise marriage and choose out other people's children, while they are impressionable and teachable, and they regard them as their own kindred, and conform them to their own customs. They do not absolutely repudiate marriage. There is also another order of Essenes, who agree with the rest in regard to their way of living, customs and laws, but differ from them in regard to marriage, for they think that by not marrying they will cut off the most important element in human life, which is the succession of mankind.

7. Their sharing of property (3, 4)

These men are despisers of riches and are wonderfully communistic among themselves. No one is to be found among them who has more than the others, for it is a law among them that those who join their sect must share with them what they have, so that among them all there is no evidence of poverty or excess of riches, but everyone's possessions are shared in common, so there is, as it were, but one property among all the brothers. They also have directors appointed by vote to manage their common affairs. These have no other interest, but each devotes himself to the needs of all. They possess no one city, but many of them dwell in every city, and if any of their sect come from other places, what they have lies open for them, just as if it were their own. They do not change garments or sandals until they first are entirely torn to pieces or worn out by time. Nor do they either buy or sell anything to each other, but every one of them gives to him who wants it and receives from him again in return for it what he wants; and even though no return is made, they are free to take what they want from whom they wish.

And their piety toward God is very extraordinary; for before sunrise they speak not a word about profane matters, but offer up certain inherited prayers as if they made a supplication to it for its rising. After this everyone is sent away by their directors to engage in some of those arts in which they are skilled, and at which they labor with great diligence until the fifth hour; after which they assemble again in one place. And when they have clad themselves in linen coverings, they bathe their bodies in cold water. After this purification is over they meet together in an apartment of their own in which none of another sect is permitted to enter. Then they go ceremonially pure into the dining room, as if into a temple. And when they have quietly sat down, the baker lays loaves in order for them, and a cook also brings a single plate of one kind of food and sets it before each of them. And a priest offers a prayer before eating. It is unlawful for any one to taste the food before the prayer. When he has dined he offers prayer again. When they begin and when they end they praise God as the giver of the necessities of life. After this they lay aside their garments as though they were sacred, and devote themselves to their labor again until evening. Then they return home to dine in the same manner and if any strangers be there they sit down with them. There is never any clamor or disturbance

9.
Their
manner
of living
(b)

249

to pollute their household, but they give everyone permission to speak in turn. The silence of the inmates appears to outsiders like some awful mystery.

10. Their high moral standards and practical knowledge (6)

They do nothing except in accordance with the injunctions of their directors. Only these two things are done among them as each wishes, namely, they assist the needy and show mercy; but they cannot assist their kindred without the permission of their directors. They dispense their anger justly and restrain their passion. They are eminent for fidelity and are the advocates of peace. Also whatever they say is mightier than an oath, but swearing is avoided by them, and they regard it worse than perjury, for they say that he who cannot be believed without swearing by God is already condemned. They also devote great attention to the study of the works of the ancients and select from them those things that are profitable for soul and body. Also they seek out such roots as may be effective for the cure of their diseases and inquire into the properties of stones.

11. Conditions of admission to their sect (7)

To one who desires to enter their sect, admission is not immediately granted; but he is prescribed the same method of living as they use for a year during which he is still excluded, and they give him a small hatchet, and girdle and the white garment. And when during that time he has given evidence of self-control, he approaches nearer to their way of living and is allowed to share the waters of purification. However, he is not even now allowed to live with them, for after this demonstration of his fortitude, his character is tried two years more, and if he appears to be worthy, they then admit him into the society. But before he is allowed to touch their common food, he is obliged to swear to them awful oaths that in the first place he will show piety toward God and then that he will observe justice toward men, and that he will do no harm to any one either voluntarily or at the command of others, and that he will always hate the wicked, and help the righteous, and that he will show fidelity to all men and especially to those in authority, that he will be a lover of truth and denounce those who tell lies, and that he will keep his hands clean from theft, and his soul from unlawful gain. Moreover he swears to communicate their doctrines to no one otherwise than he received them himself, and that he will abstain from robbery, and that he will faithfully preserve the books of their sect and the names of the angels.

Those who are caught in any heinous sins they cast out of their society; and he who is thus expelled often dies miserably. And in the judgments they pronounce they are most exacting and just, nor do they pass sentence by the votes of a court having less than one hundred members, and what is determined by them is unalterable. What they most of all honor, after God himself, is the name of their legislator [Moses], whom, if any one blasphemes, he is punished by death. They also think it a good thing to obey their elders and the majority. They are stricter than any others of the Jews in resting from their labors on the seventh day, for they not only prepare their food the day before, that they may not be obliged to kindle a fire on that day, but they will not venture to move any vessel out of its place.

12. Their legal and religious standards (8a, 9a-c)

They are also long-lived, insomuch that most of them live over a hundred years because of the simplicity of their diet and as a result of their regular course of life. They despise the miseries of life and are above pain because of their noble thoughts. And as for death, if it come with glory, they regard it as better than immortality. They think also, like the Greeks, that the good have their habitation beyond the ocean in a region that is never oppressed by storms of rain or of snow, or with heat, and that this place is refreshed by the gentle breath of the west wind that is continually blowing from the ocean; while they allot to the bad a dark and cold den which is never free from unceasing punishment.

13. Longevity and belief in immortality (10b, e, 11b)

There are also those among them who undertake to foretell things to come by reading the holy books, by using several different forms of purifications and by being constantly familiar with discourses of the prophets; and it is only seldom that they fail in their predictions.

14. Ability to predict (12)

I. **Influences that Gave Rise to the Jewish Parties.** The Maccabean period witnessed the birth of the great parties that henceforth distinguished Judaism. They represented the crystallizing of the different currents of thought that were traceable in the Greek period and even earlier. These diverse points of view were in part the result of that democratic spirit which has always characterized Israel's life. In the striking antithesis between the idealists and the legalists and the practical men of affairs it is also possible to detect the potent influence which the prophets had exerted upon the thought of their nation. In the Greek period the Chronicler and certain of the psalmists, with their intense devotion to the temple and its services to the practical exclusion of all other interests, were the forerunners of the later Pharisees. Ben Sira, with his hearty appreciation of the good things of life, with his devotion to the scriptures of his race, with his evident failure to accept the new doctrine of individual immortality, and with his great admiration for the high priests, was an earlier type of the better class of Sadducees. The persecutions of Antiochus Epiphanes developed these parties. As has already been noted, the Hasideans who followed Judas in the struggle to restore the law and the temple service were the immediate predecessors of the early Pharisees. The word "Pharisees" means separatists, and is used first in the days of Jonathan (Jos. *Ant.* III 5⁹). In the same connection Josephus refers to the Sadducees. The name of this second party is probably derived, not from the Hebrew word sadīk, meaning righteous, but from Zadok (later written Sadōk or Saddūk), who was placed by Solomon in charge of the Jerusalem temple. It was thus the designation of the aristocratic, high-priestly party. In the Persian and Greek periods the high priests had ruled the Judean state without opposition. It was the rise of the party of the Pharisees that apparently developed that of the Sadducees. This party included the hereditary nobles who supported and sympathized with the Maccabean leaders. The Essenes evidently represent a reaction against the prevailing moral corruption. In many respects they were simply extreme Pharisees. They were zealots in religion, just as the later party of the Zealots were extremists in their hatred of Rome and in the methods which they were ready to use in order to attain their ends.

II. **Character and Beliefs of the Pharisees.** Originally the Pharisees were not a political but a religious party. The opposition of the Sadducees in time led them to enter public life. In politics they were conservatives. They had little sympathy with the popular ambition for political independence, and probably regarded with alarm the tendency toward national expansion. Alliances with the heathen nations seemed to them disloyalty to Jehovah. In belief they were progressives. While they stood squarely on the ancient law, they recognized the importance of interpreting it so as to meet the many questions that rose in public and private life. To this great and practically endless task much of their time was devoted. They thus recognized the fact that Israel's law was still in process of development. To their later interpretations of the law they attributed great authority. One of their maxims was: "It is a worse offence to teach things contrary to the ordinances of the scribes than to teach things contrary to the written law." Naturally their attempt to anticipate by definite regulations each individual problem led them to absurd extremes and in time obscured the real intent of the older laws, but the spirit which actuated it was progressive. They also did not hesitate to accept the growing popular belief in angels and spirits. Like the earlier prophets, they recognized the presence of Jehovah directing the life of the nation and of the individual. They accepted the new-born belief in the immortality of the individual, clinging, however, to the hope of a bodily resurrection. They also held to the popular messianic hopes which became more and more prominent during the Maccabean and Roman periods.

The Pharisees were the most democratic party in Judaism. While for their own members they insisted upon a most rigorous ceremonial régime, they allowed the common people to ally themselves with them as associates. In their acceptance of the popular hopes and in their endeavor to adapt Israel's law to the life of the nation and thus establish a basis for the realization of Israel's hopes they appealed to the masses and exerted over them a powerful influence. Josephus asserts that so great was the influence of the Pharisees with the people that the Sadducees, in order to carry through their policies, were obliged, nominally, at least, to adopt the platform of their rivals. The Pharisees were also zealous in teaching the people and thus kept in close touch with the masses. They, therefore, stood as the true representatives of Judaism. Their principles have survived and are still the foundations of orthodox Judaism.

III. **Character and Beliefs of the Sadducees.** The Sadducees were few in numbers compared with the Pharisees. They represented, on the one side, the old priestly aristocracy, and on the other the new nobility that rallied about the Maccabean leaders. They depended for their authority upon their wealth, their inherited prestige, and the support of the throne. They were in reality a political rather than a religious party. In politics they were progressives and opportunists. Any policy that promised to further their individual or class interests was acceptable to them. As is usually the case with parties that represent wealth and hereditary power, they were conservatives in belief. They stood squarely on the earlier scriptures of their race and had no sympathy with the later Pharisaic interpretations and doctrines. Whether or not, as Josephus asserts, they entirely rejected fate, that is, the providential direction of human affairs, is not clear. Probably in this belief they did not depart from the earlier teachings of priests and prophets. Their selfish and often unscrupulous acts suggest a basis for Josephus's claim, even though allowance must be made for his hostile attitude toward them. While they were conservatives in theory, the Sadducees were of all classes in Judaism most open to Greek and heathen influence, for foreign alliances and Hellenic culture offered opportunities for advancement and power.

IV. **Character and Beliefs of the Essenes.** Less important but even more interesting are the Essenes. They were a sect, or monastic order, rather than a political or religious party. Josephus, who asserts that for a time he was associated with them, has given a full account of their peculiar customs. They evidently represented a strong reaction against the prevailing corruption and a return to the simple life. Their spirit of humility, fraternity, and practical charity are in marked contrast to the aims of the Sadducees and the later Maccabean rulers. In their beliefs they were idealists. Their invocation of the sun, their extreme emphasis on ceremonial cleanliness, their tendency toward celibacy, and their distinction between soul and body, all suggest the indirect if not the direct influence of the Pythagorean type of philosophy. If the Essenes represented simply an extreme type of Pharisaism, the peculiar form of its development was undoubtedly due to the Greek atmosphere amidst which it flourished. The Essenes do not appear to have had any direct influence in the politics of their day. They were a current apart from the main stream of Judaism, and yet they could not fail to exert an indirect influence. Many of their ideals and doctrines were closely similar to the teachings of John the Baptist and Jesus. Yet there is a fundamental difference between Essenism and primitive Christianity, for one sought to attain perfection apart from life and the other in closest contact with the currents of human thought and activity. While according to Josephus the party of the Essenes at one time numbered four thousand, like all ascetic movements it soon disappeared or else was deflected into that greater stream of monasticism which rose in the early Christian centuries.

§ CXV. THE LIFE AND FAITH OF THE JEWS OF THE DISPERSION

The Jews obtained honor from the kings of Asia when they became their auxiliaries; for Seleucus Nicator made them citizens of those cities which he built in Asia and in lower Syria, and in Antioch, the metropolis, and gave them privileges equal to those of the Macedonians and the Greeks who were its inhabitants.

1. Privileges in Asia Minor and Syria (Jos. Ant. XII, 3¹ᵃ)

For the Jewish race is widely dispersed among the inhabitants of all the world; and especially was it intermingled with the population of Syria, because of the nearness of that country. Above all, in Antioch, because of the size of the city, it had great numbers. There the kings who followed Antiochus gave the Jews a place where they might live in the most undisturbed security; for although Antiochus, who was called Epiphanes, laid waste Jerusalem and plundered the temple, the kings who succeeded him restored all the gifts of brass that had been made to the Jews of Antioch, and dedicated them to their synagogue.

2. In Antioch (Jew. War, VII, 3³ᵃ)

The succeeding kings also treated them in the same way, so that they became very numerous, and adorned their temple with ornaments and at great expense with those things which had been given them. They also continued to attract a great many of the Greeks to their services, making them in a sense part of themselves.

3. Proselyting activity of the Jews (3ᵇ)

Now Onias, the son of Simon, one of the Jewish high priests, fled from Antiochus [Epiphanes] the king of Syria, when he made war with the Jews, and came to Alexandria. And after Ptolemy [Philometor] received him very kindly on account of his hatred to Antiochus, Onias assured him that if he would comply with his proposal, he would bring all the Jews to his assistance. Now when the king agreed to do whatever he was able, Onias desired him to give him permission to build a temple somewhere in Egypt and to worship God according to the customs of his own nation. So Ptolemy complied with his proposals and gave them a place about twenty miles distant from Memphis. That province was called the province of Heliopolis. There Onias built a for-

4. The Jewish temple in northern Egypt (10²ᵈ⁻³ᵉ)

tress and a temple like that at Jerusalem except that it resembled a tower. He built it of large stones to the height of sixty cubits, but he made the structure of the altar an imitation of that in his own country. In like manner also he adorned it with gifts, excepting that he did not make a candlestick but had a single lamp hammered out of a beaten piece of gold, which illuminated the place with its rays, and which he hung by a chain of gold. The entire temple was surrounded by a wall of burnt brick, although it had a gateway of stone. The king also gave him a large territory for a revenue in money, that both the priests might have plentiful provision for themselves, and that God might have abundance of those things which were necessary for his worship.

5. Jews prominent in public service in Egypt (Ant. XIII, 10⁴)

Now in the days of John Hyrcanus, not only did the Jews in Jerusalem and Judea enjoy prosperity but also those who were at Alexandria in Egypt and Cyprus. For Cleopatra the queen was at variance with her son Ptolemy, who is called Lathyrus, and appointed as her generals Chelcias and Ananias, the son of that Onias who built the temple in the province of Heliopolis similar to that of Jerusalem. Cleopatra intrusted these men with her army and did nothing without their advice. Strabo of Cappadocia also attests that only those who were called Onias's party, being Jews, continued faithful to Cleopatra because their countrymen, Chelcias and Ananias, were in highest favor with the queen.

6. Ease with which wisdom may be attained (Wisd. of Sol. 6¹²⁻¹⁶)

Wisdom is brilliant and fades not away,
And she is easily seen by those who love her,
And found by those who seek her.
She anticipates those who desire her, making herself first known.
He who eagerly seeks her shall have no toil,
For he shall find her sitting at his gates.
For thinking upon her brings perfect wisdom,
And he who lies awake for her sake shall quickly be free from care.
For she herself goes about seeking those who are worthy of her,
And in their paths she graciously appears to them,
And in every purpose she meets them.

For she is breath of the power of God,
And a clear effluence of the glory of the Almighty;
Therefore nothing defiled can find entrance into her.
For she is a reflection of everlasting light,
And a spotless mirror of the working of God,
And an image of his goodness.
And though she is but one, she has power to do all
    things;
And remaining the same renews all things,
And from generation to generation passing into holy
    souls,
She makes them friends of God and prophets.
For God loves nothing except him who dwells with
    wisdom.
For she is fairer than the sun,
And surpasses all the order of the stars;
Compared with light, she is found to be superior to it.
For night succeeds the light of day,
But evil does not prevail against wisdom.
But she reaches from one end of the world to the
    other,
And she directs all things graciously.
The fruits of her labors are virtues;
For she teaches moderation and good sense,
Justice and fortitude,
And nothing in life is more profitable for men than
    these.

7. Nature and effects of wisdom (7²⁵—8¹, 7)

Love righteousness, O rulers of the earth,
Think of the Lord with sincerity,
And seek him in singleness of heart.
For he is found by those who do not tempt him,
And manifests himself to those who do not distrust
    him.
For perverse thoughts separate from God,
And his power, when it is tried, convicts the foolish;
For wisdom will not enter into a soul that devises evil,
Nor dwell in a body that is pledged to sin.
For a holy spirit which disciplines will flee deceit,
And will start away from senseless thoughts,

8. Purity in thought and word necessary to attain divine wisdom (1¹⁻⁵)

And will be frightened away when unrighteousness
    comes in.
For wisdom is a spirit that loves man,
And she will not absolve a blasphemer for his words,
Because God is a witness of his innermost feelings,
And a true overseer of his heart,
And a hearer of his tongue.
For the spirit of the Lord hath filled the world,
And that which holdeth all things together knoweth
    every voice.
Therefore no one who speaks unrighteous things can be
    hid,
Nor will justice, when it convicts, pass him by.

9. Man
created
not to
die but
to live
(12-15)

Do not court death by leading an erring life,
And do not by the deeds of your hands draw destruction
    upon yourselves.
For God did not make death,
And he hath no pleasure when the living perish;
For he created all things that they might exist,
And the created things of the world are not baneful.
And there is no destructive poison in them,
Nor has Hades dominion on earth,
For righteousness is immortal.

10.
Death
the re-
sult of
sin
(2²³-3¹)

For God created man for incorruption,
And made him an image of his own peculiar nature;
But through the envy of the devil death entered into
    the world,
And they who belong to him experience it.
But the souls of the righteous are in the hand of God,
And no torment can touch them.

.. Im-
mor-
tality
of the
right-
eous
(5¹⁵, ¹⁶)

But the righteous live forever,
And in the Lord is their reward,
And the care for them with the Most High.
Therefore they shall receive the glorious kingdom,
And the diadem of beauty from the Lord's hand;
Because he will cover them with his right hand,
And with his arm he will shield them.

For thou, O Lord, lovest all things that are,
And thou dost not abhor any of the things which thou hast
made,
For thou wouldest never have formed anything that thou
didst hate.
And how would anything have endured, if thou didst not
wish it?
Or how could that which was not called into being by thee
have been preserved?
But thou sparest all things, because they are thine,
O Sovereign Lord, thou lover of men's lives!
For thine incorruptible spirit is in all things.
Therefore thou convictest the fallen little by little,
And, reminding them of the things in which they sin, thou
dost warn them,
That freed from wickedness, they may believe on thee, O Lord.

12. God's love and tender care for man (11²⁴—12²)

But thou, our God, art gracious and true,
Long suffering, and in mercy directing all things.
For even if we sin, we are thine, since we know thy might.
But we shall not sin, knowing that we have been counted as
thine;
For to know thee is perfect righteousness,
And to know thy might is the root of immortality.

13. Man's relation to God (15¹⁻³)

I. Conditions of the Jews in Antioch and Asia Minor. Seleucus Nicanor, who in 311 B.C. founded the city of Antioch, like Alexander, granted many privileges to the Jewish colonies whom he thus sought to attract hither. They not only possessed the rights of citizenship, but lived in their separate quarter. Their synagogue was one of the architectural glories of the city. There they engaged in trade and undoubtedly grew rich, taking on largely the complexion of that opulent Hellenic city. Later the Jewish colony was enlarged by the apostates who fled from Judea when the Maccabean rulers gained the ascendancy. The corrupt and materialistic atmosphere of Antioch doubtless explains why its Jewish citizens apparently contributed little to the development of the thought and faith of later Judaism. Similar colonies were found throughout the great commercial cities of Asia Minor. In many of these cities—for example, Tarsus—they seem to have enjoyed the same privileges as those at Antioch.

II. The Jews in Egypt. The chief intellectual and religious centre of the Jews of the dispersion, however, was in Alexandria. It is probable that fully a million Jews were to be found in Egypt during the latter part of the Maccabean period. Industry and commerce had made many of them extremely wealthy and had given them the leisure to study not only their own scriptures but also the literature of the Greeks. The prevailingly friendly way in which the Ptolemaic rulers treated the Jews naturally led them to take a more favorable attitude toward Greek culture. Alexandria itself was the scene of an intense intellectual activity. Attracted by the munificence of the Ptolemies and by the opportunities offered by its great library, many of the most famous Greek philosophers and rhetoricians of the age found their home in the Egyptian capital. Public lectures, open discussions, and voluminous literature were only a few of the many forms in which this intellectual life was expressed. Hence it was at Alexandria that Hebrew and Greek thought met on the highest plane and mingled most closely.

III. The Jewish Temple at Leontopolis. After the murder of his father Onias III near Antioch, whither he had fled from the persecutions of Antiochus Epiphanes, Onias IV sought refuge in Egypt. Here, as the legitimate head of the Jewish high-priesthood, he was favorably received by Ptolemy and granted territory in the Nile Delta to the north of Memphis in which to rear a temple to Jehovah. In the light of recent discoveries at Elephantine it is evident that this step was not without precedent (§ XCI[vii]). Ptolemy's object was to please his Jewish subjects and to attract others to the land of the Nile. Josephus's statement in *The Jewish War*, VII, 10[4] favors the conclusion that the temple was built two hundred and forty-three years (not 343) before its final destruction in 73 A.D., that is, in 170 B.C. In any case it was probably built between 170 and 160 B.C., at the time when the persecutions of Antiochus Epiphanes made pilgrimages to the Jerusalem temple impossible, and threatened its continued existence. The plan of the Leontopolis temple indicates that it was not intended to be a rival to the Jerusalem sanctuary, but rather a common place of meeting for the Egyptian Jews and of defence in case of attack. It never seriously rivalled the Jerusalem sanctuary, although in later days it was viewed with jealousy by the Jews of Palestine.

IV. Translation of the Hebrew Scriptures into Greek. Far more significant than the building of the Leontopolis temple was the translation of the Hebrew Scriptures into Greek. The tradition preserved by Josephus that the translation was made in seventy-two days by seventy-two scholars, sent from Jerusalem by Eleazar the high priest at the request of Ptolemy, is clearly unhistorical. The impossibility of completing so vast a task in this limited time is obvious. Moreover, the character of the translation indicates that it was the work not of Palestinian but of Alexandrian Jews familiar with the peculiar Greek of Egypt and the lands of the dispersion. It was also the work not of one but of many different groups of translators, as is shown by the variant synonyms employed in different books to translate the same Hebrew words and idioms. In the case of several books the work of two or more distinct translators is readily recognized. The quality of the translation also varies greatly in different books. It is probable that the one historical fact underlying the tradition is that the work of translation was begun in the days of Ptolemy Philadelphus, who may have encouraged his Jewish subjects in their undertaking. From the character of the translations and the nature of the situation it is probable that the first books to be translated were certain historical writings, as Samuel-Kings and the books of the Law. The remaining books were probably translated by the end of the succeeding century (between 250 and 150 B.C.), for the grandson of Ben Sira implies in his prologue that he was acquainted with the Law, the Prophets, and the other writings in their Greek version.

The primary aim of this Greek translation was to put the Hebrew scriptures themselves into the hands of their Greek persecutors as the best possible answer to their false and malicious charges. Evidence of this apologetic purpose is found in the fact that glaring inconsistencies and expressions, where Jehovah is described in the likeness of a human being, were usually left out. Where the Hebrew text was corrupt the translators restored or else freely paraphrased what they thought was the original meaning. In time, however, the translation gained a new importance, for the Jews of Egypt soon began to forget the language of their fathers and so became increasingly dependent for a knowledge of their scriptures upon the Greek translation. In the end it almost completely superseded the original Hebrew version not only in the lands of the dispersion, but even in Palestine itself. A large proportion of the quotations from the Old Testament in the New are from the Greek rather than the Hebrew text. Although it is only a translation, the Greek version, or Septuagint (the Version of the Seventy), as it is popularly known, still possesses a great value for the modern translator, inasmuch as it is based upon Hebrew texts centuries older than any which now exists. At many points, especially in the historical prophetic books it makes possible the restoration of the original reading where the He brew has become corrupt in the long process of transmission.

V. Apologetic Jewish Writings. During the centuries immediately preceding the Christian era the Jews of the dispersion, and especially of Egypt, were the object of constant attack. Manetho, an Egyptian priest, wrote a history purporting to give the origin and the early experiences of the Jews. Portions of this have been preserved and reveal the bitter and unjust spirit with which this race was regarded by the Greek and Egyptian scholars of the day. To defend themselves from these attack) the Jews not only translated their scriptures, but employed many different types of writing. A certain Jew by the name of Demetrius about 215 B.C. wrote a commendatory history of the Jewish kings. Aristobulus, the teacher of Ptolemy Philometor, wrote an "Explanation of the Mosaic Laws," in which he anticipated, in many ways, the modern interpretation of the early traditions found in the opening books of the Old Testament. Like all Alexandrian scholars, however, he overshot the mark under the influence of the allegorical or symbolic type of interpretation. Other Jewish writers appealed to the older Greek historians and poets. Adopting the unprincipled methods of their persecutors, they expanded the original writings of such historians as Hecatæus, who had spoken in a commendatory way of the Jews. They even went so far as to insert long passages into the writings of the famous Greek poets, such as Orpheus, Hesiod, Æschylus, Sophocles, and Menander, so as to transform them into ardent champions of the persecuted race. The culmination of this illegitimate form of defence was to insert in the famous Sibylline Books (III) a long passage describing the glories of the Jewish race and voicing the hopes with which they regarded the future. It was in this atmosphere and under the influence of these methods that the anti-Semitic spirit was born in ancient Alexandria. Thence it was transmitted, as a malign heritage, to the Christian church.

VI. The Wisdom of Solomon. The noblest literary product of the Jews of the dispersion was the apocryphal book known as the Wisdom of Solomon. It was so called because the author assumed the point of view of Solomon. In so doing he did not intend to deceive his contemporaries, but rather followed the common tendency of his day. Although the book has many characteristic Hebrew idioms, which are due to its Jewish authorship, it was without doubt originally written in Greek. Its author was evidently acquainted with the writings of many of the Greek poets and philosophers. He accepted Plato's doctrine of the pre-existence of the soul ($8^{19, 20}$), of the limitations of the body

(9¹⁵), and of the creation of the world out of formless matter (11¹⁷). He was especially influenced by the beliefs of the Epicureans and Stoics. He was acquainted with Hellenic art, astronomy, and science (7¹⁷⁻²⁰) and throughout shows the influence of Greek methods of thinking. His rejection of the teachings of the book of Ecclesiastes, his wide learning and his conception of immortality indicate that he lived some time after the beginning of the Maccabean struggle. His reference in 3¹⁻⁴ is probably to the persecutions through which the Jews of Egypt passed during the reign of Ptolemy Psycon (140–117 B.C.). On the other hand the book clearly antedates the writings of the Jewish philosopher Philo, who lived during the latter part of the first century B.C. The Wisdom of Solomon, therefore, may be dated somewhere between 100 and 50 B.C.

VII. **Its Important Teachings.** The author of the Wisdom of Solomon aimed, first, to commend Israel's faith to the heathen by showing that it was in substantial accord with the noblest doctrines of the Greek philosophers, and second, to furnish the Jews of the dispersion, who were conversant with Hellenic thought and yet trained in the religion of their race, a working basis for their thought and practice. From the first it appears to have been highly esteemed by the Jews outside Palestine, although it never found a place in the Palestinian canon. Like most wisdom books, it describes at length the beauty and value of wisdom. The figure of Proverbs 8 and 9 is still further developed under the influence of the Greek tendency to personify abstract qualities. In the mind of the author, however, wisdom is simply an attribute of the Deity which he shares in common with men. The book is unique in two respects: (1) it contains the earliest references in Jewish literature to a personal devil and identifies him with the serpent that tempted the woman in the garden (2²⁴, cf. Gen. 3) Elsewhere, however, the author traces sin and evil to men's voluntary acts (e. g., 1¹⁶). (2) It teaches the immortality of righteousness and hence, by implication, the immortality of the individual. "God created man for incorruption," and "the souls of the righteous are in his hand." The doctrine here presented is ethical and spiritual rather than the belief in a bodily resurrection already formulated in the twelfth chapter of Daniel. It also teaches that both the good and bad will be rewarded according to their deeds. Its conceptions of God are exalted. He is the incorruptible spirit in all things, just and yet merciful, the lover of men. The book also places side by side with the Jewish teachings regarding men's duties to God and their fellow-men the Greek virtues of moderation, good sense, justice, and courage or fortitude. It also teaches that, like God, each of his children should be a lover of men. Thus the book unites most effectively that which is best in the thought of Judaism and Hellenism and is an earnest of that still nobler union that was later realized in the thought and teachings of Christianity.

§ CXVI. THE DECLINE OF THE MACCABEAN KINGDOM

1. Alexander Janneus made king (Jos. War, I, 4¹)

After Aristobulus died, his wife Salome, who by the Greeks was called Alexandra, released his brothers from prison (for Aristobulus had kept them in confinement), and made Alexander Janneus, who was the oldest, king.

2. His conquests on the maritime plain (2)

Now there was a battle between him and Ptolemy, who was called Lathyrus, who had taken the city of Asochis. He indeed slew many of his enemies, but the victory rather inclined to Ptolemy. But when this Ptolemy was pursued by his mother, Cleopatra, and retired into Egypt, Alexander besieged and took Gadara and Amathus, which was the strongest of all the fortresses that were beyond the Jordan, and the most valued of all the possessions of Theodorus, the son of Zeno, were therein. Thereupon Theodorus marched suddenly against him and took what belonged to himself, and slew ten thousand of the Jews. Alexander, however, recovered from this blow and turned his force toward the maritime districts and took Gaza, Raphia, and Anthedon.

3. Suppression of a rebellion and conquests east of the Jordan (3)

But when he had enslaved all these cities, the Jews made an insurrection against him at a festival and it looked as though he would not have been able to escape the plot they had laid for him, had not his foreign auxiliaries come to his aid. And when he had slain more than six thousand of the rebels, he invaded Arabia, and when he had conquered the Gileadites and Moabites, he commanded them to pay him tribute and returned to Amathus and took the fortress and demolished it.

4. Cruel massacres of his subjects (4a, b)

However, when he fought with Obedas, king of the Arabians, who had laid an ambush for him near Golan, he lost his entire army, which was crowded together in a deep valley and trampled to pieces by the multitude of camels. And fleeing to Jerusalem because of the greatness of the calamity that had overtaken him, he provoked the multitude, which had hated him before, to make an insurrection against him. He was, however, too strong for them in the various battles that were fought between them and he slew no fewer than fifty thousand of the Jews in the interval of six years. Yet he had no reason to rejoice in these victories, since he did but consume his own country, until he at length ceased fighting and desired to come to an agreement with them. But his changeability and the irregularity of his conduct made them hate him still more. And when he asked them why they so hated him and what he should do to appease them they said, "Die."

At the same time they invited Demetrius to assist them, and as he readily complied with their request and came with his army, the Jews joined with these their auxiliaries about Shechem. In the battle which followed, Demetrius was the conqueror, although Alexander's mercenaries performed the greatest exploits. Nevertheless the outcome of this battle proved different from what was expected by both sides, for those who had invited Demetrius to come to them did not continue loyal to him although he was the conqueror, and six thousand Jews out of pity because of the change in Alexander's condition, when he fled to the mountains, went over to him. Demetrius, supposing that all the nation would run to Alexander, left the country and went his way. The rest of the Jewish multitude, however, did not lay aside their quarrels with Alexander when the auxiliaries were gone, but had perpetual war with them until he had slain the greater part of them. Then such a terror seized the people that eight thousand of his opponents fled away the following night out of all Judea and did not return until Alexander died. **5.** His unpopularity and policy of terrorization (4c, 5e, 6a, e)

Alexander also subdued Golan, Seleucia, and what was called the Valley of Antiochus; besides which he took the strong fortress of Gamala. Then he returned into Judea after he had spent three years on this expedition. Now he was gladly received by the nation because of his success. So when he was at rest from war, he fell ill and died, terminating his troubles after he had reigned twenty-seven years. **6.** The closing years of his reign (5e, d)

Now Alexander left the kingdom to Alexandra, his wife, and trusted the Jews would readily submit to her, for in opposing his habitual violation of their laws she gained the good-will of the people. Nor was he mistaken in his hopes, **7.** Alexandra's policy (51) for this woman retained the rulership because of her reputation for piety. For she chiefly studied the ancient customs of her country and cast those men out of the government who offended against their holy laws. And as she had two sons by Alexander, she made the older, Hyrcanus, high priest, on account of his age and also on account of his inactive temperament.

8. The mistakes of the Pharisees (2, 3a, b)

And the Pharisees joined themselves to her in the government and Alexandra henceforth hearkened to them to a great degree. But these Pharisees artfully insinuated themselves into her favor little by little and presently became the real administrators of public affairs. They banished and recalled whom they pleased. While she governed the people, the Pharisees governed her. Accordingly, they slew Diogenes, a person of prominence, because he had been a friend of Alexander; they also urged Alexandra to put the rest of those to death who had stirred up Alexander against them. But the chief of those who were in danger fled to Aristobulus. He persuaded his mother to spare the men on account of their rank, but to expel them from the city. So when they were given their freedom, they were dispersed over all the country.

9. Alexandra's successors (5–6^{1b})

In the meantime Alexandra fell sick and Aristobulus, her younger son, seized this opportunity to get possession of all the fortresses. He also used the sums of money he found in them to gather together a number of mercenaries and to set himself up as king. But Alexandra, after she had lived nine years, died before she could punish Aristobulus. Hyrcanus was heir to the kingdom and to him his mother intrusted it while she was living. But Aristobulus was superior to him in ability and spirits, and when there was a battle between them near Jericho to decide the dispute about the kingdom, the majority deserted Hyrcanus and went over to Aristobulus. But they came to an agreement that Aristobulus should be the king, and that Hyrcanus should resign, but retain all the rest of his dignities.

10. Result of Antipater's intrigues (2, 3)

Now the others who opposed Aristobulus were afraid, when he thus unexpectedly came to power. This was especially true of Antipater, whom Aristobulus hated of old. He was by birth an Idumean and one of the chief men of that nation on account of his ancestry and riches and other

266

authority that belonged to him. He urged Hyrcanus to flee to Aretas, king of Arabia, and to retrieve the kingdom. When he had prepared them both beforehand he took Hyrcanus by night away from the city and escaped to Petra, which is the royal capital of Arabia. Here he put Hyrcanus into Aretas's care. He prevailed with him to give him an army to restore him to his kingdom. This army consisted of fifty thousand footmen and horsemen which Aristobulus was not able to withstand, but was defeated in the first encounter and was driven out of Jerusalem. He would have been taken by force, if Scaurus, the Roman general, had not come and opportunely raised the siege. This was the Scaurus who was sent into Syria from Armenia by Pompey the Great when he was fighting against Tigranes. As soon, therefore, as Scaurus arrived in the country, ambassadors came from both the brothers, each of them desiring his assistance. But Aristobulus's three hundred talents blocked the way of justice. When Scaurus had received this sum, he sent a herald to Hyrcanus and the Arabians, and threatened them with the resentment of the Romans and Pompey unless they raised the siege. So Aretas was terrified and retired from Judea to Philadelphia.

When Hyrcanus and Antipater were thus deprived of their hopes from the Arabians, they fled to Pompey for assistance and besought him to show his disapproval of the violent action of Aristobulus and to restore to him the kingdom, as it justly belonged to him. Aristobulus was also there himself, dressed in regal attire, but Pompey was indignant at his behavior. When Hyrcanus's friends also interceded strongly with Pompey, he took not only his Roman forces but also many of his Syrian auxiliaries and marched against Aristobulus. But when he had passed by Pella and Scythopolis and had come to Korea, he heard that Aristobulus had fled to Alexandrium, which was a stronghold fortified with the greatest magnificence, and situated upon a high mountain, and he sent to him and commanded him to come down. So Aristobulus came down to Pompey and when he had made a long defence of the justness of his rule, he returned to the fortress. Pompey however commanded him to give up his fortified places and forced him to write to each of his govern-

11. The appeal to Pompey (4, 1)

ors to surrender. Accordingly he did what he was ordered to do, but being displeased, he retired to Jerusalem and prepared to fight with Pompey.

12. The folly and perfidy of Aristobulus (6⁶–7²ᵇ) But Pompey gave him no time to make any preparations and followed at his heels. And Aristobulus was so frightened at his approach that he came and met him as a suppliant. He also promised him money and to deliver up both himself and the city. Yet he did not keep any one of his promises. At this treatment Pompey was very angry and took Aristobulus into custody. And when he had entered the city he looked about to see where he might make his attack, for he saw that the walls were so firm that it would be hard to overcome them and the valley before the walls was terrible and the temple which was in that valley was itself surrounded by such a strong wall that if the city was taken the temple would be a second place of refuge for the enemy. Inasmuch as Pompey deliberated a long time, a sedition arose among the people within the city. Aristobulus's party was willing to fight to save their king, while the party of Hyrcanus was ready to open the gates to Pompey. Then Aristobulus's party was defeated and retired into the temple and cut off the communications between the temple and the city by breaking down the bridge which joined them together, and they prepared to resist to the utmost.

13. Siege of the temple (3) Pompey himself filled up the ditch which was on the north side of the temple and the entire valley also, the army being obliged to carry the material for this purpose. Indeed, it was difficult to fill up that valley because of its great depth and especially as the Jews from their superior position used all possible means to repel them. As soon as Pompey had filled up the valley, he erected high towers upon the bank.

14. The final carnage (4, 5) Now Pompey admired not only the other examples of the Jews' fortitude, but especially that they did not at all intermit their religious services, even when they were surrounded with darts on all sides; for, as if the city were in full peace, their daily sacrifices and purifications and all their religious rites were still carried out before God with the utmost exactness. Nor when the temple was taken and they were slain about the altar daily, did they cease from those things that are appointed by their law to be observed. For it was in the third month of the siege before the Romans could even with a great struggle overthrow one of the towers and get into the temple. The greater part of the Jews were slain by their own countrymen of the opposite faction and an innumerable multitude threw themselves down from the walls. Of the Jews twelve thousand were slain, but of the Romans very few, although a greater number were wounded.

But there was nothing that affected the nation so much in the calamities which they then suffered as that their holy place, hitherto unseen, should be laid open to strangers. For Pompey and those who were about him went into the temple itself, where it was lawful for the high priest alone to enter, and saw what was deposited therein; but he commanded the ministers about the temple to purify it and to perform their accustomed sacrifices.

15. Desecration of the temple (6a, b)

Moreover he reappointed Hyrcanus high priest, by which he acted the part of a good general and reconciled the people to him rather by kindness than by terrorizing them. He took away from the nation all those cities that they had formerly taken and reduced Judea to its own bounds. Then he made all the haste he could to go through Cilicia on his way to Rome, taking Aristobulus and his two children along with him as captives. One of Aristobulus's sons, Alexander, ran away on the journey, but the younger, Antigonus, with his sisters, was carried to Rome.

16. Fate of the Maccabean family (7)

I. The Character and Policy of Alexander Janneus. For the picture of the character of Alexander Janneus we are chiefly dependent upon Josephus, and it is not clear how far this late Jewish historian was influenced by the prevailing prejudices against that ruler who figured as the arch enemy of the Pharisees. The incidents recorded reveal, however, a most sinister character. He was ambitious, but his ambitions were selfish and low. He was energetic and tireless, but his energy was wasted in futile undertakings. Furthermore, he was unscrupulous, vindictive, and merciless. There is not the slightest indication that he was actuated by any worthy ideal of service. To the Jewish state and race it was a great calamity that a man of this type should gain control of the nation at the moment when it had attained its greatest material strength. Under the kindly and wise guidance of Simon the subsequent history of the Jewish state would doubtless have been far different. Janneus's first aim was to establish his power as an absolute despot. He ardently accepted the ideal of an Oriental ruler that had been imposed upon the Jews during the short reign of his brother Aristobulus. In realizing this ambition he met, as did every other king in Israel's history, the strong opposition of the people and a bold assertion of their inherited liberties. His second aim was to break completely the power of the Pharisees. They were the party of the people and had no sympathy with his policies. In them, therefore, he recognized his chief opponents. His third am- bition was to extend the territory of the Jewish state to its farthest natural bounds. Soon after the beginning of his reign he succeeded in arousing the bitter hostility of the Greek cities on his eastern and western borders, of the reigning kings of Egypt, and of the rising Arabian power to the south of the Dead Sea. The objects for which he strove were comparatively petty: possession of the cities of Ptolemais and Gaza and of certain east-Jordan cities, such as Gadara and Amathus. He was more often defeated than victorious, but his love of struggle and advent- ure and lust for conquest ever goaded him on. In desperation his sub- jects even ventured to call in Demetrius, the governor of Damascus, but when Alexander was driven away in defeat the nation's gratitude and loyalty to the Maccabean house reasserted itself and he was recalled. Instead of granting a general armstice and thus conciliating his dis- tracted people, he treacherously used his new-won power to crucify publicly eight hundred of the Pharisees. Horror and fear seized the survivors, so that, according to Josephus, eight thousand of them fled into exile. After six years of civil war and the loss of fifty thousand lives, Alexander Janneus finally realized his first ambition and became absolute master of his kingdom. In achieving his ambitions, how- ever, he well earned the title by which his contemporaries described him, "the Son of a Thracian," that is, Barbarian.

II. The Effects of His Rule. The disastrous effects of the reign of Alexander Janneus may be briefly recapitulated. They were: (1) the destruction of the loyalty of the majority of the Jews to the Maccabean house; (2) the intensifying of the opposition between Pharisees and Sadducees to the point of murderous hate; (3) the extension of the sphere of Jewish influence from the Mediterranean on the west to the desert on the east, and from the Lebanons to the southern desert; but (4) the drain- ing of the life-blood and energies of the Jewish kingdom, so that it was far weaker and more disorganized than when Janneus came to the throne.

III. Alexandra's Reign (78–69 B.C.). Alexandra was the second queen who reigned in Israel's history. Her policy, unlike that of

Athaliah of old, was on the whole constructive. Although she was the wife of Janneus, she reversed his policy, and placed the Pharisees in control. The return of the exiles and the restoration of the prophetic party promised peace and prosperity. The ancient law was expanded and rigorously enforced. According to the Talmud it was during this period that elementary schools were introduced in connection with each synagogue. Their exact nature is not known, but it is probable that the law was the subject studied and that the scribes were the teachers. This change of policy was undoubtedly very acceptable to the people, but the Pharisees made the grave mistake of using their new power to be revenged upon the Sadducean nobles who had supported the bloody policy of Alexander Janneus. They soon suffered the evil consequences of attempting to right wrong by wrong. The Sadducees found in Aristobulus, the ambitious and energetic younger son of Janneus, an effective champion. Alexandra, in permitting them to take possession of the many strongholds throughout the land, also committed a fatal error, for it gave them control of the military resources of the kingdom. Aristobulus was not slow in asserting his power, with the result that even before Alexandra died he had seized seventy-two of the fortresses and had aroused a large part of the people to revolt. While her reign was on the whole peaceful, it was but the lull before the great storm that swept over the nation.

IV. **Quarrels between Hyrcanus and Aristobulus.** Unfortunately Alexandra's older son, Hyrcanus, was indolent and inefficient. He had been appointed high priest and, when Aristobulus assumed the title of king, he compelled Hyrcanus II to be content with this humbler title. Aristobulus's reign might have been comparatively peaceful had not at this time a new and sinister influence appeared in the troubled politics of Palestine. It was one of the results of John Hyrcanus's forcible judaizing of the Idumeans. Antipater, the son of the Idumean whom Alexander Janneus had made governor of Idumea, recognized in the rivalry between Hyrcanus and Aristobulus an opportunity to mount to power. He first persuaded Hyrcanus to flee to Petra. Then, with the aid of the Arabian king, Aretas, he finally compelled Aristobulus and his followers to seek refuge on the temple hill in Jerusalem. The picture of the Jews divided into two hostile camps and engaged in bitter civil war in the very precincts of the temple under the leadership of the great-grandsons of the patriotic Simon presents a sad contrast to the noble spirit and valiant achievements of the founders of the Maccabean kingdom who had first taken up the sword in defence of the temple and its service.

DECLINE OF THE MACCABEAN KINGDOM

V. Rome's Intervention. This situation gave Rome its desired opportunity for intervention. Pompey in 70 B.C. made a successful campaign against Mithridates, king of Pontus, and against Tigranes, king of Armenia. Rome's policy was to conquer all of southwestern Asia as far as the Euphrates. Ignoring the peril of the situation, both Aristobulus and Hyrcanus appealed to Pompey's lieutenant, Scaurus. As a result the Arabians were ordered to withdraw, and Aristobulus for a brief time was left master of the situation. In the spring of 63 B.C., however, when Pompey came to Damascus, there appeared before him three embassies, one representing the cause of Aristobulus, another that of Hyrcanus, and still a third presented the request of the Pharisees that Rome assume political control of Palestine and leave them free to devote themselves to the study and application of the their law. The fall of Aristobulus hastened what was now inevitable. Although he was held a prisoner by Pompey, his followers remained intrenched on the temple hill and were conquered only after a protracted siege and the loss of many lives. Aristobulus and his family were carried off captives to Rome to grace Pompey's triumph, and the request of the Pharisees was granted: Rome henceforth held Palestine under its direct control. Thus after a little more than a century (165–63 B.C.) the Jews again lost their independence, and the Maccabean kingdom became only a memory, never to be revived save for a brief moment.

VI. Causes of the Fall of the Jewish Kingdom. The Jewish kingdom fell as the result of causes which can be clearly recognized. It was primarily because the ideals and ambitions of the Maccabean leaders themselves became material and selfish. They proved unable to resist the temptations of success. Greed for power quenched their early patriotism. The material spirit of their age obscured the nobler ideals of their spiritual teachers. The result was a tyranny and corruption that made the later kings misleaders rather than true leaders of their nation. Parallel to the bitter struggle between the kings and their subjects was the bitter feud between the Sadducees and the Pharisees. Normal party rivalry grew into murderous hatred, and in taking revenge upon each other they brought ruin upon the commonwealth. The final end was hastened by the suicidal feud between the brothers Hyrcanus and Aristobulus, fomented by the unprincipled machinations of the Idumean Antipater. In the final crisis the Pharisaic policy of submission and of peace at any cost paved the way for the realization of Rome's ambition and made the ultimate conquest of Palestine practically inevitable. Thus the kingdom, founded in the face of almost insuperable obstacles

272

and consecrated with the life-blood of many heroes, fell ignominiously as the result of the same causes that throughout the ages have proved the ruin of even stronger empires.

VII. Political, Intellectual, and Religious Effects of the Maccabean Struggle. This century of valiant achievement, colossal errors, and overwhelming failure left its deep impression upon the Jewish race. It witnessed the return of many Jews of the dispersion to Jerusalem and Judea and the development of a strong sense of racial unity. Henceforth the Jews throughout the world looked to Jerusalem as their true political and religious capital. The events of this period intensified the ancient feud between Jew and Samaritan and gave the latter ample reason for that hostility toward their southern kinsmen which appears in the Gospel narratives. It was during this age that the parties of the Pharisees and Sadducees finally crystallized and formulated those tenets and policies which guided them during the next century. At this time the foundations were laid for the rule of the house of Herod which exerted such a baleful influence upon the fortunes and destinies of the Jews. It likewise marked the beginning and culmination of Rome's influence over the lands of the eastern Mediterranean and that subjection of the Jews to Gentile rulers which has continued until the present.

The Maccabean period gave to the Jews a greatly enlarged intellectual vision and led them to adopt many of the ideas of their Greek conquerors. In their literature it is easy to recognize the influence of the more logical Greek methods of reasoning and of the scientific attitude toward the universe. It was during this period that the wise were transformed into scribes, and the rule of the scribal method of thinking and interpretation began. The struggles through which the Jews passed intensified their love for the law and the temple services. Duty was more and more defined in the terms of ceremonial, and the Pharisees entered upon that vast and impossible task of providing rules for man's every act. Out of the struggles of the Maccabean period came that fusion of Hellenic and Jewish ideas that has become an important factor in all human thought. At last under the influence of the great crises through which they had passed, the belief in individual immortality gained wide acceptance among the Jews. Side by side with this came the belief in a personal devil and a hierarchy of demons opposed to the divine hierarchy at whose head was Jehovah. Last of all the taste of freedom under a Jewish ruler brought again to the front the kingly messianic hopes of the race, and led them to long and struggle for their realization. Thus in this brief century Judaism attained in many ways its final form, and only in the light of this process is it possible fully to understand and appreciate the background of the New Testament history.

THE RULE OF ROME

§ CXVII. THE RISE OF THE HERODIAN HOUSE

Now Alexander, that son of Aristobulus who ran away from Pompey, after a time gathered together a considerable body of men and made a strong attack upon Hyrcanus, and overran Judea, and was on the point of dethroning him. And indeed he would have come to Jerusalem, and would have ventured to rebuild its wall that had been thrown down by Pompey, had not Gabinius, who was sent as Scaurus's successor in Syria, showed his bravery by making an attack on Alexander. Alexander, being afraid at his approach, assembled a larger army composed of ten thousand armed footmen and fifteen hundred horsemen. 1. The rebellion led by Alexander (Jos. War, I, 8²)

Now when Gabinius came to Alexandrium, finding a great many encamped there, he tried by promising them pardon for their former offences to attach them to him before it came to fighting; but when they would listen to nothing reasonable, he slew a great number of them and shut up the rest in the citadel. Therefore when Alexander despaired of ever obtaining the rulership, he sent ambassadors to Gabinius and besought him to pardon his offences. He also surrendered to him the remaining fortresses, Hyrcanium and Macherus. After this Gabinius brought Hyrcanus back to Jerusalem and put him in charge of the temple. He also divided the entire nation into five districts, assigning one to Jerusalem, another to Gadara, another to Amathus, a fourth to Jericho, and the fifth to Sepphoris, a city of Galilee. 2. Its suppression by Gabinius (4a, 5)

Not long after Aristobulus became the cause of new disturbances by fleeing from Rome. He again assembled many of the Jews who were desirous of a change and those who were devoted to him of old; and when he had taken Alexandrium in the first place, he attempted to build a wall about it. But the Romans followed him, and when it came to battle, Aristobulus's party for a long time fought bravely, but at last 3. Suppression of the rebellion led by Aristobulus (6)

275

they were overcome by the Romans and of them five thousand fell. Aristobulus was again carried to Rome by Gabinius.

4. Antipater's aid in putting down a third rebellion (7)

Now when Gabinius set out to make war against the Parthians, Antipater furnished him with money and weapons and corn and auxiliaries, but during Gabinius's absence the other parts of Syria were in insurrection, and Alexander, the son of Aristobulus, stirred the Jews again to revolt. But at the battle fought near Mount Tabor ten thousand of them were slain and the rest of the multitude scattered in flight. So Gabinius came to Jerusalem and settled the government as Antipater desired.

5. Antipater's family (9b)

Now this Antipater married a wife of an eminent family among the Arabians, whose name was Cypros. And she bore him four sons, Phasælus and Herod, who was afterward king, and besides these Joseph and Pheroras. And he had a daughter by the name of Salome.

6. Death of Aristobulus (9¹)

But after the flight of Pompey and of the senate beyond the Ionian Sea, Cæsar gained possession of Rome and of the Empire and released Aristobulus from his bonds. He also intrusted two legions to him and sent him in haste into Syria, hoping that by his efforts he would easily conquer that country and the territory adjoining Judea. But he was poisoned by Pompey's sympathizers.

7. Antipater's services to Cæsar (3a, c, 4a, c, 5a)

Now after Pompey died, Antipater changed sides and cultivated a friendship with Cæsar. And when Mithridates of Pergamus with the force he led against Egypt was shut out from the roads about Pelusium and was forced to stay at Ascalon, Antipater persuaded the Arabians among whom he had lived to assist him and came himself at the head of three thousand armed Jews. He also urged the men of power in Syria to come to his assistance. In the attack on Pelusium Antipater distinguished himself pre-eminently, for he pulled down that part of the wall which was opposite him and leaped first of all into the city with the men who were about him. Thus was Pelusium taken. Moreover, as he was marching on, those Jews who inhabited the district called Onias stopped him, but Antipater not only persuaded them not to hinder but also to supply provisions for their army. Thereupon in the Delta Antipater fell upon those

276

who pursued Mithridates and slew many of them and pursued the rest till he captured their camp, while he lost no more than eighty of his own men. Thereupon Cæsar encouraged Antipater to undertake other hazardous enterprises for him by giving him great commendations and hopes of reward. In all these enterprises Antipater showed himself a most venturesome warrior, and he had many wounds almost all over his body as proofs of his courage.

And when Cæsar had settled the affairs of Egypt and returned again into Syria, he gave Antipater the rights of a Roman citizen and freedom from taxes, and made him an object of admiration because of the other honors and marks of friendship that he bestowed upon him. It was on this account that he also confirmed Hyrcanus in the high priesthood. <small>8. His rewards (5b)</small>

It was about this time that Antigonus, the son of Aristobulus, came to Cæsar and became in a surprising manner the cause of Antipater's further advance. For he proceeded to denounce Hyrcanus and Antipater. Then Antipater threw off his garments and showed the many wounds he had, and said that regarding his good will to Cæsar it was not necessary for him to say a word because his body cried aloud, though he himself said nothing. When Cæsar heard this he declared Hyrcanus to be most deserving of the high priesthood, and Antipater was appointed procurator of all Judea and also obtained permission to rebuild those walls of his country that had been thrown down. <small>9. His vindication (10^1, 2a, 3a)</small>

As soon as Antipater had conducted Cæsar out of Syria, he returned to Judea, and the first thing he did was to rebuild the walls of his own country. Then he went over the country and quieted the tumults therein. And at this time he settled the affairs of the country by himself, because he saw that Hyrcanus was inactive and not capable of managing the affairs of the kingdom. So Antipater appointed his oldest son, Phasælus, governor of Jerusalem and the surrounding territory. He also sent his second son, Herod, who was very young, with equal authority into Galilee. <small>10. His rule of Judea (4)</small>

Now Herod was a very active man and soon found a field for his energy. When, therefore, he found that Hezekias, the leader of the robbers, overran the adjoining parts of Syria with a great band of men, he caught him and slew him <small>11. Herod's effective work in Galilee (5a, b)</small>

and many more of the robbers. This exploit was especially pleasing to the Syrians, so that songs were sung in Herod's commendation both in the villages and in the cities, because he had secured peace for them and had preserved their possessions.

12. The murder of Cæsar and the death of Antipater (11¹, ⁴) At this time a mighty war arose among the Romans after the treacherous murder of Cæsar by Cassius and Brutus Accordingly Cassius came into Syria and assumed command of the army, and went about exacting tribute of the cities to such a degree that they were not able to endure it. During the war between Cassius and Brutus on the one side, against the younger Cæsar (Augustus) and Antony on the other, Cassius and Murcus gathered an army out of Syria. And because Herod had furnished a great part of the necessities, they made him procurator of all Syria and gave him an army of infantry and cavalry. Cassius promised him also that after the war was over he would make him king of Judea. But it so happened that the power and hopes of his son became the cause of Antipater's destruction. For inasmuch as a certain Malichus was afraid of this, he bribed one of the king's cup-bearers to give a poisoned potion to Antipater. Thus he became a sacrifice to Malichus's wickedness and died after the feast.

13. Herod's growing power (11⁶, 12³) Herod, however, avenged himself upon Malichus. And those who hitherto did not favor him now joined him because of his marriage into the family of Hyrcanus, for he had formerly married a wife from his own country of noble blood, Doris by name, who bore to him Antipater. Now he planned to marry Mariamne, the daughter of Alexander, the son of Aristobulus and the grandson of Hyrcanus.

14. Confirmation of his authority by Antony (⁴, ⁵) But when Cæsar and Antony had slain Cassius near Philippi and Cæsar had gone to Italy and Antony to Asia, the great men of the Jews came and accused Phasælus and Herod that they held the government by force and that Hyrcanus had nothing more than an honorable name. Herod appeared ready to answer this accusation, and having made Antony his friend by the large sums of money which he gave him, influenced him not to listen to the charges spoken against him by enemies. After this a hundred of the principal men among the Jews came to Antony at Daphne near

Antioch and accused Phasælus and Herod. But Massala opposed them and defended the brothers with the help of Hyrcanus. When Antony had heard both sides, he asked Hyrcanus which party was best fitted to govern. Hyrcanus replied that Herod and his party were the best fitted. Therefore Antony appointed the brothers tetrarchs, and intrusted to them the rulership of Judea.

Now two years after, when Barzaphanes, a Parthian governor, and Pacorus, the king's son, had captured Syria, they were persuaded by the promise of a thousand talents and five hundred women to bring back Antigonus to his kingdom and to turn Hyrcanus out of it. Thus Antigonus was brought back into Judea by the king of the Parthians, and received Hyrcanus and Phasælus as prisoners. Being afraid that Hyrcanus, who was under the guard of the Parthians, might have his kingdom restored to him by the multitude, Antigonus cut off his ears and thereby guarded against the possibility that the high priesthood would ever come to him again, inasmuch as he was maimed, and the law required that this dignity should belong to none but those who had all their members intact. Phasælus, perceiving that he was to be put to death, dashed his head against a great stone and thereby took away his own life. {15. Restoration of the Jewish kingship by the Persians (13^{1a}, Ant. XIV, 13^{10})}

Herod, however, went off by night, taking those nearest related to him. As soon as the Parthians perceived it, they pursued after him, but when at every assault he had slain a great many of them, he came to the stronghold of Masada, and there he left eight hundred of his men to guard the women, and provisions sufficient for a siege; but he himself hastened to Petra in Arabia. He was not able, however, to find any friendship among the Arabians, for their king sent to him and commanded him to turn back immediately from the country. So when Herod found that the Arabians were his enemies, he turned back to Egypt. And when he came to Pelusium, he could not obtain passage from those who lay with the fleet. Therefore he besought their captains to let him go with them. So out of respect for the fame and rank of the man they carried him to Alexandria. And when he came to the city, he was received with great splendor by Cleopatra, who hoped he might be persuaded to be the com- {16. Herod's escape (Jew. War, I, 13^{7, 8c}, 14^{1b, 2})} mander of her forces in the expedition she was about to undertake. But he rejected the queen's entreaty and sailed for Rome, where first of all he went to Antony and laid before him the calamities that had overtaken himself and his family.

17. Appointed king of the Jews at Rome (4)

Thereupon Antony's pity was aroused because of the change that had come about in Herod's affairs, so he then resolved to have him made king of the Jews. Herod found Cæsar even more ready than Antony because he recalled the campaigns through which he had gone with Herod's father, Antipater, in Egypt, and his hospitable treatment and good will in all things. Besides he recognized the energy of Herod. Accordingly he called the senate together. There Messala, and after him Atratinus, introduced Herod to them and gave a full account of his father's merits and of his own good will to the Romans. Antony also came in and told them that it was to their advantage in the Parthian war that Herod should be king. So they all gave their votes for it. And when the senate disbanded, Antony and Cæsar went out with Herod between them. Antony also made a feast for Herod on the first day of his reign.

18. His campaigns for the reconquest of Palestine (15[3a, b], 4, 16[1])

Herod then sailed from Italy and came to Ptolemais. And as soon as he had assembled a considerable army of foreigners and of his own countrymen, he marched through Galilee against Antigonus. The number of his forces increased each day as he went along, and all Galilee with few exceptions joined him. After this Herod took Joppa, and then he marched to Masada to free his kinsmen. Then he marched to Jerusalem, where the soldiers who were with the Roman general Silo joined his own, as did many from the city because they feared his power. Herod did not lie idle, but seized Idumea and held it with two thousand footmen and four hundred horsemen. He also removed his mother and all his kinsmen, who had been at Masada, to Samaria. And when he had settled them securely, he marched to capture the remaining parts of Galilee, and to drive away the garrisons of Antigonus.

19. Death of his brother Joseph (17[1])

In the meantime Herod's fortunes in Judea were not in a favorable condition. He had left his brother Joseph with full authority, but had commanded him to make no attacks against Antigonus until his return. But as soon as Joseph heard that his brother was at a great distance, he disregarded the command he had received and marched toward Jericho with five cohorts. But when his enemies attacked him in the mountains and in a place where it was difficult to pass, he was killed as he was fighting bravely in the battle, and all the Roman cohorts were destroyed.

Now near the end of winter Herod marched to Jerusalem and brought his army up to its wall. This was the third year after he had been made king at Rome. So he pitched his camp before the temple, for on that side it might be besieged and there Pompey had formerly captured the city. Accordingly he divided the work among the army and laid waste the suburbs, and gave orders to raise three mounds and to build towers upon these mounds. But he himself went to Samaria to marry the daughter of Alexander, the son of Aristobulus, who had been betrothed to him before. And when he was thus married, he came back to Jerusalem with a greater army.

20. Advance against Jerusalem (8, 9)

Now the multitude of the Jews who were in the city were divided into several factions. For the people that crowded about the temple, being the weaker party, became fanatical and raved wildly over the situation. But some of the bolder men gathered together in companies, and began robbing in many different ways and especially plundering the provisions that were about the city, so that no food was left over for the horses or the men. After a siege of five months some of Herod's chosen men ventured upon the wall and fell into the city. They first captured the environs of the temple, and as the army poured in there was a slaughter of vast multitudes everywhere, on account of the rage in which the Romans were because of the length of the siege, and because the Jews who were about Herod were eager that none of their opponents should remain. Thereupon Herod made those who were on his side still more his friends by the honors he conferred upon them; but those of Antigonus's party he slew.

21. Capture of the capital city (18¹, 2c, 4a)

I. **The Fruitless Struggle against Rome.** The first quarter century of Roman rule was in many ways the most complex in Israel's intricate history. There were three chief actors in the drama: (1) Rome, represented first by the leaders of the Republic and later by

Pompey, Cæsar, and their successors; (2) the popular Jewish party led by Aristobulus and his son Alexander, and Antigonus; and (3) Antipater, supported by his able sons Phasælus and Herod. Rome's general policy was to allow the Jews as much freedom as possible, but above all to hold Palestine under firm control, for it lay on the eastern border and faced Parthia, the one foe that had successfully defied the powerful mistress of the Mediterranean. The popular Jewish party bitterly resented Rome's interference. True, the Pharisees welcomed the relief from civil war, but they could not hold the majority of the people in leash. The inoffensive Hyrcanus was left in possession of the high-priesthood and from time to time was elevated to positions of nominal civil authority, but he was little more than the plaything of circumstance and party intrigue. The ambitions of Aristobulus and his sons kept Palestine in a state of constant political ferment. Three times in five years they stirred the Jews to rebellion against Rome. The first rebellion was in 57 B.C. and was led by Alexander. He was ultimately driven by the Roman general to Alexandria, the fortress that overlooks the middle-Jordan Valley, and was finally forced to surrender. The three great fortressses, Alexandria, Machærus, and Hyrcanium, were thrown down, and the Jewish state was divided into five districts. Each of these was under a local council consisting of the leading citizens. These reported directly to the Roman proconsul. To neutralize still further the Jewish national spirit, the Hellenic cities in and about Palestine were restored, given a large measure of independence, and placed directly under the control of Rome's representative in the East.

The second rebellion followed quickly and was led by Aristobulus. He was soon obliged, however, to take refuge in the fortress of Machærus, east of the Dead Sea, where he was captured and sent back again as a captive to Rome. The third rebellion was led by Alexander. It was more formidable, and in the end more disastrous, for the Jews were signally defeated in a battle near Mount Tabor. The only permanent results of these uprisings were the intensifying of Jewish hatred of Roman rule and the increasing of Rome's suspicion of this rebellious people. It was this suspicion that made it possible for the high-priestly party at a later time to force the Roman governor Pilate to put to death one whom he recognized to be an inoffensive Galilean peasant simply because he was accused of having assumed the historic title, King of the Jews.

II. **Antipater's Policy.** Through the troublesome first quarter-century of Roman rule Antipater and his family prospered because they were able at every turn in the political fortunes of Syria to make themselves increasingly useful to Rome. At many critical periods he was able to save the Jews from calamity and to secure for them valuable privileges. There is a certain basis for Josephus's over-enthusiastic assertion that he was "a man distinguished for his piety, justice, and love of his country" (Ant. XIV, 11⁴ᵉ).

Although Hyrcanus was but a tool in Antipater's hands, he never attempted to depose him, and apparently always treated him with respect. To steer successfully through the stormy period during which Rome made the transition from the republican to the monarchical form of government was a difficult task. When Crassus came as the representative of the First Triumvirate, Antipater's gifts and tact were not sufficient to prevent the Roman from plundering the treasures of the temple. Fortunately for the peace of Judea, during the civil war that followed between Pompey and Cæsar, the deposed Jewish king Aristobulus and his son Alexander were both put to death. After the decisive battle of Pharsalia in 48 B.C. Antipater quickly espoused the cause of Cæsar, and performed valuable services for him at a time when the great Roman was threatened by overwhelming forces. By his influence with the people of Syria and Egypt and by his personal acts of bravery he won the favors that Cæsar heaped upon him and upon the Jewish people. The old territorial division instituted by Gabinius was abolished, Hyrcanus was confirmed in the high-priesthood, and Antipater was made procurator of Judea. Joppa was restored to the Jewish state, the gerusia, the chief assembly of the Jews, was given certain of its old judicial rights, and permission was granted to rebuild the wall of Jerusalem. The Jews were also freed from the duty of supporting Roman soldiers and of serving the Roman legions. The tribute was also in part remitted on the sabbatical year, and the Jews of Palestine and throughout the Roman Empire were confirmed in their religious privileges. Thus Cæsar proved himself a friend of the Jews and established precedents to which they frequently appealed in later crises.

III. **Herod's Early Record.** Among the many rewards conferred upon Antipater was the appointment of his son Phasælus as governor of Jerusalem and his younger son Herod as governor of Galilee. Thus while still a young man Herod was given an opportunity to demonstrate his ability and energy. He at once took measures to put down the robber bands that infested Galilee, and executed their leader, Hezekias. He won thereby the gratitude of the Galileans and the approval of Rome. Hyrcanus and the sanhedrin at Jerusalem, however, viewed this assumption of authority with suspicion and alarm. When Herod was summoned before them, he appeared in full military armor and was accompanied by a military following. Provoked by his boldness, the sanhedrin would have sentenced him to death had not the local Roman governor interfered. The action of the sanhedrin aroused Herod's spirit of revenge, and before long, gathering his forces, he marched against Jerusalem and would have put to death the Jewish leaders had not his father dissuaded him.

The assassination of Cæsar in 44 B.C., followed by the battle of Philippi in 42, changed the political horizon of Palestine. Antipater and his sons, however, following their usual policy, pledged in succession their loyalty to Cassius and Antony, with the result that greater honors were conferred upon them. It was at this crisis that Malichus, a certain Jewish noble, inspired by jealousy and suspicion, treacherously murdered his rival, Antipater. Herod retaliated by instigating the assassination of the murderer, but soon a series of calamities swept over Judea which threatened to obliterate completely the house of Antipater.

IV. **The Parthian Conquest.** During the struggle between Antony and the assassins of Julius Cæsar Rome's eastern outposts were left exposed. Their old foes, the Parthians, improved this opportunity to seize northern Syria. Encouraged by the presence of the Parthians, Antigonus, the younger son of Aristobulus, in 41 B.C. entered Palestine. With the aid of the Parthians and of the Jews who were opposed to Herod he ultimately succeeded in establishing himself as king. Antipater and Herod's brother Phasælus became the victims of the Parthian treachery, and Herod after many adventures succeeded in escaping with his family to the strong fortress of Masada at the southwestern end of the Dead Sea. Leaving them under the care of his brother Joseph, Herod after many discouragements and vicissitudes finally found his way to Rome. Unfortunately for the cause of Jewish independence, Antigonus lacked the essential qualities of leadership. Instead of arousing the loyalty of his subjects his chief concern was to take vengeance upon Herod's followers and upon all who had supported the house of Antipater.

V. **Herod Made King of the Jews.** Herod went to Rome to urge the appointment of Aristobulus III, the grandson of Hyrcanus and the brother of Herod's betrothed wife Mariamne, as king of Judea. Antony and Octavian, to whom he appealed, were rightly suspicious of the survivors of the Maccabean house and appreciative of the services of Herod and his father Antipater. Therefore, to his complete surprise, they offered him the kingship, and their nomination was speedily confirmed by the senate. History presents no stranger nor more dramatic sight than Herod, the Idumean, accompanied by Antony and Octavian, going to the temple of Jupiter on the Capitoline Hill to offer sacrifices in connection with his assumption of the historic title, King of the Jews. At first it was an empty title, but the energy of Herod and the resources of Rome sufficed in time to make it real. In the spring of 39 B.C. Herod landed at Ptolemais and with the apathetic aid of the Roman generals in Palestine began to organize the Jews who rallied about him. Marching down the Mediterranean coast, he succeeded at last in relieving his family, who were besieged at Masada. Idumea and Galilee were then brought into subjection, and after two years of fighting he won an important battle at Isana, a little north of Bethel, which gave him possession of all of Judea except Jerusalem. The final contest for the capital city continued through several months, for Antigonus and his followers realized that they could expect little mercy from Herod and the Romans. Thousands of Jews were slaughtered, but at last the temple itself was captured, and Herod was in fact as well as in name King of the Jews. Antigonus pled in vain for mercy. Departing from their usual policy of clemency toward native rulers, the Romans caused him first to be scourged as a common criminal and then ignominiously beheaded. Thus the Maccabean dynasty, which had risen in glory, went down in shame, a signal illustration of the eternal principle that selfish ambitions and unrestrained passions in an individual or family sooner or later bring disgrace and destruction. While the siege of Jerusalem was still in progress, Herod went north to Samaria and there consummated his long-delayed marriage with Mariamne, the daughter of Hyrcanus, thus in part attracting to himself the loyalty which the Jews had bestowed so lavishly and disastrously upon the unworthy sons of Alexander Janneus.

§ CXVIII. HEROD'S POLICY AND REIGN

Now when the war about Actium broke out, Herod prepared to come to the assistance of Antony, but he was treacherously hindered from sharing the dangers of Antony by Cleopatra, for she persuaded Antony to intrust the war against the Arabians to Herod. This plan, however, proved of advantage to Herod, for he defeated the army of the Arabians, although it offered him strong resistance.

1. Herod's loyalty to Antony (Jos. Jew. War, I, 19⁴, ²ᵃ)

285

2. His
defence
before
Augustus
(29¹)
Now Herod was immediately concerned about his entire fortunes because of his friendship with Antony, who had been defeated at Actium by Cæsar [Augustus]. Herod, however, resolved to face the danger: so he sailed to Rhodes where Cæsar was then staying, and came to him without his diadem and in the dress and guise of a private person, but in the spirit of a king. And he concealed nothing of the truth, but spoke straight out as follows: "O Cæsar, I was made king of the Jews by Antony. I confess that I have been useful to him, nor will I conceal this added fact, that you would certainly have found me in arms, and so showing my gratitude to him, had not the Arabians hindered me. I have been overcome with Antony, and sharing the same fortune as his, I have laid aside my diadem. Now I have come to you fixing my hopes of safety upon your virtue, and I ask that you will consider how faithful a friend, and not whose friend, I have been."

3. The
confirmation of
his authority
(2)
Cæsar answered him as follows: "Nay, you shall not only be safe, but you shall reign more firmly than before, for you are worthy to reign over many subjects because of the steadfastness of your friendship. Endeavor to be equally constant in your friendship to me in the hour of my success, since I have the brightest hopes because of your noble spirit. I therefore assure you that I will confirm the kingdom to you by decree. I will also endeavor to do you some further kindness hereafter, that you may not miss Antony."

4.
Added
honors
and
territory
(b-ia)
After this, when Cæsar went to Egypt through Syria, Herod received him lavishly and royally. It was, therefore, the opinion both of Cæsar and his soldiers that Herod's kingdom was too small a return for what he had done. For this reason, when Cæsar had returned from Egypt, he added to Herod's other honors, and also made an addition to his kingdom by giving him not only the country which had been taken from him by Cleopatra, but also Gadara, Hippos, and Samaria, and also the coast cities Gaza, Anthedon, Joppa, and Straton's Tower. He also made him a present of four hundred Gauls as a body-guard, which had before belonged to Cleopatra. Moreover he added to his kingdom Trachonitis and the adjacent Batanea, and the district of Auranitis.

Now Herod had a body suited to his soul and was ever a most excellent hunter, in which sport he generally had great success owing to his skill in riding, for in one day he once captured forty wild beasts. He was also a warrior such as could not be withstood. Many also marvelled at his skill in his exercises when they saw him throwing the javelin and shooting the arrow straight to the mark. In addition to these advantages of mind and body, fortune was also very favorable to him, for he seldom failed in war, and when he failed, he was not himself the cause, but it happened either through the treachery of some one or else through the rashness of his own soldiers.

5. Herod's personal qualities (21¹⁵)

Herod also built for himself at Jerusalem in the upper city a palace, which contained two very large and most beautiful apartments to which not even the temple could be compared. One apartment he named Cæsareum and the other Agrippeum [after his friends Cæsar Augustus and Agrippa]. But he did not preserve their memory by particular buildings only and the names given them, but his generosity also went as far as entire cities. For when he had built a most beautiful wall over two miles long about a city in the district of Samaria and had brought six thousand inhabitants into it and had allotted to them a most fertile territory and in the midst of this city had erected a large temple to Augustus, he called the city Sebaste [from Sebastus, the Greek of Augustus]. And when Augustus had bestowed upon him additional territory, he built there also a temple of white marble in his honor near the fountains of the Jordan. The place is called Panium. The king erected other buildings at Jericho and named them after the same friends. In general there was not any place in his kingdom suited to the purpose that was allowed to remain without something in Augustus's honor.

6. Buildings at Jerusalem and throughout his kingdom in honor of Augustus (1ᵇ-4ᵃ)

And when he observed that there was a city by the seaside that was much decayed, called Straton's Tower, and that the place, because of its fair situation, was capable of great improvements, through his love of honor he rebuilt it all of white stone and adorned it with magnificent palaces and in it showed his natural munificence. For all the seashore between Dora and Egypt (between which places the city is situated) had no good harbor, so that every one who sailed

7. Cæsarea by the sea (5a-8a)

to Phœnicia from Egypt was obliged to toss about in the sea because of the south wind that threatened them. But the king by great expense and liberality overcame nature and built a harbor larger than was the Piræus, and in its recesses built other deep roadsteads. He let down stones into one hundred and twenty-one feet of water. And when the part below the sea was filled up, he extended the wall which was already above the sea until it was two hundred feet long. The entrance to the harbor was on the north, because the north wind was there the most gentle of all the winds. At the mouth of the harbor on each side were three colossi supported by pillars. And the houses, also built of white stone, were close to the harbor, and the narrow streets of the city led down to it, being built at equal distances from one another. And opposite the entrance of the harbor upon an elevation was the temple of Cæsar Augustus, excellent both for beauty and size, and in it was a colossal statue of Cæsar Augustus as big as the Olympian Zeus, which it was made to resemble, and a statue of Rome as big at that of Hera at Argos. And he dedicated the city to the province, and the harbor to those who sailed there. But the honor of founding the city he ascribed to Cæsar Augustus and accordingly called it Cæsarea. He also built other edifices, the amphitheater, the theater, and market-place in a manner worthy of that name.

8. Cities in the Jordan valley (9a-10a)

Herod was also a lover of his father, for he built as a memorial of his father a city in the finest plain that was in his kingdom [the lower Jordan valley], which had rivers and trees in abundance, and called it Antipatris. He also fortified a citadel that lay above Jericho and was very strong and handsome, and dedicated it to his mother, and called it Cypros. Moreover, he dedicated a tower at Jerusalem to his brother Phasælus. He also built another city in the valley which leads north from Jericho and named it Phasælis. As a memorial for himself he built a fortress upon a mountain toward Arabia and called it after himself Herodium.

9. Building enterprises outside his kingdom (11a)

And when he had built so much, he showed the greatness of his soul to many foreign cities. He built gymnasiums at Tripolis, Damascus, and Ptolemaïs. He built a wall around Byblus, and arcades, colonnades, temples, and market-places at Berytus and Tyre, and theaters at Sidon and Da-

288

mascus. He also built an aqueduct for those Laodiceans, who lived by the seaside; and for the inhabitants of Ascalon he built baths and costly fountains, as also encircling colonnades that were admirable for their workmanship and size.

Herod, however, began to be unhappy on account of his wife, of whom he was very fond. For when he attained the kingship, he divorced her whom he had married when he was a private person, a native of Jerusalem by the name of Doris, and married Mariamne, the daughter of Alexander, the son of Aristobulus. Because of Mariamne disturbances arose in his family, and that very soon, but chiefly after his return from Rome. For the sake of his sons by Mariamne he banished Antipater, the son of Doris. After this he slew his wife's grandfather, Hyrcanus, when he returned to him out of Parthia, on suspicion of plotting against him. Now of the five children which Herod had by Mariamne two of them were daughters and three were sons. The youngest of these sons died while he was being educated at Rome, but the two elder sons he treated as princes because of their mother's honorable rank and because they had been born after he became king. But what was stronger than all this was the love he bore to Mariamne.

But Mariamne's hatred toward him was as great as his love for her. She, indeed, had a just cause for indignation for what he had done, while her freedom of speech was the result of his affection for her. So she openly reproached him for what he had done to her grandfather Hyrcanus and to her brother Aristobulus. For he had not spared this Aristobulus, though he was but a lad, for after he had given him the high priesthood at the age of seventeen, Herod caused him to be slain immediately after he had conferred that honor upon him; for when Aristobulus had put on the holy garments and had approached to the altar at a festival, the assembled multitude wept for joy. Thereupon the lad was sent by night to Jericho, and there in a swimming-pool at Herod's command was held under water by the Gauls until he was drowned. For these reasons Mariamne reproached Herod, and railed at his sister and his mother most abusively. He was dumb on account of his affection for her, but the

10. His love fo Mariamne (22 in,c-2b)

11. His insane jealous and final murde of Mariamne (2c-4)

289

women were vexed exceedingly at her and charged her with being false to him, for they thought that this would be most likely to arouse Herod's anger. When, therefore, he was about to take a journey abroad, he intrusted his wife to Joseph, his sister Salome's husband. He also gave him a secret injunction that, if Antony should slay him [Herod], Joseph should slay Mariamne. But Joseph without any evil intention and in order to demonstrate the king's love for his wife disclosed this secret to her. And when Herod came back, and when they talked together, he confirmed his love to her by many oaths and assured her that he had never loved any other woman as he had her. "To be sure," said she, "you proved your love to me by the injunctions you gave Joseph when you commanded him to kill me!" When Herod heard that this secret was discovered, he was like a distracted man, and said that Joseph would never have disclosed his injunction unless he had seduced her. Made insane by his passion and leaping out of bed, he ran about the palace in a wild manner. Meantime his sister Salome improved the opportunity for false accusations and to confirm the suspicion about Joseph. So in his ungovernable jealousy and rage Herod commanded both of them to be slain immediately. But as soon as his passion was over, he repented for what he had done; and indeed his passionate desire for Mariamne was so ardent that he could not think that she was dead, but in his distress he talked to her as if she were still alive.

12. His suspicions of Mariamne's sons (23[1a, d, 2a, c-3a])   Now Mariamne's sons inherited their mother's hate; and when they considered the greatness of Herod's crime toward her, they were as suspicious of their father as of an enemy. This state of theirs increased as they grew to be men. And when Herod had been poisoned with calumnies against them, he recalled Antipater, his son by Doris, from exile as a defence against his other sons, and began to treat him in every way with more distinction than them. But these sons were not able to bear this change, for when they saw Antipater, who was the son of a private woman, advanced, the nobility of their own birth made them unable to restrain their indignation. For Antipater was already publicly named in his father's will as his successor. The two weapons

which he employed against his brothers were flattery and calumny, whereby he brought matters privately to such a point that the king thought of putting his sons to death. So Herod dragged Alexander with him as far as Rome and charged him before Augustus with attempting to poison him, but Alexander very ably cleared himself of the calumnies laid against him and brought Augustus to the point of rejecting the accusation and of reconciling Herod to his sons at once. After this the king returned from Rome and seemed to have acquitted his sons of these charges, but still he was not without some suspicion of them, for Antipater, who was the cause of the hatred, accompanied them. But he did not openly show his enmity toward them, for he stood in awe of the one who had reconciled them. But the dissensions between the brothers still accompanied them, and the suspicions they had of one another grew worse.

Alexander and Aristobulus were much vexed that the privilege of the first-born was confirmed to Antipater, and Antipater was very angry because his brothers were to succeed him. Moreover, Salome incited Herod's cruelty against his sons, for Aristobulus was desirous of bringing her who was his mother-in-law and aunt into the same dangers as himself. So he sent to her to advise her to save herself, and told her that the king was preparing to put her to death. Then Salome came running to the king and informed him of the warning. Thereupon Herod could restrain himself no longer, but caused both of his sons to be bound, and kept them apart from one another, and speedily sent to Augustus written charges against them. Augustus was greatly troubled in regard to the young men, but he did not think he ought to take from a father the power over his sons. So he wrote back to him, and gave him full authority over his sons, and said he would do well to make an examination of the plot by means of a common council consisting of his own kinsmen and the governors of his province, and if his sons were found guilty to put them to death. With these directions Herod complied. Then he sent his sons to Sebaste and ordered them there to be strangled, and his orders being executed immediately, he commanded their bodies to be brought to the fortress of Alexandrium.

13. Final result of the intrigues in Herod's court (24¹ᵃ, 27¹, 2ᵃ, 6ᵇ)

14.
Popular hatred of Antipater (28ᵗᵃ, 29²ᶜ)'

But an unconquerable hatred against Antipater rose up in the nation now that he had an indisputable title to the succession, because they well knew that he was the person who had contrived all the calumnies against his brothers. Later he secured permission by means of his Italian friends to go and live at Rome. For when they wrote that it was proper for Antipater to be sent to Augustus after some time, Herod made no delay but sent him with a splendid retinue and a large amount of money, and gave him his testament to carry in which Antipater was inscribed as king.

15.
Herod's discovery of Antipater's perfidy (30⁵ᵃ, 31¹ᵃ)

And after the death of Herod's brother Pheroras, the king devoted himself to examining his son Antipater's steward; and upon torturing him he learned that Antipater had sent for a potion of deadly poison for him from Egypt, and that the uncle of Antipater had received it from him and delivered it to Pheroras, for Antipater had charged him to destroy his father the king, while [Antipater] was at Rome, and so free him from the suspicion of doing it himself. Antipater's freedman was also brought to trial, and he was the concluding proof of Antipater's designs. This man came and brought another deadly potion of the poison of asps and of other serpents, that if the first potion did not accomplish its end, Pheroras and his wife might be armed with this also against the king.

16.
Death of Antipater and Herod (33¹, ⁷, ⁵ᵃ)

Now Herod's illness became more and more severe because his various ailments attacked him in his old age and when he was in a melancholy state, for he was already almost seventy years of age and was depressed by the calamities that had happened to him in connection with his children, so that he had no pleasure in life even when he was in health. The fact that Antipater was still alive aggravated his disease, and he preferred to destroy him, not incidentally but by crushing him completely. When letters came from his ambassadors at Rome containing the information that Antipater was condemned to death, Herod for a little while was restored to cheerfulness; but presently being overcome by his pains, he endeavored to anticipate destiny, and this because he was weakened by want of food and by a convulsive cough. Accordingly he took an apple and asked for a knife, for he used to pare his apples before eating them. He then looked around to see that there was no one to hinder him and lifted up his right hand as if to stab himself. But Achiabus, his cousin, ran up to him and, holding his hand, hindered him from so doing. Immediately a great lamentation was raised in the palace, as if the king was dying, and as soon as Antipater heard that, he took courage and with joy in his looks besought his keepers for a sum of money to loose him and let him go. But the head keeper of the prison not only prevented that but also ran and told the king what his design was. Thereupon the king cried louder than his disease could well bear, and immediately sent some of his body-guards and had Antipater slain. He also gave orders to have him buried at Hyrcanium, and altered his testament again and therein made Archelaus, his eldest son, and the brother of Antipas, his successor, and made Antipas tetrarch. Herod, after surviving the death of his son only five days, died, having reigned thirty-four years, since he had obtained control of affairs; but it was thirty-seven years since he had been made king by the Romans.

I. Herod's Character. The character of Herod is comparatively easy to understand, for it is elemental and one that constantly recurs in history. We in America are familiar with this type which is represented by our unscrupulous captains of industry or political bosses—energetic, physically strong, shrewd, relentless toward all who threaten to thwart their plans, skilful in organization, not troubled about the rightness of their methods, provided they escape the toils of the law, able to command men and successfully to carry through large policies. They are not without their personal attractions, for it is instinctive to admire that which is big and able to achieve. Many of them also make permanent contributions to the upbuilding of the nation. Oriental history is also full of analogies: Nebuchadrezzar, Cyrus, Alexander, and in more recent times Mohammed Ali of Egypt. Herod was largely the product of his inheritance and training. His father, Antipater, had taught him to regard the Jews with secret but well-concealed contempt, and to hate Aristobulus and his ambitious sons. His religion was loyalty to Rome, for this meant wealth and success. He delighted in public approval, and his ambition was to be known as a great builder. As is true with this type of man, he was a natural tyrant. Power was his ruling passion, and he regarded with extreme suspicion any who might take it from him. In this respect the contemporary rulers of the Roman Empire set an example which he was not slow to follow. His Idumean and Arabian blood coursed hot and fierce through his veins. It was an age when moral standards were exceedingly low, and Herod never learned to rule his passions. The Oriental institution of the harem gave him full license, and he lived and loved as he fought and reigned—vehemently. Such a man is especially susceptible to the weaknesses and crimes that come from jealousy, and the influences of his family and court intensified these fatal faults.

Herod is not without his attractive qualities. A man who is able to execute on a large scale and win the title Great is never commonplace. In giving Palestine the benefits of a strong and stable government he performed a real service. In his love for Mariamne and for the sons she bore him he was mastered by a passion that for a time ennobled him. Like every man, moreover, who fails to taste the joys of disinterested service for his fellow-men, Herod paid the bitter penalty for his own unrestrained selfishness. He awakes pity rather than denunciation. He never found life, because he never learned to lose his life in the service of his people.

II. **His Attitude toward Rome.** Herod's policy was loyalty at any cost to the man who at the moment ruled Rome. During the first part of his reign Antony's power on the eastern Mediterranean was still in the ascendancy. Notwithstanding the powerful intrigues of Cleopatra, Herod succeeded in retaining the favor of his patron. When the battle of Actium in 32 B.C. revealed Antony's weakness, Herod forthwith cast off his allegiance, and his treachery was one of the chief forces that drove Antony to suicide. Octavian, who henceforth under the title of Augustus attained to the complete control of Rome, recognized in Herod a valuable servant. Herod's title as king of the Jews was confirmed, and Augustus gradually increased his territory until it included practically all of Palestine with the exception of certain Greek cities along the coast and east of the Jordan. Herod's task was to preserve peace in the land thus intrusted to him and to guard the eastern border of the empire against its Parthian foes. This task he faithfully performed.

III. **His Building Activity.** The spirit and policy of Augustus were clearly reflected in Herod's court and kingdom. When his position was firmly established, Herod devoted himself to magnificent building enterprises. In Antioch, Athens, and Rhodes, he reared great public buildings. Jerusalem, his capital, was provided with a theatre and amphitheatre, and other buildings that characterize the

Græco-Roman cities of the period. The two crowning achievements of Herod's reign were the rebuilding of Samaria and Cæsarea, as its port on the Mediterranean coast. Both of these cities were renamed in honor of his patron Augustus. On the acropolis of Samaria he built a huge Roman temple, the foundations of which have recently been uncovered by the American excavators. The city itself was encircled by a colonnade, over a mile long, consisting of pillars sixteen feet in height. Cæsarea, like Samaria, was adorned with magnificent public buildings, including a temple, a theatre, a palace, and an amphitheatre. The great breakwater two hundred feet wide that ran out into the open sea was one of the greatest achievements of that building age. By these acts Herod won still further the favor of Augustus and the admiration of the Eastern world.

IV. **His Attitude toward His Subjects.** The peace which Herod brought to Palestine was won at the point of the sword. The fear which he felt for his subjects was surpassed only by the fear which he inspired in them. He was unscrupulous and merciless in cutting down all possible rivals. The treacherous murder of Aristobulus III, the grandson of Hyrcanus, and last of all the murder of the inoffensive and maimed Hyrcanus, are among the darkest deeds in Herod's bloody reign. The power of the sanhedrin, the Jewish national representative body, was almost completely crushed. Following the policy of Augustus, Herod developed a complex system of spies, or espionage, so that, like an Oriental tyrant, he ruled his subjects by means of two armies, the spies who watched in secret and the soldiers who guarded them openly. His lavish building enterprises led him to load his people with an almost intolerable burden of taxation, and yet for the common people Herod's reign was one of comparative peace and prosperity. At last they were delivered from destructive wars and free to develop the great agricultural and commercial resources of the land. While outside of Judea Herod built heathen temples, he faithfully guarded the temple of Jerusalem, and was careful not to override the religious prejudices of his subjects. His measures to relieve their suffering in time of famine reveal a generosity which under better environment and training might have made him a benign ruler.

V. **The Tragedy of His Domestic Life.** The weakness of Herod's character is most glaringly revealed in his domestic life. Undoubtedly he loved the beautiful Maccabean princess, Mariamne, with all the passion of his violent nature. It was a type of love, however, which passes over easily into insensate jealousy. Accordingly, when he left Judea just before the battle of Actium, and later when he went to meet Octavian, he had his wife Mariamne shut up in a strong fortress. Unfortunately Herod, like most despots, was unable to command the services of loyal followers. The discovery of Herod's suspicions toward her aroused the imperious spirit of Mariamne. She was also the victim of the plots of his jealous family. Human history presents no greater tragedy than that of Herod putting to death the one woman whom he truly loved, and later a victim of his own suspicions and of the intrigues of his son Antipater, finally obtaining royal permission to put to death the two noble sons whom Mariamne had borne to him. It is difficult to find in all history a more pitiable sight than Herod in his old age, hated by most of his subjects, misled by the members of his own family, the murderer of those whom he loved best, finding his sole satisfaction in putting to death his son Antipater, who had betrayed him, and in planning in his last hours how he might by the murder of hundreds of his subjects arouse wide-spread lamentation.

VI. **Effects of Herod's Reign.** One of the chief results of Herod's policy and reign was the complete extinction of the Maccabean house. Herod's motive and method were thoroughly base, but for the Jewish people the result was beneficial, for it removed one of the most active causes of those suicidal rebellions that had resulted disastrously for the Jews and brought them under the suspicion and iron rule of Rome. With his heavy hand Herod also put a stop to the party strife that had undermined the native Jewish kingdom and brought loss and suffering to thousands of Jews. The Pharisees and Sadducees at last were taught the lesson of not resorting to arms, however widely they might differ. By removing the Pharisees from public life Herod directed their energies to developing their ceremonial regulations and to instructing the people. Thus the influence of the Pharisees became paramount with the great majority of the Jews. As Herod extended his rule over all Palestine, he brought into close relations the Jews scattered throughout its territory and so strengthened the bonds of race and religion. In building the temples he also emphasized the ceremonial side of their religious life and centralized it so that even the Jews of the dispersion henceforth paid their yearly temple tax, made frequent pilgrimages to Jerusalem, and regarded themselves as a part of the nation. Furthermore, Herod brought peace and prosperity to his people and gave the Jews an honorable place in the rôle of nations. Thus, while his career is marked by many unpardonable crimes, he proved on the whole an upbuilder and a friend rather than a foe of the Jews.

§ CXIX. HEROD'S TEMPLE

Now Herod, in the eighteenth year of his reign, undertook a very great work, that is, to rebuild the temple of God at his own expense, and to make it larger in circumference and to raise it to a more magnificent height. He thought rightly that to bring the temple to perfection would be the most glorious of all his works, and that it would suffice as an everlasting memorial.

1. Herod's aim (Jos. Ant. XV, 11ᴵᵃ)

So he prepared a thousand wagons to bring stones, chose ten thousand of the most skilful workmen, bought a thousand priestly garments for as many of the priests, and had some of them taught how to work as builders, and others as carpenters. Then he began to build, but not until everything was well prepared for the work.

2. His preparations (2c)

And Herod took up the old foundations, and laid others. He erected a temple upon these foundations: its length was one hundred cubits and its height twenty additional cubits. Now the temple was built of stones that were white and strong. Each was about twenty-five cubits long, eight cubits high, and twelve cubits wide. The whole temple enclosure on the sides was on much lower ground, as were also the royal colonnades; but the temple itself was much higher, being visible for many furlongs in the country round about. It had doors at its entrance as high as the temple itself with lintels over them. These doors were adorned with variegated veils, into which were interwoven pillars and purple flowers. Over these, but under the crown-work, was spread out a golden vine, with its branches hanging far down, the great size and fine workmanship of which was a marvel to those who saw it.

3. Dimensions and decorations of the temple (8a-e)

Herod also built very large colonnades all around the temple, making them in proportion. He exceeded all who had gone before him in his lavish expenditure of money. There was a large wall about the colonnades. The hill, on which the temple stood, was rocky, ascending gradually toward the east of the city to its highest point. At the bottom, which was surrounded by a deep valley, he laid rocks that were bound together with lead. He also cut away some of

4. Its foundations and encircling court (3f-l)

the inner parts, carrying the wall to a great height, until the size and height of the square construction was immense, and until the great size of the stones in front were visible on the outside. The inward parts were fastened together with iron and the joints were preserved immovable for all time. When this work was joined together to the very top of the hill, he finished off its upper surface and filled up the hollow places about the wall and made it level and smooth on top. Within this wall, on the very top, was another wall of stone that had on the east a double colonnade of the same length as the wall. Inside was the temple itself. This colonnade faced the door of the temple and had been decorated by many kings before. Around about the entire temple were fixed the spoils taken from the barbarous nations. All these were dedicated to the temple by Herod, who added those that had been taken from the Arabians.

5. Tower of Antonia (4a, g)

Now in an angle on the north side of the temple was built a citadel, well fortified and of extraordinary strength. This citadel had been built before Herod by the kings and high priests of the Hasmonean race, and they called it the Tower. In it were deposited the garments of the high priest, which he put on only at the time when he was to offer sacrifice. Herod fortified this tower more strongly than before, in order to guard the temple securely, and gave the tower the name of Antonia to gratify Antony, who was his friend and a Roman ruler.

6. The temple gates and colonnades (5a-g)

In the western side of the temple enclosure were four gates; one led to the king's palace, two others led to the suburbs of the city, and the fourth led by many steps down into the valley and up on the other side to the entrance to the other part of the city. The fourth front of the temple, that on the south, had gates in the middle; before this front were the three royal colonnades, which reached from the valley on the east to that on the west. These colonnades were especially remarkable for their great height, which seemed more because the hill at their base dropped abruptly into a very deep valley. There were four rows of pillars, placed side by side. The fourth was built into the stone wall. Each pillar was about twenty-seven feet high, with a double spiral at the base,

298

and was so thick that three men joining hands could just reach around it. The number of the pillars was one hundred and sixty-two. The columns had Corinthian capitals, which aroused great admiration in those who saw them because of their beauty. These four rows of pillars made three parallel spaces for walking. Two of these parallel walks were thirty feet wide, six hundred and six feet in length, and fifty feet in height, while the middle walk was half as wide again and twice as high. The roofs were adorned with deep sculptures in wood, representing many different things; the middle was much higher than the rest, and the front wall, which was of polished stone, was adorned with beams set into the stone on pillars.

The second enclosure, which was reached by ascending a few steps, was not very far within the first. This inner enclosure had a stone wall for a partition. Upon this wall it was forbidden any foreigner to enter under penalty of death. This inner enclosure had on its northern and southern sides three gates at intervals from each other. On the east, however, there was one large gate, through which those of us who were ceremonially pure could enter with our wives. Within this enclosure was another forbidden to women. Still further in there was a third court, into which only the priest could go. Within this court was the temple itself; before that was the altar, upon which we offer sacrifices and burnt-offerings to God.

Herod himself took charge of the work upon the colonnades and outer enclosures; these he built in eight years. But the temple itself was built by the priest in a year and five months. Thereupon all the people were filled with joy and returned thanks, in the first place to God for the speed with which it was finished, and in the second place for the zeal which the king had shown. They feasted and celebrated this rebuilding of the temple; the king sacrificed three hundred oxen to God, as did the others, each according to his ability. The time of this celebration of the work about the temple also fell upon the day of the king's inauguration, which the people customarily observed as a festival. The coincidence of these anniversaries made the festival most notable.

7. The inner courts (sh.-i)

9. Dedication of the temple (sk. 6)

HEROD'S TEMPLE

I. Herod's Motives. It is not difficult to appreciate the reasons which influenced Herod to begin the rebuilding of the temple. Chief among these was doubtless the desire to win still further the approval of his master Augustus. It is also a characteristic of a man of Herod's type to seek to gain popular approval by the munificence of his public gifts. Throughout his reign he was painfully aware of the suspicions of his Jewish subjects. He trusted, and the event proved the wisdom of his judgment, that he might conciliate them by giving them that about which their interest most naturally gathered. The methods which he employed in building the temple clearly indicate that this was one of his leading motives. He also gratified that love of construction which had found expression in many of the cities of Palestine and the eastern Mediterranean. He desired to rear a great memorial for himself, and in this hope he was not disappointed, for later generations continued to think of him with gratitude because of the temple which bore his name.

II. Preparations for the Rebuilding of the Temple. Herod's temple was begun in 20 or 19 B.C. and was not entirely completed until a few years before its destruction in 70 A.D. The task in itself was a difficult one, for on the north the city prevented the extension of the temple area, and on the south the hill rapidly descended toward the juncture of the Tyropœan and Kidron valleys. Herod met the difficulty by filling in to the south with vast stone constructions which rose to the height of seventy to ninety feet above the virgin rock. To economize building materials he built the huge underground vaults and arches known to-day as Solomon's Stables. Thus with a vast expense of labor and wealth he extended the temple area to the south until it was double that which surrounded Solomon's temple. It was also important to regard in every detail the ceremonial scruples of the Jews. To this end a small army of priests were trained as masons and carpenters in order to do the work in the immediate proximity of the temple. To bring the ancient temple into proportions with the rest of his buildings, a huge porch or façade was reared in front of it on the east, rising, according to Josephus, to the height of one hundred and twenty feet. For the roof that covered the porches he apparently brought cedar from the distant Lebanons. Only with all the resources of the kingdom at his command was it possible to carry through this vast enterprise.

III. The Approaches to the Temple. The entire temple area was rectangular in form, about twelve hundred feet in length and six hundred feet wide. Its chief approaches were on the south and west. A small gate through which sacrificial animals were introduced immediately

300

into the temple precincts opened from the north. The one gate on the east, which opened into the Kidron Valley, was apparently opposite the eastern entrance to the temple. The two gates on the south opened toward the City of David. The one was a double gate with an incline leading into the temple area, and the other farther to the east was a triple gate. The main approaches were from the west. The southern of these was a low viaduct spanning the Kidron Valley and thence by steps or inclined approach ascending to the temple area. Remnants of the arches that spanned the valley at this point and a little farther north are still traceable on the present walls of the temple area far down in the Tyropœan Valley. The third approach farther to the north was probably also a viaduct leading directly into the temple area, while the extreme northern approach, according to Josephus, led from the palace of Herod directly to the temple. The entire temple area was encircled by a colonnade. One row of pillars was built into the high wall that surrounded the area. On the south was found the royal porch with its four rows of columns, the first and second about thirty feet apart, the second and third forty-five, and the third and fourth thirty. The pillars on the sides were about twenty-seven feet in height, while the two rows in the middle were double this height. Each of these colonnades was covered with a richly ornamented cedar roof, thus affording grateful shelter from the sun and storm. The great space at the south of the temple area was the Court of the Gentiles, the common park of the city where all classes of its population freely gathered. The colonnade on the east of the temple area bore the name of Solomon's Porch, and from it the steps led up to the raised platform of native rock twenty or more feet above the Court of the Gentiles. Somewhere to the east of the temple was found the famous Beautiful Gate. The series of steps led into the so-called Court of the Women. West of this was the Court of the Israelites, to which only men were admitted. Thence a broad, high floor led to the open space before the temple. Surrounding the altar and cutting off approach to the temple proper was a stone balustrade. The space within this was known as the Court of the Priests. Here no laymen were admitted except as the ritual of private sacrifice required. These inner courts were surrounded by a high wall and adjoining chambers for the storing of the paraphernalia used in connection with the sacrifice and for the residence of the priests. On the southern side of the temple was the room where the national council, the sanhedrin, held its public meetings. Four gates on the north and four gates on the south led from the temple court to the lower Court of the Gentiles.

IV. The Organization of the Temple Service. At the head of the temple organization was the high priest. Since the deposition of the ill-fated Hyrcanus the high priests had been appointed by Herod, for to them was intrusted large civil as well as religious authority. The one duty which the high priests could not neglect, unless prevented by illness, was to perform the sacrifice in behalf of the people and to enter the Holy of Holies on the day of atonement. Frequently he also offered the sacrifice or presided at the special services on the sabbath, the new moons, or at the great annual festivals. Otherwise the temple duties were performed by the army of priests and assistants who were associated with the temple. According to Josephus there were twenty thousand priests. They were divided into twenty-four courses. Each course included certain priestly families to which were intrusted for a week the performing of the sacrifices. Corresponding to the twenty-four courses of the priests were the courses of the people, who were represented by certain of their number at each of the important services. The priests not only performed the sacrifices but also guarded the temple treasures and the private wealth placed in their keeping. The Levites attended to the more menial duties in connection with the temple service. They aided the priests in preparing the sacrifices and in caring for the utensils that were used in connection with the sacrifice. Some of them were doorkeepers. Probably from the Levites were drafted the temple police at whose head was the captain of the temple. Their task was to preserve order and to prevent Gentiles from entering the sacred precincts of the temple. The singers constituted a third group of Levites.

Two public services were held each day, the first, at sunrise, consisted in the offering of a sacrificial ram with the accompaniment of prayer and song. The same rites were repeated at sunset. After the morning sacrifice the private offerings were presented. On the sabbaths, new moons, and great festivals, the number of sacrifices was greatly increased and the ritual made more elaborate. Upon the Jews, instructed in the synagogue in the details of the law and taught to regard the temple and its services with deepest reverence, the elaborate ceremonies of this great and magnificent sanctuary must have made a profound impression. As the people streamed up to Jerusalem by thousands at the great feasts, their attention was fixed more and more upon the ritual and the truths which it symbolized. Herod's temple also strengthened the authority of the Jewish hierarchy with the people, and gave the scribes and Pharisees the commanding position which they later occupied in the life and thought of Judaism.

§ CXX. THE MESSIANIC HOPES AND THE RELIGIOUS BELIEFS OF JUDAISM

Then a kingdom over all mankind for all times shall God raise up, who once gave the holy law to the pious, for whom he pledged to open every land, the world and the portals of the blessed, and all joys, and an eternal, immortal spirit and a joyous heart. And out of every land they shall bring frankincense and gifts to the house of the great God. And to men there shall be no other house where men may learn of the world to be than that which God hath given for faithful men to honor; for mortals shall call it the temple of the mighty God. And all pathways of the plain and rough hills and high mountains and wild waves of the deep shall be easy in those days for crossing and sailing; for perfect peace for the good shall come on earth. And the prophets of the mighty God shall remove the sword; for they are the rulers of mortals and the righteous kings. And there shall be righteous wealth among mankind; for this is the judgment and rule of the mighty God.

1. God's coming reign of peace (Sibyl. Oracles, III, 767–784)

Behold, O Lord, and raise up to them their king, the son of David, in the time which thou, O God, knowest, that he may reign over Israel thy servant; and gird him with strength that he may break in pieces those who rule unjustly. Purge Jerusalem with wisdom and with righteousness, from the heathen who trample her down to destroy her. He shall thrust out the sinners from the inheritance, utterly destroy the proud spirit of the sinners, and as potters' vessels he shall break in pieces with a rod of iron all their substance. He shall destroy the ungodly nations with the word of his mouth, so that at his rebuke the nations will flee before him, and he shall convict the sinners in the thoughts of their hearts. And he shall gather together a holy people, whom he shall lead in righteousness; and shall judge the tribes of the people that has been sanctified by the Lord his God. And he shall not suffer iniquity to lodge in their midst; and none that knoweth wickedness shall dwell with them. For he shall take knowledge of them, that they are all the sons of their God, and shall divide them

2. Rule of the messianic king (Ps. Sol. 17^{23-35a})

upon earth according to their tribes, and the sojourner and the stranger shall dwell with them no more. He shall judge the nations and the peoples with the wisdom of his righteousness. And he shall possess the nations of the heathen to serve him beneath his yoke; and he shall glorify the Lord in a place to be seen by the whole earth; and he shall purge Jerusalem and make it holy, even as it was in the days of old.

3. Character and effects of his rule (35b-46)

And a righteous king and taught of God is he who reigneth over them; and there shall be no iniquity in his days in their midst, for all shall be holy and their king is the Lord Messiah. For he shall not put his trust in horse and rider and bow, nor shall he multiply unto himself gold and silver for war, nor by ships shall he gather confidence for the day of battle. The Lord himself is his King, and the hope of him who is strong in the hope of God. And he shall have mercy upon all the nations that come before him in fear. For he shall smite the earth with the word of his mouth, even for evermore. He shall bless the people of the Lord with wisdom and gladness. He himself also is pure from sin, so that he may rule a mighty people, and rebuke princes and overthrow sinners by the might of his word. And he shall not faint all his days, because he leaneth upon his God; for God shall cause him to be mighty through the spirit of holiness, and wise through the counsel of understanding, with might and righteousness. And the blessing of the Lord is with him in might, and his hope in the Lord shall not faint. And who can stand up against him; he is mighty in his works and strong in the fear of God, tending the flock of the Lord with faith and righteousness. And he shall allow none of them to faint in their pasture. In holiness shall he lead them all, and there shall be no pride among them that any should be oppressed.

4. Appearance of the Son of Man (Enoch 46¹⁻³)

And there I saw One who had a head of days, and his head was white like wool, and with him was another being whose countenance had the appearance of a man, and his face was full of graciousness, like one of the holy angels. And I asked the angel who went with me and showed me all the hidden things, concerning that Son of Man, who he was, and whence he was, and why he went with the Head of

304

Days? And he answered and said to me, "This is the Son of Man who hath righteousness, with whom dwelleth righteousness, and who reveals all the treasures of that which is hidden, because the Lord of Spirits hath chosen him, and his lot before the Lord of Spirits hath surpassed everything in uprightness for ever."

Before the sun and the signs were created, before the stars of the heaven were made, his name was named before the Lord of Spirits. He will be a staff to the righteous on which they will support themselves and not fall, and he will be the light of the Gentiles, and the hope of those whose hearts are troubled. All who dwell on earth will fall down and bow the knee before him and will bless and laud and magnify with song the Lord of Spirits. And for this reason hath he been chosen and hidden before him before the creation of the world and for evermore. ^{5. His pre-existence and world-wide mission (48³⁻⁶)}

And he sat on the throne of his glory, and the sum of judgment was committed to him, and the Son of Man caused the sinners and those who have led the world astray to pass away and be destroyed from off the face of the earth. With chains they shall be bound, and in their assembling-place of destruction shall they be imprisoned, and all their works will vanish from the face of the earth. And henceforth there will be nothing that is corruptible; for the Son of Man hath appeared and sitteth on the throne of his glory, and all evil will pass away before his face and depart; but the word of the Son of Man will be strong before the Lord of Spirits. ^{6. His work as judge (49²⁷⁻²⁹)}

And in those days will the earth also give back those who are treasured up within it, and Sheol also will give back that which it has received, and hell will give back that which it owes. And he will choose the righteous and holy from among them; for the day of their redemption is at hand. ^{7. Resurrection and glorification of the righteous (51¹, ²)}

I. The Growth of Israel's Messianic Hopes.

Eternal hopefulness is a marked characteristic of the Hebrew race. Throughout most of their history the greater the calamities that overtook them the greater was their assurance that these were but the prelude to a glorious vindication and deliverance. This hopefulness was not merely the result of their natural optimism, but of the belief, formed by their experiences in

305

many a national crisis, that a God of justice was overruling the events of history, and that he was working not for man's destruction but for his highest happiness and well-being. It was their insight into the divine purpose that led the Hebrew prophets to break away from the popular traditions that projected backward to the beginnings of history the realization of man's fondest hopes. Instead they proclaimed that the golden era lay in the future rather than the past. The hopes of Israel's prophets regarding that future took many different forms. Often the form was determined by the earlier experiences of the nation. At many periods the people looked for a revival of the glories of the days of David. In later days, when they were oppressed by cruel persecutions, they revived in modified form the dreams that had been current in the childhood of the Semitic race, and thought of a supernatural kingdom that was to be inaugurated after Jehovah and his attendant angels, like Marduk in the old Babylonian tradition of the creation, had overcome Satan and the fallen angels. Israel's messianic hopes were also shaped and broadened by the teachings of the great ethical prophets. A growing realization of the imperfections of the existing order led them to look ever more expectantly to the time when the prophetic ideals of justice and mercy would be realized in society, as well as in the character of the individual. These different expectations regarding the future are broadly designated as messianic prophecies. The word "messianic," like its counterpart "Messiah" (Greek, "Christ"), comes from the Hebrew word meaning to smear or to anoint. It designated in ancient times the weapons consecrated for battle or the king chosen and thus symbolically set aside to lead the people as Jehovah's representative, or a priest called to represent the people in the ceremonial worship. The common underlying idea in the word is that of consecration to a divine purpose. In its narrower application it describes simply the agent who is to realize God's purpose in history, but in its broader and prevailing usage it designates all prophecies that described the ideal which Jehovah is seeking to perfect in the life of Israel and of humanity, and the agents or agencies, whether individual or national, material or spiritual, natural or supernatural, by which he is to realize that ideal.

II. **The Kingly, Nationalistic Type of Messianic Hope.** The messianic prophecies of the Old Testament seem only confusing and contradictory until the three distinct types are recognized. These different types of messianic prophecy naturally shade into each other, and yet they are fundamentally distinct and were represented throughout Israel's history by different classes of thinkers. The first is the kingly, nationalistic type of hope. It came into existence as soon as Israel became a nation, and may be traced in the Balaam oracles in Numbers 24$^{17-19}$, where the seer is represented as beholding Israel's victorious king smiting its foes, the Moabites and Edomites, and ruling gloriously over a triumphant people. It is echoed in II Samuel 7$^{10-16}$ in the promise that the house of David should rule peacefully and uninterruptedly through succeeding generations. Ezekiel, in his picture of the restored nation in 37$^{21-28}$, declares in the name of Jehovah that "my servant David shall be king over them and they shall dwell in the land that I have given to my servant Jacob wherein their fathers dwelt, and they shall dwell therein, they and their sons forever, and David my servant shall be their prince forever." In such passages as Isaiah 9 and 11 the Davidic ruler is represented as reigning not despotically or selfishly, but in accordance with the principles of justice and mercy, bringing peace to all his subjects. As has already been noted, in the prophecies of Haggai and Zechariah and in connection with the rebuilding of the second temple Israel's kingly, nationalistic hope reached its culmination, but through the victories of Darius was rudely cast to the ground (XCV^{vi}). For the next three centuries and a half, throughout the Persian and Greek periods, this type of Israel's messianic hope was apparently silenced. The Maccabean struggles and victories, however, and the oppressive rule of Rome stirred this smouldering hope into a flame and gave it wide currency among the people at the beginning of the Christian era. Again the nation came to the forefront. In the beautiful prophecy of Zechariah 9$^{9,\,10}$, which apparently comes from the earlier part of the Maccabean era, is found the noble picture of a peasant king, humble yet victorious, establishing with the sword a world-wide kingdom. Memories of the glorious achievements of the Maccabean leaders kindled the popular imagination. When in 63 B.C. Rome's iron hand closed upon Palestine, the eyes of the Jews looked expectantly for the advent of a champion like David of old, who would crush the heathen, convict the sinful Jews, and gather the faithful people, ruling over them in justice and with tender care. These hopes are most plainly expressed in the Psalms of Solomon, which were written near the beginning of the Roman period. These expectations in their more material form inspired the party of the Zelots during the earlier part of the first Christian century repeatedly to unsheathe the sword in the vain effort to overthrow Rome and to establish at once the rule of the Messiah. It was because this type of hope was so strong in the minds of the common people that the false messiahs who rose from time to time were able quickly to gather thousands about them in the vain expectation that the moment of deliverance had at last arrived.

III. The Apocalyptic, Catastrophic Type of Messianic Hope. Another class of thinkers in Israel looked not for a temporal but for a supernatural kingdom. It is usually described in the symbolic language of the apocalypse. The inauguration of this kingdom was not dependent upon man's activity but solely upon the will of God. The exact time and manner of its institution was clothed in mystery. Traces of this belief are found in the references in Amos to the popular expectations regarding the day of Jehovah. Evidently the Northern Israelites lived in anticipation of a great universal judgment day, in which their heathen foes would be suddenly destroyed and they themselves would be exalted. It was a belief which Amos and the ethical prophets who followed him strongly combated, for they were fully aware of the fundamental weakness in the apocalyptic or catastrophic type of prophecy: it took away from the nation and individual all personal responsibility. Furthermore, its roots went back to the old Semitic mythology. This type of hope, however, was too firmly fixed in the popular mind to be dispelled even by the preaching of Israel's greatest prophets. As a result of the calamities that gathered about the fall of the Hebrew state it was revived. It is found in Ezekiel, Zechariah, and Joel. Each of these prophets looked forward to the time when Jehovah would miraculously overthrow their heathen foes, restore his scattered people, and establish for them a world-wide, eternal kingdom. In the closing chapters of the book of Daniel this form of belief attains its fullest expression in the Old Testament. In the Similitudes of Enoch (37–71), which come either from the latter part of the Maccabean era or else from the days of Herod, these messianic hopes are still further developed. Instead of Israel's guardian angel Michael, represented as coming on the clouds from heaven and in appearance like a son of man, a heavenly Messiah is introduced. He is known by the title of the Messiah, the Elect One, and the Son of Man (probably taken from the book of Daniel). In Enoch the term Son of Man has evidently become, as in IV Esdras, the title of a personal Messiah. He is described as pre-existent and gifted with the divine authority. When he appears, the dead are to rise, and angels, as well as men, are to be tried before his tribunal. The sinners and the fallen angels he will condemn to eternal punishment. All sin and wrong shall be driven from the earth. Heaven and earth shall be transformed, and an eternal kingdom shall be established in which all the righteous, whether dead or living, shall participate. This was evidently the type of messianic hope held by the Pharisees as well as the Essenes. As the result of the teaching of the Pharisees it was held widely by the Jews of the first Christian century. It was clearly in the minds of Jesus' disciples when he made his last journey to Jerusalem. It was both the background and the barrier to all his work. It is the key to the interpretation of Paul's conception of the Christ, or the Messiah, for he had been educated a Pharisee. This apocalyptic type of messianic hope powerfully influenced the life and thought of the early Christian Church and even permeated the Gospel narratives. The question of how far Jesus himself was influenced by it is one of the most vital and difficult problems of early Christian history.

IV. **The Ethical and Universalistic Type of Messianic Prophecy.** Far removed from the kingly, messianic hopes of the people and the supernatural visions of the apocalypses were the plain, direct, practical ideals of Israel's great ethical prophets. Amos, Hosea, Isaiah, and Jeremiah all united in declaring that the realization of Jehovah's purpose in history depended primarily upon the response of his people. They regarded the kingdom of God as a natural growth. It represented the gradual transformation of the characters of men under the influence of God's truth and spirit working in their minds. They hoped and labored to see the nation Israel living in full accord with the demands of justice, mercy, and service. The II Isaiah, under the influences which grew out of the destruction of the temple and the closer contact with the heathen world, voiced this type of messianic hope in its broadest and most spiritualized form. He declared that the Israelites had been called and trained for a unique service and that that service was to be performed by them quietly and unostentatiously, as prophets and teachers of men. He also presented most clearly Israel's missionary ideal, and showed that its task was not to destroy but to bring light to the Gentile world. He and the more enlightened prophets who followed him saw an ever-widening kingdom established without the aid of the sword and freed from all racial barriers—the eternal, universal, spiritual kingdom of God on earth. It is evident that in contrast to the other types of messianic prophecy this form was comprehensible, practicable, and alone capable of realization.

V. **The Messianic Hopes of Judaism at the Beginning of the Christian Era.** Unfortunately, as a result of the varied experiences through which Judaism passed in the centuries immediately preceding the Christian era, its ethical and universal messianic hopes were largely eclipsed. The ideal of the suffering servant appears to have been almost forgotten. As the later Jews read the earlier scriptures of their race in order to determine what the future held in store for them, they fixed their eyes upon the kingly and apocalyptic prophecies. Regarding all scriptures as equally authoritative, they attempted the impossible task of blending these fundamentally different types of prophecy. The result was that their beliefs became, indeed, a complex labyrinth with paths leading in opposite directions. Later events have proved beyond question that these popular types were the dreams of religious enthusiasts rather than true pictures of the way in which the divine purpose was to be perfected in human history, and yet the apocalyptic type of prophecy was not without its significance. It tended to correct the narrow national hopes of the Jews and to lift them to the consideration of that which was spiritual and eternal. It also led them to appreciate the unity of all history, and in times of distress it kept alive their faith in a God who was wisely guiding their destinies. Underlying all these different types of prophecy is the appreciation of the broad truth that God was working out in the lives of men and nations a definite purpose, and that that purpose was good, and that the God back of all history was a God not only of power but also of love. It was inevitable that the ethical and more spiritual expectations of the early Hebrew prophets should find the fullest response in the heart and life of the Great Teacher. In the face of opposition from the leaders of his race, from the multitudes that gathered about him, and even from the disciples who loved and followed him, he proclaimed that the kingdom of God would not come by observation, but that its growth would be natural and gradual like that of the mustard seed, that it was not external but within the hearts of men, that membership in that kingdom depended not upon the arbitrary will of God, but upon men's acting in accord with that will in the every-day relations of life. Thus Jesus prepared the way for the complete fulfilment of all that was noblest and best in Israel's messianic hopes, and in his character and teachings far surpassed the highest expectations of the inspired teachers of his race.

APPENDIX

I

A PRACTICAL REFERENCE LIBRARY

Books for Constant Reference. The complete text of the biblical writings of the post-exilic period are found in Volumes II to VI of the *Student's Old Testament*. A careful, thorough résumé of the history is contained in Riggs's *History of the Jewish People during the Maccabean and Roman Periods*. Professor Bevan, in his *Jerusalem Under the High Priests*, presents, especially from the ecclesiastical point of view, a fresh survey of the history during the Greek and Maccabean periods. The geographical background may be studied either in George Adam Smith's *Historical Geography of the Holy Land* or in Kent's *Biblical Geography and History*.

Additional Books of Reference: Introductions and Commentaries. In addition to the standard Old Testament introductions by McFadyen, Cornill, and Driver, the collection of monographs in Professor Torrey's *Ezra Studies* will be found especially valuable. The introduction, as well as the critical notes, in the brief yet scholarly volumes of the *New Century Bible* are exceedingly useful for the general reader. More fundamental are the volumes in the *International Critical Commentary*. The introductions to the different books in Hastings' *Dictionary of the Bible* and the *Encyclopædia Biblica* are clear, concise, and written from the modern point of view.

Jewish and Contemporary History. The thorough student of this period will find a wealth of suggestive material in Smith's *Old Testament History* and in Schürer's monumental work, *A History of the Jewish People in the Time of Jesus Christ*. The later development of Israel's religion is presented in Marti's *Religion of the Old Testament*, in the first part of Toy's *Judaism and Christianity*, in Bousset's *Judaism*, and in Charles's *Eschatology, Hebrew, Jewish and Christian*. An excellent survey of the contemporary history of the period is to be found in the *History of the Ancient World* by Goodspeed or in Meyer's *Ancient History*. A more detailed treatment of the contemporary history will

311

be found in the *History of Greece* by Curtius or by Holm. The *History of Rome* is fully traced in the monumental works of Mommsen or Gibbon or the more recent study in *The Greatness and Decline of Rome* by Ferrero. Briefer but equally reliable histories of Rome are those by Botsford, Horton, and Seignobos.

II

GENERAL QUESTIONS AND SUBJECTS FOR SPECIAL RESEARCH

The GENERAL QUESTIONS, as in the preceding volumes, follow the main divisions of the book, and are intended to guide the student in collecting and co-ordinating the more important facts presented in the biblical text or in the notes.

The SUBJECTS FOR SPECIAL RESEARCH are intended to guide the reader to further study in related lines, and, by means of detailed references, to introduce him to the most helpful passages in the best English books of reference. In class-room work many of these topics may be profitably assigned for personal research and report. The references are to pages, unless otherwise indicated. Ordinarily, several parallel references are given that the student may be able to utilize the book at hand. More detailed classified bibliographies will be found in the appendices of Volumes II–VI of the author's *Student's Old Testament.*

THE EXILE AND REVIVAL OF THE JUDEAN COMMUNITY

§ XCI. **The Jews in Palestine and Egypt.** GENERAL QUESTIONS: 1. What did the final destruction of Jerusalem in 586 mean to the Jewish people? 2. Describe the structure and contents of the book of Lamentations. 3. Its probable authorship and date. 4. Its theme and historical value. 5. The condition of the Jews who were left in Palestine. 6. The numbers of the Jews in Egypt. 7. The life of the Jewish colony at Elephantine. 8. The character and service of the temple of Jahu.

SUBJECTS FOR SPECIAL RESEARCH: 1. The literary history of the book of Lamentations. McFadyen, *Introd.*, 294–7; Driver, *Lit. of the O. T.*, 456–65. 2. History of Egypt from 600 to 560 B.C. Breasted,

APPENDIX

Hist. of the Ancient Egyptians, 404–18. 3. The discoveries at Elephantine. Sayce and Cowley, *Aramaic Papyri Discovered at Assuan;* Sachau, *Drei aramäische Papyrururkunden aus Elephantine.*

§ XCII. **Ezekiel's Message to His Scattered Countrymen.** GENERAL QUESTIONS: 1. Describe the situation of the Jewish colony in Babylon. 2. Their opportunities and occupations. 3. Their religious life. 4. The prophecies of Ezekiel after the destruction of Jerusalem. 5. Meaning of his description of the valley of dry bones in chapter 37. 6. His conception of the way in which the scattered exiles were to be restored. 7. His plan of the restored temple. 8. The meaning and significance of this detailed plan.

SUBJECTS FOR SPECIAL RESEARCH: 1. Babylon under Nebuchadrezzar. Goodspeed, *Hist. of Babs. and Assyrs.,* 336–50; *En. Bib.,* III, 3369–71. 2. The religious institutions of the Babylonians. Goodspeed, *Hist. of Babs. and Assyrs.,* 351–66; Jastrow, *Relig. of Bab. and Assyr.;* Johns, *Bab. and Assyr. Laws, Letters, and Contracts,* 208–17. 3. Influence of Babylonian institutions upon Ezekiel. Toy, *Ezek.* (Introd.).

§ XCIII. **The Closing Years of the Babylonian Rule.** GENERAL QUESTIONS. 1. Describe the different influences that transformed the Jews into a literary people. 2. The nature of their literary activity. 3. The Old Testament books that were written or re-edited during this period. 4. The general character of the Holiness Code. 5. The national hopes inspired by the liberation of Jehoiachin. 6. The character of Nabonidus. 7. The effects of his rule. 8. The early conquests of Cyrus. 9. His capture of Babylon. 10. His policy toward conquered peoples.

SUBJECTS FOR SPECIAL RESEARCH: 1. Contents and history of the Holiness Code. *St. O. T.,* IV, 36–42; McFadyen, *Introd. to O. T.,* 31–4. 2. The last decade of Babylonian history. Goodspeed, *Hist. of Babs. and Assyrs.,* 367–76; Kent, *Hist. J. P.,* 66–77. 3. Character and reign of Cyrus. Herodotus, I, 95, 108–30, 177–214; Hastings, *D. B.,* I, 541–2; Rawlinson, *Anc. Monarchies,* IV, VII; Duncker, *Hist. of Antiq.,* V.

§ XCIV. **The Rebuilding of the Temple.** GENERAL QUESTIONS: Describe the contents and literary history of the books of Ezra and Nehemiah. 2. Their authorship. 3. The Chronicler's peculiar ideas regarding the restoration. 4. Revolutions in the Persian Empire that aroused the Jews to action. 5. Haggai's appeal to the Judean community. 6. Measures taken to stop the rebuilding of the temple. 7. Meaning of the rebuilding of the temple to the Jewish race.

APPENDIX

SUBJECTS FOR SPECIAL RESEARCH: 1. The historical value of Ezra and Nehemiah. Torrey, *Composition and Historical Value of Ezra and Nehemiah*, or *Ezra Studies*, 62–251. 2. The first two decades of Persian history. Goodspeed, *Hist. of Ancient World*, 60–2; Ragozin, *The Story of Media*, II; Meyer, *Anc. Hist.*, 88–93. 3. Evidence that there was no general return of the Jews in 536 B.C. Kent, *Hist. J. P.*, 126–36; Torrey, *Ezra Studies*, 297–307.

§ XCV. **Zechariah's Visions and Encouraging Addresses.** GENERAL QUESTIONS: 1. Describe the evidence that Zechariah wrote from the point of view of a priest. 2. The structure and contents of his book. 3. The problems of the Judean community. 4. Their hopes of a national revival. 5. Zechariah's assurances. 6. The steps that were taken to make Zerubbabel king. 7. Evidence that the popular kingly hopes were disappointed. 8. The content of Zechariah's later sermons. 9. The hopes which he inspired in his fellow-countrymen.

SUBJECTS FOR SPECIAL RESEARCH: 1. Origin of the apocalyptic type of prophecy. *Jewish Encyc.*, I, 669–73; *St. O. T.*, III, 42–3; Hastings, *D. B.*, I, 109–10. 2. The popular messianic hopes of the period. *St. O. T.*, III, 44–5, 472–86. 3. The establishment of Darius' authority. Herodotus, II, 67–86; Ragozin, *Media*, XIII; Hastings, *D. B.*, I, 558.

§ XCVI. **Israel's Training and Destiny.** GENERAL QUESTIONS: 1. Describe the conditions in the Judean community during the seventy years following the rebuilding of the temple. 2. The forces that kept alive the spiritual life of the Jews. 3. The indications that Isaiah 40–66 were written in Palestine. 4. The probable date of these chapters. 5. Their distinctive literary characteristics. 6. The purpose for which they were written.

SUBJECTS FOR SPECIAL RESEARCH: 1. The organization of the Persian Empire under Darius. Goodspeed, *Hist. of Anc. World*, 62–3; Ragozin, *Media*, 384–91; Sayce, *Anc. Empires*, 247–50; *En. Bib.*, I, 1016–7. 2. The Persian invasions of Europe. Goodspeed, *Anc. Hist.*, 122–8; Herodotus, IV, 1–142; Ragozin, *Media*, 412–29; Bury, *Hist. of Greece*, 265–96; Botsford, *Hist. of Greece*, 127–36. 3. Contents and literary characteristics of Isaiah 40–48. *St. O. T.*, III, 27–30; Cobb, in *Jour. of Bib. Lit.*, XXVII, 48–64; Box, *Isaiah*, 179–237.

§ XCVII. **Conditions and Problems in the Jewish Community.** GENERAL QUESTIONS: 1. What is the probable date of the book of Malachi? 2. Describe its teachings regarding the temple service. 3. The need of a great moral awakening. 4. The doubts expressed by the faithful in the community. 5. The encouraging promises held

314

out to them. 6. Presentation of the problem of the faithful in the psalms of the period.

SUBJECTS FOR SPECIAL RESEARCH: 1. Contemporary Greek history and literature. Goodspeed, *Anc. Hist.*, 159–96; Bury, *Hist. of Greece*, 507–90; Jebb, *Greek Lit.*, 109–20. 2. The earliest psalms. Briggs, *Psalms*, I, LXXXIX–XCII; Cobb, *Bk. of Pss.*, XI–XIV; Driver, *Lit. of the O. T.*, 371–2; McFadyen, *Introd. to O. T.*, 238–50. 3. Psalm literature among contemporary peoples. Breasted, *Hist. of Anc. Egyptians*, 273–7; Jastrow, *Relig. of Bab. and Assyr.*, 294–327.

§ XCVIII. **The Problems and Teachings of the Book of Job.** GENERAL QUESTIONS: 1. Describe the structure of the book of Job. 2. The different literary units which have entered into it. 3. The probable dates of these different sections. 4. Contents of the original prose story. 5. The theme and contents of the great poem in 3–31, 38^1–42^6. 6. The different lines of progress in Job's thought. 7. The meaning of the speeches of Jehovah. 8. The contribution of the book to the solution of the problem of evil.

SUBJECTS FOR SPECIAL RESEARCH: 1. The Babylonian prototype of Job. Jastrow, in *Jour. of Bib. Lit.*, XXV, Pt. II, 135–91. 2. Comparison of Job with other great skeptical dramas. Owen, *The Five Great Skeptical Dramas of History.* 3. The modern explanations of the problem of evil. Royce, *Studies of Good and Evil.*

§ XCIX. **The Training and Mission of the True Servant of Jehovah.** GENERAL QUESTIONS: 1. Describe the different characteristics of Jehovah's servant in Isaiah 49–53. 2. What was the prophet's purpose in presenting this vivid portrait of Jehovah's ideal servant? 3. Describe the class to whom the prophet appealed. 4. His interpretation of the task of the servant. 5. His training. 6. The different methods whereby he was to accomplish his mission. 7. Did the prophet have in mind an individual, a class, or simply an ideal character? 8. In what ways were his predictions fulfilled? 9. In what sense is his ideal of service of present-day application?

SUBJECTS FOR SPECIAL RESEARCH: 1. The meaning and history of the different messianic titles. *St. O. T.*, III, 39, 47; *En. Bib.*, III, 3057–61. 2. Contents and unity of Isaiah 49–55. *St. O. T.*, III, 28–30; Box, *Isaiah*, 238–83. 3. How far was Jesus influenced by the ideal of the suffering servant?

§ C. **Nehemiah's Work in Rebuilding the Walls of Jerusalem.** GENERAL QUESTIONS: 1. What is the historical value of Nehemiah's memoirs? 2. In what way was he informed of conditions in Jerusalem?

3. How did he secure permission to go to Jerusalem? **4.** Describe the obstacles that there confronted him. **5.** His plan of work. **6.** His diplomacy in dealing with his opponents. **7.** The task of rebuilding the walls. **8.** Their dedication. **9.** The significance of the rebuilding of the walls.

SUBJECTS FOR SPECIAL RESEARCH: **1.** Contemporary events in Greek history. Goodspeed, *Anc. Hist.*, 141–72; Bury, *Hist. of Greece*, 336–75; Botsford, *Hist. of Greece*, 151–85. **2.** The topography of Jerusalem. Kent, *Bib. Geog. and Hist.*, 64–72; Smith, *Jerusalem*, I, 1–249; Hastings, *D. B.*, II, 591–6. **3.** Recent excavations at Jerusalem. *Jerusalem Vol. of P. E. F. Memoirs*; Bliss and Dickey, *Excavations at Jerusalem*; Smith, *Jerusalem*, I.

§ CI. Nehemiah's Social and Religious Reforms. GENERAL QUESTIONS: **1.** Describe the cruel oppression of the leaders of the Jewish community. **2.** The effect upon the mass of the people. **3.** The way in which Nehemiah corrected these evils. **4.** The evidence for and against the historical accuracy of Nehemiah 13. **5.** Nehemiah's measures to improve the temple service. **6.** His emphasis upon Sabbath observance. **7.** His opposition to foreign marriages. **8.** The importance of his work as a whole.

SUBJECTS FOR SPECIAL RESEARCH: **1.** In what respects was Nehemiah a worthy successor of the earlier Hebrew prophets? **2.** The later Jewish laws regarding the Sabbath. *St. O. T.*, IV, 263–4. **3.** Regarding marriage with foreigners. *St. O. T.*, IV, 54–5.

§ CII. Traditional Account of the Adoption of the Priestly Law. GENERAL QUESTIONS: **1.** Describe the present literary form of the tradition regarding Ezra. **2.** Its probable history. **3.** Its historical value. **4.** The facts underlying it. **5.** Origin of the later priestly laws. **6.** Their general purpose. **7.** Their more important regulations. **8** Their transforming influence upon the Jewish community.

SUBJECTS FOR SPECIAL RESEARCH: **1.** The difficulties in accepting the Ezra narrative as strictly historical. Torrey, *Ezra Studies*, 208–78; Smith, *O. T. Hist.*, 390–8. **2.** History of the later priestly codes. *St. O. T.*, IV, 43–8. **3.** Income and duties of the priests and Levites according to the late priestly codes. *St. O. T.*, IV, 187–92, 197–202.

§ CIII. The Jewish State during the Last Century of Persian Rule. GENERAL QUESTIONS: **1.** Describe the indications that the Judean community enjoyed unusual prosperity during the half-century following the work of Nehemiah. **2.** The effect of this prosperity upon the intellectual life of the Jews. **3.** The growth of the

APPENDIX

Psalter during this period. 4. The date of the prophecy of Joel.
5. Its theme. 6. The hopes of the Jews at this time. 7. Nature of
the rule of the high priests. 8. The evidence regarding the date of the
Samaritan schism. 9. Its causes. 10. Its effect upon Judaism.

SUBJECTS FOR SPECIAL RESEARCH: 1. History of the Persian Empire
between 400 and 332 B.C. Cox, *The Greeks and the Persians*. 2. Contemporary events in Greek history. Goodspeed, *Hist. of Anc. World*,
173–204; Meyer, *Anc. Hist.*, 244–74. 3. The history of the Samaritans. *En. Bib.*, IV, 4256–64; Montgomery, *The Samaritans*.

THE GREEK AND MACCABEAN AGE

§ CIV. **The Jews under Their Greek Rulers.** GENERAL QUES-
TIONS: 1. Describe the character of the Jewish historian, Josephus.
2. The extent of his histories. 3. Their historical value. 4. Alexander's Asiatic conquests. 5. His attitude toward the Jews. 6. The
Jews in Alexandria. 7. The general character of the rule of the Ptolemies. 8. Their policy in the treatment of the Jews. 9. Fortunes of
the Jews of Palestine during the first century of Greek rule. 10. The
Seleucid kingdom with its capital at Antioch. 11. The subjugation of
Palestine by the Seleucids.

SUBJECTS FOR SPECIAL RESEARCH: 1. Josephus's rank as a historian.
Hastings, *D. B.*, extra Vol., 461–73. 2. Alexander the Great. Mahaffy,
The Story of Alexander's Empire, 1–11; Hogarth, *Philip and Alex-
ander of Macedon*; Wheeler, *Alexander the Great*. 3. Character of the
Ptolemaic rulers. Bevan, *Jerusalem under the High Priests*, 21–30;
Mahaffy, *The Ptolemaic Dynasty*, Vol. IV of Petrie's *Hist. of Egypt*.

§ CV. **The Wise and Their Teachings.** GENERAL QUESTIONS:
1. Describe the literary structure of the book of Proverbs. 2. The
evidence that it is the work of many different wise men. 3. The probable date of the different collections. 4. The references to the wise
in the pre-exilic literature. 5. The influence of the Babylonian exile
upon their activity. 6. The reasons why they attained their greatest
prominence in the Greek period. 7. The character of the wise. 8.
Their aims. 9. Their methods. 10. Their important social and moral
teachings.

SUBJECTS FOR SPECIAL RESEARCH: 1. The book of Proverbs.
McFadyen, *Introd. to O. T.*, 256–63; Driver, *L. O. T.*, 392–407; Toy,
Proverbs, Introd. 2. The sages of Egypt and Greece. The Wisdom
of Ptah-hotep, in the *Wisdom of the East Series*; Symonds, *Studies of the*

APPENDIX

Greek Poets, I, 161–273; Jebb, *Classical Greek Poetry*. 3. The social teachings of the book of Proverbs. *St. O. T.*, VI, *in loco*; Kent, *The Wise Men of Ancient Israel and Their Proverbs*, 100–14, 158–75; Root, *The Profit of the Many*, 17–126.

§ CVI. **The Different Currents of Thought in Judaism during the Greek Period.** GENERAL QUESTIONS: 1. Why were there many different currents of thought in Judaism during this period? 2. Describe the character and aims of the ritualists. 3. Of the legalists. 4. Of those who laid especial emphasis upon the teaching of the earlier prophets. 5. The evidence regarding the date of the book of Jonah. 6. The meaning of the story. 7. Its teaching. 8. The history of the book of Ecclesiastes. 9. Its point of view. 10. Its philosophy of life.

SUBJECTS FOR SPECIAL RESEARCH: 1. The Chronicler's conception of the origin of Israel's institutions. Curtis, *Chronicles*, Introd.; Torrey, *Ezra Studies*, 208–38; *St. O. T.*, II, 22–8. 2. Greek myths parallel to the story of Jonah. *En. Bib.*, II, 2568–9; Taylor, *Primitive Culture*, I, 306. 3. A comparison of Koheleth's philosophy and teaching with those of the author of Omar Khayyam.

§ CVII. **The Teachings of Jesus the Son of Sirach.** GENERAL QUESTIONS: 1. Describe the evidence regarding the date of Jesus the son of Sirach. 2. The character of the man. 3. The history of his writings. 4. The nature of the Greek translation. 5. The recovery of the Hebrew original. 6. Its picture of the Jewish life of the period. 7. Its description of the wise men and scribes. 8. Its social teachings. 9. Its religious teachings.

SUBJECTS FOR SPECIAL RESEARCH: 1. The Hebrew fragments of Ben Sira. Cowley and Neubauer, *The Original Heb. of a Portion of Ecclus.*; Schechter and Taylor, *The Wisdom of Ben-Sira*; Hastings, *D. B.*, IV, 546–9; *En. Bib.*, II, 1166–9. 2. The character of Ben Sira as revealed in his writings. Hastings, *D. B.*, IV, 550; *En. Bib.*, II, 1175–8; Bevan, *Jerusalem under the High Priests*, 49–51. 3. A comparison of the moral and social teachings of Ben Sira with those of the book of Proverbs. Bevan, *Jerusalem under the High Priests*, 52–68.

§ CVIII. **The Causes of the Maccabean Struggle.** GENERAL QUESTIONS: 1. Describe the general character of I Maccabees. 2. Its historical value. 3. II Maccabees. 4. The attractive and aggressive qualities in the contemporary Hellenic culture. 5. Its superiority to the teachings of Judaism. 6. The elements in which Judaism was superior. 7. The conquest of Hellenism in the ranks of Judaism. 8.

APPENDIX

The influence of the apostate Jewish high priests. 9. The history and character of Antiochus Epiphanes. 10. Reasons why he attempted to hellenize the Jews. 11. The measures which he adopted.

SUBJECTS FOR SPECIAL RESEARCH: 1. The characteristics of Greek religion. Gulick, *Life of the Ancient Greeks*, 262–83; Dyer, *The Gods in Greece*; Goodspeed, *Hist. of Anc. World*, 148–51; Hastings, *D. B.*, extra Vol., 109–56. 2. The historical value of II Maccabees. Hastings, *D. B.*, III, 189–92; *En. Bib.*, III, 2869–79. 2. Contemporary portraits of Antiochus Epiphanes. *Livy*, XLI–XLV; *Polybius*, XXVI–XXXI; *Appian*, *Syr.*, 45, 66; *Justin*, XXIV, 3.

§ CIX. **The Effect of Persecution on the Jews.** GENERAL QUESTIONS: 1. Describe the uprising led by Mattathias. 2. The methods adopted by the rebels. 3. The origin and political principles of the Hasideans or Pious. 4. The evidence regarding the date of the visions in Daniel 7–12. 5. Their literary character. 6. Their meaning and aims. 7. The identification of the four heathen kingdoms. 8. The message of hope presented in these chapters. 9. Its effect upon the persecuted Jews.

SUBJECTS FOR SPECIAL RESEARCH: 1. The town of Modein. Kent, *Bib. Geog. and Hist.*, 210–2; Smith, *Hist. Geog. of Holy Land*, 212. 2. Contents and literary history of the book of Daniel. McFadyen, *Introd. to O. T.*, 316–31; Driver, *L. O. T.*, 438–515; Hastings, *D. B.*, I, 552–7.

§ CX. **The Victories that Gave the Jews Religious Liberty.** GENERAL QUESTIONS: 1. Describe the characteristics that fitted Judas to be a great political leader. 2. The odds against which he and the Jews contended. 3. The physical contour of western Palestine. 4. The defeat of Apollonius. 5. Of the Syrian army under Seron. 6. The details of the battle of Emmaus. 7. The significance of the victory at Bethsura. 8. The restoration of the temple service. 9. The effect of the persecutions upon the Jews.

SUBJECTS FOR SPECIAL RESEARCH: 1. Greek military equipment and methods of warfare. Gulick, *Life of the Anc. Greeks*, 188–205. 2. The western headlands of Judah. Kent, *Bib. Geog. and Hist.*, 40–2; Smith, *Hist. Geog. of Holy Land*, 286–320. 3. Comparison of Judas with other great military commanders. Conder, *Judas Maccabæus*; Bevan, *Jer. under the High Priests*, 97–9; Smith, *O. T. Hist.*, 465.

§ CXI. **The Long Contest for Political Independence.** GENERAL QUESTIONS: 1. Describe the attitude of the heathen nations toward the Jews. 2. The political problems that confronted them.

APPENDIX

3. The Jewish attitude toward the heathen reflected in the book of Esther. 4. Judas's east-Jordan campaign. 5. Results of the battle of Beth-zacharias. 6. The re-establishment of Syrian authority. 7. The victories over Nicanor. 8. The causes which resulted in the death of Judas. 9. Conditions in the Syrian court which gave the Jews their great opportunity. 10. The character and policy of Jonathan. 11. The honors and authority granted him by the rival Syrian kings.

SUBJECTS FOR SPECIAL RESEARCH: 1. The history and value of the book of Esther. Paton, *Esther*; Hastings, *D. B.*, I, 773–6; *En. Bib.*, II, 1400–5. 2. The Syrian history of the period. Bevan, *Jer. under the High Priests*, 100–6; Smith, *O. T. Hist.*, 465–9. 3. The scenes of Judas's east-Jordan campaign. Kent, *Bib. Geog. and Hist.*, 214–7.

§ CXII. **Peace and Prosperity under Simon.** GENERAL QUESTIONS: 1. Describe the political intrigues which resulted in the death of Jonathan. 2. The character and rule of Simon. 3. His extension of the Jewish territory. 4. The authority granted him by the Jews. 5. His development of the temple service. 6. The causes that led to the completion of the Psalter. 7. The religious life and faith reflected in the later psalms.

SUBJECTS FOR SPECIAL RESEARCH: 1. Compare the characters of the three brothers, Judas, Jonathan, and Simon. 2. The guilds of temple singers. Hastings, *D. B.*, IV, 92–3; Wellhausen, *The Book of Psalms* (in *S. B. O. T.*), 217–9. 3. The evidence that many of the psalms come from the Maccabean period. Hastings, *D. B.*, IV, 152–3; Cheyne, *Origin of the Psalter*.

§ CXIII. **The Rule of John Hyrcanus and Aristobulus.** GENERAL QUESTIONS: 1. Describe the intrigue that resulted in the death of Simon. 2. The Syrian invasion under Antiochus Sidetes. 3. The character of John Hyrcanus. 4. His military policy. 5. His conquests in the north and south. 6. The reasons why he lost the support of the Pharisees. 7. The significant events in the reign of Aristobulus.

SUBJECTS FOR SPECIAL RESEARCH: 1. Contemporary conditions in the Syrian kingdom. *En. Bib.*, IV, 4356–60; Gardner, *The Seleucid Kings of Syria*. 2. The history of the Idumeans. Hastings, *D. B.*, I, 644–6; *En. Bib.*, II, 1181–8; Buhl, *Edomites*. 3. Compare the policy of John Hyrcanus with that of David.

§ CXIV. **The Pharisees, Sadducees, and Essenes.** GENERAL QUESTIONS: 1. Describe the influences that gave rise to the party of the Pharisees. 2. Of the Sadducees. 3. The characteristics and beliefs of the Pharisees. 4. Of the Sadducees. 5. The political influence

APPENDIX

or these parties. 6. The characteristics of the sect of the Essenes. 7. Their beliefs.

SUBJECTS FOR SPECIAL RESEARCH: 1. The party of the Pharisees. Hastings, *D. B.*, III, 821–8; *En. Bib.*, IV, 4321–9. 2. The Sadducees. Hastings, *D. B.*, IV, 349–51; *En. Bib.*, IV, 4234–40. 3. The points of contact between Essenism and Christianity. Hastings, *D. B.*, I, 767–72; *En. Bib.*, II, 1396–1400; Thomson, *Books which Influenced Our Lord*, 75–122; Cheyne, *Origin of the Psalter*, 418–21, 446–9.

§ CXV. **The Life and Faith of the Jews of the Dispersion.** GENERAL QUESTIONS: 1. Describe the life of the Jews in Antioch and Asia Minor. 2. The privileges granted them by the Syrian king. 3. The number of the Jews in Egypt. 4. The privileges granted them by the Ptolemies. 5. The founding of the Jewish temple at Leontopolis. 6. Its significance. 7. The occasion of the translation of the Hebrew scriptures into Greek. 8. The important apologetic Jewish writings. 9. The theme and date of the Wisdom of Solomon. 10. Its important teachings. 11. Its reflections of Greek and Jewish thought.

SUBJECTS FOR SPECIAL RESEARCH: 1. Characteristics and value of the Greek translation of the Old Testament. Hastings, *D. B.*, IV, 864–6; Swete, *Introd. to the Old Testament in Greek*; *En. Bib.*, IV, 5016–22. 2. The history and contents of the Wisdom of Solomon. Hastings, *D. B.*, IV, 928–31; *En. Bib.*, IV, 5336–49; Deane, *The Book of Wisdom*, 1–41; Gregg, *The Wisd. of Sol.*

§ CXVI. **The Decline of the Maccabean Kingdom.** GENERAL QUESTIONS: 1. Describe the character of Alexander Janneus. 2. His military policy. 3. His treatment of his subjects. 4. The extension of Jewish territory. 5. The effects of his rule. 6. Alexandra's policy. 7. The fatal mistakes of the Pharisees. 8. The suicidal quarrels between her sons, Hyrcanus and Aristobulus. 9. The intrigues of Antipater. 10. The appeal to Rome. 11. Pompey's intervention and capture of Jerusalem. 12. The causes of the fall of the Maccabean kingdom. 13. The political effects of the Maccabean struggle. 14. The impression which it made upon Israel's faith. 15. The new spirit that it inspired in the Jews.

SUBJECTS FOR SPECIAL RESEARCH: 1. Rome's policy and campaigns in the East. Goodspeed, *Hist. of Anc. World*, 311–9; Seignobos, *Hist. of Rom. People*, 126–30. 2. Rome's earlier relation to the Jewish kingdom. 3. The character and career of Pompey. Goodspeed, *Hist. of Anc. World*, 343–9; Botsford, *Hist. of Rome*, 175–80, 183–9; Morey, *Outlines of Roman Hist.*, ch. 20.

APPENDIX

THE RULE OF ROME

§ CXVII. The Rise of the Herodian House. GENERAL QUES-
TIONS: 1. Describe the repeated rebellions against Rome that were instigated and led by Aristobulus and his sons. 2. The reasons why the
Jews rallied about their standard. 3. Antipater's character and policy.
4. Herod's career as governor of Galilee. 5. The Parthian conquest
and the temporary restoration of the Maccabean rule. 6. The immediate effect upon Herod and his family. 7. Reasons why he was appointed king of the Jews by Antony and Octavian.

SUBJECTS FOR SPECIAL RESEARCH: 1. The fortresses of Alexandrium
and Macherus. Smith, *Hist. Geog. of the Holy Land*, 352–3, 569–71;
Kent, *Bib. Geog. and Hist.*, 229, 244–5; Schürer, *H. J. P.*, I, i, 250–1.
2. The history of Rome from 60 to 40 B.C. Botsford, *Hist. of Rome*,
183–97; Fowler, *Julius Cæsar*; Mahaffy, *Gk. World under Roman
Sway*, ch. IV. 3. The Parthians. Hastings, *D. B.*, III, 680–1.

§ CXVIII. Herod's Policy and Reign. GENERAL QUESTIONS:
1. Describe the strength and weakness of Herod's character. 2. The
ways in which he won the favor of Augustus. 3. His building activity
within his kingdom. 4. Outside of Palestine. 5. His treatment of his
subjects. 6. His record as husband and father. 7. The effects of his
reign.

SUBJECTS FOR SPECIAL RESEARCH: 1. Rome under Augustus. Bots-
ford, *Hist. of Rome*, 204–22; Bury, *Student's Rom. Emp.*, chs. I–XIV;
Capes, *Early Empire*, chs. I–III, XII–XIX. 2. Herod's Cæsarea.
Smith, *Hist. Geog. of the Holy Land*, 138–41; *En. Bib.*, I, 617–8;
Kent, *Bib. Geog. and Hist.*, 233. 3. The various sides of Herod's
character. Hastings, *D. B.*, II, 356–7; *En. Bib.*, II, 2025–9; Bevan,
Jer. under the High Priests, 148–51.

§ CXIX. Herod's Temple. GENERAL QUESTIONS: 1. Describe the
motives that inspired Herod to rebuild the temple at Jerusalem. 2. His
preparations for the work. 3. The extension of the temple area. 4.
The different gates leading to it. 5. The surrounding porches. 6. The
temple proper. 7. The temple officials. 8. The temple service.

SUBJECTS FOR SPECIAL RESEARCH: 1. The detailed plan and di-
mensions of Herod's temple. Hastings, *D. B.*, IV, 711–6; *En Bib.*,
IV, 4943–7; Warren, *The Temple and the Tomb*; Smith, *Jerusalem*,
II, 499–520. 2. The administration of the temple finances. Hastings,
D. B., IV, 92–7; *En. Bib.*, IV, 4949–51; Smith, *Jerusalem*, I, 351–66.

APPENDIX

3. The inscription forbidding foreigners to enter the inner courts. Hastings, *D. B.*, IV, 713–4.

§ CXX. **The Messianic Hopes and Religious Beliefs of Juda= ism.** GENERAL QUESTIONS: 1. Describe the influences that determined the growth of Israel's messianic hopes. 2. The different forms which these hopes assumed. 3. The kingly nationalistic type of messianic hope. 4. The characteristics and development of the apocalyptic, catastrophic type of hope. 5. The type proclaimed by the great ethical prophets. 6. The broadening and universalizing of Israel's messianic hopes. 7. The influence of the Maccabean struggle upon Israel's messianic beliefs. 8. The messianic expectations of the Jews at the beginning of the Christian era.

SUBJECTS FOR SPECIAL RESEARCH: 1. The origin of Israel's messianic hopes. *St. O. T.*, III, 39–48; Goodspeed, *Israel's Messianic Hope*; Oesterley, *Evolution of the Messianic Idea*. 2. The Sibylline Oracles. Deane, *Pseudepigrapha*; Hastings, *D. B.*, extra Vol., 66–8. 3. The Psalms of Solomon. Ryle and James, *The Pss. of Sol.*; Deane, *Pseudepigrapha*, 25–48.